An Intimate Por
Australia

Debra Doenges Andrew Teakle

NEW HOLLAND

Acknowledgements

I would like to thank my good friends Michael Snedic, Damien and Penny Woods, and Mark Wallace for their valuable contributions to this book. There is nothing so valuable as a fresh pair of eyes.

First published in Australia in 2008 by
New Holland Publishers (Australia) Pty Ltd
Sydney • Auckland • London • Cape Town

1/66 Gibbes Street Chatswood NSW 2067 Australia
218 Lake Road Northcote Auckland New Zealand
86 Edgware Road London W2 2EA United Kingdom
80 McKenzie Street Cape Town 8001 South Africa

A record of this book is held at the National Library of Australia

ISBN 9781741107494

Publisher: Fiona Schultz
Publishing Manager: Lliane Clarke
Designer: Andrew Teakle
Production manager: Linda Bottari
Production Assistant: Liz Malcolm
Printer: Tien Wah Press

10 9 8 7 6 5 4 3 2 1

Cover: Rainbow Lorikeets Grooming, Brisbane River, QLD, Andrew Teakle
Title Page: Sand Dune, Simpson Desert National Park, QLD, Andrew Teakle
Page 3: Elabana Falls, Lamington National Park, QLD, Andrew Teakle
Page 4: Cleaved Boulder, Devils Marbles Conservation Reserve, NT, Debra Doenges

www.tesseraphoto.com www.tesseratravel.com

In loving memory of Debra Lynne Doenges
I miss you every moment of every day
I miss your cheeky laugh, wise words, beautiful eyes, artistic eye
I miss your love

Introduction

Australia is rightly known for its stunning landscapes. Everyone can recall visions of Uluru set amongst a vast expanse of desert oak and mulga, or of a grand sweep of limestone cliffs littered with the discarded hunks of rock we call the Twelve (or is it seven) Apostles. Australia's landscapes are beautiful and awe-inspiring...and found in other books. *An Intimate Portrait of Australia* showcases the jewels found within these landscapes: the flowers, cascades and animals that are easy to miss if you're not paying attention.

The Australian landscape rewards a keen eye, patience and the curiosity to examine the details of nature's handiwork by revealing vignettes of sublime beauty. Splashes of colour, textures and exquisite patterns lie hidden in the visual chaos of the world around us. Walking through it with an open eye and open mind is all that is required to be treated to these visual feasts.

Once, like many people I suppose, I'd set out on a walking trail and stride purposefully until I'd reached the featured destination: a waterfall, rock formation or lookout, only cursorily glancing at the details around me. Dutifully I'd then pull out the camera and get a few snaps. Photography then started to become more important to me and I began to look for opportunities along the trails, but it wasn't until I met Debra Doenges in the US that my skills at distinguishing the patterns from the chaos became more refined. One of her mantras was "it is the journey, not the destination". We've all heard it before, but she truly incorporated it into all aspects of her life, especially photography. Hiking the trails became slower and more deliberate. We'd stop to study the flowers, fungi, bark patterns and secretive animals that were obvious only to those who took the time to see them. One of the great joys of photography is in seeing these patterns of nature repeated in different elements of nature and at different scales: similar patterns to those seen etched on a beach when the tide recedes (page 81) can be found in the veins of a leaf (page 18), the shape of stranded seaweed (page 58) and in a river system when viewed from the air (page 36).

Another of the important lessons that Debra unconsciously taught me was to look beyond the obvious. I remember very vividly on our first trip around Australia driving from Brisbane to see the highlights of my home country. One of the iconic views I desperately wanted to capture was the Three Sisters in the Blue Mountains. We pulled up at Echo Point and my heart fell when a bank of cloud rolled in and blocked the gorgeous late afternoon light from illuminating the famous landforms. Compounding the problem were the eight or nine other photographers who had arrived early and had taken the prime positions at the lookout, crowding us laggards out. At a glance, Debra saw we were not going to "get the shot", and looked west. The sun was lighting up those errant clouds as they surged around the cliffs. Quietly she set up her medium format camera and captured an image that is still one of my favourites (page six, Jamison Valley in Golden Fog). Not one of the other photographers turned around to see why the light was gone.

The concept that it is these details within nature, rather than simply the grand scenic view, that give rise to the majesty of the world around us, is so important to us that we named our business Tessera Photographic Arts. Tesserae are the individual tiles that make up the whole mosaic. I hope you enjoy this collection of tesserae from our vast, diverse and beautiful continent.

Andrew Teakle

JAMISON VALLEY IN GOLDEN FOG
Blue Mountains National Park, NSW

Debra Doenges

Andrew Teakle

WISTARI REEF

Great Barrier Reef Marine Park, QLD

AUTUMN VINEYARD
Bowral, NSW

Debra Doenges

Debra Doenges

CLARET ASH IN AUTUMN
Southern Highlands, NSW

ABOVE AND BELOW
Mossman River, Daintree National Park, QLD

Debra Doenges

Andrew Teakle

STONE AND KELP

Bluestone Bay, Freycinet National Park, TAS

Debra Doenges

EBOR FALLS

Guy Fawkes River Nature Reserve, NSW

WEEPING ROCK

Blue Mountains National Park, NSW

Debra Doenges

SPOTTED GUMS AND CYCADS
Mimosa Rocks National Park, NSW

Debra Doenges

Debra Doenges

ANTARCTIC BEECH FOREST
Lamington National Park, QLD

16

MORNING FOG IN PARKES PLACE
Canberra, ACT

Debra Doenges

Andrew Teakle

SNOW GUMS

Kosciuszko National Park, NSW

RAINFOREST FLOOR
Tarra-Bulga National Park, VIC

Andrew Teakle

19

Debra Doenges

FERN GULLY

Kosciuszko National Park, NSW

LOCH ARD GORGE
Port Campbell National Park, VIC

Andrew Teakle

WEEPING BOTTLEBRUSH
Paluma Range National Park, QLD
Andrew Teakle

FOG LIFTS OVER BITHRY INLET
Mimosa Rocks National Park, NSW

Debra Doenges

Debra Doenges

PICCABEEN PALM AERIAL ROOTS
Eungella National Park, QLD

LITTLE MILLSTRAM FALLS

Millstream Falls National Park, QLD

Andrew Teakle

Debra Doenges

WENTWORTH FALLS

Blue Mountains National Park, NSW

GREATER BILBIES
Adelaide Zoo, SA

Andrew Teakle

Andrew Teakle

SEA LION PUP AND MOTHER
Kangaroo Island, SA

ROCK POOLS
Blackdown Tableland National Park, QLD

Debra Doenges

Debra Doenges

BRINDLE CREEK
Border Ranges National Park, NSW

KING PARROT
Lamington National Park, QLD

Andrew Teakle

Andrew Teakle

CHAIN OF HOLLOWS
Uluṟu-Kata Tjuṯa National Park, NT

CYCAD FROND AND BURNT TRUNK
Carnarvon Gorge National Park, QLD

Andrew Teakle

Andrew Teakle

PALM FROND SHADOW

Carnarvon Gorge National Park, QLD

CARNIVAL OF FLOWERS
Toowoomba, QLD

Debra Doenges

Andrew Teakle

KANGAROO AND FLOWERS
Warrumbungle National Park, NSW

FITZROY RIVER PATTERNS
Rockhampton, QLD

Andrew Teakle

Debra Doenges

EUCALYPT BARK
New England Plateau, NSW

WANGI FALLS
Litchfield National Park, NT

Andrew Teakle

Debra Doenges

JOUNAMA CREEK
Kosciuszko National Park, NSW

FAN PALM CANOPY
Licuala State Forest, QLD

Debra Doenges

Andrew Teakle

BIRDS NEST FERN

Lamington National Park, QLD

MORNING FOG THROUGH MULGRAVE VALLEY
Atherton Tableland, QLD

Debra Doenges

Debra Doenges

COASTLINE
Daintree National Park, QLD

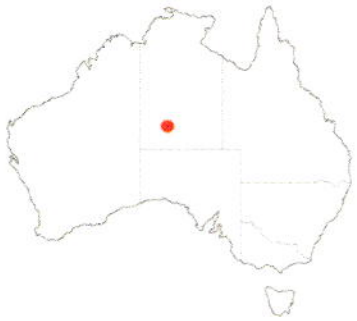

SPRING FLOWER

Kings Canyon, Watarrka National Park, NT

Andrew Teakle

Debra Doenges

ROSE MALLEE
Kings Park, Perth, WA

TOOLONA CREEK
Lamington National Park, QLD

Andrew Teakle

Andrew Teakle

CHALAHN FALLS
Lamington National Park, QLD

SPINIFEX AND RUBY DOCK
Finke Gorge National Park, NT

Debra Doenges

Debra Doenges

RUBY DOCK AND PTILOTIS
Finke Gorge National Park, NT

MELALEUCAS
Bombah Broadwater, Myall Lakes National Park, NSW

Andrew Teakle

GHOST GUM
Finke Gorge National Park, NT
Debra Doenges

TWINING FRINGE LILY
Harvey, WA

Andrew Teakle

Andrew Teakle

WHITE ARUM LILY

Baden Powell Reserve, WA

CYCAD IN THE GARDEN OF EDEN

Debra Doenges

Kings Canyon, Watarrka National Park, NT

Debra Doenges

STRINGY GUM BARK
Hunter Valley, NSW

WILD CATTLE CREEK AT DAWN
Tannum Sands, QLD

Debra Doenges

Andrew Teakle

FLOWERING GUM
Brisbane River, QLD

KELP ON SQUEAKY BEACH
Wilsons Promontory National Park, VIC

Andrew Teakle

Andrew Teakle

LICHENS ON SNOW GUMS
Kosciuszko National Park, NSW

FERN FROND VORTEX
Carnarvon Gorge National Park, QLD

Andrew Teakle

Debra Doenges

SUNFLOWERS
Clifton, QLD

PANDANUS OVER LAWN HILL CREEK
Boodjamulla National Park, QLD

Andrew Teakle

Debra Doenges

FAN PALM RAINFOREST
Daintree National Park, QLD

GHUNGALU ART SITE
Blackdown Tableland National Park, QLD

Andrew Teakle

65

Andrew Teakle and Debra Doenges

ARKAROO ROCK ART
Flinders Ranges, SA

PTILOTIS IN FULL BLOOM
Uluṟu-Kata Tjuṯa National Park, NT

Andrew Teakle

Andrew Teakle

SPOTTED GUMS AND CYCADS
Mimosa Rocks National Park, NSW

CHESTNUT TEAL BATHING
Kuranda, QLD

Andrew Teakle

Debra Doenges

BLACK SWANS IN MIST
Canberra, ACT

KINGS CANYON WALL
Watarrka National Park, NT

Debra Doenges

Andrew Teakle

CASCADE IN DALES GORGE
Karijini National Park, WA

PLAYING ON THE BEACH

Byron Bay, NSW

Andrew Teakle and Debra Doenges

◀ UPPER WENTWORTH FALLS

Blue Mountains National Park, NSW

Debra Doenges

Debra Doenges

LAKE ALLOM

Fraser Island, Great Sandy National Park, QLD

SNOW GUMS AFTER STORM
Kosciuszko National Park, NSW

Andrew Teakle

Debra Doenges

KNYVET FALLS

Cradle Mountain-Lake Saint Clair National Park, TAS

RAINBOW ROCKS
Daintree National Park, QLD

Debra Doenges

Debra Doenges

NOAH CREEK
Daintree National Park, QLD

SEA EAGLE OVER TALLOW BEACH
Byron Bay, NSW

Debra Doenges

Debra Doenges

LEAVES AND CRAB BALLS
Bustard Bay, Town of 1770, QLD

SPRING BLOSSOMS
Margaret River, WA

Andrew Teakle

Andrew Teakle

NEW SHOOTS AFTER FIRE
Bundjalung National Park, NSW

BLACK SWANS AND CYGNETS
Kangaroo Island, SA

Andrew Teakle

Andrew Teakle

SCALY-BREASTED LORIKEETS
Brisbane River, QLD

PANDANUS AND DECIDUOUS BEECH
Cradle Mountain-Lake Saint Clair National Park, TAS

Debra Doenges and Andrew Teakle

Andrew Teakle

FAN PALMS

Bundjalung National Park, NSW

SPOTTED GUMS
Mimosa Rocks National Park, NSW

Andrew Teakle

Andrew Teakle

BROOMFIELD REEF
Great Barrier Reef Marine Park, QLD

BRACKET FUNGI

Lamington National Park, QLD

Andrew Teakle

AUTUMN FOLIAGE
Southern Highlands, NSW
Andrew Teakle ▶

COASTLINE

Daintree National Park, QLD

Debra Doenges

Debra Doenges

WATER-STREAKED ROCK

Uluṟu-Kata Tjuṯa National Park, NT

CATTLE BUSH
Finke Gorge National Park, NT

Andrew Teakle

Andrew Teakle

HONEY GREVILLEA AND NATIVE BEE
Uluṟu-Kata Tjuṯa National Park, NT

BLACK BOOYONG BUTTRESS ROOTS
Lamington National Park, QLD

Debra Doenges and Andrew Teakle

Debra Doenges

FAN PALM FRONDS
Daintree National Park, QLD

AUTUMN LEAVES
Bright, VIC

Debra Doenges

Debra Doenges

AUTUMN VINEYARD
Bright, VIC

GRANITE BOULDERS ALONG TIDAL RIVER
Wilsons Promontory National Park, VIC

Debra Doenges

Debra Doenges

ROCKS AND ANTARCTIC BEECH IN FOG

Lamington National Park, QLD

SULPHUR-CRESTED COCKATOO
Brisbane, QLD

Andrew Teakle

Andrew Teakle

KOALA

Currumbin Wildlife Sanctuary, Gold Coast, QLD

PTILOTIS PATTERNS
Mereenie Loop, NT

Andrew Teakle

Debra Doenges

DUNE PATTERNS

Port Denison, WA

PALM TRUNKS AGAINST SANDSTONE
Finke Gorge National Park, NT

Andrew Teakle

Debra Doenges

LAKE ALLOM REFLECTIONS
Fraser Island, Great Sandy National Park, QLD

VINEYARD
Hunter Valley, NSW

Andrew Teakle

Andrew Teakle and Debra Doenges

GRAND CANYON TRAIL
Blue Mountains National Park, NSW

DRIFTWOOD
Kingscliff, NSW

Debra Doenges and Andrew Teakle

Andrew Teakle

WATERLILIES

James River, Avon Downs, NT

TULIP OAK BLOSSOMS ON PALM FRONDS
Eungella National Park, QLD

Debra Doenges

Debra Doenges

DESERT SUCCULENT
Brisbane Botanic Gardens, QLD

Debra Doenges

SPINIFEX AND RUBY DOCK
Finke Gorge National Park, NT

◀ BOULDER AND MULGA IN BLOOM
Uluru-Kata Tjuta National Park, NT
Debra Doenges

MOSS GARDEN
Carnarvon Gorge National Park, QLD

Debra Doenges

Debra Doenges

STEPS TO LAKE ALLOM

Fraser Island, Great Sandy National Park, QLD

SNOW GUMS DURING STORM
Kosciuszko National Park, NSW

Andrew Teakle

Debra Doenges

ROCK WALLABY

Atherton Tableland, QLD

NAMBUCCA RIVER
Nambucca Heads, NSW

Debra Doenges

Andrew Teakle

STONES AND LEAVES
Daintree National Park, QLD

PURPLE SWAMP HENS
Brisbane Botanic Gardens, QLD

Andrew Teakle

Andrew Teakle

RAINBOW LORIKEETS GROOMING
Brisbane, QLD

EVERLASTING DAISIES
Kings Canyon, Watarrka National Park, NT

Andrew Teakle

Debra Doenges

LEUCOSPERMUM
Kings Park, Perth, WA

MOSSMAN RIVER
Daintree National Park, QLD

Andrew Teakle

Debra Doenges

TULLAWALLAL CIRCUIT
Lamington National Park, QLD

WHITE-PLUMED HONEYEATER
Birdsville Billabong, QLD

Andrew Teakle

Student's Study Guide
Part II

Calculus and Analytic Geometry
8th Edition

Student's Study Guide
Part II

Calculus and Analytic Geometry
8th Edition

Thomas/Finney

Maurice D. Weir

U.S. Naval Postgraduate School

ADDISON-WESLEY PUBLISHING COMPANY

Reading, Massachusetts Menlo Park, California New York
Don Mills, Ontario Wokingham, England Amsterdam Bonn
Sydney Singapore Tokyo Madrid San Juan Milan Paris

Reproduced by Addison-Wesley from camera-ready copy supplied by the author.

ISBN: 0-201-53308-1

1 2 3 4 5 6 7 8 9 10-BA-95949392

PREFACE TO THE STUDENT

This study guide has been designed especially for you, the student. It conforms with the eighth edition of CALCULUS AND ANALYTIC GEOMETRY, by George B. Thomas and Ross L. Finney. It is intended as a self-study workbook to assist you in mastering the basic ideas in calculus. Although this manual was written to conform to the Thomas/Finney CALCULUS AND ANALYTIC GEOMETRY, it can be used to accompany any standard calculus textbook and course.

ORGANIZATION AND LEARNING OBJECTIVES

The study manual is organized section by section to correspond with the Thomas/Finney text. For each section we specify its main ideas by stating appropriate learning OBJECTIVES. Each objective states a particular task for you to perform in order to master that objective. Usually the task requires you to solve a certain type of problem related to the discussion in the text; sometimes the task requires you to demonstrate proficiency with certain key terms or concepts. In every case the objective is highly specific and states exactly what you must do.

One or more examples follows each objective and illustrates its requirements. Each example is written in a semi-programmed format; that is, the example is only partially worked out, so you must supply some of the intermediate results yourself. Correct answers to each intermediate result are supplied at the bottom of the page. Thus, each example is broken down into a sequence of steps to guide you through the procedures and techniques associated with its solution. Each example has been carefully selected not to repeat examples or problems in the Thomas/Finney text; thus you retain the full array of the text problems for practice and further learning.

SELF-TESTS

At the end of each chapter there is a SELF-TEST. Each test is followed by complete solutions to all the test problems. The test problems cover the objectives and are similar in scope and difficulty to the examples in this manual and the examples and problems in the Thomas/Finney text. The test should be useful in preparing for class examinations.

HOW TO USE THIS STUDY GUIDE

We recommend that this manual be used in the following way:

1. Read the textbook: Carefully read the section of Thomas/Finney assigned you by your calculus instructor.

2. Study the learning objectives and examples: Read each objective and work through the associated example(s) in the corresponding section of this manual. You should conceal the answers to the examples at the bottom of the page. Work with pencil and scratch paper as you are guided through each solution, writing in the intermediate results in the blanks provided.

3. Check your answers: After all the blanks for a given problem are filled in, compare your answers with the correct answers at the bottom of the page. If you have difficulty or do not fully understand the answers given, review the material in the textbook or consult with your instructor.

4. Do the chapter self-test: After you complete a chapter in Thomas/Finney, review the objectives for that chapter in this manual. Then take the chapter self-test and compare your solutions with those provided. Problems in the self-test sometimes bring together several ideas from the chapter.

GUIDANCE FROM YOUR INSTRUCTOR

We caution you that the learning objectives given in this manual by no means exhaust all the possible objectives that could be written for a careful study of calculus; we have tried to identify the main ones. However, your instructor may have additional requirements. For instance, he or she may want you to be able to prove certain theorems or derive results in the text. We have not stated objectives of this sort. Also, your instructor may consider some objectives far more important than others and not require that you master some objectives at all. So it is imperative that you find out specifically what your instructor considers essential, and study accordingly. This manual should be helpful to you both in identifying the tasks and successfully mastering them. The problems assigned by your instructor should help you discover those concepts and applications of calculus that your instructor wishes to stress.

MAURICE D. WEIR
Monterey, California

TABLE OF CONTENTS

CHAPTER 8 INFINITE SERIES

INTRODUCTION

An ancient Greek paradox, due to the mathematician Zeno, concerned the following problem. Suppose that a man wants to walk a certain distance, say two miles, along a straight line from A to B. First he must pass the half-way point, then the 3/4 point, then the 7/8 point, and so on as illustrated in the following figure.

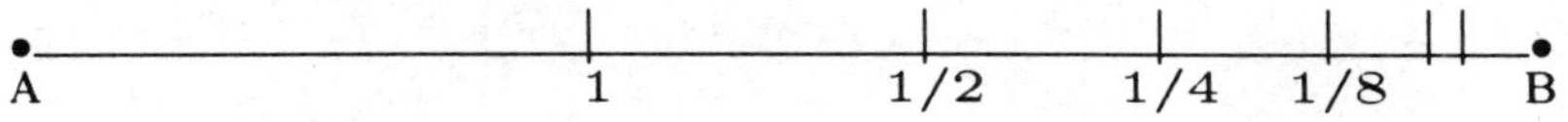

The fractional numbers in the figure indicate the distance in miles remaining to be covered. Therefore, on the assumption that a finite length contains an infinite number of points, the man must pass an infinite number of distance markers along the way. But that seems impossible. The paradox is that the man does get to B, and in a finite amount of time, assuming he walks at some steady pace.

An analysis of the problem is not difficult. The total distance s from A to B is an infinite sum expressible as,

$$s = 1 + \left(\frac{1}{2}\right) + \left(\frac{1}{2}\right)^2 + \left(\frac{1}{2}\right)^3 + \dots ,$$

and the paradox is dispelled if this infinite sum equals the finite number of 2 miles. That turns out to be exactly the case, as you will see further on in this chapter when it is established that

$$\frac{1}{1-x} = 1 + x + x^2 + \dots + x^n + \dots , \quad \text{if} \quad |x| < 1.$$

For then,

$$2 = \frac{1}{1-\frac{1}{2}} = 1 + \frac{1}{2} + \left(\frac{1}{2}\right)^2 + \left(\frac{1}{2}\right)^3 + \dots + \left(\frac{1}{2}\right)^n + \dots .$$

8.1 LIMITS OF SEQUENCES OF NUMBERS

OBJECTIVE A: Given a defining rule for the sequence $\{a_n\}$, write the first few items of the sequence.

1. An infinite sequence is a __________ whose domain is the set of __________ greater than or equal to some integer n.

2. The numbers in the range of a sequence are called the __________ of the sequence. The number a_n is called the __________ of the sequence, or the term with __________ n.

---

1. function, integers   2. terms, nth term, index

3. For the sequence whose defining rule is $a_n = 2 + \frac{1}{n}$, the first four terms are
$a_1 = 3$, $a_2 =$ ______, $a_3 =$ ______, and $a_4 =$ ______.

4. For the sequence whose defining rule is $a_n = \frac{4^n}{n!}$, the first four terms are
$a_1 = 4$, $a_2 =$ ______, $a_3 =$ ______, and $a_4 =$ ______.

5. For the sequence whose defining rule is $a_n = (-1)^{n+1}\left(\frac{n+1}{n^3}\right)$, the first four terms are
$a_1 = 2$, $a_2 =$ ______, $a_3 =$ ______, and $a_4 =$ ______.

6. For the sequence defined by the recursion formula
$x_{n+1} = \left(\frac{2}{n+1}\right)x_n$, where $x_1 = 2$, the next four terms are
$x_2 =$ ______, $x_3 =$ ______, $x_4 =$ ______, and $x_5 =$ ______.

OBJECTIVE B: Given a sequence $\{a_n\}$ determine if it converges or diverges. If it converges, use the theorems presented in this article of the text, or l'Hôpital's rule, or Table 8.1, to find the limit.

7. The sequence $\{a_n\}$ converges to the number L if to every ______ ϵ there corresponds an ______ N such that if $n > N$, then ______. If no such limit L exists, we say that $\{a_n\}$ ______.

8. If $0 < b < 1$, then $\{b^n\}$ converges to 0. To see why, consider the inequality

$$|b^n - 0| = b^n < \epsilon.$$

Thus, we seek an integer N such that if $n > N$, then

______.

Since the natural logarithm $y = \ln x$ is an increasing function for all x,

$b^n < \epsilon$ is equivalent to $n \ln b < \ln \epsilon$.

Also, because $\ln b$ is a negative number for $0 < b < 1$, this latter inequality is equivalent to

$n >$ ______.

Therefore, we need only choose an integer N satisfying

______,

and the criterion set forth in Problem 7 for convergence to 0 is satisfied.

---

3. $\frac{5}{2}, \frac{7}{3}, \frac{9}{4}$ 4. $8, \frac{32}{3}, \frac{32}{3}$ 5. $-\frac{3}{8}, \frac{4}{27}, -\frac{5}{64}$ 6. $2, \frac{4}{3}, \frac{2}{3}, \frac{4}{15}$

7. positive number, integer, $|a_n - L| < \epsilon$, diverges 8. $b^n < \epsilon$, $\frac{\ln \epsilon}{\ln b}$, $N > \frac{\ln \epsilon}{\ln b}$

9. Consider the sequence defined by $a_n = \frac{4^n}{n!}$. Thus, if $n > 5$,

$$a_n = \frac{4 \cdot 4 \cdot 4 \cdot 4 \cdots 4}{1 \cdot 2 \cdot 3 \cdot 4 \cdots n} = \underline{\qquad} \left(\frac{4 \cdot 4 \cdots 4}{5 \cdot 6 \cdots n}\right)$$
$$\leq \frac{32}{3}\left(\frac{4}{5}\right)^{\underline{\qquad}} = \left(\frac{32}{3}\right)\left(\frac{5}{4}\right)^4\left(\frac{4}{5}\right)^n$$

Since $0 \leq a_n$ for all n, the Sandwich Theorem 2 of the Thomas/Finney text gives $a_n \to$ ______ because $\left(\frac{4}{5}\right)^n \to 0$ from Problem 8.

10. For the sequence $\left\{\frac{n^3 + 5}{n^2 - 1}\right\}$, $\lim_{n\to\infty} \frac{n^3 + 5}{n^2 - 1} = \lim_{n\to\infty} \frac{n + (5/n^2)}{1 - (1/n^2)} =$ ______.

Therefore, the sequence ____________.

11. For the sequence defined by $a_n = (-1)^{n+1}\left(\frac{n - 1}{n^3}\right)$,

$0 \leq |a_n| =$ ________ $= \frac{1}{n^2} +$ ________.

Therefore,

$$(-1)^{n+1}\frac{n + 1}{n^3} \to \underline{\qquad\qquad} \text{ as } n \to \infty,$$

by the sequence version of the Sandwich Theorem.

12. Let $a_n = \left(\frac{3n - 1}{5n + 1}\right)^n$. Then,

$\frac{3n - 1}{5n + 1} < \frac{3n}{5n + 1} <$ ________ implies $0 \leq \left(\frac{3n - 1}{5n + 1}\right)^n <$ __________.

Therefore $a_n \to$ ________ because $\left(\frac{3}{5}\right)^n \to 0$.

13. Let $a_n = \left(\frac{3n + 1}{5n - 1}\right)^{1/n}$. Then, applying the natural logarithm to each side, $\ln a_n = \frac{1}{n}(3n + 1) -$ __________. By l'Hôpital's rule,

$$\lim_{n\to\infty} \frac{\ln(3n + 1)}{n} = \lim_{n\to\infty} \frac{\underline{\qquad}}{1} = \underline{\qquad\qquad}, \text{ and}$$
$$\lim_{n\to\infty} \frac{\ln(5n - 1)}{n} = \lim_{n\to\infty} \frac{\underline{\qquad}}{1} = \underline{\qquad\qquad}.$$

Then, $\ln a_n \to 0$ so that taking $f(x) = e^x$ and $L = 0$ in Theorem 3, $a_n = e^{\ln a_n} \to$ __________.

14. Consider the sequence defined by $a_n = \left(1 + e^{-n}\right)^n$. Then,

$\ln a_n =$ ____________________ ,

and by l'Hôpital's rule,

---

9. $\frac{32}{3}$, n - 4, 0 10. ∞, diverges 11. $\frac{n + 1}{n^3}$, $\frac{1}{n^3}$, 0

12. $\frac{3}{5}$, $\left(\frac{3}{5}\right)^n$, 0 13. $\frac{1}{n}\ln(5n - 1)$, $\frac{3}{3n + 1}$, 0, $\frac{5}{5n - 1}$, 0, $e^0 = 1$

$$\lim_{n\to\infty} \frac{\ln(1+e^{-n})}{1/n} = \lim_{n\to\infty} \frac{\rule{2cm}{0.4pt}}{-1/n^2} \qquad (0/0)$$

$$= \lim_{n\to\infty} \frac{n^2}{e^n+1} \qquad (\infty/\infty)$$

$$= \lim_{n\to\infty} \rule{2cm}{0.4pt} \qquad (\text{still } \infty/\infty)$$

$$= \lim_{n\to\infty} \frac{2}{e^n} = \rule{2cm}{0.4pt}.$$

Therefore,

$$a_n = e^{\ln a_n} \to \rule{2cm}{0.4pt}.$$

15. Let $a_n = \sqrt[n]{n^3}$. Then, $a_n = \left(n^3\right)^{1/n} = n^{\rule{1cm}{0.4pt}} = \left(\sqrt[n]{n}\right)^{\rule{1cm}{0.4pt}}$.
Now, $\sqrt[n]{n} \to$ ________ by Rule 2 in Table 8.1 in the text.
Thus, if $f(x) = x^3$, then

$$a_n = f(\sqrt[n]{n}) \to \rule{2cm}{0.4pt}.$$

8.2 INFINITE SERIES

16. If $\{a_n\}$ is a sequence, and

$$s_n = a_1 + a_2 + \ldots + a_n,$$

then the sequence $\{s_n\}$ is called an ________________.

17. The number s_n is called the ________________ of the series.

18. Instead of $\{s_n\}$ we usually use the notation ________ for the series.

19. The series $\sum_{n=1}^{\infty} a_n$ is said to converge if the sequence ________ converges to a finite limit L. In that case we write ________________ or $a_1 + a_2 + \ldots + a_n + \ldots = L$. If no such limit exists, the series is said to ____________.

OBJECTIVE A: For a given geometric series $\sum_{n=1}^{\infty} ar^{n-1}$, determine if the series converges or diverges. If it does converge, then compute the sum of the series. The indexing of the series may be changed for a given problem.

20. Consider the series $\sum_{n=1}^{\infty} \frac{3}{5^{n-1}}$. This is a geometric series with $a =$ ________ and $r =$ ________. Since $|r| < 1$, the geometric

---

14. $n \ln(1+e^{-n})$, $\left(\frac{1}{1+e^{-n}}\right)(-e^{-n})$, $\frac{2n}{e^n}$, 0, $e^0 = 1$ 15. $\frac{3}{n}$, 3, 1, $1^3 = 1$ 16. infinite series
17. nth partial sum 18. $\sum_{n=1}^{\infty} a_n$ 19. $\{s_n\}$, $\sum_{n=1}^{\infty} a_n = L$, diverge

series ___________, and its sum is given by

$$\sum_{n=1}^{\infty} \frac{3}{5^{n-1}} = \_\_\_\_\_\_\_\_\_\_ = \_\_\_\_\_\_\_\_\_\_ .$$

21. The series $\sum_{n=3}^{\infty} (-1)^{n-1} \frac{4}{3^{n-1}}$ is a geometric series with $a =$ ______ and $r =$ _______. Since $|r| < 1$, the geometric series __________. However, the index begins with $n = 3$ instead of $n = 1$. Now,

$$\sum_{n=3}^{\infty} (-1)^{n-1} \frac{4}{3^{n-1}} = \sum_{n=1}^{\infty} (-1)^{n-1} \frac{4}{3^{n-1}} - (\_\_\_\_\_\_\_\_)$$
$$= \_\_\_\_\_\_\_\_\_\_ - \frac{8}{3} = \_\_\_\_\_\_\_\_\_\_ .$$

22. The series $\sum_{n=3}^{\infty} \frac{2^n}{7}$ is a geometric series with $a =$ _______ and $r =$ _______. Since __________ the series diverges.

23. The repeating decimal 0.15 15 15 ... is a geometric series in disguise. It can be written as

$$0.15\ 15\ 15 \ldots = \frac{15}{100} + \frac{15}{\_\_\_\_} + \frac{15}{\_\_\_\_} + \ldots$$
$$= \sum_{n=1}^{\infty} \_\_\_\_\_\_\_\_\_\_$$
$$= \frac{1}{100} \sum_{n=1}^{\infty} \_\_\_\_\_\_\_\_\_\_$$
$$= \frac{1}{100} (\_\_\_\_\_\_\_\_) = \frac{15}{\_\_\_\_\_\_} = \frac{15}{99} .$$

24. If you write in the first four terms of the following geometric series you have

$$\sum_{n=0}^{\infty} ar^n = \_\_\_\_\_ + \_\_\_\_\_ + \_\_\_\_\_ + \_\_\_\_\_ + \ldots .$$

Thus, $\sum_{n=0}^{\infty} ar^n$ is simply another way of writing the geometric series $\sum_{n=1}^{\infty} ar^{n-1}$. Therefore, if $|r| < 1$ we conclude that

$$\sum_{n=0}^{\infty} ar^n = \_\_\_\_\_\_\_\_\_\_\_\_ .$$

---

20. 3, $\frac{1}{5}$, converges, $\frac{3}{1 - \frac{1}{5}}$, $\frac{15}{4}$

21. 4, $-\frac{1}{3}$, converges. $4 - \frac{4}{3}$, $\frac{4}{1 + \frac{1}{3}}$, $\frac{1}{3}$

22. $\frac{1}{7}$, 2, $|r| > 1$

23. 100^2, 100^3, $\frac{15}{100^n}$, $\frac{15}{100^{n-1}}$, $\frac{15}{1 - \frac{1}{100}}$, 100 - 1

24. a, ar, ar^2, ar^3, $\frac{a}{1 - r}$

25. Sometimes the terms of a given series are a sum or difference of terms, each of which beongs to a geometric series. For example,

$$\sum_{n=0}^{\infty}\left(\frac{7}{3^n} - \frac{1}{2^n}\right) = \sum_{n=0}^{\infty}\frac{7}{3^n} - \sum_{n=0}^{\infty}\frac{1}{2^n}$$

$$= \_\_\_\_\_\_\_\_ - \_\_\_\_\_\_\_\_ = \_\_\_\_\_\_\_\_ - \frac{4}{2} = \_\_\_\_\_\_\_\_.$$

OBJECTIVE B: Use the nth-term test for divergence to test a given series $\sum_{n=1}^{\infty} a_n$ for divergence.

26. For the series $\sum_{n=1}^{\infty} \frac{n^n}{n!}$, we have for every index n,

$$a_n = \frac{n^n}{n!} = \frac{n \cdot n \cdot n \cdots n}{1 \cdot 2 \cdot 3 \cdots n} = \left(\frac{n}{1}\right)\left(\frac{n}{2}\right)(\_\_\_\_\_)\cdots\left(\frac{n}{n}\right) > \_\_\_\_\_\_\_\_.$$

Therefore, $\lim_{n\to\infty} a_n \neq 0$. We conclude that the series ________.

27. Consider the series $\sum_{n=1}^{\infty} (-1)^{n+1}\left(1 + \frac{1}{3^n}\right)$. For large values of the index n, the absolute value of the nth term,

$$|a_n| = 1 + 3^{-n}$$

is close to ________. Therefore, the limit

$\lim_{n\to\infty} (-1)^{n+1}\left(1 + \frac{1}{3^n}\right)$ ________ exist. We conclude that the series __________.

28. For the series $\sum_{n=1}^{\infty} \left(\frac{n+2}{n}\right)^n$, we have

$\lim_{n\to\infty} \left(\frac{n+2}{n}\right)^n = \lim_{n\to\infty}\left(1 + \frac{2}{n}\right)^n = \_\_\_\_\_\_$. Thus, the series __________ because the limit of the nth term is not zero.

29. For the series $\sum_{n=1}^{\infty} \frac{2n^2 + 1}{n^3 - 1}$ the limit of the nth-term is

$$\lim_{n\to\infty}\left(\frac{2n^2+1}{n^3-1}\right) = \lim_{n\to\infty}\left(\frac{\frac{2}{n} + \frac{1}{n^3}}{\_\_\_\_\_\_}\right) = \frac{0+0}{\_\_\_\_\_\_} = 0 .$$

Since the limit is equal to zero, the nth-term test gives no information concerning convergence or divergence.

---

25. $\frac{7}{1 - \frac{1}{3}}$, $\frac{1}{1 - \frac{1}{2}}$, $\frac{21}{2}$, $\frac{17}{2}$

26. $\frac{n}{3}$, 1, diverges

27. 1, does not, diverges

28. e^2, diverges

29. $1 - \frac{1}{n^3}$, $1 + 0$

OBJECTIVE C: Use partial fractions to find the sum of a series, if appropriate.

30. Consider the series $\sum_{n=1}^{\infty} \frac{1}{(2n - 1)(2n + 1)}$. This is not a geometric series. However, we can use partial fractions to re-write the kth term:

$$\frac{1}{(2k - 1)(2k + 1)} = \frac{1}{2}\left[\_\_\_\_\_\_ - \frac{1}{2k + 1}\right].$$

This permits us to write the partial sum

$$\sum_{n=1}^{k} \frac{1}{(2n - 1)(2n + 1)} = \frac{1}{1 \cdot 3} + \frac{1}{3 \cdot 5} + \cdots + \frac{1}{(2k - 1)(2k + 1)}$$

as

$$s_k = \frac{1}{2}\left(\frac{1}{1} - \frac{1}{3}\right) + \frac{1}{2}\left(\_\_\_\_\_\_\right) + \frac{1}{2}\left(\_\_\_\_\_\_\right)$$
$$+ \cdots + \frac{1}{2}\left(\frac{1}{2k - 1} - \frac{1}{2k + 1}\right).$$

By removing parentheses on the right, and combining terms, we find that

$$s_k = \_\_\_\_\_\_\_\_\_\_\_\_.$$

Therefore, $s_k \to$ ______ and the series ______ converge. Hence,

$$\sum_{n=1}^{\infty} \frac{1}{(2n - 1)(2n + 1)} = \_\_\_\_\_\_.$$

8.3 SERIES WITHOUT NEGATIVE TERMS: THE COMPARISON AND INTEGRAL TESTS

OBJECTIVE A: Know the Nondecreasing Sequence Theorem and how it applies to an infinite series of nonnegative terms.

31. A nondecreasing sequence $\{s_n\}$ is a sequence with the property that ________ for every n.

32. A sequence $\{s_n\}$ is said to be ________ from above if there is a finite constant M such that $s_n \le M$ for every n.

33. If $\{s_n\}$ is a nondecreasing sequence that is bounded from above, then it ____________.

34. If a nondecreasing sequence $\{s_n\}$ fails to be bounded, then it ____________.

35. If Σa_n is a series of nonnegative terms, then its sequence $\{s_n\}$ of partial sums is ________.

---

30. $\frac{1}{2k - 1}$, $\frac{1}{3} - \frac{1}{5}$, $\frac{1}{5} - \frac{1}{7}$, $\frac{1}{2}\left(1 - \frac{1}{2k + 1}\right)$, $\frac{1}{2}$, does, $\frac{1}{2}$
31. $s_n \le s_{n+1}$
32. bounded
33. converges
34. diverges to plus infinity
35. nondecreasing

36. If Σa_n is a series of nonnegative terms, then it converges if and only if its sequence $\{s_n\}$ of partial sums is ______________ ______________.

OBJECTIVE B: Use the comparison and integral tests for convergence and divergence to determine whether a given series with no negative terms converges or diverges.

37. $\sum_{n=1}^{\infty} \frac{n+5}{n^2 - 3n + 5}$

For every index n, $5n > -3n + 5$ because n is a positive integer. Then, $n^2 + 5n >$ ______________, and since $n^2 - 3n + 5$ is positive for every index it follows that

$$\frac{n+2}{n^2 - 3n + 5} > \text{\_\_\_\_\_\_\_\_}.$$

We conclude that the given series ____________ by comparison with the series $\Sigma \frac{1}{n}$.

38. $\sum_{n=2}^{\infty} \frac{1}{n(\ln n)^2}$

We apply the integral test $\int_2^{\infty} \frac{dx}{x(\ln x)^2} = \lim_{b\to\infty}$ ________$\Big]_b^2$ = ________.

Therefore, the integral ____________ and hence the series ____________.

39. $\sum_{n=1}^{\infty} \frac{(\ln n)^2}{n^3}$

The following argument shows that $\ln n < \sqrt{n}$ for every index n. First, define the function $g(x) = \sqrt{x} - \ln x$. Now $g'(x) =$ ____________ is nonnegative if $x \geq$ ________, and it follows that g is an increasing function of x for $x \geq 4$. Also, $g(4) = 2 - \ln 4 \approx 0.613$ is positive. Therefore, $g(x) > 0$ for $x \geq 4$. A simple verification using tables, or a calculator, shows that $g(1)$, $g(2)$, and $g(3)$ are positive. Hence, we have established that $\ln n < \sqrt{n}$ for every positive integer n. Using this fact,

$$\frac{(\ln n)^2}{n^3} < \frac{(\sqrt{n})^2}{n^3} = \text{\_\_\_\_\_\_\_\_}.$$

We conclude that the series $\sum_{n=1}^{\infty} \frac{(\ln n)^2}{n^3}$ ____________ by the comparison test.

---

36. bounded from above

37. $n^2 - 3n + 5$, $\frac{1}{n}$, diverges

38. $\frac{1}{\ln x}$, $\frac{1}{\ln 2}$, converges, converges

39. $\frac{1}{2\sqrt{x}} - \frac{1}{x}$, 4, $\frac{1}{n^2}$, converges

8.4 SERIES WITHOUT NEGATIVE TERMS: THE RATIO AND ROOT TESTS

OBJECTIVE: Given a series without negative terms, investigate its convergence or divergence using the ratio and root tests.

40. $\sum_{n=1}^{\infty} \frac{n!}{3^n}$

We try the ratio test. Thus, $\frac{a_{n+1}}{a_n} = \frac{(n+1)!/3^{n+1}}{n!/3^n} =$ __________.

Hence, $\rho = \lim_{n\to\infty} \frac{a_{n+1}}{a_n} =$ __________, and the series __________.

41. $\sum_{n=1}^{\infty} (\sqrt[n]{n} - 1)^n$

We try the nth-root test. Thus, for $a_n = (\sqrt[n]{n} - 1)^n$,

$$\sqrt[n]{a_n} = \_\_\_\_\_\_ \rightarrow \_\_\_\_\_\_.$$

Because $\rho =$ ______ we conclude that the series __________ according to the root test.

42. $\sum_{n=1}^{\infty} \frac{n \ln n}{(n+1)^2}$

We try the ratio test. Thus,

$$\frac{a_{n+1}}{a_n} = \frac{(n+1)\ln(n+1)}{(n+2)^2} \cdot \_\_\_\_\_\_\_\_ .$$

Hence,

$$\rho = \lim_{n\to\infty} \frac{a_{n+1}}{a_n} = \lim_{n\to\infty} \left[\frac{(n+1)^3}{n(n+1)^2} \cdot \_\_\_\_\_\_\right] = \_\_\_ \cdot 1 = \_\_\_\_.$$

In this case the root test says the series ____________________ ____________________.

8.5 ALTERNATING SERIES AND ABSOLUTE CONVERGENCE

OBJECTIVE A: Use the Alternating Series Theorem (Leibniz's Theorem) to investigate the convergence of an alternating series.

43. $\sum_{n=1}^{\infty} (-1)^{n+1} \frac{n}{n^2+1}$

First we see that $a_n = \frac{n}{n^2+1}$ is positive for every n. Also, $\lim_{n\to\infty} a_n =$ ______. Next, we compare a_{n+1} with a_n for

---

40. $\frac{1}{3} \cdot (n+1)$, $+\infty$, diverges

41. $\sqrt[n]{n} - 1$, 0, 0, converges

42. $\frac{(n+1)^2}{n \ln n}$, $\frac{\ln(n+1)}{\ln n}$, 1, 1, may converge or may diverge

arbitrary n. Now, $\frac{n + 1}{(n + 1)^2 + 1} \le \frac{n}{n^2 + 1}$ if and only if

$(n + 1)(n^2 + 1) \le n[(n + 1)^2 + 1]$. This last inequality is equivalent to $n^3 + n^2 + n + 1 \le$ __________ or, $1 \le n^2 + n$ which is true. We conclude that the alternating series __________.

44. $\sum_{n=1}^{\infty} (-1)^{n+1} \frac{1}{n^{1+ 1/n}}$

It is clear that $a_n = \frac{1}{n^{1 + 1/n}} = \frac{1}{n \cdot \sqrt[n]{n}}$ is positive for every n. Also, $\lim_{n\to\infty} a_n = \lim_{n\to\infty} \frac{1}{n} \cdot \lim_{n\to\infty} \frac{1}{\sqrt[n]{n}} =$ __________. We would like to show that $\{a_n\}$ is a __________ sequence. One way is to replace n by the continuous variable x and show that the resultant function

$$y = f(x) = x^{1+ 1/x}, \quad x > 0,$$

which is the reciprocal of a_n for $x = n$, is an <u>increasing</u> function of x for every x. If we take the logarithm of both sides of this last equation, and differentiate implicitly with respect to x, we obtain

$$\ln y = \left(1 + \frac{1}{x}\right) \ln x, \quad \text{and} \quad \frac{y'}{y} = \frac{1}{x^2} (\text{\_\_\_\_\_\_\_\_\_\_}) + \frac{1}{x}.$$

Simplifying algebraically, $y' = \frac{y}{x^2}(1 +$ ______ $- \ln x)$.

Thus, since $x > \ln x$ for all $x > 0$, we find that y' is positive, and $y = f(x)$ is increasing for all x (so the reciprocal is __________). Therefore we have established that

$$\frac{1}{(n + 1) \cdot \sqrt[n+1]{n + 1}} < \frac{1}{n \cdot \sqrt[n]{n}} \quad \text{for every index } n.$$

We conclude that the alternating series ______________.

OBJECTIVE B: Use the Alternating Series Estimation Theorem to estimate the magnitude of the error if the first k terms, for some specified number k, are used to approximate a given alternating series.

45. It can be shown, with a little work, that the alternating harmonic series

$$\sum_{n=1}^{\infty} \frac{(-1)^{n+1}}{n}$$

converges to $\ln 2$. If we wish to approximate $\ln 2$ correct to four decimal places using this series, the alternating series error estimation gives

---

43. 0, $n^3 + 2n^2 + 2n$, converges 44. $0 \cdot 1 = 0$, decreasing, $1 - \ln x$, x, decreasing, converges

______ $< 0.5 \times 10^{-5}$, or $n >$ ____________.

Therefore, we would need to sum the first 200,000 terms of the alternating harmonic series to ensure four decimal place accuracy in approximating ln 2. This does not mean that fewer terms would not provide that accuracy. A more efficient approximation for ln 2, accurate to four decimal places, uses Simpson's rule with $n = 6$ to estimate

$$\int_1^2 \frac{dx}{x}.$$

OBJECTIVE C: Given an infinite series, use the tests studied in this chapter of the text to determine if the series is absolutely convergent, conditionally convergent, or divergent.

46. A series $\sum_{n=1}^{\infty} a_n$ is said to converge absolutely if

_________________________.

47. True or False:
(a) If a series converges absolutely, then it converges.
(b) If a series converges, then it converges absolutely.

48. If a series $\sum a_n$ converges, but the series of absolute values $\sum |a_n|$ diverges, we say that the original series $\sum a_n$ is _________________________.

49. $\displaystyle\sum_{n=1}^{\infty} \frac{(-1)^{n+1}\, n \ln n}{3^n}$

The absolute value of the nth term of the series is $|a_n| = \dfrac{n \ln n}{3^n}$. Applying the ratio test,

$$\frac{|a_{n+1}|}{|a_n|} = \frac{(n+1)\ \ln\ (n+1)/3^{n+1}}{n \ln n/3^n} = \text{____________}.$$ By l'Hôpital's

rule, $\displaystyle\lim_{n\to\infty} \frac{\ln\ (n+1)}{\ln n} = \lim_{n\to\infty}$ _______________ = __________.

Therefore, $\displaystyle\lim_{n\to\infty} \frac{|a_{n+1}|}{|a_n|} =$ __________, so we conclude that

$\displaystyle\sum_{n=1}^{\infty} \frac{(-1)^{n+1}\, n \ln n}{3^n}$ ______________ converge absolutely.

---

45. $\frac{1}{n}$, 2×10^5

46. $\sum_{n=1}^{\infty} |a_n|$ converges

47. (a) True (b) False

48. conditionally convergent

49. $\frac{1}{3}\left(\frac{n+1}{n}\right)\frac{\ln\,(n+1)}{\ln n}$, $\frac{1/(n+1)}{1/n}$, 1, $\frac{1}{3}$, does

50. $\sum_{n=1}^{\infty} \frac{2n - n^2}{n^3}$

The nth term of the series is $a_n = \frac{2n - n^2}{n^3} = \frac{n(2 - n)}{n^3}$ which is negative if $n >$ ________. Thus, $-a_n = \frac{n - 2}{n^2}$ is positive for $n > 2$. Now, $\frac{n - 2}{n^2} > \frac{1}{2n}$ whenever $n >$ ________. Since the series $\sum_{n=1}^{\infty} \frac{1}{2n}$ ________, we conclude that the series

$\sum_{n=1}^{\infty} |a_n| = \sum_{n=1}^{\infty} \frac{n - 2}{n^2}$ ________ by the comparison test.

Therefore, the original series ________ converge absolutely.

51. In Problem 44 above, the series $\sum_{n=1}^{\infty} (-1)^{n+1} \frac{1}{n^{1+1/n}}$ was shown to be convergent. We want to know if the series converges absolutely. Using the same technique as in Problem 44, it is easy to establish that

$$\sqrt[n+1]{n + 1} < \sqrt[n]{n} \quad \text{if} \quad n \geq 3:$$

we define the function $y = x^{1/n}$, $x \geq 3$, and show that y' is always negative; whence we conclude that y is a ________ function of x. In particular, $\sqrt[n]{n} < \sqrt[3]{3} \approx 1.44 < \frac{3}{2}$ if $n \geq$ ________. It follows that

$$\frac{1}{n \cdot \sqrt[n]{n}} > \text{________} \quad \text{if} \quad n \geq 4.$$

Since the harmonic series $\sum \frac{1}{n}$ diverges, we find that the series $\sum_{n=1}^{\infty} \frac{1}{n^{1+1/n}}$ ________ by the comparison test.

Therefore, the original series $\sum_{n=1}^{\infty} (-1)^{n+1} \frac{1}{n^{1+1/n}}$ is ________________.

52. $\sum_{n=1}^{\infty} (-1)^{n+1} \left(\frac{n + 1}{n}\right)^n$

In this case, $a_n = \left(\frac{n + 1}{n}\right)^n = \left(1 + \frac{1}{n}\right)^n \to$ ________. Therefore the series ________.

53. $\sum_{n=2}^{\infty} \frac{\cos n\pi}{n\sqrt{\ln n}}$

Since $\cos n\pi$ is 1 when n is even, and -1 when n is odd, the series is alternating in sign. Let us see if the series converges absolutely. Now,

---

50. 2, 4, diverges, diverges, does not

51. decreasing, 4, $\frac{2}{3n}$, diverges, conditionally convergent

52. e, diverges

$|a_n| = \left|\frac{\cos n\pi}{n\sqrt{\ln n}}\right| =$ ____________. Applying the integral test,

$$\int_1^{\infty} \frac{dx}{x\sqrt{\ln x}} = \lim_{b\to\infty} \text{\_\_\_\_\_\_\_\_\_\_\_\_}\Big]_1^b = \text{\_\_\_\_\_\_\_\_\_\_\_\_}.$$

Therefore, the series $\sum |a_n|$ ____________. To see if the original series converges we check the three conditions of the Alternating Series Theorem (remember that the numerator $\cos n\pi$ simply determines the sign of the nth term of the series):

$\frac{1}{n\sqrt{\ln n}}$ is positive for all n, and converges to ________.

It is clear that $\frac{1}{(n+1)\sqrt{\ln (n+1)}} < \frac{1}{n\sqrt{\ln n}}$ because $y = \ln x$ is an ____________ function of x. Therefore, the series $\sum_{n=1}^{\infty} \frac{\cos n\pi}{n\sqrt{\ln n}}$ is ________________________.

8.6 POWER SERIES

54. A series of the form

$$\sum_{n=0}^{\infty} c_n x^n = c_0 + c_1 x + c_2 x^2 + c_3 x^3 + \ldots + c_n x^n + \ldots$$

is called a ________________________.

55. For the power series

$$\sum_{n=0}^{\infty} c_n (x-a)^n = c_0 + c_1(x-a) + c_2(x-a)^2 + \ldots + c_n(x-a)^n + \ldots$$

the constant a is called the ____________. The coefficients $c_0, c_1, c_2, \ldots, c_n, \ldots$ are all ______________.

OBJECTIVE A: Given a power series $\sum_{n=0}^{\infty} c_n(x-a)^n$, find its interval of convergence. If the interval is finite, determine whether the series converges at each endpoint.

56. $\sum_{n=1}^{\infty} \frac{1}{\sqrt{n}\ 3^n} x^n$

We apply the ratio test to the series of absolute values, and find

$$\rho = \lim_{n\to\infty} \left| \frac{x^{n+1}}{\sqrt{n+1}\ 3^{n+1}} \cdot \text{\_\_\_\_\_\_\_\_} \right| = \lim_{n\to\infty} \frac{\sqrt{n}}{\text{\_\_\_\_\_\_\_\_}} |x| = \text{\_\_\_\_\_\_\_\_}.$$

---

53. $\frac{1}{n\sqrt{\ln n}}$, $2\sqrt{\ln x}$, $+\infty$, diverges, 0, increasing, conditionally convergent

54. power series

55. center, constants

Therefore the original series converges absolutely if $|x| <$ ______ and diverges if ________. When $x = 3$, the series becomes

$$\sum_{n=1}^{\infty} \text{\_\_\_\_\_\_\_\_\_\_},$$ the p-series with $p =$ __________;

this series __________. When $x = -3$, the series becomes

$$\sum_{n=1}^{\infty} \text{\_\_\_\_\_\_\_\_\_\_\_},$$

and this series __________, by the Alternating Series Theorem. Therefore, the interval of convergence of the original power series is ______________.

57. $\displaystyle\sum_{n=1}^{\infty} \frac{2^n}{n(3^{n+2})} x^{n+1}$

The power series converges for $x = 0$. For $x \neq 0$, we apply the root test to the series of absolute values, and find

$$\rho = \lim_{n\to\infty} \sqrt[n]{\frac{2^n\ |x|^n\ |x|}{n \cdot 3^n \cdot 3^2}} = \lim_{n\to\infty} \text{\_\_\_\_\_\_\_\_\_\_\_\_\_\_\_\_\_\_\_\_\_\_\_\_}$$

$$= \frac{2|x| \cdot 1}{\text{\_\_\_\_\_\_\_}} < 1, \quad \text{if} \quad |x| < \text{\_\_\_\_\_\_\_}.$$

Therefore, the original series converges absolutely if $|x| < \frac{3}{2}$ and diverges if $|x| > \frac{3}{2}$. When $x = \frac{3}{2}$, the series becomes

$$\sum_{n=1}^{\infty} \frac{2^n}{n(3^{n+2})} \left(\frac{3}{2}\right)^{n+1} = \sum_{n=1}^{\infty} \text{\_\_\_\_\_\_\_\_\_\_},$$

and this series _________. When $x = -\frac{3}{2}$, the series becomes

$$\sum_{n=1}^{\infty} \frac{(-1)^{n+1}}{6n},$$

and this series __________, by the Alternating Series Theorem. Therefore, the interval of convergence of the original power series is ____________.

58. $\displaystyle\sum_{n=1}^{\infty} [\sin(5n)](x - \pi)^n$

For every value of x, $|[\sin(5n)](x - \pi)^n| \leq |x - \pi|^n$. The geometric series $\displaystyle\sum_{n=1}^{\infty} |x - \pi|^n$ converges if ___________ and diverges if ____________. Therefore, by the comparison test, the original series converges absolutely if ____________.

---

56. $\frac{\sqrt{n}\,3^n}{x^n}$, $3\sqrt{n+1}$, $\frac{1}{3}|x|$, 3, $|x| > 3$, $\frac{1}{\sqrt{n}}$, $\frac{1}{2}$, diverges, $\frac{(-1)^n}{\sqrt{n}}$, converges, $-3 \leq x < 3$

57. $\frac{2\,|x| \cdot \sqrt[n]{|x|}}{\sqrt[n]{n} \cdot 3 \cdot \sqrt[n]{9}}$, $1 \cdot 3 \cdot 1$, $\frac{3}{2}$, $\frac{1}{6n}$, diverges, converges, $-\frac{3}{2} \leq x < \frac{3}{2}$

Suppose $|x - \pi| = 1$. Then the series becomes,

$$\sum_{n=1}^{\infty} \sin(5n) \quad \text{or} \quad \sum_{n=1}^{\infty} \underline{\hspace{4cm}} .$$

However, $\lim_{n\to\infty} \sin(5n)$ fails to exist, so neither of these series can converge. We conclude that the interval of convergence of the original series is ____________________.

OBJECTIVE B: Given a power series $f(x) = \sum a_n x^n$, find the power series for $f'(x)$.

59. From Example 5 of the text we deduce that

$$\frac{1}{1 + x^2} = 1 - x^2 + x^4 - x^6 + \ldots , \quad \text{for} \quad -1 < x < 1.$$

Therefore, using the term-by-term differentiation theorem,

$$\frac{-2x}{\left(1 + x^2\right)^2} = \underline{\hspace{4cm}}, \quad \text{for} \quad \underline{\hspace{3cm}} .$$

OBJECTIVE C: If f is a function having a known power series $f(x) = \sum a_n x^n$, use the series and a calculator to estimate the integral $\int_0^b f(x)dx$, assuming that b lies within the interval of convergence.

60. Let us find $\int_0^{0.2} \cos\sqrt{x}\, dx$ accurate to five decimal places.

Now,

$$\cos x = 1 - \frac{x^2}{2!} + \frac{x^4}{4!} - \frac{x^6}{6!} + \frac{x^8}{8!} - \ldots ,$$

so the power series for $\cos\sqrt{x}$ is given by

$$\cos\sqrt{x} = \underline{\hspace{6cm}}, \quad x \geq 0.$$

Thus, using term-by-term integration,

$$\int_0^{0.2} \cos\sqrt{x}\, dx = \underline{\hspace{6cm}}\Big]_0^{0.2}$$

$$= 0.2 - \frac{0.04}{4} + \frac{0.008}{72} - \frac{0.0016}{2880} + \frac{0.00032}{201600} - \ldots$$

$$\approx 0.2 - 0.01 + 0.00011 - 0.00000056 + \ldots$$

Hence, $\int_0^{0.2} \cos\sqrt{x}\, dx \approx$ ____________

with an error of less than 5×10^{-6}.

---

58. $|x - \pi| < 1$, $|x - \pi| \geq 1$, $|x - \pi| < 1$, $(-1)^n \sin(5n)$, $\pi - 1 < x < \pi + 1$

59. $-2x + 4x^3 - 6x^5 + \ldots$, $-1 < x < 1$

60. $1 - \frac{x}{2!} + \frac{x^2}{4!} - \frac{x^3}{6!} + \frac{x^4}{8!} - \ldots$, $x - \frac{x^2}{2 \cdot 2!} + \frac{x^3}{3 \cdot 4!} - \frac{x^4}{4 \cdot 6!} + \frac{x^5}{5 \cdot 8!} - \ldots$, 0.19011

8.7 TAYLOR SERIES AND MACLAURIN SERIES

OBJECTIVE A: Find the Taylor Series at $x = a$, or the Maclaurin series, for a given function $y = f(x)$. Assume that $x = a$ is specified and that f has finite derivatives of all orders at $x = a$.

61. If $y = f(x)$ has finite derivatives of all orders at $x = a$, the particular power series

$$f(a) + f'(a)(x - a) + \frac{f''(a)}{2!}(x - a)^2 + \ldots + \frac{f^{(n)}(a)}{n!}(x - a)^n + \ldots$$

is called the ______________________________. If $a = 0$, the series is known as the ______________ for f. The Taylor series for a function may or may not converge to the function.

62. If $y = f(x)$ has finite derivatives of order up to and including n, then the polynomial

$$P_n(x) = f(a) + f'(a)(x - a) + \frac{f''(a)}{2!}(x - a)^2 + \ldots + \frac{f^{(n)}(a)}{n!}(x-a)^n$$

is called the ______________________________ ______________. The graph of this polynomial passes through the point _______, and its first n derivatives match the first n derivatives of _______ at _______. Each nonnegative integer n corresponds to a Taylor polynomial for f at $x = a$, provided the first n derivatives of f exist at $x = a$.

63. Let us find the Maclaurin series for the function $f(x) = x^5 + 4x^4 + 3x^3 + 2x + 1$. We need to find the derivatives of f of all orders, and evalute them at $x = 0$:

$f'(x)$ = ________________, $f'(0) = 2$

$f^{(2)}(x)$ = ________________, $f^{(2)}(0)$ = ______

$f^{(3)}(x)$ = ________________, $f^{(3)}(0)$ = ______

$f^{(4)}(x) = 120x + 96$, $f^{(4)}(0) = 96$

$f^{(5)}(x)$ = _____, $f^{(5)}(0)$ = ______

$f^{(6)}(x) = 0$, $f^{(6)}(0) = 0$

In general, $f^{(k)}(0)$ = _____ if $k \geq 6$. Thus, the Maclaurin series is

______________________________________ ,

---

61. Taylor series generated by f at $x = a$, Maclaurin series

62. Taylor polynomial of order n generated by f at $x = a$, $(a, f(a))$, $y = f(x)$, $x = a$

63. $5x^4 + 16x^3 + 9x^2 + 2$, $20x^3 + 48x^2 + 18x$, 0, $60x^2 + 96x + 18$, 18, 120, 120, 0,

$1 + 2x + 0x^2 + \frac{18}{3!}x^3 + \frac{96}{4!}x^4 + \frac{120}{5!}x^5$

which simplifies to $1 + 2x + 3x^3 + 4x^4 + x^5$. Therefore, the Maclaurin series for a polynomial expressed in powers of x is the polynomial itself.

64. Suppose we want to express the polynomial in Problem 63 in powers of $(x + 1)$ instead of powers of x. We find the Taylor series of f at $x =$ ______. From our previous calculations of the derivatives, we find that

$f(-1) = -1$, $f'(-1) = 0$, $f^{(2)}(-1) =$ ______, $f^{(3)}(-1) =$ ______, $f^{(4)}(-1) =$ ______, $f^{(5)}(-1) =$ ______, and $f^{(k)}(-1) =$ ______ if $k \geq 6$. Thus the Taylor series of f at $x = -1$ is

______________________________,

which simplifies to

$$-1 + 5(x + 1)^2 - 3(x + 1)^3 - (x + 1)^4 + (x + 1)^5.$$

65. Let us find the Taylor polynomials $P_3(x)$ and $P_4(x)$ for the function $f(x) = a^x$, $a > 0$, at $x = 1$. To do this we complete the following table:

n	$f^{(n)}(x)$	$f^{(n)}(1)$
0	a^x	a
1	$a^x \ln a$	$a \ln a$
2	______	______
3	______	______
4	______	______

Then,

$P_3(x) = a + a(\ln a)(x - 1) + \dfrac{a(\ln a)^2}{2!}(x - 1)^2 +$ ______,

$P_4(x) =$ ______________________________.

66. For the function $f(x) = a^x$ in Problem 65, the Taylor series at $x = 1$ is

$$\sum_{n=0}^{\infty} \text{\_\_\_\_\_\_\_\_\_\_}.$$

---

64. -1, 10, -18, -24, 120, 0, $-1 + 0(x + 1) + \frac{10}{2!}(x + 1)^2 - \frac{18}{3!}(x + 1)^3 - \frac{24}{4!}(x + 1)^4 + \frac{120}{5!}(x + 1)^5$

65. For $n = k$, $f^{(k)}(1) = a(\ln a)^k$; $\dfrac{a(\ln a)^3}{3!}(x - 1)^3$,

$a + a(\ln a)(x - 1) + \dfrac{a(\ln a)^2}{2!}(x - 1)^2 + \dfrac{a(\ln a)^3}{3!}(x - 1)^3 + \dfrac{a(\ln a)^4}{4!}(x - 1)^4$

66. $\dfrac{a(\ln a)^n}{n!}(x - 1)^n$

OBJECTIVE B: Know the statement of Taylor's Theorem and a formula for the remainder of order n.

67. The statement of Taylor's Theorem in the text gives the remainder term as

$$R_n(x) = \_\_\_\_\_\_\_\_\_\_\_\_\_\_\_\_\_\_\_\_,$$

where the number c lies between ________________. This remainder term measures the error in the approximation of $y = f(x)$ by the nth-degree Taylor polynomial at ________. Thus, the Taylor series expansion for $f(x)$ will converge to $f(x)$ provided that

____________________ .

68. This remainder form is very useful because often we can bound the derivative $f^{(n+1)}(c)$ by some constant M: $|f^{(n+1)}(c)| \le M$. This ensures that $R_n(x)$ converges to _____ as $n \to \infty$.

OBJECTIVE C: Use the Remainder Estimation Theorem to estimate the truncation error when a Taylor polynomial is used to approximate a given function. Assume that the function has derivatives of all orders.

69. We will calculate $\cos\sqrt{2}$ with an error less than 10^{-6}. By Taylor's Theorem, $\cos\sqrt{2} = \_\_\_\_\_\_\_\_\_\_\_\_\_\_\_\_\_\_\_\_ + R_{2k}(x)$. The Remainder Estimation Theorem, with M = ______, x = _____, and r = 1 gives $|R_{2k}| \le 1 \cdot \_\_\_\_\_\_\_\_\_\_\_\_$. By trial we find that $\frac{(\sqrt{2})^{11}}{11!} = 0.0000011337 > 10^{-6}$ and $\frac{(\sqrt{2})^{13}}{13!} = 0.0000000145 < 10^{-6}$. Thus, we should take $(2k + 1)$ to be at least ______, or k to be at least 6. With an error less than 10^{-6},

$$\cos\sqrt{2} = 1 - \frac{2}{2!} + \frac{4}{4!} - \frac{8}{6!} + \dots + \_\_\_\_\_\_$$

↑ last term

$$\approx 0.155944.$$

70. Let us determine for what values of $x > 0$ we can replace e^x by $1 + x + \left(\frac{x^2}{2}\right) + \left(\frac{x^3}{3!}\right)$ with an error of magnitude less than 5×10^{-5}. In Example 4 in this section of the text, if $x > 0$,

$$|R_3(x)| < \_\_\_\_\_\_\_\_\_\_\_\_\_\_\_\_\_\_\_\_.$$

---

67. $f^{(n+1)}(c)\,\frac{(x-a)^{n+1}}{(n+1)!}$, a and x, $x = a$, $\lim_{n\to\infty} R_n(x) = 0$ 68. 0

69. $1 - \frac{2}{2!} + \frac{4}{4!} - \frac{8}{6!} + \dots + (-1)^k \frac{2^k}{(2k)!}$, 1, $\sqrt{2}$, $\frac{(\sqrt{2})^{2k+1}}{(2k+1)!}$, 13, 6, $\frac{64}{12!}$

We desire $|R_3(x)| < 5 \times 10^{-5}$. This is the case if $e^x|x|^4 <$ __________ or, since $x > 0$, $x + 4 \ln x < -5.116$. By calculator experimentation this inequality holds if $0 < x < 0.26$. Thus, for instance,

$$e^{0.1} \doteq 1 + (0.1) + \frac{(0.1)^2}{2} + \frac{(0.1)^3}{6} \approx 1.10517$$

is correct to five decimal places.

OBJECTIVE D: Using the Maclaurin series for the functions e^x, $\sin x$, and $\cos x$, write the Maclaurin series for functions which are combinations of sines, cosines, exponentials, or powers of x.

71. The Maclaurin series for e^x, $\sin x$, and $\cos x$ are $e^x =$ __________, $\sin x =$ __________, and $\cos x =$ __________.

72. Let us find the Maclaurin series for $\sin^3 x$. A trigonometric identity gives

$$\sin^3 x = \frac{1}{4}(3 \sin x - \sin 3x).$$

We use Maclaurin series for the terms on the right side:

$3 \sin x = 3x - \frac{3x^3}{3!} + \frac{3x^5}{5!} - \frac{3x^7}{7!} + \ldots,$

$\sin 3x =$ ____________________,

$3 \sin x - \sin 3x = 4x^3 - 2x^5 + \frac{52}{5!}x^7 - \ldots$

Therefore, $\sin^3 x =$ ____________________

$$= \sum_{n=0}^{\infty} \frac{(-1)^n(3 - 3^{2n+1})}{4(2n+1)!} x^{2n+1}.$$

73. Euler's formula asserts that

$$e^{i\theta} = \text{\_\_\_\_\_\_\_\_\_\_\_\_\_\_\_\_\_\_\_\_}.$$

8.8 CALCULATIONS WITH TAYLOR SERIES

OBJECTIVE A: Use a suitable series to calculate a given quantity to three decimal places. Show that the remainder term does not exceed 5×10^{-4}. (Assume the quantity is the value of a function whose series expansion has been studied in this chapter of the text.)

74. Replacing x by $-x$ in the Taylor series expansion for $\ln(1 + x)$ gives the expansion

$$\ln(1 - x) = \text{\_\_\_\_\_\_\_\_\_\_\_\_\_\_\_\_\_\_\_\_}$$

---

70. $e^x \cdot \frac{x^4}{4!}$, 6×10^{-3}

71. $\sum_{n=0}^{\infty} \frac{x^n}{n!}$, $\sum_{n=0}^{\infty} \frac{(-1)^n x^{2n+1}}{(2n+1)!}$, $\sum_{n=0}^{\infty} \frac{(-1)^n x^{2n}}{(2n)!}$

72. $3x - \frac{(3x)^3}{3!} + \frac{(3x)^5}{5!} - \frac{(3x)^7}{7!} + \ldots$, $x^3 - \frac{1}{2}x^5 + \frac{13}{5!}x^7 - \ldots$

73. $\cos\theta + i \sin\theta$

which is also valid for $|x| < 1$. Subtracting this result from the expansion for $\ln(1 + x)$ gives

$$\ln(1 + x) - \ln(1 - x) = \ln \frac{1 + x}{1 - x} = \underline{\hspace{6cm}}.$$

75. Let N be a positive integer. Then

$$\ln(N + 1) = \ln N + \ln \frac{N + 1}{N}.$$

Now, solve the equation

$$\frac{1 + x}{1 - x} = \frac{N + 1}{N}$$

for x to obtain $x = \underline{\hspace{2.5cm}}$. Substitution into the result from Problem 74 yields

$$\ln \frac{N + 1}{N} = \underline{\hspace{7cm}}.$$

76. Let's use the result of Problem 74 to calculate $\ln 2$ by setting $N = 1$. Thus,

$$\ln 2 = 2\left(\frac{1}{3} + \frac{1}{3(3)^3} + \frac{1}{3(3)^5} + \frac{1}{7(3)^7} + \frac{1}{9(3)^9} + \frac{1}{11(3)^{11}} + \dots\right)$$

$$\approx 2(0.3333333 + 0.0123457 + 0.0008230 + 0.0000653 + 0.0000056 + 0.0000005)$$

$$\approx \underline{\hspace{4cm}}.$$

The error satisfies

$$|R_{11}(x)| \le \frac{1}{12} \cdot \frac{|x|^{12}}{1 - |x|} \quad \text{where} \quad x = \frac{1}{2N + 1} = \underline{\hspace{1.5cm}}.$$

Thus,

$$|R_{11}(x)| \le \frac{1}{12} \cdot \frac{3}{2}\left|\frac{1}{3}\right|^{12} = 0.00000023252 < 5 \times 10^{-6}.$$

It follows that $\ln 2 \approx 0.69315$, accurate to five decimal places.

77. Now let's calculate $\ln 0.75$ using the result in Problem 74. First use the identity

$$\ln 0.75 = \ln \frac{3}{4} = \ln \frac{3}{2} - \underline{\hspace{4cm}}.$$

We can use the calculation for $\ln 2$ obtained in Problem 76: $\ln 2 \approx 0.69315$. To obtain the first term on the right side of the previous equation we use the series

$$\ln \frac{N + 1}{N} = 2\left(\underline{\hspace{6cm}}\right) \quad \text{with} \quad N = 2.$$

Then,

---

74. $-x - \frac{x^2}{2} - \frac{x^3}{3} - \dots - \frac{x^n}{n} - \dots$, $2\left(x + \frac{x^3}{3} + \frac{x^5}{5} + \dots + \frac{x^{2k-1}}{2k - 1} + \dots\right)$

75. $\frac{1}{2N + 1}$, $2\left(\frac{1}{2N + 1} + \frac{1}{3(2N + 1)^3} + \frac{1}{5(2N + 1)^5} + \dots\right)$

76. 0.6931468, $\frac{1}{3}$

$$\ln \frac{3}{2} = 2\left(\frac{1}{5} + \frac{1}{3(5)^3} + \frac{1}{5(5)^5} + \frac{1}{7(5)^7} + \cdots\right)$$
$$= 2(0.2 + 0.00266667 + 0.000064 + 0.00000183 + \ldots)$$
$$\approx 0.40547.$$

The error satisfies

$$|R_7(x)| \le \frac{1}{8} \cdot \frac{|x|^8}{1 - |x|}, \quad \text{where} \quad x = \frac{1}{2N + 1} = \underline{\qquad}.$$

Thus,

$$|R_7(x)| \le \frac{5}{32}\left|\frac{1}{5}\right|^8 < 5 \times 10^{-6}.$$

It follows that

$$\ln \frac{3}{4} \approx 0.40547 - 0.69315 = -0.28768,$$

accurate to five decimal places.

OBJECTIVE B: If f is a function having a known power series $f(x) = \sum a_n x^n$, use the series and a calculator to estimate the integral $\int_0^b f(x)\,dx$, assuming that b lies within the interval of convergence.

78. Let us find $\int_0^{0.2} \cos\sqrt{x}\,dx$ accurate to five decimal places. Now,

$$\cos x = 1 - \frac{x^2}{2!} + \frac{x^4}{4!} - \frac{x^6}{6!} + \frac{x^8}{8!} - \cdots,$$

so the power series for $\cos\sqrt{x}$ is given by

$$\cos\sqrt{x} = \underline{\qquad\qquad\qquad}, \quad x \ge 0.$$

Thus, using term-by-term integration,

$$\int_0^{0.2} \cos\sqrt{x}\,dx = \underline{\qquad\qquad\qquad}\Big]_0^{0.2}$$
$$= 0.2 - \frac{0.04}{4} + \frac{0.008}{72} - \frac{0.0016}{2880} + \frac{0.00032}{201600} - \cdots$$
$$\approx 0.2 - 0.01 + 0.00011 - 0.00000056 + \ldots$$

Hence, $\int_0^{0.2} \cos\sqrt{x}\,dx \approx \underline{\qquad}$ with an error less than 5×10^{-6}.

8.9 A COMPUTER MYSTERY

79. Why did the computer or calculator produce the answer 1 for calculating $(1 + \frac{1}{n})^n$ when $n = 10^{13}$, $n = 10^{14}$, etc., in this section of the text?

---

77. $\ln 2$, $\frac{1}{2N+1} + \frac{1}{3(2N+1)^3} + \frac{1}{5(2N+1)^5} + \ldots$, $\frac{1}{5}$

78. $1 - \frac{x}{2!} + \frac{x^2}{4!} - \frac{x^3}{6!} + \frac{x^4}{8!} - \ldots$, $x - \frac{x^2}{2\cdot 2!} + \frac{x^3}{3\cdot 4!} - \frac{x^4}{4\cdot 6!} + \frac{x^5}{5\cdot 8!} - \ldots$, 0.19011

79. The number $\frac{1}{n}$ is so small that when added to 1 the computer cannot show any digits beyond the 12th decimal place. Thus the computer effectively sets $1 + \frac{1}{n}$ equal to 1. and $1^n = 1$.

CHAPTER 8 SELF-TEST

1. Determine if each sequence $\{a_n\}$ converges or diverges. Find the limit of the sequence if it does converge.

   (a) $a_n = \sqrt{n+1} - \sqrt{n}$ (b) $a_n = \dfrac{1 + (-1)^n}{n\sqrt{n}}$

   (c) $a_n = \left(\dfrac{n - 0.05}{n}\right)^n$ (d) $a_n = \dfrac{2^n}{5^{3 + 1/n}}$

2. Find the sum of each series.

   (a) $\displaystyle\sum_{n=0}^{\infty} (-1)^n \frac{3}{5^n}$ (b) $\displaystyle\sum_{n=4}^{\infty} \frac{2}{(4n - 3)(4n + 1)}$

   (c) $\displaystyle\sum_{n=0}^{\infty} \left(\frac{5}{3^n} - \frac{2}{7^n}\right)$

   (d) $\dfrac{127}{1000} + \dfrac{127}{1000^2} + \dfrac{127}{1000^3} + \dots + \dfrac{127}{1000^n} + \dots$

In Problems 3-8, determine whether the given series converges or diverges. In each case, give a reason for your answer.

3. $\displaystyle\sum_{n=1}^{\infty} \frac{\sqrt{n}}{n^2 + 3}$ 4. $\displaystyle\sum_{n=1}^{\infty} \frac{n!3^n}{10^n}$ 5. $\displaystyle\sum_{n=1}^{\infty} \sin\left(\frac{n\pi - 2}{3n}\right)$

6. $\displaystyle\sum_{n=1}^{\infty} \left(\frac{n}{2n + 5}\right)^n$ 7. $\displaystyle\sum_{n=1}^{\infty} \frac{1}{n + \sqrt{n}}$ 8. $\displaystyle\sum_{n=1}^{\infty} \frac{\tan^{-1} n}{n^2 + 1}$

In Problems 9-12, determine whether the series are absolutely convergent, conditionally convergent, or divergent.

9. $\displaystyle\sum_{n=1}^{\infty} (-1)^{n+1} \frac{\sin n}{n^2 + 1}$ 10. $\displaystyle\sum_{n=1}^{\infty} (-1)^{n+1} \frac{1}{(n + 1)^{1/n}}$

11. $\displaystyle\sum_{n=2}^{\infty} (-1)^n \frac{1}{(\ln n)^2}$ 12. $\displaystyle\sum_{n=1}^{\infty} (-1)^{n+1} \frac{n + 1}{7n - 2}$

13. Estimate the magnitude of the error if the first five terms are used to approximate the series,

$$\sum_{n=1}^{\infty} (-1)^{n+1} \frac{2^n}{3^n}$$

   Sum the first five terms, and state whether your approximation underestimates or overestimates the sum of the series.

14. Find the interval of convergence for the power series

$$\sum_{n=2}^{\infty} \frac{\ln n}{n} x^n$$

15. Find the Taylor series of $f(x) = \sqrt{x}$ at $a = 9$. Do not be concerned with whether the series converges to the given function f.

16. Find the Maclaurin series for the function $f(x) = x \ln(1 + x^2)$ using series that have already been obtained in the Thomas/Finney text.

17. Use series to estimate the number $e^{-1/3}$ with an error of magnitude less than 0.001.

18. Find the first three nonzero terms in the Maclaurin series for the function $f(x) = \sec^2 x$ using the Maclaurin series for $\tan x$.

19. (Calculator) Use series and a calculator to estimate the integral

$$\int_0^{0.5} \cos x^2 \, dx$$

with an error of magnitude less than 0.0001.

SOLUTIONS TO CHAPTER 8 SELF-TEST

1. (a) $a_n = \sqrt{n+1} - \sqrt{n} = \dfrac{(\sqrt{n+1} - \sqrt{n})(\sqrt{n+1} + \sqrt{n})}{(\sqrt{n+1} + \sqrt{n})} = \dfrac{(n+1) - n}{\sqrt{n+1} + \sqrt{n}}$

$= \dfrac{1}{\sqrt{n+1} + \sqrt{n}} \to 0$ as $n \to \infty$

(b) $\sqrt[n]{n} \to 1$, but $1 + (-1)^n$ alternates back and forth between 0 and 2. Thus, for n large, a_n alternates between numbers very close to 2 and 0; hence the sequence diverges.

(c) $a_n = \left(\frac{n - 0.05}{n}\right)^n = \left(1 + \frac{-0.05}{n}\right)^n \to e^{-0.05} \approx 0.951.$

(d) $5^{3+1/n} = 125\sqrt[n]{5} \to 125$, but $2^n \to +\infty$. Therefore, the sequence $\{a_n\}$ is unbounded and diverges.

2. (a) $\displaystyle\sum_{n=0}^{\infty} (-1)^n \frac{3}{5^n} = \sum_{n=0}^{\infty} 3\left(-\frac{1}{5}\right)^n = \frac{3}{1 + \frac{1}{5}} = \frac{5}{2}.$

(b) Using the partial fraction decomposition,

$\dfrac{2}{(4k-3)(4k+1)} = \dfrac{1}{2}\left(\dfrac{1}{4k-3}\right) - \dfrac{1}{2}\left(\dfrac{1}{4k+1}\right)$, we write the partial sum

$$s_k = \sum_{n=4}^{k} \frac{2}{(4n-3)(4n+1)}$$

as

$$s_k = \frac{1}{2}\left(\frac{1}{13} - \frac{1}{17}\right) + \frac{1}{2}\left(\frac{1}{17} - \frac{1}{21}\right) + \frac{1}{2}\left(\frac{1}{21} - \frac{1}{25}\right) + \cdots$$
$$+ \frac{1}{2}\left(\frac{1}{4k-3} - \frac{1}{4k+1}\right).$$

Thus,

$$s_k = \frac{1}{2}\left(\frac{1}{13} - \frac{1}{4k+1}\right) \to \frac{1}{26} \quad \text{as} \quad k \to \infty$$

so that

$$\sum_{n=4}^{\infty} \frac{2}{(4n-3)(4n+1)} = \frac{1}{26}.$$

(c) $\displaystyle\sum_{n=0}^{\infty}\left(\frac{5}{3^n} - \frac{2}{7^n}\right) = \sum_{n=0}^{\infty}\frac{5}{3^n} - \sum_{n=0}^{\infty}\frac{2}{7^n} = \frac{5}{1 - \frac{1}{3}} - \frac{2}{1 - \frac{1}{7}} = \frac{31}{6}.$

(d) $\displaystyle\sum_{n=1}^{\infty} 127\left(\frac{1}{1000}\right)^n = \sum_{n=0}^{\infty} 127\left(\frac{1}{1000}\right)^n - 127 = \frac{127}{1 - \frac{1}{1000}} - 127$

$$= \frac{127{,}000 - 126{,}873}{999} = \frac{127}{999}.$$

3. $\frac{\sqrt{n}}{n^2 + 3} < \frac{\sqrt{n}}{n^2} = \frac{1}{n^{3/2}}$ so that $\sum_{n=1}^{\infty} \frac{\sqrt{n}}{n^2 + 3}$ converges by comparison with the convergent p-series for $p = \frac{3}{2}$.

4. Using the ratio test, $\lim_{n\to\infty} \frac{(n+1)!3^{n+1}}{10^{n+1}} \cdot \frac{10^n}{n!3^n} = \lim_{n\to\infty} \frac{(n+1)3}{10} = \infty$. Thus, $\sum_{n=1}^{\infty} \frac{n!3^n}{10^n}$ diverges by the ratio test.

5. $\lim_{n\to\infty} \sin\left(\frac{n\pi - 2}{3n}\right) = \lim_{n\to\infty} \sin\left(\frac{\pi}{3} - \frac{2}{3n}\right) = \sin\frac{\pi}{3} = \frac{\sqrt{3}}{2} \neq 0$, so the series $\sum_{n=1}^{\infty} \sin\left(\frac{n\pi - 2}{3n}\right)$ diverges by the nth-term test for divergence.

6. If $a_n = \left(\frac{n}{2n+5}\right)^n$, then $\sqrt[n]{a_n} = \frac{n}{2n+5} \to \frac{1}{2}$. Thus, the series $\sum_{n=1}^{\infty} \left(\frac{n}{2n+5}\right)^n$ converges by the root test.

7. $\frac{1}{n + \sqrt{n}} > \frac{1}{n + n} = \frac{1}{2n}$ so that $\sum_{n=1}^{\infty} \frac{1}{n + \sqrt{n}}$ diverges by comparison to the divergent series $\sum_{n=1}^{\infty} \frac{1}{2n}$.

8. $\int_1^{\infty} \frac{\tan^{-1} x\, dx}{x^2 + 1} = \lim_{b\to\infty} \frac{1}{2}\left(\tan^{-1} x\right)^2\Big]_1^b = \lim_{b\to\infty} \frac{1}{2}\left(\tan^{-1} b\right)^2 - \frac{1}{2}\tan^{-1} 1$
$= \frac{1}{2}\left(\frac{\pi}{2}\right)^2 - \frac{1}{2}\left(\frac{\pi}{4}\right)$

Therefore, the improper integral converges, so the original series $\sum_{n=1}^{\infty} \frac{\tan^{-1} n}{n^2 + 1}$ converges by the integral test.

9. $\left|(-1)^{n+1} \frac{\sin n}{n^2 + 1}\right| \leq \frac{1}{n^2 + 1}$, so the original series $\sum_{n=1}^{\infty} (-1)^{n+1} \frac{\sin n}{n^2 + 1}$ converges absolutely by the comparison test.

10. Since $\frac{1}{n^2} < \frac{1}{n+1} < \frac{1}{n}$, it follows that $\left(\frac{1}{\sqrt[n]{n}}\right)\left(\frac{1}{\sqrt[n]{n}}\right) < \frac{1}{\sqrt[n]{n+1}} < \frac{1}{\sqrt[n]{n}}$. Thus, $\lim_{n\to\infty} \frac{1}{\sqrt[n]{n+1}} = 1$ so the original series $\sum_{n=1}^{\infty} (-1)^{n+1} \frac{1}{(n+1)^{1/n}}$ diverges by the nth-term test.

11. $\lim_{n\to\infty} \frac{1}{(\ln n)^2} = 0$, and $\frac{1}{[\ln (n+1)]^2} < \frac{1}{(\ln n)^2}$ because $y = \ln x$ is an increasing function of x. Therefore the alternating

series $\sum_{n=2}^{\infty} (-1)^n \frac{1}{(\ln n)^2}$ converges by the Alternating Series Theorem. However, since $\ln n < \sqrt{n}$ implies $\frac{1}{(\ln n)^2} > \frac{1}{n}$ if $n \geq 2$, series of absolute values $\sum_{n=2}^{\infty} \frac{1}{(\ln n)^2}$ diverges by comparison with the divergent harmonic series. Therefore, $\sum_{n=2}^{\infty} (-1)^n \frac{1}{(\ln n)^2}$ is conditionally convergent.

12. $\lim_{n\to\infty} \frac{n+1}{7n-2} = \frac{1}{7}$ so that $\sum_{n=1}^{\infty} (-1)^{n+1} \frac{n+1}{7n-2}$ diverges by the nth-term test.

13. $\sum_{n=1}^{\infty} (-1)^{n+1} \frac{2^n}{3^n} \approx \frac{2}{3} - \frac{4}{9} + \frac{8}{27} - \frac{16}{81} + \frac{32}{243} \approx 0.4527$ with an error of magnitude less than $2^6/3^6 < 0.0878$. Since the sign of the first unused term is negative, the sum 0.4527 overestimates the value of the series. In fact, the given geometric series sums to 0.4.

14. Using the ratio test,

$$\lim_{n\to\infty} \frac{\ln (n+1)\ |x|^{n+1}}{(n+1)} \cdot \frac{n}{\ln n\ |x|^n}$$

$$= \lim_{n\to\infty} \frac{\ln (n+1)}{\ln n} \cdot \frac{n+1}{n} |x| = |x|.$$

Thus, the given power series converges absolutely for $|x| < 1$ and diverges for $|x| > 1$. Test the endpoints of the interval:

For $x = 1$, the power series is $\sum_{n=2}^{\infty} \frac{\ln n}{n}$. Now $\int_2^{\infty} \frac{\ln x}{x}\,dx = \lim_{b\to\infty} \frac{1}{2}(\ln x)^2\Big]_2^b = +\infty$ diverges, so the series $\sum_{n=2}^{\infty} \frac{\ln n}{n}$ is divergent by the integral test.

For $x = -1$, the power series is $\sum_{n=2}^{\infty} \frac{(-1)^n \ln n}{n}$. Since $0 \leq \lim_{n\to\infty} \frac{\ln n}{n} \leq \lim_{n\to\infty} \frac{\sqrt{n}}{n} = 0$, and $\frac{d}{dx}\left(\frac{\ln x}{x}\right) = \frac{1 - \ln x}{x^2} < 0$ for $x \geq 3$ implies that $\frac{\ln (n+1)}{n+1} < \frac{\ln n}{n}$, the alternating series $\sum_{n=2}^{\infty} \frac{(-1)^n \ln n}{n}$ converges by the Alternating Series Theorem.

Therefore, the power series $\sum_{n=2}^{\infty} \frac{\ln n}{n} x^n$ converges for all x satisfying $-1 \leq x < 1$.

15. We calculate the derivatives of $f(x) = \sqrt{x}$, and evaluate f and these derivatives at $a = 9$:

$$f(x) = \sqrt{x} \qquad f(9) = 3$$

$$f'(x) = \tfrac{1}{2}x^{-1/2} \qquad f'(9) = \tfrac{1}{6}$$

$$f^{(2)}(x) = (-1)\left(\tfrac{1}{2}\right)\left(\tfrac{1}{2}\right)x^{-3/2} \qquad f^{(2)}(9) = -\frac{1}{108}$$

$$f^{(3)}(x) = (-1)^2\left(\tfrac{1}{2}\right)\left(\tfrac{1}{2}\right)\left(\tfrac{3}{2}\right)x^{-5/2} \qquad f^{(3)}(9) = \frac{1}{648}$$

$$f^{(4)}(x) = (-1)^3\,\frac{3\cdot 5}{2^4}\,x^{-7/2} \qquad f^{(4)}(9) = -\frac{5}{11664}$$

$$\vdots \qquad\qquad \vdots$$

$$f^{(k)}(x) = (-1)^{k+1}\,\frac{3\cdot5\cdots(2k-3)}{2^k}\,x^{-(2k-1)/2}$$

$$f^{(k)}(9) = (-1)^{k+1}\,\frac{3\cdot5\cdots(2k-3)}{2^k\;3^{2k-1}}$$

Therefore, the Taylor series for $f(x) = \sqrt{x}$ at $a = 9$ is

$$3 + \tfrac{1}{6}(x-9) - \frac{1}{216}(x-9)^2 + \dots + (-1)^{k+1}\,\frac{3\cdot5\cdots(2k-3)}{2^k\;3^{2k-1}\cdot k!}\,(x-9)^k + \dots$$

16. $\ln(1 + x) = x - \frac{x^2}{2} + \frac{x^3}{3} - \frac{x^4}{4} + \dots, \qquad -1 < x \le 1$

$\ln(1 + x^2) = x^2 - \frac{x^4}{2} + \frac{x^6}{3} - \frac{x^8}{4} + \dots, \qquad -1 < x \le 1$

$x\ln(1 + x^2) = x^3 - \frac{x^5}{2} + \frac{x^7}{3} - \frac{x^9}{4} + \dots, \qquad -1 < x \le 1$

or, in closed form, $x\ln(1 + x^2) = \sum_{n=0}^{\infty} (-1)^n\,\frac{1}{n+1}\,x^{2n+3}$, valid for all x satisfying $-1 < x \le 1$.

17. $e^{-1/3} = 1 - \frac{1}{3} + \frac{(-1/3)^2}{2!} + \frac{(-1/3)^3}{3!} + \frac{(-1/3)^4}{4!} + \dots$

By trial, $\frac{(-1/3)^4}{4!} < 0.00052$ and $\frac{(1/3)^3}{3!} > 0.001$.

Since the series is an alternating series,

$e^{-1/3} \approx 1 - \frac{1}{3} + \frac{1/9}{2!} - \frac{1/27}{3!} = 0.71605$ with an error in magnitude less than 0.00052.

18. The Maclaurin series for $\tan x$, through the first three nonzero terms, is

$$\tan x = x + \frac{x^3}{3} + \frac{2x^5}{15} + \dots$$

Hence, $\sec^2 x = \frac{d}{dx}\tan x = 1 + x^2 + \frac{2}{3}x^4 + \dots$.

19. The Maclaurin series for $\cos x^2$ is

$$\cos x^2 = 1 - \frac{x^4}{2!} + \frac{x^8}{4!} - \frac{x^{12}}{6!} + \dots + (-1)^k \frac{x^{4k}}{(2k)!} + \dots$$

Hence,

$$\int_0^{0.5} \cos x^2\, dx = x - \frac{x^5}{5 \cdot 2!} + \frac{x^9}{9 \cdot 4!} - \frac{x^{13}}{13 \cdot 6!} + \dots \Big]_0^{0.5}$$

$$\approx 0.5 - 0.00313 + 0.0000090 - \dots = 0.49687,$$

with an error in magnitude less than 0.000009 because the series is an alternating series.

NOTES.

CHAPTER 9 CONIC SECTIONS, PARAMETRIZED CURVES AND POLAR COORDINATES

9.1 EQUATIONS FOR CONIC SECTIONS

OBJECTIVE A: Given an equation of an ellipse $Ax^2 + Cy^2 = F$, where A, C and F are positive numbers, put the equation in standard form and find the ellipse's eccentricity. Sketch the ellipse and include the foci in your sketch.

1. The standard equation for an ellipse centered at the origin with foci on the x-axis is

   ______________________________ , $a > b$.

   The foci are located at the points ____________ where $c =$ ______________. The points $(\pm a, 0)$ are called the ____________ of the ellipse, and a is the ___________________ axis.

2. If the foci lie on the y-axis, the standard equation for an ellipse centered at the origin is

   ______________________________ , $a > b$.

   The points $(0, \pm a)$ are the ______________ and the foci are ______________ where $c = \sqrt{a^2 - b^2}$.

3. The ratio

   $$\frac{\text{Distance between foci}}{\text{Distance between vertices}} = \frac{c}{a}$$

   is called the ______________________________ of the ellipse. If $c = 0$ the ellipse takes the shape of a ______________. As c increases, the ellipse tends to ___________________, degenerating into a ________________________ when $c = a$.

4. In an elliptical mirror, light is reflected from ____.

---

1. $\frac{x^2}{a^2} + \frac{y^2}{b^2} = 1$, $(\pm c, 0)$, $\sqrt{a^2 - b^2}$, vertices, semimajor

2. $\frac{x^2}{b^2} + \frac{y^2}{a^2} = 1$, vertices, $(0, \pm c)$

3. eccentricity, circle, flatten out, line segment

4. one focus to the other

5. The equation $16x^2 + 5y^2 = 80$ represents an ellipse. In standard form it is written

________________________________.

In this case $c =$ ________________ ≈ 3.32, and the foci are located at the points ________________. The vertices are __________. The eccentricity is

$e =$ __________.

Sketch the ellipse in the coordinate system at the right, and include the foci in your sketch.

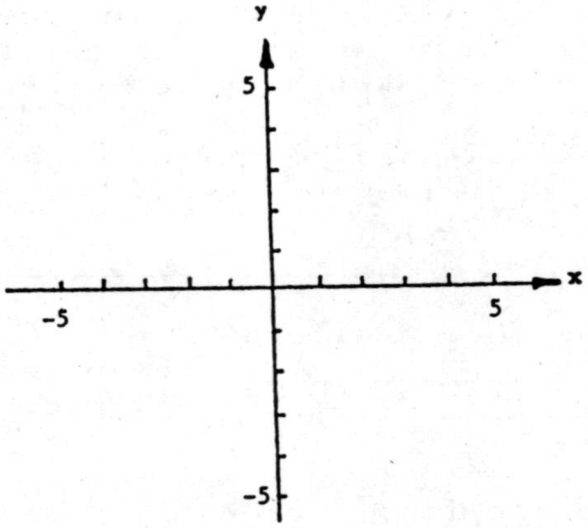

OBJECTIVE B: Given an equation of a hyperbola $Ax^2 - Cy^2 = F$ or $Cy^2 - Ax^2 = F$, where A, C and F are positive numbers, put the equation in standard form and find the hyperbola's eccentricity and asymptotes. Sketch the hyperbola, including the asymptotes and foci in your sketch.

6. The standard equation for a hyperbola centered at the origin with foci on the x-axis is

________________________________.

---

5. $\frac{x^2}{5} + \frac{y^2}{16} = 1$, $\sqrt{16 - 5}$,

$(0, \pm\sqrt{11})$, $(0, \pm 4)$, $\frac{\sqrt{11}}{4}$

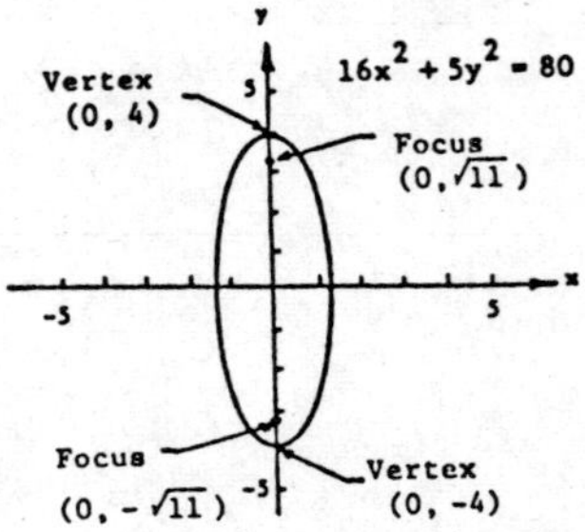

The foci are located at the points ________ where $c =$ __________. The points $(\pm a, 0)$ are called the ________ of the hyperbola. The asymptotes are straight lines passing through the origin with equations ___________. Note that in the case of the hyperbola it is not necessary for $a > b$ or $b > a$. It is also permissible for $a = b$.

7. If the foci lie on the y-axis, the standard equation for a hyperbola centered at the origin is

______________________________.

The foci are located at the points $(0, \pm c)$ where $c =$ ________. The points __________ are the vertices, and the asymptotes are given by the equations ____________.

8. The eccentricity of a hyperbola is always given by

$e =$ ________ .

For a hyperbola, it is always true that e _____ 1.

9. Light directed toward one focus of a hyperbolic mirror is reflected ______________________.

10. The equation $16y^2 - 5x^2 = 80$ represents a hyperbola. In standard form it is written

__________________________ .

In this case $c =$ ________ ≈ 4.58, and the foci are located at the points __________. The vertices are __________, and the asymptotes are given by __________. The eccentricity is $e =$ _____.

---

6. $\frac{x^2}{a^2} - \frac{y^2}{b^2} = 1$, $(\pm c, 0)$, $\sqrt{a^2 + b^2}$, vertices, $y = \pm \frac{b}{a}x$

7. $\frac{y^2}{a^2} - \frac{x^2}{b^2} = 1$, $\sqrt{a^2 + b^2}$, $(0, \pm a)$, $y = \pm \frac{a}{b}x$

8. $\frac{c}{a}$ or $\frac{\sqrt{a^2 + b^2}}{a}$, $e > 1$

9. toward the other focus

Sketch the hyperbola in the coordinate system at the right, including the foci and asymptotes in your sketch.

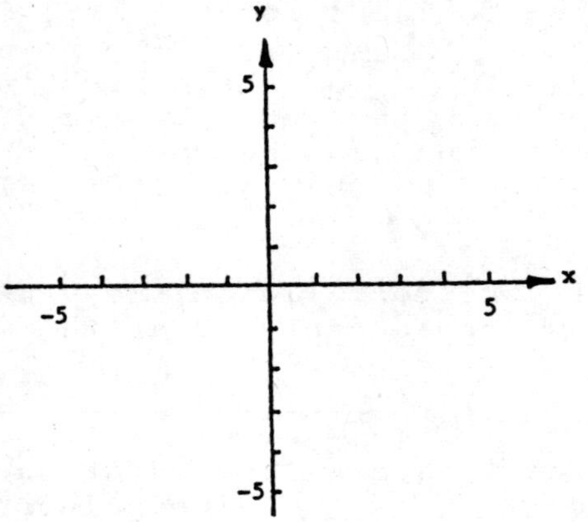

9.2 THE GRAPHS OF QUADRATIC EQUATIONS IN x AND y; ROTATIONS ABOUT THE ORIGIN

11. Any second degree equation in x and y represents a circle, parabola, ellipse, or hyperbola (although it may degenerate). To find the curve given its equation

$$Ax^2 + Bxy + Cy^2 + Dx + Ey + F = 0,$$

(1) First rotate axes, to force $B = 0$, through an angle α satisfying $\cot 2\alpha =$ ____________.

(2) Next, ____________ axes by completing the squares (if necessary) to reduce the equation to a standard form.

OBJECTIVE A: Given an equation of the form $Ax^2 + Bxy + Cy^2 + F = 0$, transform the equation by a rotation of axes into an equation that has no cross-product term. Then identify the graph of the equation.

---

10. $\frac{y^2}{5} - \frac{x^2}{16} = 1$, $\sqrt{5 + 16}$, $(0, \pm\sqrt{21})$,

$(0, \pm\sqrt{5})$, $y = \pm\frac{\sqrt{5}}{4}x$,

$\frac{\sqrt{21}}{\sqrt{5}} \approx 2.05$

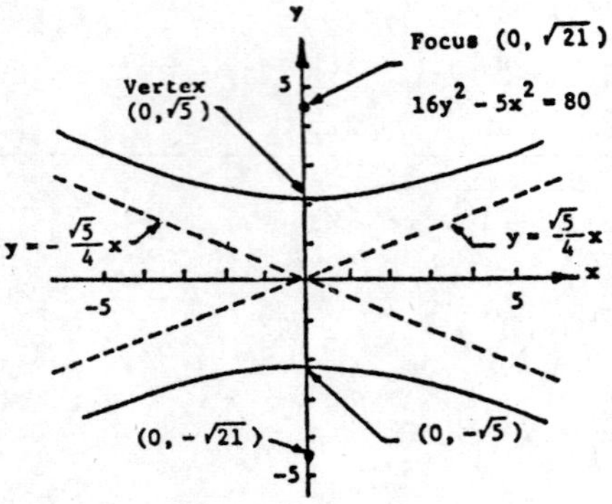

11. $\frac{A - C}{B}$, translate

12. Consider the equation $5x^2 - 2\sqrt{3}xy + 7y^2 = 6$. The required angle of rotation to eliminate the xy term satisfies $\cot 2\alpha = \dfrac{5 - 7}{\_\_\_\_} = \_\_\_\_\_\_\_\_$; hence $2\alpha =$ ______ radians, or $\alpha =$ ________. Thus, $\sin \alpha =$ _______ and $\cos \alpha =$ _______. The equations for the rotation of axes are $x = \frac{\sqrt{3}}{2}x' - \frac{1}{2}y'$ and ____________________. Substitution for x and y into the given second-degree equation gives

$$5\left(\tfrac{3}{4}x'^2 - \_\_\_\_\_\_\_\_ + \tfrac{1}{4}y'^2\right) - 2\sqrt{3}\left(\tfrac{\sqrt{3}}{4}x'^2 + \_\_\_\_\_\_\_\_\_\_ - \tfrac{\sqrt{3}}{4}y'^2\right)$$
$$+ 7\left(\tfrac{1}{4}x'^2 + \_\_\_\_\_\_\_\_\_\_ + \tfrac{3}{4}y'^2\right) = 6 .$$

Simplifying algebraically,

$$\left(\tfrac{15}{4} - \_\_\_\_\_\_\_ + \tfrac{7}{4}\right)x'^2 + \left(\_\_\_ + \tfrac{3}{2} + \tfrac{21}{4}\right)y'^2 = 6, \quad \text{or}$$

________________. This is an equation of ________________.

OBJECTIVE B: Given a second degree equation of the form $Ax^2 + Bxy + Cy^2 + Dx + Ey + F = 0$, use the discriminant to classify it as representing a circle, an ellipse, a parabola, or a hyperbola.

13. The <u>discriminant</u> is the expression ______________. The discriminant is not changed by a rotation of axes.

14. If the discriminant is positive, the equation represents ________________.

15. If the discriminant is zero, the equation represents ________________.

16. If the discriminant is negative, the equation represents ________________.

17. In order that the equation represent a circle, it is necessary that the discriminant be ___________ and that ________________.

18. Consider the equation given by

$$2x^2 - 4xy - y^2 + 20x - 2y + 17 = 0.$$

The discriminant is $B^2 - 4AC = 16 - (\_\_\_\_\_\_\_) =$ ________.
Thus, the equation represents __________________.

---

12. $-2\sqrt{3}$, $\frac{1}{\sqrt{3}}$, $\frac{\pi}{3}$, $\frac{\pi}{6}$, $\frac{1}{2}$, $\frac{\sqrt{3}}{2}$, $y = \frac{1}{2}x' + \frac{\sqrt{3}}{2}y'$, $\frac{\sqrt{3}}{2}x'y'$, $\frac{1}{2}x'y'$, $\frac{\sqrt{3}}{2}x'y'$, $\frac{3}{2}$, $\frac{5}{4}$, $4x'^2 + 8y'^2 = 6$, an ellipse

13. $B^2 - 4AC$, $A + C$ 14. a hyperbola 15. a parabola 16. an ellipse

17. negative, $A = C$ 18. -8, 24, a hyperbola

19. For $4x^2 - 12xy + 9y^2 - 52x + 26y + 81 = 0$ the discriminant is $B^2 - 4AC$ = ______ $- 4(36)$ = ______. Thus, the equation represents ______________________.

9.3 PARAMETRIZATIONS OF CURVES

OBJECTIVE A: Given parametric equations $x = f(t)$ and $y = g(t)$ for the motion of a particle in the xy-plane, eliminate the parameter t to find a Cartesian equation for the particle's path. Graph the Cartesian equation.

20. Consider the curve given by the parametric equations $x = t - 2$, $y = 2t + 3$, $-\infty < t < \infty$. Complete the following table providing some of the points $P(x,y)$ on the curve:

t	-2	-1	0	1	2	3
x	-4					
y	-1					

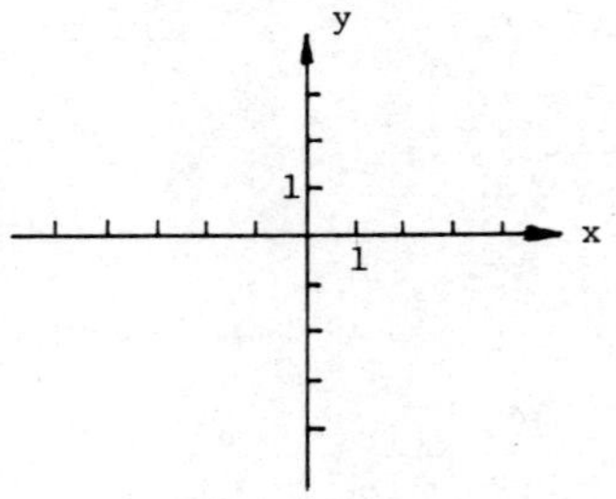

To eliminate the parameter t, note that $t = x + 2$. Substitution for t in the parametric equation for y gives y = ________. This is a Cartesian equation for a ________ with slope m = ______ and y-intercept b = _______. Sketch the curve in the coordinate system to the right.

21. For the curve given by the parametric equations $x = e^t$ and $y = e^{-t}$, $-\infty < t < \infty$, complete the following table:

t	-2	-1	0	1	2	3
x						
y						

---

19. 144, 0, a parabola

20.

t	-2	-1	0	1	2	3
x	-4	-3	-2	-1	0	1
y	-1	1	3	5	7	9

$2x + 7$, line, 2, 7

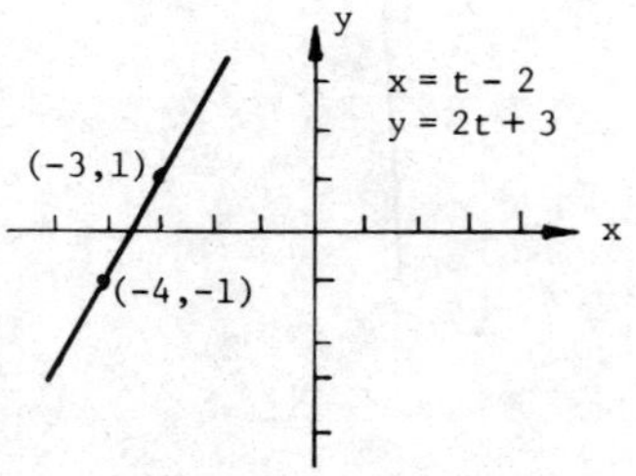

To eliminate the parameter t, notice that xy = ________. This equation describes a ______________. Sketch the graph in the coordinate system at the right.

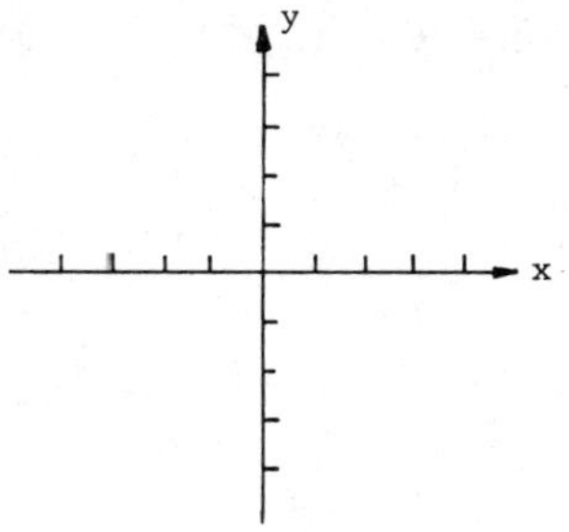

22. For the curve given parametrically in Problem 21, notice that x and y are always positive. Are the parametric equations and the cartesian equation coextensive? _______, because x and y can both be ____________ in the cartesian equation xy = 1.

OBJECTIVE B: Find parametric equations for a curve described geometrically, or by an equation, in terms of some specified or arbitrary parameter.

23. Find parametric equations for the circle with center C(-2,3) and radius $r = \sqrt{2}$.

Solution. An equation of the circle is $(x + 2)^2 +$ _________ = _______, or _______________________ = 1.

This suggests the substitutions $\frac{x+2}{\sqrt{2}} = \sin\theta$ and $\frac{y-3}{\sqrt{2}} =$ __________. Hence, parametric equations for the circle are x = __________ and y = __________, $0 \le \theta \le 2\pi$.

24. Find parametric equations for the line in the plane through the point (a,b) with slope m, where the parameter t is the change x - a.

Solution. For any point P(x,y) on the line, y - b = m(________) = ________. Thus, x = ______ and y = ______ give parametric equations of the line in terms of the specified parameter t.

21.

t	-2	-1	0	1	2	3
x	.14	.37	1	2.7	7.4	20
y	7.4	2.7	1	.37	.14	.05

(approximate values)

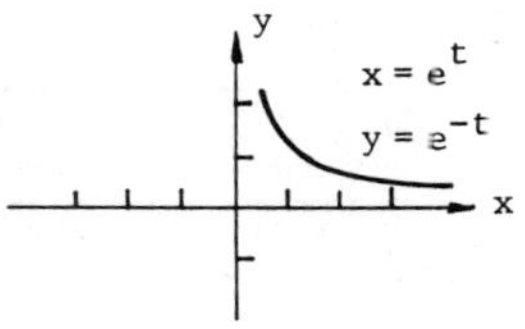

xy = 1, hyperbola

22. No, negative

23. $(y-3)^2$, 2, $\left(\frac{x+2}{\sqrt{2}}\right)^2 + \left(\frac{y-3}{\sqrt{2}}\right)^2$, $\cos\theta$, $\sqrt{2}\sin\theta - 2$, $3 + \sqrt{2}\cos\theta$

24. x - a, mt, a + t, b + mt

9.4 THE CALCULUS OF PARAMETRIZED CURVES

OBJECTIVE A: Given parametric equations $x = f(t)$ and $y = g(t)$, find $\frac{dy}{dx}$ in terms of $\frac{dy}{dt}$ and $\frac{dx}{dt}$. Find $\frac{d^2y}{dx^2}$ in terms of t.

25. The equations $x = f(t)$ and $y = g(t)$, which express x and y in terms of t, are called ____________ equations. The variable t is called a ____________. From the chain rule, the derivative $\frac{dy}{dx}$ is given by $\frac{dy}{dx}$ = ____________.

26. Let $x = t^2 - 1$ and $y = \frac{1}{t}$. Then $\frac{dx}{dt}$ = __________ and $\frac{dy}{dt}$ = __________. It follows that

$y' = \frac{dy}{dx}$ = ____________________ .

To calculate the second derivative $\frac{d^2y}{dx^2}$ we first find

$\frac{dy'}{dt}$ = ____________________ .

Then,

$\frac{d^2y}{dx^2} = \frac{dy'/dt}{\_\_\_\_}$ = __________ .

27. If $x = t^2$ and $y = t^2 - 2t$, then $\frac{dx}{dt}$ = __________ and $\frac{dy}{dt}$ = ________. Thus,

$y' = \frac{dy}{dx}$ = ____________ .

Next, $\frac{dy'}{dt}$ = __________ so that

$\frac{d^2y}{dx^2} = \frac{\_\_\_\_}{dx/dt} = \frac{\_\_\_\_}{2t}$ = __________ .

When $t = 2$, x = ______, y = ______ and $\frac{dy}{dx}$ = ______. Thus an equation of the line tangent to the curve at $(4,0)$ is

__________________________ .

---

25. parametric, parameter, $\frac{dy/dt}{dx/dt}$

26. $2t$, $-\frac{1}{t^2}$, $-\frac{1}{2t^3}$, $\frac{3}{2}t^{-4}$, $\frac{dx}{dt}$, $\frac{3}{4t^5}$

27. $2t$, $2t - 2$, $1 - \frac{1}{t}$, $\frac{dy'}{dt}$, $\frac{1}{t^2}$, $\frac{1}{2t^3}$, 4, 0, $\frac{1}{2}$, $y = \frac{1}{2}(x - 4)$ or $2y - x + 4 = 0$

OBJECTIVE B: Find the length of a curve specified parametrically by continuously differentiable equations $x = f(t)$ and $y = g(t)$ over a given interval $a \le t \le b$.

28. To compute the length of the curve given by $x = t^2 \cos t$ and $y = t^2 \sin t$ for $0 \le t \le 1$, we first calculate $\frac{dx}{dt}$ and $\frac{dy}{dt}$.

$\frac{dx}{dt} =$ ________________ ; $\frac{dy}{dt} =$ ________________ so that

$$\left(\frac{dx}{dt}\right)^2 + \left(\frac{dy}{dt}\right)^2 = t^2[(2 \cos t - t \sin t)^2 + (\_\_\_\_\_\_\_\_\_\_\_\_\_\_\_\_)^2]$$
$$= t^2[4 \cos^2 t - 4t \cos t \sin t + t^2 \sin^2 t$$
$$+ (\_\_\_\_\_\_\_\_\_\_\_\_\_\_\_\_)]$$
$$= t^2[4 + \_\_\_\_\_\_\_\_].$$

Hence the arc length is given by,

$$s = \int_0^1 \sqrt{\left(\frac{dx}{dt}\right)^2 + \left(\frac{dy}{dt}\right)^2}\, dt = \int_0^1 \_\_\_\_\_\_\_\_\_\_\_\_\_\_\_\_ \, dt$$
$$= \_\_\_\_\_\_\_\_\_\_\_\_ \Big]_0^1 = \frac{1}{3}\, (\_\_\_\_\_\_\_\_) \approx 1.0601 \text{ units.}$$

OBJECTIVE C: Find the area of a surface generated by rotating the arc of a curve specified parametrically by equations $x = f(t)$ and $y = g(t)$ over $a \le t \le b$ about an indicated axis. (Again, f and g are assumed to have continuous derivatives.)

29. Find the surface area generated when the arc $x = 2t$ and $y = \sqrt{2}t^2$ from $t = 0$ to $t = 2$ is rotated about the y-axis.

Solution. We write $dS = 2\pi$ ____ ds, since the rotation occurs about the y-axis. Next, we calculate the derivatives $\frac{dx}{dt} =$ ______ and $\frac{dy}{dt} =$ ______ so that the arc length differential is given by

$$ds = \sqrt{\_\_\_\_\_\_\_\_\_\_\_\_}\, dt = 2\sqrt{\_\_\_\_\_\_\_\_\_\_\_\_}\, dt.$$

Therefore, the surface area is

$$S = 2\pi \int_0^2 \_\_\_\_\_\_\_\_\_\_\_\_ \, dt = \frac{4\pi}{3}\, (\_\_\_\_\_\_\_\_\_\_\_\_)\Big]_0^2$$
$$= \frac{4\pi}{3}\, (\_\_\_\_\_\_\_\_) = \_\_\_\_\_\_\_\_\_\_\_\_\_\_ \approx 108.90854 \text{ sq. units.}$$

---

28. $2t \cos t - t^2 \sin t$, $2t \sin t + t^2 \cos t$, $2 \sin t + t \cos t$, $4 \sin^2 t + 4t \cos t \sin t + t^2 \cos^2 t$, t^2, $t\sqrt{4 + t^2}$, $\frac{1}{3}\left(4 + t^2\right)^{3/2}$, $5\sqrt{5} - 8$

29. x, 2, $2\sqrt{2}\,t$, $\left(\frac{dx}{dt}\right)^2 + \left(\frac{dy}{dt}\right)^2$, $2t^2 + 1$, $4t\sqrt{2t^2 + 1}$, $\left(2t^2 + 1\right)^{3/2}$, $27 - 1$, $\frac{104\pi}{3}$

9.5 POLAR COORDINATES

OBJECTIVE A: Given a point P in polar coordinates (r,θ), give the Cartesian coordinates (x,y) of P.

30\. The polar and Cartesian coordinates are related by the equations $x =$ ____________ and $y =$ ____________.

31\. If P is the point $(-2,\frac{\pi}{6})$ in polar coordinates, then $x =$ ____________ and $y =$ ____________ so that P can be expressed in Cartesian coordinates by (_____,_____).

32\. For $P = (-2,-\frac{\pi}{6})$ in polar coordinates, $x =$ ____________ and $y =$ ____________ so that P = (_____,_____) in Cartesian coordinates.

OBJECTIVE B: Graph the points $P(r,\theta)$ whose polar coordinates satisfy a given equation, inequality or inequalities.

33\. $\theta = -\frac{\pi}{4}$, $-2 \leq r$
Sketch the graph at the right.

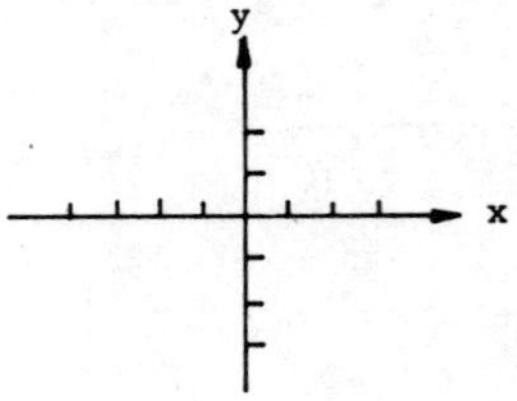

34\. $r = 2$, $-\frac{3\pi}{4} < \theta \leq \frac{\pi}{6}$
Sketch the graph at the right.

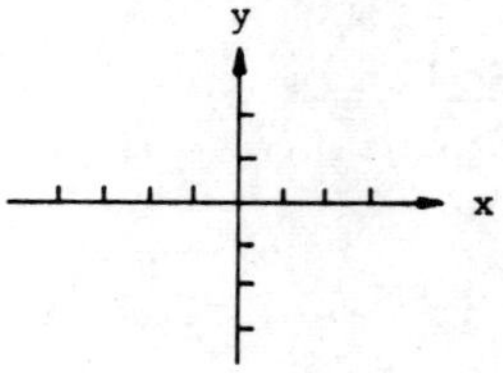

30\. $r\cos\theta$, $r\sin\theta$

31\. $-2\cos\frac{\pi}{6}$, $-2\sin\frac{\pi}{6}$, $(-\sqrt{3}, -1)$

32\. $-2\cos\left(-\frac{\pi}{6}\right)$, $-2\sin\left(-\frac{\pi}{6}\right)$, $(-\sqrt{3},1)$

33\.

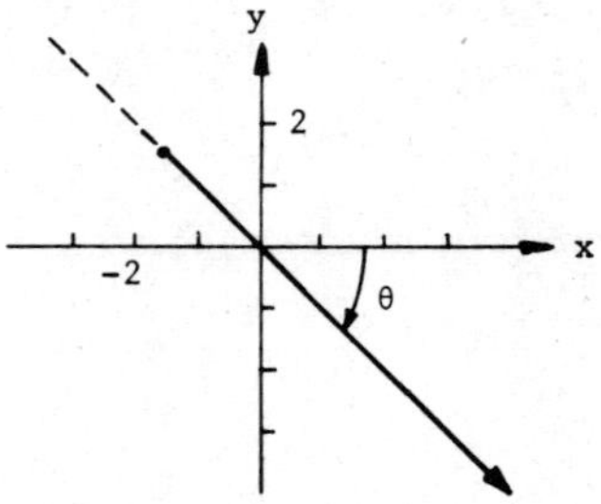

34\.

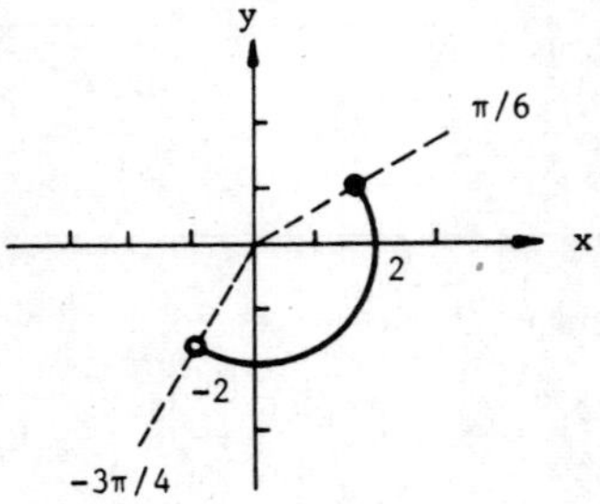

OBJECTIVE C: Given an equation in polar coordinates, replace it by an equivalent equation in Cartesian coordinates and identify the graph.

35. Consider the equation $r = -3 \sec \theta$. Then, $-3 = r$ ________, or since $x =$ ________ the equation is equivalent to ________. This is an equation of a ________ line 3 units to the left of the ______ axis.

36. Consider the equation $r \sin (\theta - \frac{\pi}{3}) = \frac{1}{2}$. By the trigonometric summation identities, $\sin (\theta - \frac{\pi}{3}) = \sin \theta \cos \frac{\pi}{3} -$ ________ $=$ ________.

Therefore, the polar equation can be written

$$\frac{1}{2} = \frac{1}{2} r \sin \theta - \text{\_\_\_\_\_\_\_\_} = \frac{1}{2} y - \text{\_\_\_\_\_\_\_\_}.$$

Simplifying algebraically, $y =$ ________. This is an equation of a line with slope $m =$ ______ and y-intercept $b =$ ______.

37. Suppose $r = \tan \theta \sec \theta$. Then, $r = \sin \theta \cdot$ ________ or $r = \frac{\sin \theta}{\text{\_\_\_\_}}$. Equivalently, $\sin \theta =$ ________ or

$r \sin \theta =$ ________. In terms of Cartesian coordinates the equation becomes ________, which is readily recognized as an equation of ____________.

38. Given the equation $r = \dfrac{1}{3 \cos \theta + 2 \sin \theta}$, clear fractions and

obtain $3r \cos \theta +$ ________ $= 1$. Next, substitute $x = r \cos \theta$ and $y =$ ________ to obtain $3x +$ ______ $= 1$. This is an equation of a straight line with slope $m =$ ______ and y-intercept $b =$ ______.

39. The equation $r^2 - 5r + 4 = 0$ factors into $(r-4)(\text{\_\_\_\_\_\_}) = 0$. Thus, $r = 4$ or $r =$ ______. The graph is two concentric circles, one of radius 4 and the other of radius 1, centered at the origin.

40. Consider $r^2 = 2 \csc 2\theta$. Then, $r^2 \sin 2\theta =$ ______. Now, $\sin 2\theta = 2$ ________, so the equation becomes $2r \sin \theta \cdot$ ________ $= 2$ or ________ $= 2$. That is, $xy = 1$ which is an equation of ________ with center ________.

---

35. $\cos \theta$, $r \cos \theta$, $x = -3$, vertical, y

36. $\cos \theta \sin \frac{\pi}{3}$, $\frac{1}{2} \sin \theta - \frac{\sqrt{3}}{2} \cos \theta$, $\frac{\sqrt{3}}{2} r \cos \theta$, $\frac{\sqrt{3}}{2} x$, $\sqrt{3}x + 1$, $\sqrt{3}$, 1

37. $\sec^2 \theta$, $\cos^2 \theta$, $r \cos^2 \theta$, $r^2 \cos^2 \theta$, $y = x^2$, a parabola

38. $2r \sin \theta$, $r \sin \theta$, 2y, $-\frac{3}{2}$, $\frac{1}{2}$

39. r - 1, 1

40. 2, $\sin \theta \cos \theta$, $r \cos \theta$, 2xy, a hyperbola, C(0, 0)

41. Given the equation $r = \frac{3}{1 - 2\cos\theta}$, clear fractions to obtain r - ________ = 3; or substituting $x = r\cos\theta$, r = ________. Hence, r^2 = ________ = 9 + 12x + ______. Since $r^2 = x^2 + y^2$ this last equation simplifies to $y^2 = 9 + 12x$ + ________ or $y^2 = 3(x + 2)^2$ + (______). Therefore, $(x + 2)^2$ - ________ = 1. This is an equation of a hyperbola.

42. For $r = 2\sin(\theta + \frac{\pi}{4})$ we can expand the right side by the summation formula for the sine: $r = 2\sin\theta\cos\frac{\pi}{4}$ + __________ or r = ______________. Hence, $r^2 = \sqrt{2}\, r\sin\theta$ + ____________. Since $x^2 + y^2 = r^2$, $x = r\cos\theta$, and $y = r\sin\theta$, substitution and algebraic simplification yields

$\left(x - \frac{\sqrt{2}}{2}\right)^2$ + __________ = 1. This equation represents __________ with center ____________ and radius $r = 1$.

9.6 GRAPHING IN POLAR COORDINATES

OBJECTIVE A: Given an equation $F(r,\theta) = 0$ in polar coordinates, analyze and sketch its graph.

43. The graph of $F(r,\theta) = 0$ is symmetric about the x-axis if the equation is unchanged when ________ is replaced by ________.

44. The graph of $F(r,\theta) = 0$ is symmetric about the origin if the equation is unchanged when r is replaced by __________, or θ is replaced by __________.

45. The graph of $F(r,\theta) = 0$ is symmetric about the y-axis if the equation is unchanged when θ is replaced by __________, or r is replaced by __________ and θ is replaced by ________.

---

41. $2r\cos\theta$, $3 + 2x$, $(3 + 2x)^2$, $4x^2$, $3x^2$, -3, $\frac{y^2}{3}$

42. $2\cos\theta\sin\frac{\pi}{4}$, $\sqrt{2}\sin\theta + \sqrt{2}\cos\theta$, $\sqrt{2}\, r\cos\theta$, $\left(y - \frac{\sqrt{2}}{2}\right)^2$, a circle, $C\left(\frac{\sqrt{2}}{2}, \frac{\sqrt{2}}{2}\right)$

43. θ, $-\theta$

44. $-r$, $\theta + \pi$

45. $\pi - \theta$, $-r$, $-\theta$

46. Consider the curve given by $r = 1 - 2 \cos \theta$. Since $\cos(-\theta) = \cos \theta$, the curve is symmetric about the ______. Next, $\frac{dr}{d\theta}$ = __________. Thus, as θ varies from 0 to $\frac{\pi}{3}$, r increases from r = ________ to r = ________; and as θ varies from $\frac{\pi}{2}$ to π, r increases from r = ________ to r = ________. Complete the following table of values for the curve, and sketch its graph using its symmetries.

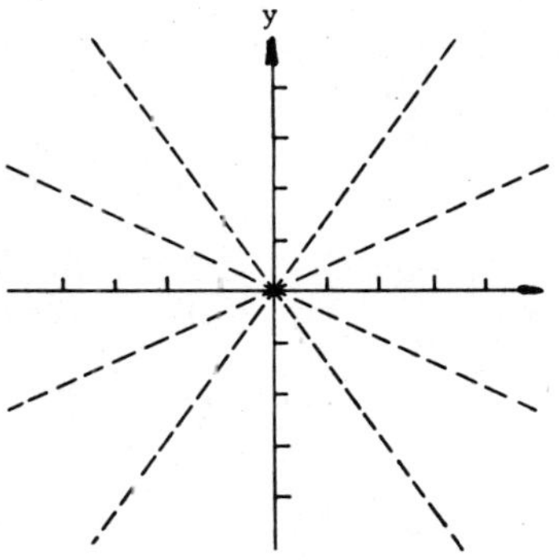

θ	0	$\pi/6$	$\pi/3$	$\pi/2$	$2\pi/3$	$5\pi/6$	π
r							

47. Consider the curve given by $r^2 = \sin \theta$. Since the $\sin \theta$ must be nonnegative in order to equal the square of a real number, we must restrict θ to the interval ____________. Since the equation remains unchanged when r is replaced by -r, the curve is symmetric about the __________. Also, since $\sin(\pi - \theta) = \sin \theta$, the curve is symmetric about the __________. Complete the following table and sketch the graph using these symmetries:

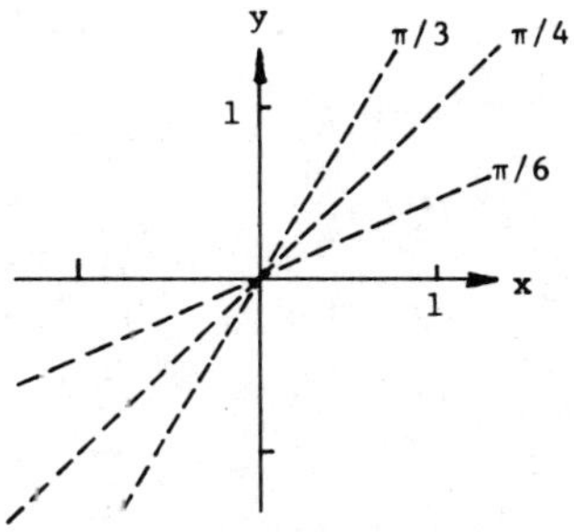

---

46. x-axis, $2 \sin \theta$, -1, 0, 1, 3

θ	0	$\pi/6$	$\pi/3$	$\pi/2$	$2\pi/3$	$5\pi/6$	π
r	-1	$1 - \sqrt{3}$	0	1	2	$1 + \sqrt{3}$	3

The dashed portion of the curve is the rest of it due to its symmetry about the x-axis.

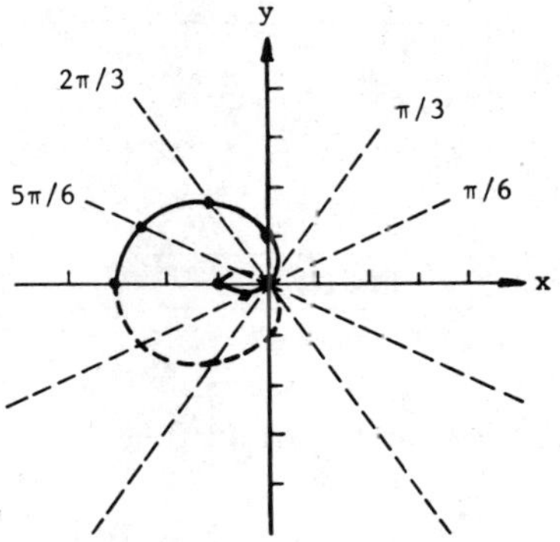

θ	0	$\pi/6$	$\pi/4$	$\pi/3$	$\pi/2$
r^2					
r					

OBJECTIVE B: If $r = f(\theta)$ is differentiable, find the slope $\frac{dy}{dx}$ at the point (r,θ) on the graph of f.

48. If $r = f(\theta)$ is differentiable and $\frac{dx}{d\theta} \neq 0$, then

slope at (r,θ) = ________________________.

49. For the polar curve $r = 1 - 2\cos\theta$ in Problem 46, $r' =$ ________. When $\theta = \frac{2\pi}{3}$ radians, $r =$ ________ and $r' =$ ________. Thus,

$$\text{Slope at } \left(2, \tfrac{2\pi}{3}\right) = \frac{\sqrt{3}\sin\left(\frac{2\pi}{3}\right) + 2\cos\left(\frac{2\pi}{3}\right)}{\_\_\_\_\_\_\_\_}$$

$$= \frac{1/2}{\_\_\_\_} = \_\_\_\_\_\_\_\_$$

$$\approx -0.192 .$$

Note that $\frac{dx}{d\theta} = \frac{dr}{d\theta}\cos\theta - r\sin\theta = \frac{-3\sqrt{3}}{2} \neq 0$ when $\theta = \frac{2\pi}{3}$ for the given polar curve.

9.7 POLAR EQUATIONS FOR CONIC SECTIONS

OBJECTIVE A: Given an equation of a straight line in polar coordinates, find a corresponding Cartesian equation.

---

47. $0 \leq \theta \leq \pi$, origin, y-axis

θ	0	$\pi/6$	$\pi/4$	$\pi/3$	$\pi/2$
r^2	0	1/2	$1/\sqrt{2}$	$\sqrt{3}/2$	1
r	0	$\pm.71$	$\pm.84$	$\pm.93$	±1

The portions of the graph in QII, QIII, and QIV are obtained by the symmetries.

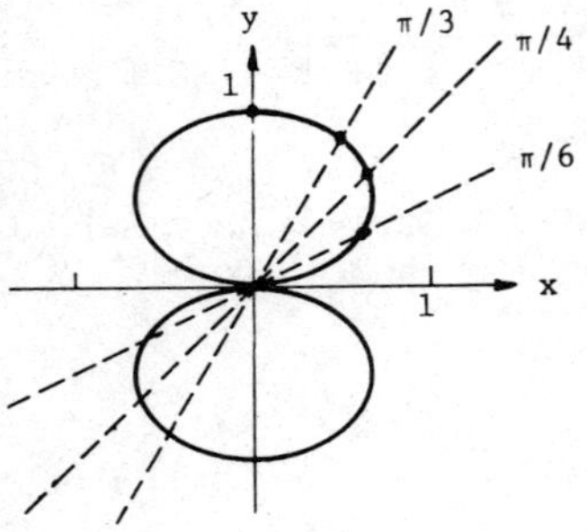

48. $\frac{r'\sin\theta + r\cos\theta}{r'\cos\theta - r\sin\theta}$ where $r' = \frac{dr}{d\theta}$

49. $2\sin\theta$, 2, $\sqrt{3}$, $\sqrt{3}\cos\left(\frac{2\pi}{3}\right) - 2\sin\left(\frac{2\pi}{3}\right)$, $\frac{-3\sqrt{3}}{2}$, $\frac{-1}{3\sqrt{3}}$

50. If $P_o(r_o, \theta_o)$ is the foot of the perpendicular from the origin to the line L with $r_o \geq 0$, then an equation for L in polar coordinates is

________________________ .

51. A polar equation for the line displayed in the figure at the right is

________________ .

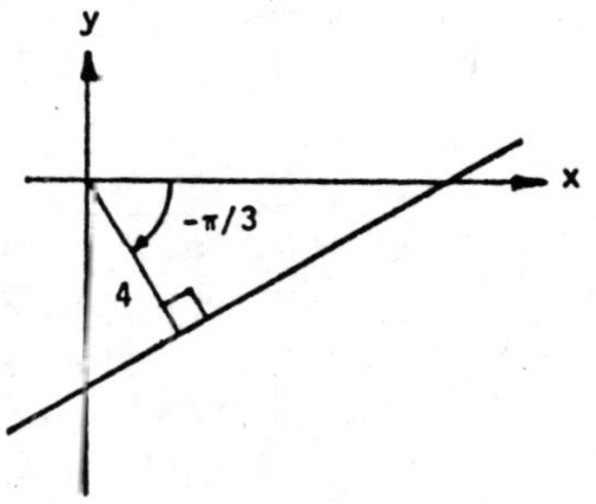

52. Using the identity for $\cos(A + B)$, we find the following Cartesian equation for the line in Problem 51:

$$r \cos\left(\theta + \frac{\pi}{3}\right) = 4$$

$$r[\_\_\_\_\_\_\_\_\_\_\_\_\_\_\_\_] = 4$$

$$\frac{1}{2} r \cos\theta - \_\_\_\_\_\_\_\_\_\_ = 4$$

$$\_\_\_\_\_\_\_\_\_\_\_\_\_\_\_\_ = 4$$

or

$$y = \_\_\_\_\_\_\_\_\_\_\_\_\_\_ .$$

OBJECTIVE B: Given the eccentricity of an ellipse together with its semimajor axis, write a polar equation for the ellipse.

53. The semimajor axis for the orbit of Saturn is 9.539 AU (astronomical units) and the eccentricity is 0.0543. Thus a polar equation of Saturn's orbit around the sun is

$$r = \frac{\_\_\_\_\_\_\left[1 - (0.0543)^2\right]}{\_\_\_\_\_\_\_\_\_\_\_\_}$$

$$= \frac{9.511}{1 + 0.0543 \cos\theta}$$

$$= \frac{\_\_\_\_\_\_\_\_}{18.42 + \cos\theta} .$$

At its most distant point (aphelion), Saturn is ____________ (astronomical units) from the sun.

---

50. $r \cos(\theta - \theta_o) = r_o$

51. $r \cos\left(\theta + \frac{\pi}{3}\right) = 4$

52. $\cos\theta \cos\frac{\pi}{3} - \sin\theta \sin\frac{\pi}{3}$, $\frac{\sqrt{3}}{2} r \sin\theta$, $\frac{1}{2}x - \frac{\sqrt{3}}{2}y$, $\frac{1}{\sqrt{3}}(x - 8)$

53. $\dfrac{9.539\left[1 - (0.0543)^2\right]}{1 + 0.0543 \cos\theta}$, 175.2, 10 AU

9.8 INTEGRATION IN POLAR COORDINATES

OBJECTIVE A: Find the total plane area enclosed by a polar graph $r = f(\theta)$ and the rays $\theta = \alpha$, $\theta = \beta$.

54. The area bounded by the polar curve $r = f(\theta)$ and the rays $\theta = \alpha$, $\theta = \beta$ is given by the integral

$$A = \underline{\hspace{4cm}}.$$

55. Find the area inside the larger loop and outside the smaller loop of the polar graph $r = 1 - 2\cos\theta$ given in Problem 46.

Solution. The graph of the curve is sketched in the figure below. That part of the curve traced out as θ varies from $\theta = 0$ to $\theta = \pi$ is drawn in with a broader ink stroke. Now, as θ varies from $\frac{\pi}{3}$ to π, the radius vector r sweeps out the larger loop of the curve including that portion of the smaller loop lying above the x-axis. By symmetry, the area of that smaller half-loop is the same as the area of the half-loop swept out by r as θ varies from 0 to $\frac{\pi}{3}$. Thus, the total area inside the larger loop and outside the smaller loop is

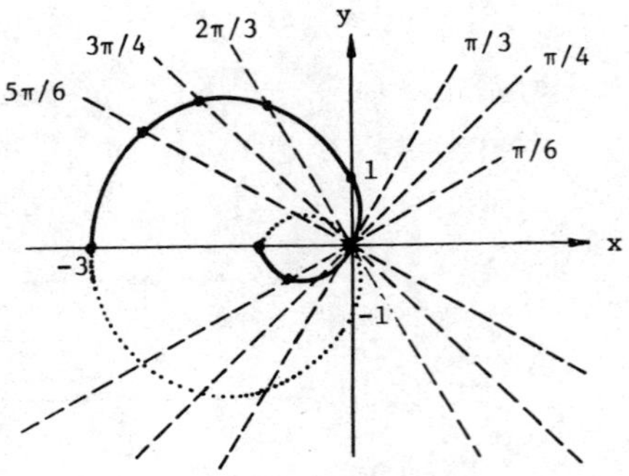

$$A = 2\left[\int_{\pi/3}^{\pi} \tfrac{1}{2} f^2(\theta)\, d\theta - \underline{\hspace{4cm}}\right]$$

$$= \int_{\pi/3}^{\pi} (1 - 4\cos\theta + 4\cos^2\theta)\, d\theta - \underline{\hspace{4cm}}$$

$$= \left[\theta - 4\sin\theta + 4\left(\tfrac{\theta}{2} + \tfrac{1}{4}\sin 2\theta\right)\right]_{\pi/3}^{\pi} - \underline{\hspace{4cm}}$$

$$= (\pi + 2\pi) - \left[\tfrac{\pi}{3} - 4\left(\tfrac{\sqrt{3}}{2}\right) + 4\left(\tfrac{\pi}{6} + \tfrac{1}{4}\cdot\tfrac{\sqrt{3}}{2}\right)\right] - \underline{\hspace{4cm}}$$

$$= \underline{\hspace{3cm}} \approx 8.338.$$

---

54. $\int_{\alpha}^{\beta} \frac{1}{2}[f(\theta)]^2\, d\theta$

55. $\int_0^{\pi/3} \frac{1}{2} f^2(\theta)\, d\theta$, $\int_0^{\pi/3} (1 - 4\cos\theta + 4\cos^2\theta)\, d\theta$, $\left[\theta - 4\sin\theta + 4\left(\frac{\theta}{2} + \frac{1}{4}\sin 2\theta\right)\right]_0^{\pi/3}$,

$\left[\frac{\pi}{3} - 4\left(\frac{\sqrt{3}}{2}\right) + 4\left(\frac{\pi}{6} + \frac{1}{4}\cdot\frac{\sqrt{3}}{2}\right)\right]$, $3\sqrt{3} + \pi$

OBJECTIVE B: Given a polar curve $r = f(\theta)$, calculate its arc length as θ varies from $\theta = a$ to $\theta = b$.

56. The differential element of arc length ds for the polar curve $r = f(\theta)$ satisfies the equation

$$ds^2 = \_\_\_\_\_\_\_\_\_\_\_\_ .$$

Thus the length of arc traced out by the curve as θ varies from $\theta = a$ to $\theta = b$ is given by

$$s = \_\_\_\_\_\_\_\_\_\_\_\_ .$$

57. To determine the length of the curve $r = 3 \sec \theta$ as θ varies from $\theta = 0$ to $\theta = \frac{\pi}{4}$, we find $\frac{dr}{d\theta} = \_\_\_\_\_\_\_\_$. Then the arc length is,

$$s = \int_0^{\pi/4} \sqrt{\_\_\_\_\_\_\_\_\_\_}\, d\theta = 3 \int_0^{\pi/4} \sec \theta \sqrt{\_\_\_\_\_\_\_\_}\, d\theta$$

$$= 3 \int_0^{\pi/4} \_\_\_\_\_\_\_\_ \, d\theta = \_\_\_\_\_\_\_\_ \Big]_0^{\pi/4} = \_\_\_\_\_\_\_\_ .$$

58. Consider the polar curve $r = \cos^4 \frac{\theta}{4}$. As θ varies from $\theta = 0$ to $\theta = 2\pi$, the equation describes the path shown in the figure at the right. As θ varies from $\theta = 2\pi$ to $\theta = 4\pi$ the curve shown is reflected across the x-axis. Thus, the total arc length is given by

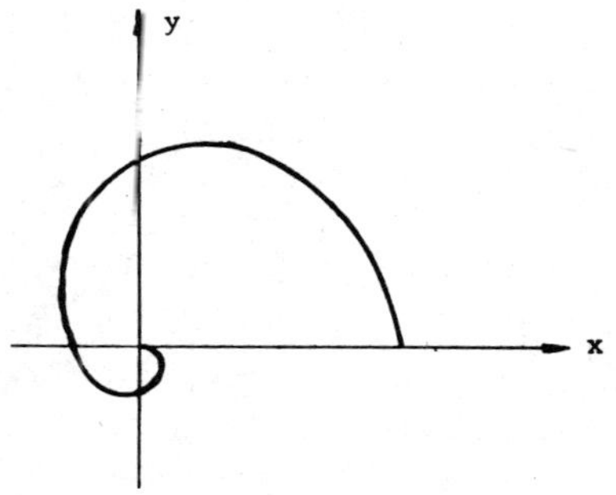

$$s = 2 \int_0^{2\pi} \sqrt{r^2 + \_\_\_\_\_\_\_\_}\, d\theta .$$

Now, $\frac{dr}{d\theta} = \_\_\_\_\_\_\_\_$ so that

$$r^2 + \left(\frac{dr}{d\theta}\right)^2 = \cos^8 \frac{\theta}{4} + \_\_\_\_\_\_\_\_ = \cos^6 \frac{\theta}{4} .$$

Thus, $s = 2 \int_0^{2\pi} \_\_\_\_\_\_\_\_ \, d\theta .$

Since $\cos \frac{\theta}{4} \geq 0$ for $0 \leq \theta \leq 2\pi$, the integral becomes

---

56. $r^2\, d\theta^2 + dr^2$, $\int_a^b \sqrt{r^2 + \left(\frac{dr}{d\theta}\right)^2}\, d\theta$

57. $3 \sec \theta \tan \theta$, $9 \sec^2 \theta + 9 \sec^2 \theta \tan^2 \theta$, $1 + \tan^2 \theta$, $\sec^2 \theta$, $3 \tan \theta$, 3

$$s = 2\int_0^{2\pi} (1 - \sin^2 \tfrac{\theta}{4}) \text{ \_\_\_\_\_\_\_\_\_\_ } d\theta$$

$$= 2\int_{\_\_}^{\_\_} \text{ \_\_\_\_\_\_\_\_\_\_ } du, \quad \text{where} \quad u = \sin \tfrac{\theta}{4}$$

$$= \text{ \_\_\_\_\_\_ } (\text{\_\_\_\_\_\_\_\_})]_{\_\_}^{\_\_} = \text{ \_\_\_\_\_\_\_\_\_\_ }.$$

OBJECTIVE C: Find the area of the surface generated when a polar graph is revolved about the x-axis or the y-axis.

59. The graph of the polar equation $r = 5 \cos \theta$ is the circle shown at the right. If the graph is rotated about the x-axis, the total surface area is generated by that portion of the graph as θ varies from $\theta = 0$ to $\theta =$ ________ because of the symmetry of the graph across the x-axis.

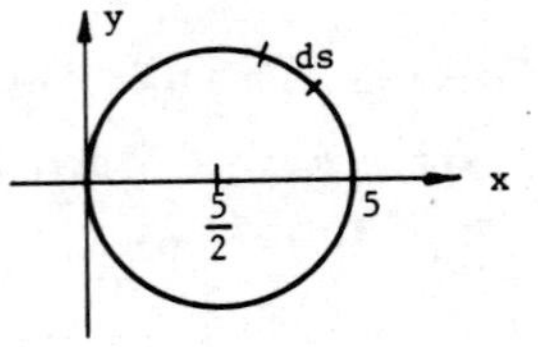

An element of arc length ds (see the figure) generates a portion of surface area dS = ________ ds, where $y = r \sin \theta$ and ds = __________. Thus,

$$dS = 2\pi \cdot \text{ \_\_\_\_\_\_\_\_\_\_\_\_\_\_\_\_\_\_\_\_ } d\theta = 2\pi(5 \cos \theta) \text{ \_\_\_\_\_\_\_\_\_\_ } d\theta.$$

Hence, the total surface area is given by

$$S = 50\pi \int_{\_\_}^{\_\_} \text{ \_\_\_\_\_\_\_\_\_\_ } d\theta = \text{ \_\_\_\_\_\_\_\_\_\_\_\_ }]_{\_\_}^{\_\_} = \text{ \_\_\_\_\_\_\_\_ }$$

$$\approx 78.54.$$

60. If the graph in Problem 59 is rotated about the axis $\theta = \frac{\pi}{2}$, the total surface area is generated by the graph as θ varies from $\theta = 0$ to $\theta =$ ________. An element of arc length ds now generates a portion of the surface area

$$dS = \text{ \_\_\_\_\_\_\_\_\_\_ } = 2\pi\left(\text{\_\_\_\_\_\_\_\_\_\_}\right) \cdot 5\, d\theta.$$

Thus, the total surface area is given by

$$S = 50\pi \int_{\_\_}^{\_\_} \text{ \_\_\_\_\_\_\_\_\_\_ } d\theta = 50\pi \left[\text{\_\_\_\_\_\_\_\_\_\_\_\_\_\_\_\_}\right]_{\_\_}^{\_\_}$$

$$= \text{ \_\_\_\_\_\_\_\_\_\_ } \approx 246.74.$$

---

58. $\left(\frac{dr}{d\theta}\right)^2$, $-\cos^3 \frac{\theta}{4} \sin \frac{\theta}{4}$, $\cos^6 \frac{\theta}{4} \sin^2 \frac{\theta}{4}$, $\left|\cos^3 \frac{\theta}{4}\right|$, $\cos \frac{\theta}{4}$, $\int_0^1 4(1 - u^2)\, du$, $8(u - \frac{1}{3} u^3)]_0^1$, $\frac{16}{3}$

59. $\frac{\pi}{2}$, $2\pi y$, $\sqrt{dr^2 + r^2\, d\theta^2}$, $r \sin \theta \sqrt{25 \sin^2 \theta + 25 \cos^2 \theta}$, $5 \sin \theta$,

$\int_0^{\pi/2} \sin \theta \cos \theta\, d\theta$, $50\pi \cdot \frac{1}{2} \sin^2 \theta]_0^{\pi/2}$, 25π

60. π, $2\pi x\, ds$, $r \cos \theta$, $\int_0^{\pi} \cos^2 \theta\, d\theta$, $\frac{1}{2}\theta + \frac{1}{4} \sin 2\theta\,]_0^{\pi}$, $25\pi^2$

CHAPTER 9 SELF-TEST

1. Find the eccentricity of the ellipse $81x^2 + 25y^2 = 2025$.

2. Consider the equation $x^2 - 2xy - y^2 = 12$.
   (a) Use the discriminant to classify it.
   (b) Transform the equation by a rotation of axes into an equation with no cross-product term.

3. Write an equation for the circle with center $C(4,6)$ and radius $r = 3$.

4. Sketch the graph of the curve described by $x = t - 2$ and $y = t^2 - t + 1$ for $-\infty < t < \infty$. Also find a Cartesian equation of the curve.

5. Find parametric equations for the circle $x^2 + y^2 = 2x$, using as parameter the arc length s measured counterclockwise from the point $(2,0)$ to the point (x,y).

6. Given the parametric equations $x = t^2 - 1$ and $y = t + 1$
   (a) Express dx and dy in terms of t and dt,
   (b) Find $\frac{d^2y}{dx^2}$ in terms of t,
   (c) Find an equation of the tangent line to the curve at the point for which $t = 1$.

7. Consider the curve given by the parametric equations $x = 3t - 1$ and $y = t^2 - t$. Eliminate the parameter t to find an equation of the form $y = F(x)$ and find $\frac{dy}{dx}$ in terms of $\frac{dy}{dt}$ and $\frac{dx}{dt}$. For what value of t is $\frac{dy}{dx} = 0$? Sketch the graph of the curve over the interval $-2 \le t \le 3$.

8. Find the length of the curve given by $x = t^3 + 3t^2$ and $y = t^3 - 3t^2$ for $0 \le t \le 2$.

9. Find the area of the surface generated by rotating the cardiod $x = 2\cos\theta - \cos 2\theta$, $y = 2\sin\theta - \sin 2\theta$, for $0 \le \theta \le \pi$, about the x-axis. First sketch the curve.

10. Convert the following from polar coordinates to Cartesian coordinates.
    (a) $\left(-6, \frac{\pi}{4}\right)$ (b) $\left(1, -\frac{5\pi}{6}\right)$ (c) $\left(-2, -\frac{7\pi}{12}\right)$

11. Write the following simple polar equations in Cartesian form.
    (a) $r = 5$ (b) $\theta = \frac{3\pi}{4}$ (c) $r = -5\csc\theta$

In Problems 12 and 13, graph the polar equation.

12. $r = 2\cos 4\theta$

13. $r^2 = -\sin 2\theta$

14. Determine a Cartesian equation, and sketch the curve, for $r = \cos\theta + 5\sin\theta$.

15. Find a polar equation of the line with slope $m = -2$ passing through the Cartesian point $(1,-3)$.

16. Find a polar equation of the circle centered at the Cartesian point $(\frac{1}{3},0)$ and passing through the origin.

17. Find the length of the polar curve $r = a\cos(\theta + b)$ from $\theta = 0$ to $\theta = \pi$, where a and b are constants.

18. Find the area of the region bounded on the outside by the graph of $r = 2 + 2\sin\theta$ for $\theta = 0$ to $\theta = \pi$, and on the inside by the graph of $r = 2\sin\theta$.

19. Write an integral expressing the surface area generated by rotating the portion of the polar curve $r = 1 + \cos\theta$ in the first quadrant about $\theta = \frac{\pi}{2}$.

SOLUTIONS TO CHAPTER 9 SELF-TEST

1. The standard form of the ellipse is

$$\frac{x^2}{25} + \frac{y^2}{81} = 1 \ .$$

Thus, since $81 > 25$, the foci lie along the y-axis at $(0, \pm c)$ where $c = \sqrt{81 - 25} = 2\sqrt{14}$. The eccentricity is $e = \frac{c}{a} = \frac{2\sqrt{14}}{9} \approx 0.83$.

2. (a) The discriminant is $B^2 - 4AC = (-2)^2 - 4(1)(-1) = 8 > 0$. Therefore, the equation represents a hyperbola.

(b) $\cot 2\alpha = \frac{A - C}{B} = \frac{1 + 1}{-2} = -1$; thus $2\alpha = \frac{3\pi}{4}$ radians.

Hence, $\cos 2\alpha = \frac{-1}{\sqrt{2}}$. Using the half-angle formulas,

$$\sin \alpha = \sqrt{\frac{1 - \cos 2\alpha}{2}} = \sqrt{\frac{1 + \sqrt{2}}{2\sqrt{2}}} = \frac{1}{2}\sqrt{2 + \sqrt{2}}, \quad \text{and}$$

$$\cos \alpha = \sqrt{\frac{1 + \cos 2\alpha}{2}} = \sqrt{\frac{1 - \sqrt{2}}{2\sqrt{2}}} = \frac{1}{2}\sqrt{2 - \sqrt{2}}.$$

Now,
$$A' = A \cos^2\alpha + B \cos\alpha \sin\alpha + C \sin^2\alpha$$
$$= \frac{1}{4}(2 - \sqrt{2}) - \frac{2}{4}(\sqrt{-2 + 4}) - \frac{1}{4}(2 + \sqrt{2}) = -\sqrt{2}$$

$$C' = A \sin^2\alpha - B \cos\alpha \sin\alpha + C \cos^2\alpha$$
$$= \frac{1}{4}(2 + \sqrt{2}) + \frac{2}{4}(\sqrt{-2 + 4}) - \frac{1}{4}(2 - \sqrt{2}) = \sqrt{2}.$$

Thus, since $B' = 0$ because of the choice $\alpha = \frac{3\pi}{8}$, the original equation is reduced to $A'x'^2 + C'y'^2 = F$, or $-\sqrt{2}\,x'^2 + \sqrt{2}\,y'^2 = 12$, or $y'^2 - x'^2 = 6\sqrt{2}$.

3. $(x - 4)^2 + (y - 6)^2 = 9$, or $x^2 + y^2 - 8x - 12y + 43 = 0$.

4. We have the following table giving some of the points on the curve:

t	-1	0	1	2	3
x	-3	-2	-1	0	1
y	3	1	1	3	7

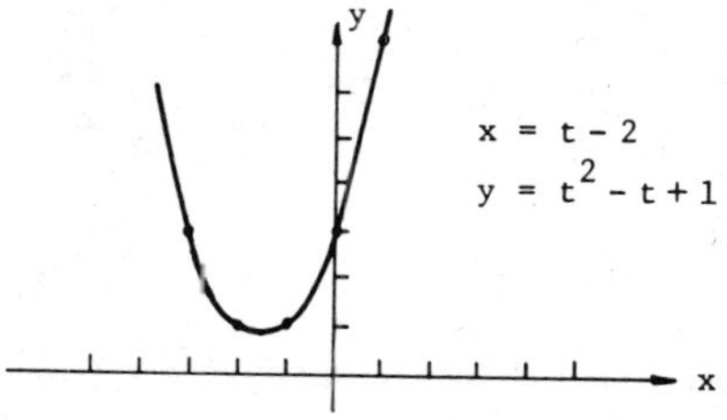

Substitution of $t = x + 2$ into the parametric equation for y gives

$y = (x + 2)^2 - (x + 2) + 1$, or simplifying algebraically, $y = x^2 + 3x + 3$. This is a Cartesian equation of the parabola sketched in the figure above.

5. Completing the square gives the equation $(x - 1)^2 + y^2 = 1$ which we recognize as an equation of a unit circle centered at (1,0) (see the figure at the right). Hence, $x - 1 = 1 \cos s$ and $y - 0 = 1 \sin s$ or,

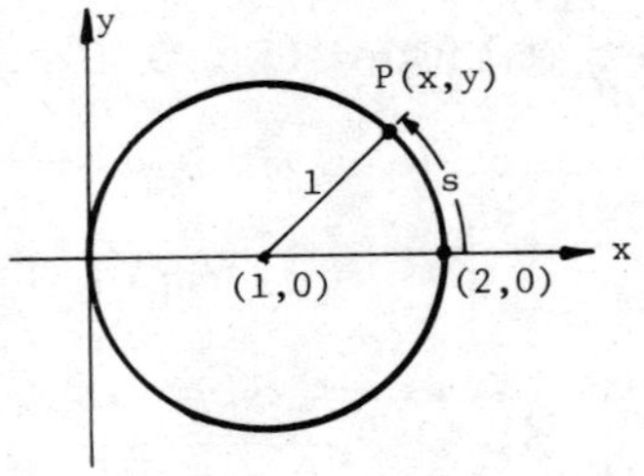

$$x = 1 + \cos s \quad \text{and} \quad y = \sin s$$

are parametric equations for the circle in terms of the arc length parameter s.

6. (a) $\frac{dx}{dt} = 2t$ and $\frac{dy}{dt} = 1$, so that $dx = 2t\,dt$ and $dy = dt$.

(b) $\frac{dy}{dx} = \frac{1}{2t}$ so that $\frac{d^2y}{dx^2} = \frac{dy'/dt}{dx/dt} = \frac{-1/2t^2}{2t} = -\frac{1}{4t^3}$

(c) When $t = 1$, $x = 0$, $y = 2$, and $\frac{dy}{dx} = \frac{1}{2}$; thus $y - 2 = \frac{1}{2}(x - 0)$ or $2y - x = 4$ is an equation of the tangent line.

7. $\frac{dx}{dt} = 3$ and $\frac{dy}{dt} = 2t - 1$, so that $\frac{dy}{dx} = \frac{dy/dt}{dx/dt} = \frac{1}{3}(2t - 1)$. When $t = \frac{1}{2}$, $\frac{dy}{dx} = 0$ which occurs at the point $(x,y) = \left(\frac{1}{2}, -\frac{1}{4}\right)$. To eliminate the parameter t, use the parametric expression for x, $t = \frac{1}{3}(x + 1)$, and substitute into the parametric expression for y giving

$$y = \frac{1}{9}(x + 1)^2 - \frac{1}{3}(x + 1)$$
$$= \frac{1}{9}(x^2 - x - 2).$$

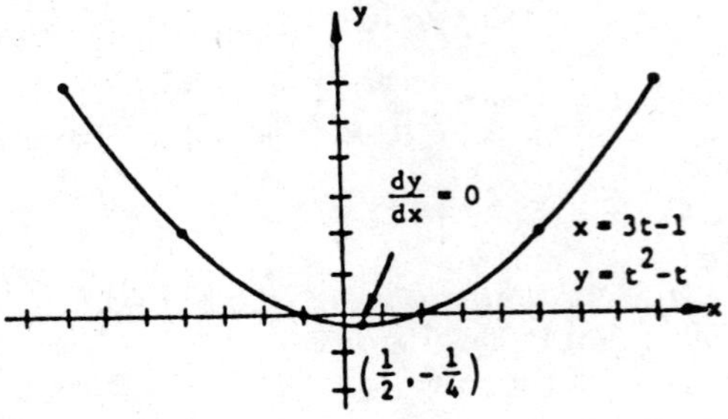

A table of coordinate values is as follows:

t	-2	-1	0	1/2	1	2	3
x	-7	-4	-1	1/2	2	5	8
y	6	2	0	-1/4	0	2	6

8. $\frac{dx}{dt} = 3t^2 + 6t$ and $\frac{dy}{dt} = 3t^2 - 6t$ so that

$$\left(\frac{dx}{dt}\right)^2 + \left(\frac{dy}{dt}\right)^2 = (9t^4 + 36t^3 + 36t^2) + (9t^4 - 36t^3 + 36t^2)$$
$$= 18t^2(t^2 + 4).$$

Thus, the arc length is given by

$$s = \int_0^2 3\sqrt{2}\, t\sqrt{t^2 + 4}\, dt = 3\sqrt{2}\left(\frac{1}{3}\right)\left(t^2 + 4\right)^{3/2} \Big]_0^2$$
$$= 8(4 - \sqrt{2}) \approx 20.7 \text{ units.}$$

9. The required surface is obtained by rotating the arc from $\theta = 0$ to $\theta = \pi$ about the x-axis. The arc is shown in the figure at the right.

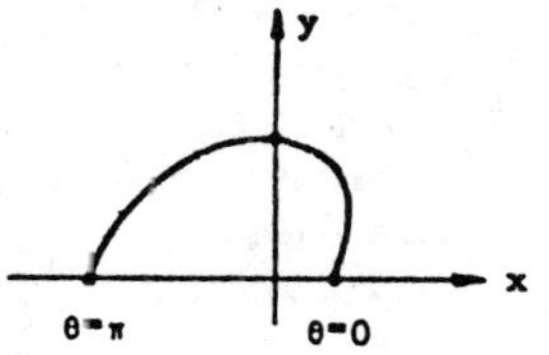

$\frac{dx}{d\theta} = -2 \sin \theta + 2 \sin 2\theta,$

$\frac{dy}{d\theta} = 2 \cos \theta - 2 \cos 2\theta$ so that

$$\left(\frac{dx}{d\theta}\right)^2 + \left(\frac{dy}{d\theta}\right)^2 = \left(4 \sin^2 \theta - 8 \sin \theta \sin 2\theta + 4 \sin^2 2\theta\right) + \left(4 \cos^2 \theta - 8 \cos \theta \cos 2\theta + 4 \cos^2 2\theta\right)$$
$$= 8(1 - \sin \theta \sin 2\theta - \cos \theta \cos 2\theta)$$
$$= 8[1 - \cos(2\theta - \theta)]$$
$$= 8(1 - \cos \theta)$$

Therefore, the surface area is given by

$$S = \int_0^{\pi} 2\pi(2 \sin \theta - \sin 2\theta) \cdot 2\sqrt{2} \sqrt{1 - \cos \theta}\, d\theta$$
$$= \int_0^{\pi} 8\sqrt{2}\, \pi \sin \theta (1 - \cos \theta)^{3/2}\, d\theta, \quad \text{with } \sin 2\theta = 2 \sin \theta \cos \theta$$
$$= \frac{16\sqrt{2}}{5} \pi (1 - \cos \theta)^{5/2}\Big]_0^{\pi} = \frac{128\pi}{5} \approx 80.4 \text{ square units.}$$

10. (a) $x = -6 \cos \frac{\pi}{4} = -6 \cdot \frac{\sqrt{2}}{2} = -3\sqrt{2};\quad y = -6 \sin \frac{\pi}{4} = -3\sqrt{2}$

(b) $x = 1 \cos \left(-\frac{5\pi}{6}\right) = \cos \frac{5\pi}{6} = -\frac{\sqrt{3}}{2};$

$y = 1 \sin \left(-\frac{5\pi}{6}\right) = -\sin \frac{5\pi}{6} = -\frac{1}{2}$

(c) $x = -2 \cos \left(-\frac{7\pi}{12}\right) = -2 \cos \frac{7\pi}{12} = \frac{\sqrt{2}}{2} (\sqrt{3} - 1) \approx 0.518$

$y = -2 \sin \left(-\frac{7\pi}{12}\right) = 2 \sin \frac{7\pi}{12} = \frac{\sqrt{2}}{2} (\sqrt{3} + 1) \approx 1.932$

11. (a) $\pm \sqrt{x^2 + y^2} = 5$ or $x^2 + y^2 = 25$

(b) $y = -x$

(c) Equivalently, $r \sin \theta = -5$, or $y = -5$

12. $r = 2 \cos 4\theta$ is symmetric about the x-axis, the y-axis, and the origin.
The graph is the eight-leafed rose sketched at the right.

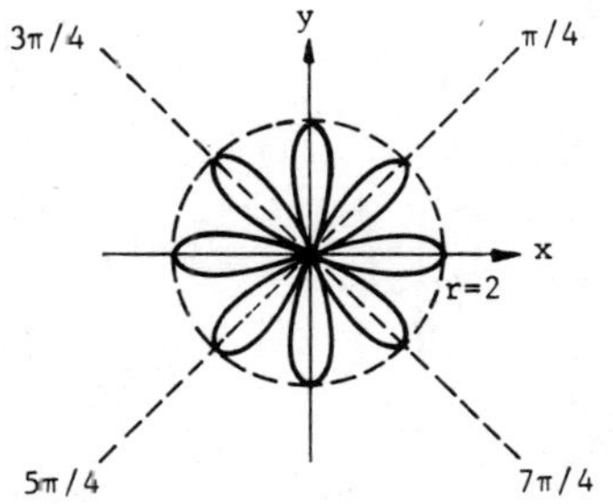

13. $r^2 = -\sin 2\theta$ is symmetric about the origin since the equation is unchanged when r is replaced by $-r$. Notice that $-\sin 2\theta$ must be nonnegative. If θ is restricted to the interval $[0, 2\pi]$, then $-\sin 2\theta \geq 0$ if and only if θ is in $[\frac{\pi}{2}, \pi]$ or $[\frac{3\pi}{2}, 2\pi]$. Using the following table and symmetry we obtain the graph sketched at the right:

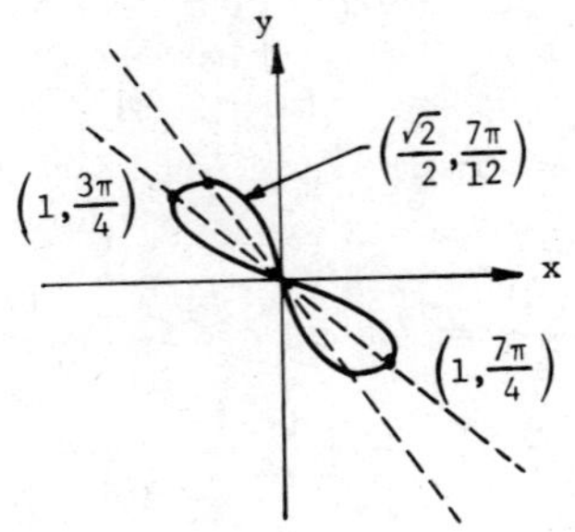

θ	$\pi/2$	$7\pi/12$	$3\pi/4$	π	$3\pi/2$
r	0	$\sqrt{2}/2$	1	0	0

The curve is a lemniscate.

14. Since $r = 5\cos\theta + 5\sin\theta$, for $r \neq 0$ ($r = 0$ is on the graph at $\theta = \frac{3\pi}{4}$), $r^2 = 5r\cos\theta + 5r\sin\theta$, or $x^2 + y^2 = 5x + 5y$. Then, completing the squares in the x and y terms gives

$$\left(x - \frac{5}{2}\right)^2 + \left(y - \frac{5}{2}\right)^2 = \frac{25}{2}.$$

This is a circle with center $\left(\frac{5}{2}, \frac{5}{2}\right)$ and radius $\frac{5}{\sqrt{2}}$.

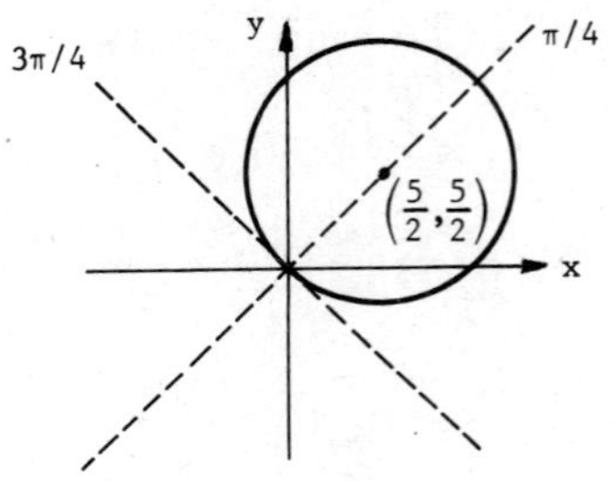

15. A Cartesian equation of the line is given by $y + 3 = -2(x - 1)$ or $2x + y = -1$. Thus, $2r\cos\theta + r\sin\theta = -1$, or solving for r, $r = \dfrac{-1}{2\cos\theta + \sin\theta}$.

16. A Cartesian equation of the circle is given by $\left(x - \frac{1}{3}\right)^2 + y^2 = \frac{1}{9}$ or $x^2 + y^2 = \frac{2}{3}x$. Thus, $3r^2 = 2r\cos\theta$, or since $r = 0$ lies on the graph $3r = 2\cos\theta$ when $\theta = \frac{\pi}{2}$, the latter gives a polar equation of the circle.

17. For $r = a\cos(\theta + b)$, $\frac{dr}{d\theta} = -a\sin(\theta + b)$ so that $r^2 + \left(\frac{dr}{d\theta}\right)^2 = a^2\cos^2(\theta + b) + a^2\sin^2(\theta + b) = a^2$. Therefore the arc length is given by the integral $s = \int_0^{\pi} \sqrt{a^2}\, d\theta = |a|\pi$.

18. A graph depicting the region is shown in the figure at the right (the shaded portion represents the area we seek). Thus the area is given by

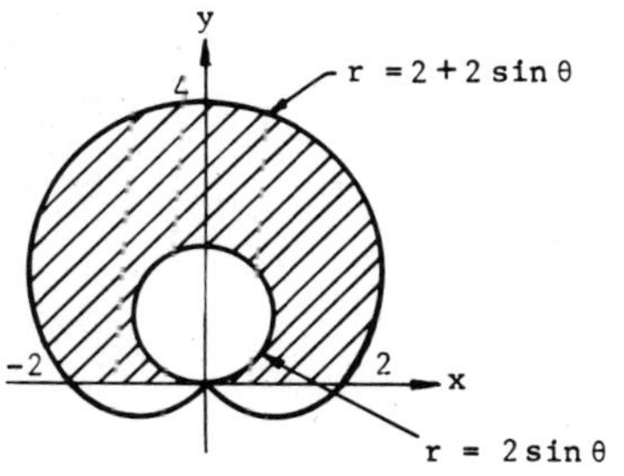

$$A = \frac{1}{2}\int_0^{\pi} (2 + 2\sin\theta)^2\, d\theta$$

$$- \frac{1}{2}\int_0^{\pi} (2\sin\theta)^2\, d\theta$$

$$= \frac{1}{2}\int_0^{\pi} (4 + 8\sin\theta)\, d\theta$$

$$= 2(\theta - 2\cos\theta)\Big]_0^{\pi}$$

$$= 2\pi + 8 \approx 14.28.$$

19. A sketch of the surface is shown in the figure at the right. An element of arc length ds generates a portion of surface area

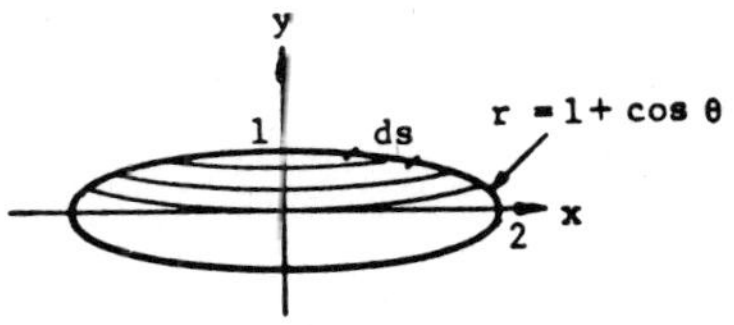

$$dS = 2\pi x\, dx.$$

Now, $\frac{ds}{d\theta} = \sqrt{r^2 + \left(\frac{dr}{d\theta}\right)^2}$

$$= \sqrt{1 + 2\cos\theta + \cos^2\theta) + \sin^2\theta} = \sqrt{2}\,\sqrt{1 + \cos\theta}$$

Hence, $dS = 2\pi x\, ds = 2\pi r\cos\theta\, ds = 2\sqrt{2}\pi(1 + \cos\theta)^{3/2}\cos\theta\, d\theta$. Therefore, the total surface area generated is given by the integral

$$S = 2\sqrt{2}\pi\int_0^{\pi/2} (1 + \cos\theta)^{3/2}\cos\theta\, d\theta.$$

(The definite integral can be evaluated by using the identity $\cos^2\frac{\theta}{2} = 1 + \cos\theta$, but it is tedious to carry out the calculations. Using Simpson's rule with $n = 12$, an approximate value to the integral is 39.31. This calculation was made using a calculator.)

CHAPTER 10 VECTORS AND ANALYTIC GEOMETRY IN SPACE

10.1 VECTORS IN THE PLANE

OBJECTIVE A: Given the points P_1 and P_2 in the plane, express the vector $\vec{P_1P_2}$ in the form $a\vec{i} + b\vec{j}$.

1. Consider the points $P_1(x_1,y_1)$ and $P_2(x_2,y_2)$. The directed change in the x-direction from P_1 to P_2 is $a =$ __________, and in the y-direction it is $b =$ __________. Hence, the vector $\vec{P_1P_2}$ can be expressed as $\vec{P_1P_2} =$ ____________________.

2. The vector from the point $P_1(-7,4)$ to the point $P_2(3,-5)$ is $\vec{P_1P_2} = (3 - \_\_)\vec{i} + (\_\_ - 4)\vec{j}$ or $\vec{P_1P_2} =$ __________.

3. The vector from $P(2,-9)$ to the origin is $\vec{PO} =$ __________.

OBJECTIVE B: Express the sum and difference of two given vectors, and multiples of given vectors by scalars, in the form $a\vec{i} + b\vec{j}$.

4. The sum of $\vec{v}_1 = a_1\vec{i} + b_1\vec{j}$ and $\vec{v}_2 = a_2\vec{i} + b_2\vec{j}$ is $\vec{v}_1 + \vec{v}_2 =$ ______________________________.

5. If $\vec{v}_1 = 3\vec{i} - 4\vec{j}$ and $\vec{v}_2 = -5\vec{i} + 2\vec{j}$, then $\vec{v}_1 + \vec{v}_2 =$ __________ and $\vec{v}_2 - \vec{v}_1 =$ __________.

6. If $\vec{v}_1 = -3\vec{i} + 7\vec{j}$, then
$-\vec{v} =$ ________, $2\vec{v} =$ ________,
$-5\vec{v} =$ ________, and $\frac{1}{4}\vec{v} =$ ________.

OBJECTIVE C: Given a vector $\vec{v} = a\vec{i} + b\vec{j}$, calculate its length or magnitude, direction, and the angle it makes with the positive x-axis.

7. The length or magnitude of the vector $\vec{v} = a\vec{i} + b\vec{j}$ is given by $|\vec{v}| =$ __________.

---

1. $x_2 - x_1$, $y_2 - y_1$, $(x_2 - x_1)\vec{i} + (y_2 - y_1)\vec{j}$
2. -7, -5, $10\vec{i} - 9\vec{j}$
3. $-2\vec{i} + 9\vec{j}$
4. $(a_1 + a_2)\vec{i} + (b_1 + b_2)\vec{j}$, $(a_2 - a_1)\vec{i} + (b_2 - b_1)\vec{j}$
5. $-2\vec{i} - 2\vec{j}$, $-8\vec{i} + 6\vec{j}$
6. $3\vec{i} - 7\vec{j}$, $-6\vec{i} + 14\vec{j}$, $15\vec{i} - 35\vec{j}$, $-\frac{3}{4}\vec{i} + \frac{7}{4}\vec{j}$
7. $\sqrt{a^2 + b^2}$

8. The angle θ that $\vec{v} = a\vec{i} + b\vec{j}$ makes with the positive x-axis satisfies

$$\cos\theta = \_\_\_\_\_\_\_\_ \quad \text{and} \quad \sin\theta = \_\_\_\_\_\_\_\_ .$$

9. The length of $\vec{v} = -\sqrt{2}\vec{i} + 7\vec{j}$ is $|\vec{v}| = \_\_\_\_\_\_\_\_\_\_\_\_$.

10. Consider the vector $\vec{v} = -\vec{i} + \sqrt{3}\vec{j}$. The length of $\vec{v}$ is $|\vec{v}| = \_\_\_\_\_\_\_\_$. The direction of $\vec{v}$ is given by Direction of $\vec{v} = \frac{\vec{v}}{|\vec{v}|} = \_\_\_\_\_\_\_\_$. Thus, if θ is the angle $\vec{v}$ makes with the positive x-axis, then

$$\cos\theta = \_\_\_\_\_ \quad \text{and} \quad \sin\theta = \_\_\_\_\_ .$$

It follows that $\theta = \frac{\pi}{2} + \_\_\_\_\_ = \_\_\_\_\_$ radians.

OBJECTIVE D: Find unit vectors tangent and normal to a given curve $y = f(x)$ at a specified point $P(a,b)$.

11. Consider the curve $y = 1 - 2e^x$. Observe that the point $P(0,-1)$ lies on the curve. The slope of the line tangent to curve at P is $y' = \_\_\_\_\_|_{x=0} = \_\_\_\_\_$. A vector $\vec{v}$ having this slope is given by $\vec{v} = \_\_\_\_\_\vec{i} + \_\_\_\_\_\vec{j}$. (Any nonzero multiple of $\vec{v}$ will also have the slope -2, so $\vec{v}$ is not unique.) A unit vector parallel to $\vec{v}$ is given by

$$\vec{u} = \frac{\vec{v}}{|\vec{v}|} = \_\_\_\_\_\_\_\_ .$$

The vector $\vec{u}$ is a unit vector tangent to the curve at $P(0,-1)$; the vector $-\vec{u}$ is also a unit vector tangent to the curve at $P(0,-1)$.

12. One unit vector normal to the curve at P for Problem 11 above is $\vec{n} = \_\_\_\_\_\_\_\_$. A second vector is $-\vec{n} = \_\_\_\_\_\_\_\_$. Either vector will do as a unit vector normal to $y = 1 - 2e^x$ at $P(0,-1)$.

10.2 CARTESIAN (RECTANGULAR) COORDINATES AND VECTORS IN SPACE

OBJECTIVE A: Given two points P_1 and P_2 in space, express the vector $\vec{P_1P_2}$ from P_1 to P_2 in the form $a\vec{i} + b\vec{j} + c\vec{k}$.

13. The vector from the point $(-1,3,0)$ to the point $(4,-2,1)$ is given by $(4 + 1)\vec{i} + \_\_\_\_\_\vec{j} + \_\_\_\_\_\vec{k}$ or $\_\_\_\_\_\_\_\_$.

---

8. $\frac{a}{\sqrt{a^2 + b^2}}$, $\frac{b}{\sqrt{a^2 + b^2}}$ 9. $\sqrt{2 + 49} = \sqrt{51}$ 10. $\sqrt{1 + 3} = 2$, $-\frac{1}{2}\vec{i} + \frac{\sqrt{3}}{2}\vec{j}$, $-\frac{1}{2}$, $\frac{\sqrt{3}}{2}$, $\frac{\pi}{6}$, $\frac{2\pi}{3}$

11. $-2e^x$, -2, 1, -2, $\frac{1}{\sqrt{5}}\vec{i} - \frac{2}{\sqrt{5}}\vec{j}$ 12. $\frac{2}{\sqrt{5}}\vec{i} + \frac{1}{\sqrt{5}}\vec{j}$, $-\frac{2}{\sqrt{5}}\vec{i} - \frac{1}{\sqrt{5}}\vec{j}$ 13. $(-2 - 3)$, $(1 - 0)$, $5\vec{i} - 5\vec{j} + \vec{k}$

OBJECTIVE B: Find the length of any space vector.

14. The length of the vector $\vec{v} = -2\vec{i} + 6\vec{j} - 5\vec{k}$ is

$$|\vec{v}| = \sqrt{(-2)^2 + (\_\_\_\_) + (\_\_\_\_\_)} = \sqrt{\_\_\_\_\_} \approx 8.06 .$$

OBJECTIVE C: Given a Cartesian equation of a sphere in space, find the coordinates of its center and the radius.

15. Consider the equation of the sphere given by

$$x^2 + y^2 + z^2 + 2x - 6y + 4z + 9 = 0.$$

Complete the squares in the given equation to obtain,

$(x^2 + 2x + 1) + (y^2 - 6y + 9) + (\_\_\_\_\_\_\_\_\_\_) = \_\_\_\_\_\_\_$, or

$$(x + 1)^2 + (y - 3)^2 + (\_\_\_\_\_\_\_\_\_) = \_\_\_\_\_\_ .$$

Thus, the center is __________ and the radius is ______.

OBJECTIVE D: Given a nonzero space vector find its direction.

16. If $\vec{A}$ is a nonzero vector, <u>the direction of</u> $\vec{A}$ is a ______ vector obtained from $\vec{A}$ by dividing $\vec{A}$ by ______.

17. To compute the direction of the vector $\vec{A} = -2\vec{i} + 6\vec{j} - 5\vec{k}$, we divide $\vec{A}$ by $|\vec{A}| =$ _____ found in Problem 14. This gives the unit vector $\vec{u} = \frac{\vec{A}}{|\vec{A}|} =$ ________________ as the direction of $\vec{A}$.

10.3 DOT PRODUCTS

OBJECTIVE A: Find the scalar product or dot product of two vectors in space and the cosine of the angle between them.

18. The scalar or dot product of the vectors $\vec{A} = 2\vec{i} + \vec{j} - 3\vec{k}$ and $\vec{B} = 3\vec{i} - 6\vec{j} + 2\vec{k}$ is $\vec{A}\cdot\vec{B} = (2)(3) + (1)(\_\_\_\_) + (\_\_\_\_)(\_\_\_\_)$ $=$ _______.

19. For the vectors in Problem 18,

$|\vec{A}| = \sqrt{4 + 1 + \_\_\_\_} = \_\_\_\_\_$ and $|\vec{B}| = \sqrt{9 + 36 + \_\_\_\_} = \_\_\_\_$.

Thus, the cosine of the angle θ between them is

$$\cos\theta = \frac{\_\_\_\_\_}{|\vec{A}||\vec{B}|} = \frac{-6}{\_\_\_\_\_} \approx -.229, \text{ or } \theta \approx 103^\circ.$$

---

14. 6^2, $(-5)^2$, 65

15. $z^2 + 4z + 4$, $1 + 4$, $(z + 2)^2$, 5, (-1,3,-2), $\sqrt{5}$

16. unit, $|\vec{A}|$

17. $\sqrt{65}$, $-\frac{2}{\sqrt{65}}\vec{i} + \frac{6}{\sqrt{65}}\vec{j} - \frac{5}{\sqrt{65}}\vec{k}$

18. -6, -3, 2, -6

19. 9, $\sqrt{14}$, 4, 7, $\vec{A}\cdot\vec{B}$, $7\sqrt{14}$

OBJECTIVE B: Given two space vectors $\vec{A}$ and $\vec{B}$ find the projection vector $\text{proj}_{\vec{A}}\,\vec{B}$ and the scalar component of $\vec{B}$ in the direction $\vec{A}$.

20. The projection of $\vec{B}$ onto $\vec{A}$ is the vector

$$\text{proj}_{\vec{A}}\,\vec{B} = \_\_\_\_\_\_\_.$$

21. The scalar component of $\vec{B}$ in the direction $\vec{A}$ is the scalar ________. Since $\vec{A}\cdot\vec{A} = |\vec{A}|^2$, the magnitude of the vector $\text{proj}_{\vec{A}}\,\vec{B}$ is given by $|\text{proj}_{\vec{A}}\,\vec{B}| = \dfrac{|\vec{B}\cdot\vec{A}|}{\_\_\_\_}\,|\vec{A}| = \_\_\_\_\_\_\_\_\_\_.$

Thus, the absolute value of the scalar component of $\vec{B}$ in the direction $\vec{A}$ is simply the magnitude of ________.

22. Consider the vectors $\vec{A} = -2\vec{i} + \vec{j} + 2\vec{k}$ and $\vec{B} = 2\vec{i} - 6\vec{j} - 3\vec{k}$. Then,

$$\text{proj}_{\vec{A}}\,\vec{B} = \left(\frac{\vec{B}\cdot\vec{A}}{\vec{A}\cdot\vec{A}}\right)\vec{A} = \frac{\_\_\_\_\_\_\_\_}{4+1+4}\,\vec{A} = \_\_\_\_\_\ \vec{A} = \_\_\_\_\_\_\_\_\_\_\_\_\_\_\_.$$

Then the scalar component of $\vec{B}$ in the direction $\vec{A}$ is the scalar $\dfrac{\vec{B}\cdot\vec{A}}{|\vec{A}|} = \_\_\_\_\_\_$. The fact that this component is negative means that the vector $\text{proj}_{\vec{A}}\,\vec{B}$ points in the _______________ direction of $\vec{A}$.

23. For the vectors in Problem 22,

$$\text{proj}_{\vec{B}}\,\vec{A} = \left(\frac{\vec{A}\cdot\vec{B}}{\vec{B}\cdot\vec{B}}\right)\_\_\_\_ = \frac{-16}{\_\_\_\_}\,\vec{B} = \_\_\_\_\_\_\_\_\_\_\_\_\_\_\_.$$

The scalar component of $\vec{A}$ in the direction of $\vec{B}$ is

$$\frac{\vec{A}\cdot\vec{B}}{\_\_\_\_} = \_\_\_\_\_.$$

OBJECTIVE C: Use vector methods to calculate the distance between a given point $P(x,y)$ and a given line L in the xy-plane.

24. Find the distance between the point $P(1,-7)$ and the line L: $5y - 7x + 14 = 0$.

---

20. $\left(\dfrac{\vec{B}\cdot\vec{A}}{\vec{A}\cdot\vec{A}}\right)\vec{A}$

21. $\dfrac{\vec{B}\cdot\vec{A}}{|\vec{A}|}$, $|\vec{A}|^2$, $\dfrac{|\vec{B}\cdot\vec{A}|}{|\vec{A}|}$, $\text{proj}_{\vec{A}}\,\vec{B}$

22. $-4-6-6$, $-\frac{16}{9}$, $\frac{32}{9}\vec{i} - \frac{16}{9}\vec{j} - \frac{32}{9}\vec{k}$, $-\frac{16}{3}$, opposite

23. $\vec{B}$, 49, $-\frac{32}{49}\vec{i} + \frac{96}{49}\vec{j} + \frac{48}{49}\vec{k}$, $|\vec{B}|$, $-\frac{16}{7}$

<u>Solution</u>. If we write the equation of the line L in the form $7x - 5y = 14$, we find a normal vector to the line is $\vec{N} =$ ________. The point B(0,_____) lies on the line. Thus, the vector $\vec{BP} =$ __________ is a vector from the line L to P. The magnitude of the projection of $\vec{BP}$ onto the normal $\vec{N}$ gives the distance between P and L:

$$d = |\text{proj}_{\vec{N}}\ \vec{BP}| = \frac{|\underline{\qquad} \cdot \vec{N}|}{|\vec{N}|} = \frac{|\underline{\qquad}|}{\sqrt{74}} = \underline{\qquad\qquad}.$$

Notice that since $|\text{proj}_{\vec{N}}\ \vec{BP}|$ is the <u>absolute</u> <u>value</u> of the scalar component of $\vec{BP}$ in the direction $\vec{N}$, we need not be concerned with whether $\vec{BP}$ points in the same or opposite direction to $\vec{N}$: either way the procedure correctly computes a positive distance between P and L.

OBJECTIVE D: Know the following five properties of the scalar product.

25. $\vec{B} \cdot \vec{A} =$ ________

26. $\vec{A} \cdot (\vec{B} + \vec{C}) =$ ______________

27. $\vec{A} \cdot \vec{A} = 0$ if and only if _________.

28. $\vec{A} \cdot (c\vec{B}) = (c\vec{A}) \cdot \vec{B} =$ ____________.

29. $\vec{A} \cdot \vec{A}$ is __________ for every nonzero vector $\vec{A}$.

OBJECTIVE E: Find an equation for the line in the xy-plane that passes through a given point and is perpendicular to a specified vector.

30. The line through the point P(-3,1) perpendicular to $\vec{N} = -\vec{i} + 4\vec{j}$ is

_________________ $= (-1)(-3) + (4)(1)$

or

$y =$ ____________________________ .

---

24. $7\vec{i} - 5\vec{j}$, $-\frac{14}{5}$, $\vec{i} - \frac{21}{5}\vec{j}$, $\vec{BP}$, $7 + 21$, $\frac{14\sqrt{74}}{37}$

25. $\vec{A} \cdot \vec{B}$

26. $\vec{A} \cdot \vec{B} + \vec{A} \cdot \vec{C}$

27. $\vec{A} = \vec{0}$

28. $c(\vec{A} \cdot \vec{B})$

29. positive

30. $-x + 4y$, $\frac{1}{4}(x + 7)$

10.4 CROSS PRODUCTS

OBJECTIVE A: Define the vector product or cross product of two vectors in space, and give at least five properties of the cross product.

31. $\vec{A} \times \vec{B} = (\_\_\_\_\_\_\_\_\_\_)\vec{n}$, where $\vec{n}$ is a _____ vector __________ to the plane of $\vec{A}$ and $\vec{B}$, and pointing in the direction a right-threaded screw advances when its head is rotated from ____ to ____ through the angle θ from $\vec{A}$ to $\vec{B}$.

32. $\vec{B} \times \vec{A} = \_\_\_\_\_\_\_\_$.

33. $\vec{A} \times (\vec{B} + \vec{C}) = \_\_\_\_\_\_\_\_\_\_\_\_$.

34. $(\vec{B} + \vec{C}) \times \vec{A} = \_\_\_\_\_\_\_\_\_\_\_\_$.

35. $(r\vec{A}) \times (s\vec{B}) = \_\_\_\_\_\_\_\_\_\_$.

36. If $\vec{A} \times \vec{B} = \vec{0}$, then $\vec{A} = \vec{0}$ or $\vec{B} = \vec{0}$, or $\vec{A}$ and $\vec{B}$ are __________ vectors.

37. $\vec{i} \times \vec{j} = \_\_\_\_$, $\vec{j} \times \vec{k} = \_\_\_\_$, and $\vec{k} \times \vec{i} = \_\_\_\_$.
These three equations are easily remembered by writing the vectors in cyclic order $\vec{i}, \vec{j}, \vec{k}, \vec{i}, \vec{j}$ and realizing that the cross product of any two results is the next one in line.

OBJECTIVE B: Use the determinant formula to calculate the cross product of any two vectors in space whose $\vec{i}, \vec{j}, \vec{k}$ components are given.

38. Let $\vec{A} = \vec{i} + \vec{j} + \vec{k}$ and $\vec{B} = -5\vec{i} + 3\vec{j} - 2\vec{k}$. Then

$$\vec{A} \times \vec{B} = \begin{vmatrix} \vec{i} & \vec{j} & \vec{k} \\ \_\_ & \_\_ & \_\_ \\ \_\_ & \_\_ & \_\_ \end{vmatrix} = (-2 - 3)\vec{i} + (-5 + \_\_\_)\vec{j} + (\_\_\_\_\_)\vec{k}$$

$$= \_\_\_\_\_\_\_\_\_\_\_\_.$$

---

31. $|\vec{A}|\,|\vec{B}| \sin\theta$, unit, perpendicular, $\vec{A}$, $\vec{B}$

32. $-\vec{A} \times \vec{B}$

33. $(\vec{A} \times \vec{B}) + (\vec{A} \times \vec{C})$

34. $(\vec{B} \times \vec{A}) + (\vec{C} \times \vec{A})$

35. $rs(\vec{A} \times \vec{B})$

36. parallel

37. $\vec{k}, \vec{i}, \vec{j}$

38. $\begin{vmatrix} \vec{i} & \vec{j} & \vec{k} \\ 1 & 1 & 1 \\ -5 & 3 & -2 \end{vmatrix}$, 2, 3 + 5, $-5\vec{i} - 3\vec{j} + 8\vec{k}$

39. For the vectors in Problem 38, the magnitude $|\vec{A} \times \vec{B}|$ = ______ represents the area of the ______________ with sides ______ and $\vec{B}$.

OBJECTIVE C: Find a vector that is perpendicular to two given vectors in space.

40. Let $\vec{A} = \vec{i} + \vec{k}$ and $\vec{B} = \vec{i} + 2\vec{j} - \vec{k}$. Then a vector perpendicular to both $\vec{A}$ and $\vec{B}$ is $\vec{A} \times \vec{B}$ = ______________.

41. The three points A(1,0,2), B(3,1,4), and C(-1,5,1) determine a plane in space. The vectors $\vec{AB}$ = ______________ and $\vec{AC}$ = ______________ both lie in that plane. Thus, the cross product $\vec{AB} \times \vec{AC}$ = ______________ gives a vector that is perpendicular to the plane containing A, B, and C. Other vectors perpendicular to that plane are $\vec{CB} \times \vec{CA}$, $\vec{BA} \times \vec{BC}$, $\vec{AB} \times \vec{BC}$, etc.

OBJECTIVE D: Find the area of any triangle with specified vertices in space, and find the distance between the origin and the plane determined by that triangle.

42. The area of the triangle determined by the points in Problem 41 is:

$$\text{area} = \frac{1}{2}\ \underline{\qquad\qquad} = \frac{1}{2}\sqrt{121 + \underline{\qquad} + \underline{\qquad}} = \underline{\qquad\qquad}.$$

43. To calculate the distance between the origin and the plane determined by the triangle in Problem 41, simply calculate the magnitude of the projection of any vector $\vec{OP}$ from the origin O to a point P on the plane onto a direction vector perpendicular to the plane. For instance, the point A(1,0,2) lies on the plane and $\vec{OA}$ = ________. A vector orthogonal to the plane is $\vec{N} = \vec{AB} \times \vec{AC}$ which was calculated in Problem 41. Hence,

$$|\text{proj}_{\vec{N}}\ \vec{OA}| = \frac{|\vec{OA} \cdot \underline{\qquad}|}{|\vec{N}|} = \frac{|\underline{\qquad\qquad}|}{\sqrt{269}} = \underline{\qquad\qquad\qquad}$$

gives the distance between the origin and the plane of the triangle.

---

39. $7\sqrt{2}$, parallelogram, $\vec{A}$

40. $-2\vec{i} + 2\vec{j} + \vec{k}$

41. $2\vec{i} + 2\vec{j} + 2\vec{k}$, $-2\vec{i} + 5\vec{j} - \vec{k}$, $-11\vec{i} - 2\vec{j} + 12\vec{k}$

42. $|\vec{AB} \times \vec{AC}|$, 4, 144, $\frac{1}{2}\sqrt{269}$

43. $\vec{i} + 2\vec{k}$, $\vec{N}$, -11 + 24, $\frac{13}{\sqrt{269}} \approx .79262$

10.5 LINES AND PLANES IN SPACE

OBJECTIVE A: Write parametric equations of a line in space given (a) two points on the line, or (b) a point on the line and a vector parallel to the line.

44. Consider the line L determined by the two points $P(\frac{1}{2},0,1)$ and $Q(\frac{1}{2},-1,2)$. The vector $\vec{PQ}$ = ________ lies in a direction parallel to the line. Then, using the point P on the line,

$$x = \frac{1}{2} + 0t, \quad y = \_\_\_\_\_\_, \quad \text{and} \quad z = \_\_\_\_\_\_$$

are parametric equations for the line. Using the point Q,

$$x = \frac{1}{2} + 0s, \quad y = \_\_\_\_\_\_, \quad \text{and} \quad z = \_\_\_\_\_\_$$

is another set of parametric equations representing the same line. The point $(\frac{1}{2},-2,3)$ lies on the line when $t = 2$ and when s = ______. The two sets of equations describe the same set of points (a straight line), but any particular point on that line will be given by different values of the parameters t and s in each representation.

45. A line through the point $(4,-2,2)$ in the direction parallel to the vector $\vec{A} = -2\vec{i} + \vec{j} + \vec{k}$ is given by x = ______, y = ______, and z = ______.

OBJECTIVE B: Find the distance between a given point and line in space.

46. Suppose it is desired to find the distance between the point $P(7,3,-1)$ and the line L: $x = 4 - 2t$, $y = -2 + t$, and $z = 2 + t$. The vector $\vec{v} = -2\vec{i} + \vec{j} + \vec{k}$ is __________ to L (see figure at the right). Choose any point on the line L, say $Q(4,-2,2)$. Let θ denote the angle between $\vec{v}$ and $\vec{QP}$. Then, from the diagram at the right, $d = |\vec{QP}| \sin \theta$ and

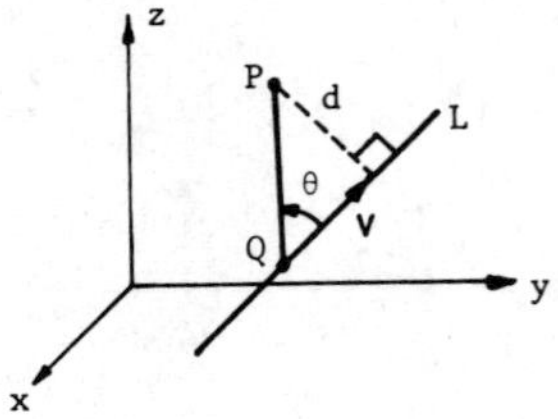

$|\vec{v}|d = |\vec{v}||\vec{QP}| \sin \theta$ = __________. Thus, $d = \frac{|\vec{v} \times \vec{QP}|}{|\vec{v}|}$ gives the desired distance. Now, $\vec{QP}$ = ______________ and

$$\vec{v} \times \vec{QP} = \begin{vmatrix} \vec{i} & \vec{j} & \vec{k} \\ -2 & 1 & 1 \\ \_ & \_ & \_ \end{vmatrix} = \_\_\_\_\_\_\_\_\_\_\_\_ .$$

Hence, $d = \frac{\_\_\_\_\_\_}{\sqrt{4 + 1 + 1}}$ = ____________________.

---

44. $-\vec{j} + \vec{k}$, $0 - t$, $1 + t$, $-1 - s$, $2 + s$, 1

45. $4 - 2t$, $-2 + t$, $2 + t$

46. parallel, $|\vec{v} \times \vec{QP}|$, $3\vec{i} + 5\vec{j} - 3\vec{k}$, 3, 5, -3, $-8\vec{i} - 3\vec{j} - 13\vec{k}$, $\sqrt{64 + 9 + 169}$, $\sqrt{\frac{121}{3}} = \frac{11}{3}\sqrt{3} \approx 6.35$

Note: Problem 46 presents a different method from the text for finding the distance between a point and line in space.

OBJECTIVE C: Write an equation of a plane in space given (a) a point on the plane and a vector normal to the plane, or (b) three noncollinear points on the plane.

47. An equation of the plane in space through the point $(1,-1,7)$ and perpendicular to the vector $\vec{v} = -2\vec{i} - 4\vec{j} + 5\vec{k}$ is given by $-2(x - 1) + (-4)(\_\_\_\_\_\_) + \_\_\_\_\_\_(z - 7) = 0$, or simplifying algebraically, $\_\_\_\_\_\_\_\_\_\_\_\_ = -37$.

48. To find an equation of the plane containing the three points $A(4,-2,3)$, $B(3,2,-1)$, and $C(-1,1,1)$ observe that the vectors $\vec{AB} = \_\_\_\_\_\_\_\_\_\_\_\_$ and $\vec{AC} = \_\_\_\_\_\_\_\_\_\_\_\_$ both lie in the plane. Hence $\vec{AB} \times \vec{AC} = \_\_\_\_\_\_\_\_\_\_\_\_$ is normal to the plane. Using the point A on the plane, an equation for it is $4(x - 4) + \_\_\_\_\_\_(y + 2) + 17(\_\_\_\_\_\_) = 0$, or $\_\_\_\_\_\_\_\_\_\_\_\_ = 31$.

OBJECTIVE D: Find the distance between a given point and plane in space.

49. To find the distance between the point P and a plane, pick any point Q on the plane and calculate the magnitude of the projection vector of $\vec{PQ}$ onto a vector perpendicular to the plane. Let us find the distance between the point $P(5,-1,0)$ and the plane $2x + 4y - 5z = -37$. The point $Q(0,0,\_\_\_\_\_\_)$ lies on the plane. A vector normal to the plane is $\vec{N} = 2\vec{i} + \_\_\_\_\_\_\_\_$, and we have the vector $\vec{PQ} = \_\_\_\_\_\_\_\_\_\_\_\_$. Thus,

$$|\text{proj}_{\vec{N}}\, \vec{PQ}| = \frac{|\vec{PQ} \cdot \vec{N}|}{\_\_\_\_\_\_} = \frac{|\_\_\_\_\_\_|}{\sqrt{45}} \approx 6.41$$

gives the distance between the point and the plane.

OBJECTIVE E: Find the point in which a given line meets a given plane.

50. The line $x = 4 - 2t$, $y = -2 + t$, $z = 2 + t$ from Problem 45 meets the plane $x - 3y + 7z = 30$ when $\_\_\_\_\_\_\_\_\_\_\_\_\_\_\_\_ = 30$ or $t = \_\_\_\_\_\_\_\_$. The point of intersection is $P(\_\_\_\_\_\_\_\_)$.

---

47. $y + 1$, 5, $2x + 4y - 5z$

48. $-\vec{i} + 4\vec{j} - 4\vec{k}$, $-5\vec{i} + 3\vec{j} - 2\vec{k}$, $4\vec{i} + 18\vec{j} + 17\vec{k}$, 18, $z - 3$, $4x + 18y + 17z$

49. $\frac{37}{5}$, $4\vec{j} - 5\vec{k}$, $-5\vec{i} + \vec{j} + \frac{37}{5}\vec{k}$, $|\vec{N}|$, -43

50. $(4 - 2t) - 3(-2 + t) + 7(2 + t)$, 3, $P(-2,1,5)$

OBJECTIVE F: Find parametric equations for the line in which two given nonparallel planes intersect. Find also the (acute) angle between the planes.

51. A vector parallel to the line of intersection of the planes $-x + 2y - z = 4$ and $3x - y - 2z = 3$ is given by the cross product of their normals:

$$\begin{vmatrix} \vec{i} & \vec{j} & \vec{k} \\ -1 & 2 & -1 \\ 3 & -1 & -2 \end{vmatrix} = \underline{\hspace{4cm}} .$$

Substituting $x = 0$ in the plane equations and solving for y and z simultaneously gives $y = 1$ and $z =$ ________. Thus the point (________) is common to both planes and lies on the line of their intersection. The line is $x =$ __________, $y = 1 - 5t$, $z =$ __________.

52. The (acute) angle between the two planes in Problem 51 is

$$\theta = \cos^{-1}\left(\frac{\vec{N}_1 \cdot \vec{N}_2}{|\vec{N}_1||\vec{N}_2|}\right)$$

$$= \cos^{-1}\left(\frac{-3 - 2 + 2}{\underline{\hspace{3cm}}}\right)$$

$$= \cos^{-1}\left(\frac{-3}{2\sqrt{21}}\right)$$

$= 71°$. (Calculator, rounded)

10.6 PRODUCTS OF THREE VECTORS OR MORE

OBJECTIVE A: Given any three vectors $\vec{A}$, $\vec{B}$, and $\vec{C}$ in space, calculate the triple scalar product $\vec{A} \cdot (\vec{B} \times \vec{C})$.

53. For the vectors $\vec{A} = 3\vec{i} + 5\vec{j} - 2\vec{k}$, $\vec{B} = -\vec{i} + 4\vec{j} - 4\vec{k}$, and $\vec{C} = 4\vec{j} - \vec{k}$, the triple scalar product $\vec{A} \cdot (\vec{B} \times \vec{C})$ is given by the determinant

$$\vec{A} \cdot (\vec{B} \times \vec{C}) = \begin{vmatrix} \_ & \_ & \_ \\ \_ & \_ & \_ \\ \_ & \_ & \_ \end{vmatrix} = \underline{\hspace{2cm}} .$$

---

51. $-5\vec{i} - 5\vec{j} - 5\vec{k}$, -2, $(0,1,-2)$, $-5t$, $-2 - 5t$ 52. $\sqrt{6}\sqrt{14}$ 53. $\begin{vmatrix} 3 & 5 & -2 \\ -1 & 4 & -4 \\ 0 & 4 & -1 \end{vmatrix}$, 39

54. $\vec{A} \cdot (\vec{B} \times \vec{C}) = (\vec{A} \times$ _____$) \cdot$ _____ so that the dot and the cross may be ________________ in the triple scalar product.

OBJECTIVE B: Find the volume of the box determined by three given vectors $\vec{A}$, $\vec{B}$, and $\vec{C}$.

55. For the three vectors given in Problem 53 above, the volume of the parallelepiped determined by them is the absolute value of the triple scalar product $\vec{A} \cdot$ (_______):

$$|\vec{A} \cdot (\_\_\_\_\_\_\_)| = \_\_\_\_\_\_\_ .$$

OBJECTIVE C: Given three vectors $\vec{A}$, $\vec{B}$, and $\vec{C}$ in space, find the triple vector product $(\vec{A} \times \vec{B}) \times \vec{C}$ by two methods.

56. $(\vec{A} \times \vec{B}) \times \vec{C} = (\vec{A} \cdot \vec{C})\vec{B}$ - __________.

57. For the vectors $\vec{A} = 2\vec{i} - 3\vec{j} + 4\vec{k}$, $\vec{B} = \frac{1}{2}\vec{i} + \vec{j} - \vec{k}$, and $\vec{C} = 3\vec{i} - 5\vec{j} + 2\vec{k}$, $\vec{A} \times \vec{B} =$ ________________ so that $(\vec{A} \times \vec{B}) \times \vec{C} =$ ________________.

58. Using the formula in Problem 56,
$\vec{A} \cdot \vec{C} =$ ______ so $(\vec{A} \cdot \vec{C})\vec{B} =$ ________________, and
$\vec{B} \cdot \vec{C} =$ ______ so $(\vec{B} \cdot \vec{C})\vec{A} =$ ________________.
Hence, $(\vec{A} \cdot \vec{C})\vec{B} - (\vec{B} \cdot \vec{C})\vec{A} =$ ________________ in agreement with $\vec{A} \times (\vec{B} \times \vec{C})$ as found in Problem 57.

OBJECTIVE D: Find the volume of a tetrahedron in space given its four vertices.

59. Consider the tetrahedron with vertices A, B, C, D shown in the figure at the right. The volume V is $V = \frac{1}{3}$ (area base) $\cdot$ height. Now, the area of the base triangle ABC is given by

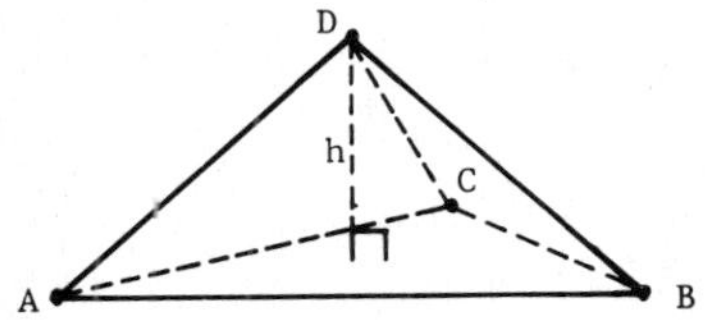

area $\Delta ABC = \frac{1}{2}|$________$|$. The vector $\vec{N} = \vec{AC} \times \vec{AB}$ is also ________ to the base. Hence, the height h of the tetrahedron is the magnitude of the projection of $\vec{AD}$ onto $\vec{N}$:

---

54. $\vec{B}$, $\vec{C}$, interchanged   55. $\vec{B} \times \vec{C}$, $\vec{B} \times \vec{C}$, 39   56. $(\vec{B} \cdot \vec{C})\vec{A}$

57. $-\vec{i} + 4\vec{j} + \frac{7}{2}\vec{k}$, $\frac{51}{2}\vec{i} + \frac{25}{2}\vec{j} - 7\vec{k}$

58. 29, $\frac{29}{2}\vec{i} + 29\vec{j} - 29\vec{k}$, $-\frac{11}{2}$, $-11\vec{i} + \frac{33}{2}\vec{j} - 22\vec{k}$, $\frac{51}{2}\vec{i} + \frac{25}{2}\vec{j} - 7\vec{k}$

$$h = |\text{proj}_{\vec{N}}\ \vec{AD}| = \frac{|\vec{AD} \cdot (\vec{AC} \times \vec{AB})|}{\_\_\_\_\_\_\_\_\_\_\_\_\_\_} .$$

Therefore,

$$V = \frac{1}{3} \cdot \frac{1}{2}|\vec{AC} \times \vec{AB}| \cdot h = \_\_\_\_\_\_\_\_\_\_\_\_\_\_\_\_ .$$

60. Given the tetrahedron with vertices A(1,2,3), B(3,2,1), C(1,0,1), and D(1,5,7),

$\vec{AD}$ = __________, $\vec{AC}$ = __________, and $\vec{AB}$ = __________.

Thus, the volume is given by

$$V = \frac{1}{6}|\vec{AD} \cdot (\vec{AC} \times \vec{AB})| = \frac{1}{6}\begin{vmatrix} \_\_ & \_\_ & \_\_ \\ \_\_ & \_\_ & \_\_ \\ \_\_ & \_\_ & \_\_ \end{vmatrix} = \_\_\_\_\_\_\_\_ .$$

OBJECTIVE E: Find the area of the orthogonal projection of a given parallelogram onto a specified plane.

61. If the parallelogram is determined by the vectors $\vec{A}$ and $\vec{B}$, and if $\vec{n}$ is a unit normal to the specified plane, then the area of the orthogonal projection is the absolute value of ____________.

62. The area of the projection of the parallelogram with sides $\vec{A} = 4\vec{i} + 6\vec{j} + 9\vec{k}$ and $\vec{B} = 2\vec{i} - 3\vec{j}$ onto the xy-plane is

$$|\_\_\_\_\_\_\_\_\_\_| = |(\_\_\_\_\_\_\_\_\_\_\_\_\_\_\_\_) \cdot \vec{k}| = \_\_\_\_\_\_ .$$

10.7 SURFACES IN SPACE

OBJECTIVE A: Discuss and sketch cylinders whose equations are given.

---

59. $\vec{AC} \times \vec{AB}$, normal, $|\vec{AC} \times \vec{AB}|$, $\frac{1}{6}|\vec{AD} \cdot (\vec{AC} \times \vec{AB})|$

60. $3\vec{j} + 4\vec{k}$, $-2\vec{j} - 2\vec{k}$, $2\vec{i} - 2\vec{k}$, $\begin{vmatrix} 0 & 3 & 4 \\ 0 & -2 & -2 \\ 2 & 0 & -2 \end{vmatrix}$, $\frac{2}{3}$

61. $(\vec{A} \times \vec{B}) \cdot \vec{n}$

62. $(\vec{A} \times \vec{B}) \cdot \vec{k}$, $27\vec{i} + 18\vec{j} - 24\vec{k}$, 24

63. Consider the surface given by $y = \sin x$. It is a cylinder with elements parallel to the ___-axis. It extends indefinitely in both the positive and negative directions along the ____-axis. Sketch the graph in the coordinate system at the right.

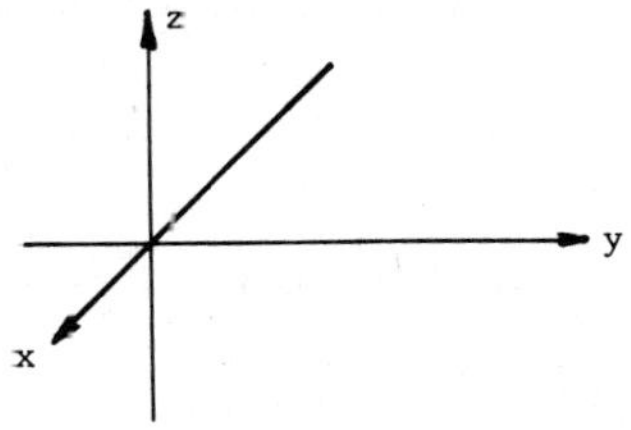

64. Consider the surface $z = x^3$. It is a cylinder with elements parallel to the ____-axis. It extends indefinitely in both the positive and negative directions along the y-axis, with parallel lines passing through the curve $z = x^3$ in the ____-plane. Sketch the graph at the right.

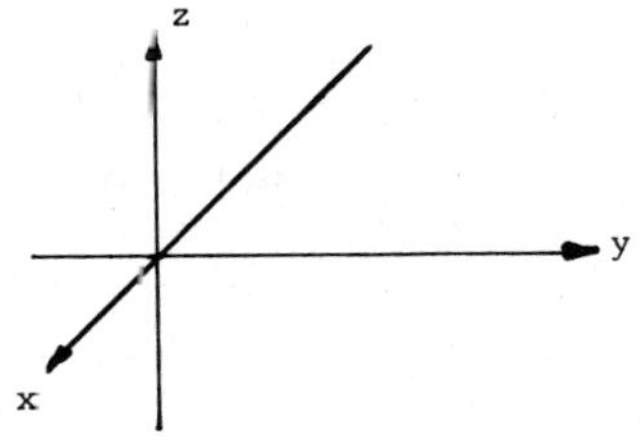

OBJECTIVE B: Discuss and sketch a given surface whose equation $F(x,y,z) = 0$ is a quadratic in the variables x, y, and z.

65. Consider the surface given by the equation $x^2 - 2y^2 + z^2 - 4x - 12y = 20$. Completing the squares we obtain $(x - 2)^2 +$ ____________ $= 6$ or, dividing by 6,

____________________________.

This is a _________ of _______ sheet. It is centered at the point __________. Cross sections parallel to the plane $y = 0$ are _________ while those parallel to

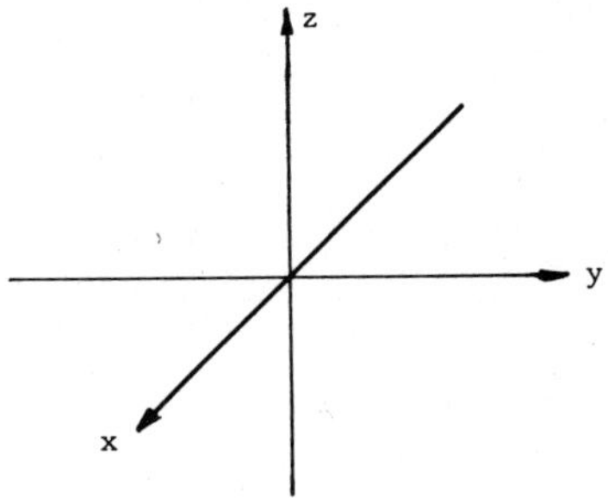

---

63. z, z

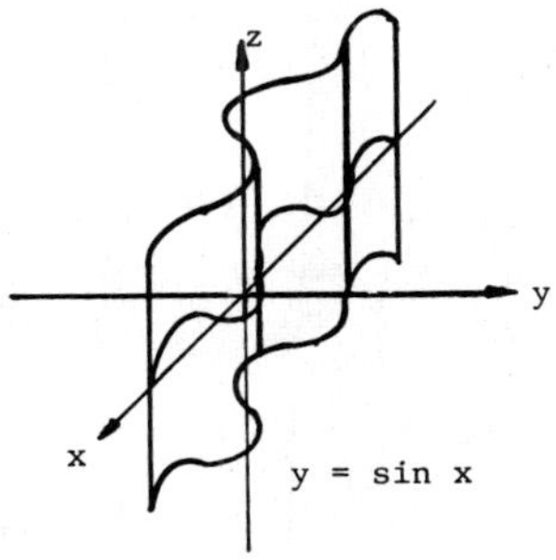

64. y, xz

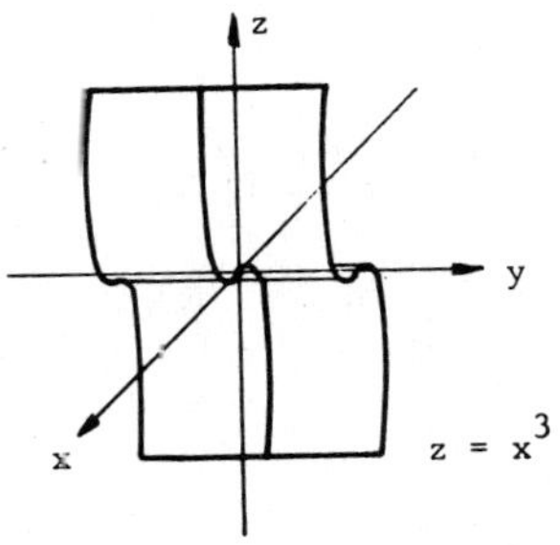

the other coordinate planes are _____________. Sketch the surface.

10.8 CYLINDRICAL AND SPHERICAL COORDINATES

OBJECTIVE A: Describe the set of points in space whose Cartesian, cylindrical, or spherical coordinates satisfy given pairs of simultaneous equations.

66. Consider the pair of Cartesian equations $y^2 - z^2 = 1$, $x = 2$. The equation $y^2 - z^2 = 1$ represents a _____________. This curve lies in the ________ $x = 2$ that is ___________ to the yz-plane and 2 units from it. The set of points representing the curve is sketched at the right.

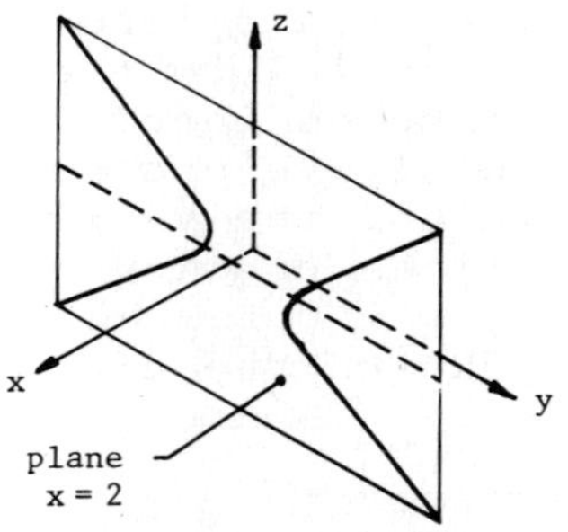

67. Consider the pair of cylindrical equations $z = 5$, $r = \theta$. The equation $z = 5$ represents a ___________ that is parallel to the ____________ and 5 units above it. The equation $r = \theta$ represents a __________ on that plane. It is sketched at the right.

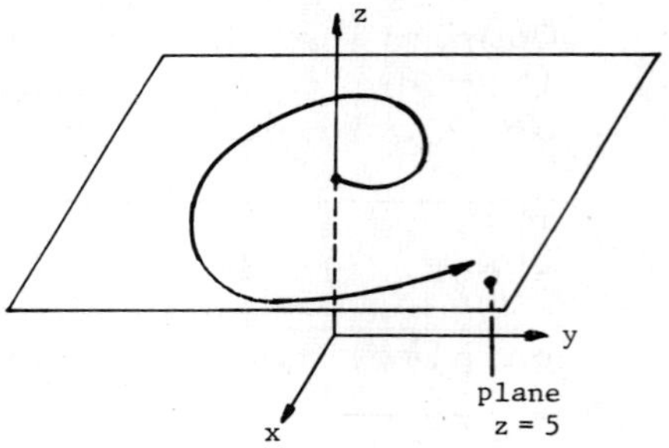

---

65. $-2(y + 3)^2 + z^2$,

$$\frac{(x - 2)^2}{6} - \frac{(y + 3)^2}{3} + \frac{z^2}{6} = 1,$$

hyperboloid, one, (2,-3,0), circles, hyperbolas

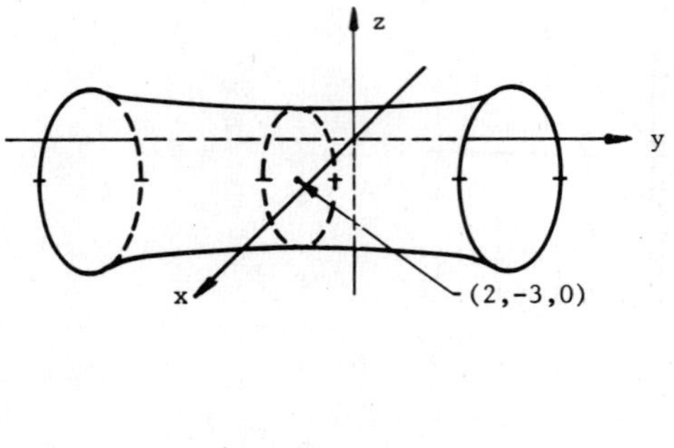

66. hyperbola, plane, parallel

67. plane, xy-plane, spiral

68. Consider the pair of equations $\theta = \frac{\pi}{4}$, $\rho = 3 \sec \phi$ representing a set of points in spherical coordinates. The equation $\rho = 3 \sec \phi$ can be written $3 =$ __________, or $3 =$ _____. Thus it represents a ________ parallel to the ____________ and 3 units above it. The equation $\theta = \frac{\pi}{4}$ represents a ______________ so the set of points described by the pair of equations is a half-line or ray at an angle $\frac{\pi}{4}$ with the _______. It is sketched at the right.

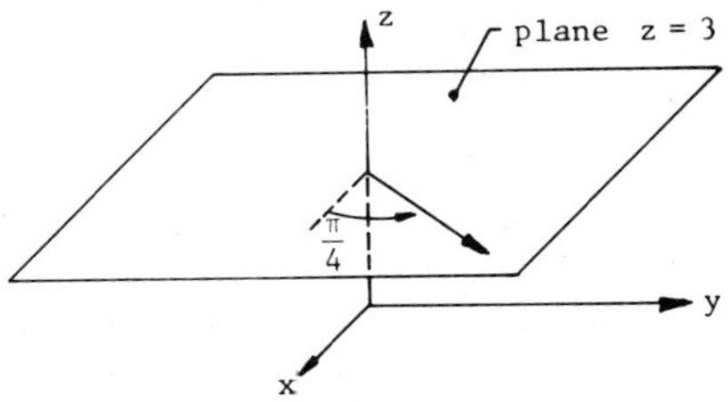

OBJECTIVE B: Translate an equation from a given coordinate system (Cartesian, cylindrical, or spherical) into forms that are appropriate to the other two systems.

69. To translate the equation $z = x^2 + y^2$ into cylindrical coordinates, let $x =$ __________ and $y =$ __________. Then, $z =$ _____ is an appropriate equation in the cylindrical coordinate system. To translate this into spherical coordinates, let $z =$ __________ and $r =$ __________ yielding the equation ______________________ or $\cos \phi =$ __________.

70. To translate the equation $\phi = \frac{\pi}{4}$ into cylindrical coordinates, let $r =$ __________ $=$ ______. Then $2r^2 =$ _____ $= z^2 +$ _____, or $r^2 =$ _____. To translate this into Cartesian equations, note that $r^2 =$ __________ so the equation becomes _______________. The equation $\phi = \frac{\pi}{4}$ describes a _______ with vertex at the origin O, axis Oz, and generating angle $\frac{\pi}{4}$.

---

68. $\rho \cos \phi$, z, plane, xy-plane, half-plane, xz-plane, $z = 3$

69. $r \cos \theta$, $r \sin \theta$, r^2, $\rho \cos \phi$, $\rho \sin \phi$, $\rho \cos \phi = \rho \sin^2\phi$, $\rho \sin^2\phi$

70. $\rho \sin \phi$, $\frac{\sqrt{2}}{2}\rho$, ρ^2, r^2, z^2, $x^2 + y^2$, $z^2 = x^2 + y^2$, cone

71. Consider the surface given in cylindrical coordinates by the equation $6z = 12 + r^2 \cos 2\theta$. Rewriting the equation in Cartesian coordinates, we find

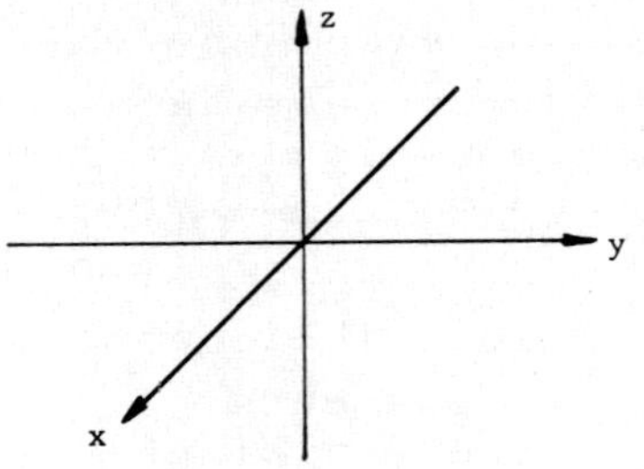

$6(z - 2) = r^2(\cos^2\theta -$ ________ $)$

$=$ ________ $- r^2 \sin^2\theta$

$=$ ________ or,

$z - 2 =$ ________.

This equation represents a ____________________. Cross sections parallel to the xy-plane are __________. If x or y is fixed we obtain ___________. The surface is centered at the point _________. Sketch the surface.

---

71. $\sin^2\theta$, $r^2 \cos^2\theta$,

$x^2 - y^2$, $\frac{x^2}{6} - \frac{y^2}{6}$,

hyperbolic paraboloid, hyperbolas, parabolas, (0,0,2)

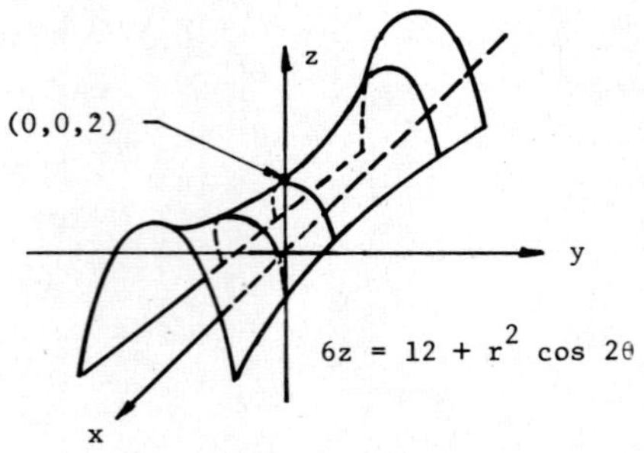

CHAPTER 10 SELF-TEST

1. Find unit vectors tangent and normal to the curve $6y = x^3 - 6x^2 + 9x + 6$ at the point $P(0,1)$.

2. Given the vectors $\vec{A} = \vec{i} - \vec{j} + \vec{k}$ and $\vec{B} = -2\vec{j} + 3\vec{k}$:
   (a) Determine the cosine of the angle between $\vec{A}$ and $\vec{B}$.
   (b) Find $\vec{A} \times \vec{B}$.
   (c) Find the projection vector $\text{proj}_{\vec{A}} \vec{B}$, and the component of $\vec{B}$ in the direction $\vec{A}$.

3. Find the distance between the point $P(5,0)$ in the xy-plane and the line L: $2y = -3x + 7$.

4. Find an equation for the line in the xy-plane that passes through $(3,-5)$ and is perpendicular to the vector $\vec{N} = 2\vec{i} - 3\vec{j}$.

5. (a) Find an equation of the plane in space containing the points $A(\frac{1}{2},0,1)$, $B(-\frac{1}{2},1,-1)$, and $C(-\frac{3}{2},2,1)$.
   (b) Find the area of the triangle with vertices A, B, C.
   (c) Find the distance between the origin and the plane determined in part (a).

6. (a) Write parametric equations for the line in space through the points $(7,1,-2)$ and $(5,-1,0)$.
   (b) Write parametric equations for the line through the point $(12,0,-2)$ and parallel to the vector $\vec{v} = \vec{i} + \vec{j} - \vec{k}$.

7. Find the distance between the point $P(-3,1,0)$ and the line L: $x = 2 + t$, $y = -3 + 2t$, $z = 4 + 2t$.

8. Find the volume of the parallelepiped ("box") determined by $\vec{u} = 2\vec{i} - \vec{j} + \vec{k}$, $\vec{v} = 3\vec{i} + 2\vec{j} - 2\vec{k}$, and $\vec{w} = 3\vec{i} + 2\vec{j}$.

9. Find parametric equations for the line of intersection of the planes $2x + z = 6$ and $y - 2z = -1$.

10. Find the volume of the tetrahedron with vertices $P(1,2,3)$, $Q(3,3,6)$, $R(4,2,-1)$, and $S(6,3,5)$.

11. Find the vector triple product $(\vec{A} \times \vec{B}) \times \vec{C}$, where $\vec{A} = \vec{i} - \vec{j} + \vec{k}$, $\vec{B} = -3\vec{i} - 6\vec{j} + 2\vec{k}$, and $\vec{C} = 4\vec{i} + \vec{j} - 3\vec{k}$ by two methods.

12. Find the area of the orthogonal projection of the parallelogram with sides determined by $A = 3\vec{i} + 4\vec{j} + 5\vec{k}$ and $\vec{B} = -2\vec{i} + \vec{j} + 3\vec{k}$ onto the plane $x + y + z = 1$.

13. Sketch the cylinder $y = -\sin z$ in space.

14. Sketch the surface $z = \frac{1}{2}\sqrt{x^2 + y^2}$.

15. Sketch the quadric surface $z = x^2 + y^2 - 2x - 2y + 2$, and identify its type.

16. Describe the set of points whose cylindrical or spherical coordinates satisfy the given pairs of simultaneous equations. Sketch.
(a) $\theta = \frac{\pi}{4}$, $z = r^2$ (b) $\phi = \frac{\pi}{3}$, $\rho = 2$

17. Translate the equation $r^2 = z(4 - z)$ from cylindrical into spherical and Cartesian coordinates.

SOLUTIONS TO CHAPTER 10 SELF-TEST

1. Observe that the point P does lie on the curve since the coordinates of P satisfy the equation for the curve. Now, $y' = \frac{1}{2}(x^2 - 4x + 3)$ so that $y'(0) = \frac{3}{2}$. One vector having this slope is $\vec{v} = 2\vec{i} + 3\vec{j}$, so a tangent vector having this slope is $\frac{\vec{v}}{|\vec{v}|} = \frac{2}{\sqrt{13}}\vec{i} + \frac{3}{\sqrt{13}}\vec{j}$. A unit normal vector is $\vec{n} = -\frac{3}{\sqrt{13}}\vec{i} + \frac{2}{\sqrt{13}}\vec{j}$.

2. (a) $\cos\theta = \frac{\vec{A}\cdot\vec{B}}{|\vec{A}|\,|\vec{B}|} = \frac{5}{\sqrt{3}\,\sqrt{13}} = \frac{5}{\sqrt{39}} \approx 0.80064.$

(b) $\vec{A} \times \vec{B} = -\vec{i} - 3\vec{j} - 2\vec{k}$

(c) $\text{proj}_{\vec{A}}\,\vec{B} = \left(\frac{\vec{B}\cdot\vec{A}}{\vec{A}\cdot\vec{A}}\right)\vec{A} = \frac{5}{3}\vec{i} - \frac{5}{3}\vec{j} + \frac{5}{3}\vec{k}$, and the component of $\vec{B}$ in the direction $\vec{A}$ is $\frac{\vec{B}\cdot\vec{A}}{|\vec{A}|} = \frac{5}{\sqrt{3}}$.

3. A normal vector to $3x + 2y = 7$ is $\vec{N} = 3\vec{i} + 2\vec{j}$. The point $B(0,\frac{7}{2})$ lies on the line. Then $\vec{BP} = 5\vec{i} - \frac{7}{2}\vec{j}$, and the distance is given by

$$d = |\text{proj}_{\vec{N}}\,\vec{BP}| = \frac{|15 - 7|}{\sqrt{9 + 4}} = \frac{8}{\sqrt{13}} \approx 2.22\ .$$

4. $2x - 3y = 2(3) + (-3)(-5) = 21$, or $y = \frac{2}{3}x - 7$.

5. (a) The vector $\vec{N} = \vec{AC} \times \vec{AB} = \begin{vmatrix} \vec{i} & \vec{j} & \vec{k} \\ -2 & 2 & 0 \\ -1 & 1 & -2 \end{vmatrix} = -4\vec{i} - 4\vec{j}$ is normal to the plane. An equation of the plane is given by

$$-4\left(x - \tfrac{1}{2}\right) - 4(y - 0) + 0(z - 1) = 0 \quad \text{or,} \quad 4x + 4y = 2\ .$$

(b) area $= \frac{1}{2}|\vec{N}| = \frac{1}{2}\sqrt{16 + 16} = 2\sqrt{2}$.

(c) The distance between the origin and the plane is given by

$$d = |\text{proj}_{\vec{N}}\,\vec{OA}| = \frac{|\vec{OA}\cdot\vec{N}|}{|\vec{N}|} = \frac{|-2 + 0 + 0|}{4\sqrt{2}} = \frac{1}{2\sqrt{2}} \approx 0.354\ .$$

6. (a) $x = 7 - 2t, \quad y = 1 - 2t, \quad z = -2 + 2t$

(b) $x = 12 + t, \quad y = t, \quad z = -2 - t$

7. The vector $\vec{v} = \vec{i} + 2\vec{j} + 2\vec{k}$ is parallel to L, and the point Q(2,-3,4) lies on L. The vector from Q to P is given by $\vec{QP} = -5\vec{i} + 4\vec{j} - 4\vec{k}$. The distance between P and the line L is then given by

$$d = \frac{|\vec{v} \times \vec{QP}|}{|\vec{v}|} = \frac{|-16\vec{i} - 6\vec{j} + 14\vec{k}|}{|\vec{i} + 2\vec{j} + 2\vec{k}|} = \frac{\sqrt{488}}{\sqrt{9}} \approx 7.36.$$

8. The volume is the absolute value of the triple scalar product $\vec{u} \cdot (\vec{v} \times \vec{w})$. Thus,

$$\vec{u} \cdot (\vec{v} \times \vec{w}) = \begin{vmatrix} 2 & -1 & 1 \\ 3 & 2 & -2 \\ 3 & 2 & 0 \end{vmatrix} = 8 + (-1)(-6) + 1(6 - 6) = 14 ,$$

so the volume is 14 cubic units.

9. The vector

$$\vec{N}_1 \times \vec{N}_2 = \begin{vmatrix} \vec{i} & \vec{j} & \vec{k} \\ 2 & 0 & 1 \\ 0 & 1 & -2 \end{vmatrix} = -\vec{i} + 4\vec{j} + 2\vec{k}$$

is parallel to the line of intersection. Substituting $z = 0$ in the plane equations gives $x = 3$ and $y = -1$, so the point (3,-1,0) lies on the line. The line is given by

$$x = 3 - t, \quad y = -1 + 4t, \quad z = 2t .$$

10. Let $\vec{u} = \vec{PQ} = 2\vec{i} + \vec{j} + 3\vec{k}$, $\vec{v} = \vec{PR} = 3\vec{i} - 4\vec{k}$, and $\vec{w} = \vec{PS} = 5\vec{i} + \vec{j} + 2\vec{k}$. Then the volume of the tetrahedron is given by the absolute value of $\frac{1}{6}[\vec{u} \cdot (\vec{v} \times \vec{w})]$. Thus,

$$\vec{u} \cdot (\vec{v} \times \vec{w}) = \begin{vmatrix} 2 & 1 & 3 \\ 3 & 0 & -4 \\ 5 & 1 & 2 \end{vmatrix} = 2(4) + 1(-26) + 3(3) = -9 .$$

Hence the volume is $V = \frac{1}{6}|-9| = \frac{3}{2}$.

11. <u>Method 1</u>. $\vec{A} \times \vec{B} = \begin{vmatrix} \vec{i} & \vec{j} & \vec{k} \\ 1 & -1 & 1 \\ -3 & -6 & 2 \end{vmatrix} = 4\vec{i} - 5\vec{j} - 9\vec{k}$ so that

$$(\vec{A} \times \vec{B}) \times \vec{C} = \begin{vmatrix} \vec{i} & \vec{j} & \vec{k} \\ 4 & -5 & -9 \\ 4 & 1 & -3 \end{vmatrix} = 24\vec{i} - 24\vec{j} + 24\vec{k} .$$

Method 2. $(\vec{A} \cdot \vec{C})\vec{B} = (4 - 1 - 3)\vec{B} = 0\vec{B} = 0\vec{i} + 0\vec{j} + 0\vec{k}$ and $(\vec{B} \cdot \vec{C})\vec{A} = (-12 - 6 - 6)\vec{A} = -24\vec{A} = -24\vec{i} + 24\vec{j} - 24\vec{k}$. Hence, $(\vec{A} \times \vec{B}) \times \vec{C} = (\vec{A} \cdot \vec{C})\vec{B} - (\vec{B} \cdot \vec{C})\vec{A} = 24\vec{i} - 24\vec{j} + 24\vec{k}$.

12. A unit normal to the plane is $\vec{n} = \frac{1}{\sqrt{3}}\vec{i} + \frac{1}{\sqrt{3}}\vec{j} + \frac{1}{\sqrt{3}}\vec{k}$,

$$\vec{A} \times \vec{B} = \begin{vmatrix} \vec{i} & \vec{j} & \vec{k} \\ 3 & 4 & 5 \\ -2 & 1 & 3 \end{vmatrix} = 7\vec{i} - 19\vec{j} + 11\vec{k},$$ and the area of the orthogonal projection is given by

$$|(\vec{A} \times \vec{B}) \cdot \vec{n}| = \left|\frac{7}{\sqrt{3}} - \frac{19}{\sqrt{3}} + \frac{11}{\sqrt{3}}\right| = \frac{1}{\sqrt{3}} \approx 0.577 .$$

13.

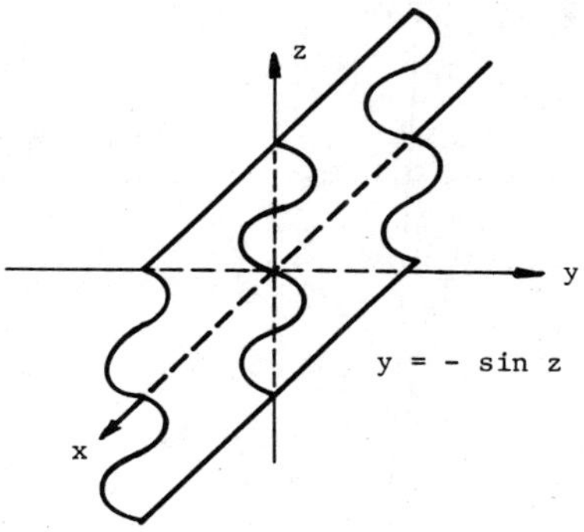

14.

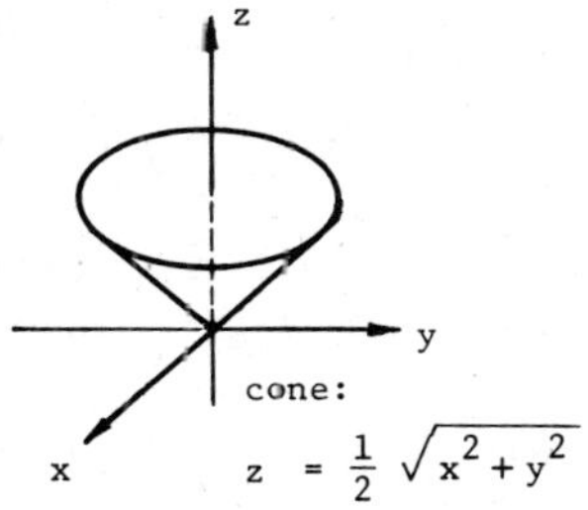

15. Completing the squares, $z = (x - 1)^2 + (y - 1)^2$, which represents the circular paraboloid sketched at the right.

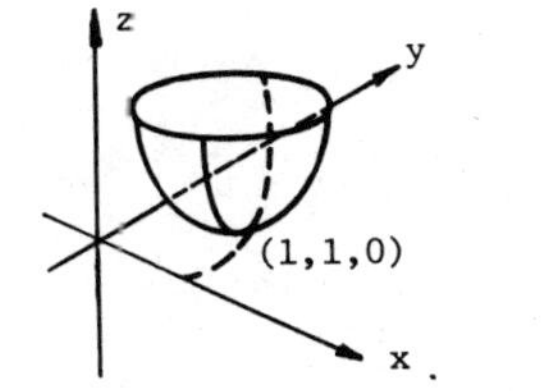

$z = x^2 + y^2 - 2x - 2y + 2$

16. (a) The equation $z = r^2$ represents a parabola with vertical axis z and horizontal axis r. The parabola lies in the plane $\theta = \frac{\pi}{4}$ and is sketched at the right.

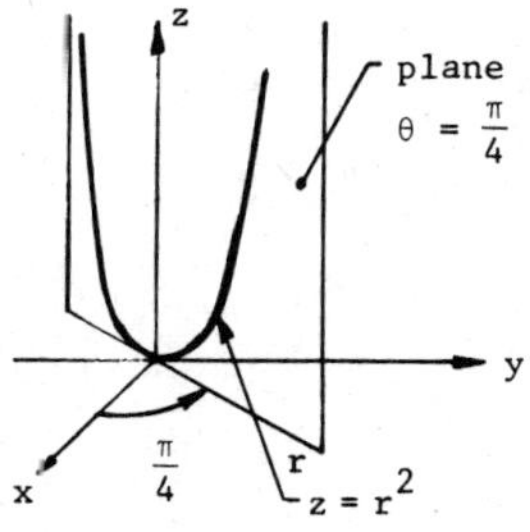

(b) The equation $\phi = \frac{\pi}{3}$ describes a cone in spherical coordinates. Also $z = \rho \cos \phi = 2 \cdot \frac{1}{2} = 1$ is constant. The intersection of the plane $z = 1$ and the cone $\phi = \frac{\pi}{3}$ results in a circle of radius $r = \rho \sin \phi = \sqrt{3}$ centered on the z-axis in the plane $z = 1$. It is sketched at the right.

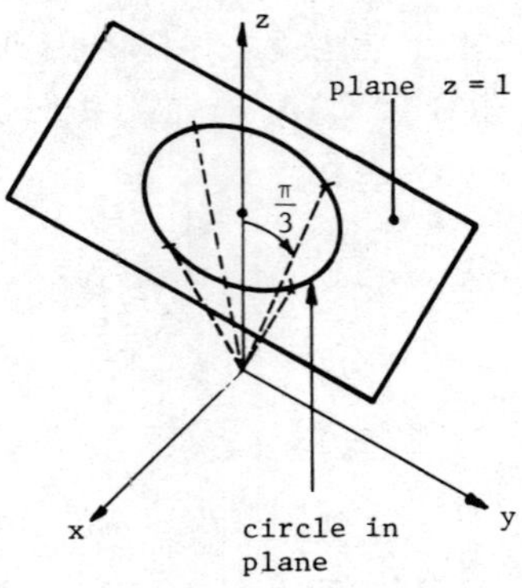

17. The equation can be written as $r^2 + z^2 = 4z$. In spherical coordinates $\rho^2 \sin^2\phi + \rho^2 \cos^2\phi = 4\rho \cos \phi$ or, $\rho = 4 \cos \phi$. (Note that $\rho = 0$ is included.)

In Cartesian coordinates, $x^2 + y^2 + z^2 = 4z$ or, completing the square, $x^2 + y^2 + (z - 2)^2 = 4$, which represents a sphere of radius 2 centered at the point $(0,0,2)$.

NOTES.

CHAPTER 11 VECTOR-VALUED FUNCTIONS AND MOTION IN SPACE

11.1 VECTOR-VALUED FUNCTIONS AND SPACE CURVES

1. A function $\vec{f}(t) = f(t)\vec{i} + g(t)\vec{j} + h(t)\vec{k}$ is called a __________ function of t.

2. The most important vector function is the radius vector

$$\vec{r}(t) = f(t)\vec{i} + g(t)\vec{j} + h(t)\vec{k}$$

from the ________ to the point ________________. This vector is also called the __________ vector of a particle moving through space.

OBJECTIVE A: Find the derivative of a given vector function and give the domain of the derived function.

3. If $\vec{f}(t) = f(t)\vec{i} + g(t)\vec{j} + h(t)\vec{k}$ is a vector function and each component is differentiable at $t = c$, then $\vec{f}$ is differentiable at $t = c$ and $\vec{f}' =$ ____________________.

4. Consider the vector function

$$\vec{f}(t) = \sqrt{1 - t^2}\,\vec{i} + \sinh t\vec{j} + 2^t\vec{k}.$$

The derivative is given by

$$\vec{f}'(t) = \_\_\_\_\_\_\_\_\_\_\_\_\_\_\_\_\_\_\_\_ .$$

The first component, $\sqrt{1 - t^2}$, is differentiable for ________. The second component, $\sinh t$, is differentiable for ________; and the third component, 2^t, is differentiable for ________. Thus, the vector function $\vec{f}$ is differentiable for __________.

OBJECTIVE B: Given the position vector of a particle at any time t, find the velocity and acceleration vectors. Evaluate these vectors and find the speed and direction of motion of the particle at any instant of time.

---

1. vector 2. origin, $P(f(t), g(t), h(t))$, position 3. $f'(c)\vec{i} + g'(c)\vec{j} + h'(c)\vec{k}$

4. $\frac{-t}{\sqrt{1 - t^2}}\vec{i} + \cosh t\vec{j} + 2^t \ln 2\vec{k}$, $-1 < t < 1$, all t, all t, $-1 < t < 1$

5. The derivative $\frac{d\vec{r}}{dt}$ of the position vector is called the ____________ vector. It is designated by $\vec{v}$. The magnitude $|\vec{v}|$ is the ____________ of the particle moving along the path defined by ________. The direction of the particle's motion at time t is the vector ____________. The acceleration is the vector ____________.

6. Consider the curve described by the position vector $\vec{r}(t) = a \cos t\vec{i} + a \sin t\vec{j} + bt\vec{k}$, where a and b are constants. The curve describes a circular helix. The velocity and acceleration vectors are given by

$\vec{v}$ = ______________________________ and $\vec{a}$ = ____________________,

respectively. When $t = \frac{\pi}{2}$, the velocity is $\vec{v}(\frac{\pi}{2})$ = ____________, and the acceleration is $\vec{a}(\frac{\pi}{2})$ = ______. The cosine of the angle θ between the velocity and acceleration vectors when $t = \frac{\pi}{2}$ is given by $\cos\theta = \frac{\vec{a} \cdot \vec{v}}{|\vec{a}||\vec{v}|}$ = ______. In fact, $\vec{a} \cdot \vec{v}$ = _____ for all t, so that the velocity and acceleration vectors are always perpendicular or orthogonal for the circular helix. Note that the acceleration vector $\vec{a}$ always points in the direction from the point $P(x,y,z)$ towards the z-axis in this example, because $a \cos t\vec{i} + a \sin t\vec{j}$ describes a circular path of radius a about the z-axis.

7. The speed of the particle moving along the curve in Problem 6 at any time t is $|\vec{v}|$ = ____________________. The direction of motion is the vector ____________________.

8. If $\vec{r}(t)$ gives the position of a particle moving along a path, and t is a differentiable function of the variable s, then according to the chain rule

$$\frac{d\vec{r}}{ds} = \underline{\hspace{3cm}} .$$

9. If $\vec{r}(t) = e^t\vec{i} + \sin t\vec{j} + t^2\vec{k}$, and $t = \sqrt{s}$ for $s > 0$, then

$$\frac{d\vec{r}}{ds} = (e^t\vec{i} + \underline{\hspace{2cm}}\vec{j} + 2t\vec{k}) \cdot \underline{\hspace{2cm}}$$

$$= \frac{e^{\sqrt{s}}}{2\sqrt{s}}\vec{i} + \underline{\hspace{2cm}}\vec{j} + \vec{k}.$$

---

5. velocity, speed, $\vec{r}$, $|\vec{v}|\,\vec{v}$, $\frac{d\vec{v}}{dt}$ or $\frac{d^2\vec{r}}{dt^2}$

6. $-a \sin t\vec{i} + a \cos t\vec{j} + b\vec{k}$, $-a \cos t\vec{i} - a \sin t\vec{j}$, $-a\vec{i} + b\vec{k}$, $-a\vec{j}$, zero, 0

7. $\sqrt{a^2 + b^2}$, $\sqrt{a^2 + b^2}(-a \sin t\vec{i} + a \cos t\vec{j} + b\vec{k})$

8. $\frac{d\vec{r}}{dt}\frac{dt}{ds}$

9. $\cos t$, $\frac{1}{2\sqrt{s}}$, $\frac{\cos\sqrt{s}}{2\sqrt{s}}$

OBJECTIVE C: Using the appropriate rules, calculate the derivatives of vector expressions involving the dot or cross products.

10. $\frac{d}{dt}(\vec{u} \cdot \vec{v}) =$ ________________.

11. $\frac{d}{dt}(\vec{u} \times \vec{v}) =$ ________________.

12. Suppose that $\vec{u}$ is a twice differentiable vector function of t. Then

$$\frac{d}{dt}\left(\vec{u} \times \frac{d\vec{u}}{dt}\right) = \frac{d\vec{u}}{dt} \times \frac{d\vec{u}}{dt} + \text{\_\_\_\_\_\_\_\_} = \text{\_\_\_\_} \times \frac{d^2\vec{u}}{dt^2}.$$

Therefore, if $\vec{u}$ is parallel to $\frac{d^2\vec{u}}{dt^2}$ for all t, $\frac{d}{dt}\left(\vec{u} \times \frac{d\vec{u}}{dt}\right)$ is the ______ vector. It follows that $\vec{u} \times \frac{d\vec{u}}{dt}$ is a ________ vector since the derivative of each component is zero (so that each component is a constant scalar function).

13. If $\vec{u}$ is a differentiable vector function of constant length, then $\vec{u}$ and $\frac{d\vec{u}}{dt}$ are ________________ to each other.

OBJECTIVE D: Find the definite or indefinite integral of a vector-valued function having continuous components.

14. $\int \left[t^3\vec{i} + e^{-2t}\vec{j} - \frac{1}{3t}\vec{k}\right] dt$

$= \text{\_\_\_\_\_\_\_\_\_\_\_\_\_\_\_\_\_\_\_\_\_\_\_\_} + \vec{c}, \quad t \neq 0.$

Here $\vec{c}$ is an arbitrary constant ____________.

OBJECTIVE E: Find the position vector $\vec{r}(t)$ when the acceleration vector $\vec{a}(t)$ is known together with initial conditions $\vec{v}(0)$ and $\vec{r}(0)$. That is, solve a vector-valued initial value problem.

15. Suppose $\vec{a} = e^t\vec{i} + e^{-t}\vec{j}$ with $\vec{v}(0) = -\vec{j}$ and $\vec{r}(0) = 2\vec{i} - \vec{j}$. Note that the $\vec{k}$-component is zero and the particles moves in the xy-plane. Integration of $\vec{a}$ gives the velocity vector

$$\vec{v} = \text{\_\_\_\_\_\_\_\_\_\_\_\_} + \vec{c}_1$$

where $\vec{c}_1$ is a constant vector. From the initial condition $\vec{v}(0) = -\vec{j}$ we find

$$-\vec{j} = \text{\_\_\_\_\_\_\_\_\_\_\_\_} + \vec{c}_1$$

---

10. $\frac{d\vec{u}}{dt} \cdot \vec{v} + \vec{u} \cdot \frac{d\vec{v}}{dt}$ 11. $\frac{d\vec{u}}{dt} \times \vec{v} + \vec{u} \times \frac{d\vec{v}}{dt}$ 12. $\vec{u} \times \frac{d^2\vec{u}}{dt^2}$, $\vec{u}$, zero, constant

13. orthogonal 14. $\frac{1}{4}t^4\vec{i} - \frac{1}{2}e^{-2t}\vec{j} - \frac{1}{3}\ln|t|\vec{k}$, vector

or, solving for the constant vector,

$$\vec{c}_1 = \underline{\hspace{3cm}} .$$

Thus,

$$\vec{v} = (e^t - 1)\vec{i} - e^{-t}\vec{j} .$$

A second integration gives

$$\vec{r} = \underline{\hspace{2cm}}\vec{i} + e^{-t}\vec{j} + \vec{c}_2$$

where $\vec{c}_2$ is a constant vector. From the initial condition $\vec{r}(0) = 2\vec{i} - \vec{j}$ we find

$$2\vec{i} - \vec{j} = \underline{\hspace{3cm}} + \vec{c}_2$$

or $\vec{c}_2 = \vec{i} - 2\vec{j}$. Thus,

$$\vec{r}(t) = (e^t - t + 1)\vec{i} + \underline{\hspace{2cm}}\vec{j} .$$

11.2 MODELING PROJECTILE MOTION

OBJECTIVE: Use the parametric equations describing the motion of a projectile fired with initial speed v_0 at an angle of elevation α to answer questions concerning the motion of the projectile. Assume that air resistance is neglected and gravity is the only force acting on the projectile.

16. For a projectile fired with an initial speed v_0 ft/sec at an angle of elevation α, the parametric equations for its motion are $x = c_1 t +$ ______ ft and $y =$ ________ $+ c_3 t + c_4$ ft, where c_1, c_2, c_3, and c_4 are constants determined from the initial conditions. Here t is measured in ________.

17. The initial conditions give the ______________________ $x(t_0)$ and $y(t_0)$, and the ______________________ $\frac{dx}{dt}(t_0)$ and $\frac{dy}{dt}(t_0)$ at some given instant $t = t_0$.

18. Suppose a person throws a ball at an angle of 45° with the horizontal and with an initial speed of 30 ft/sec toward a building 35 ft away. If the ball leaves the person's hand from a height of 3 ft above the ground, will it reach the building?

<u>Solution</u>. For this problem, the initial conditions are $t = 0$ sec, $x =$ ______ ft, $y =$ ______ ft, $\frac{dx}{dt}(0) = 30 \cos$ ______ ≈ 21.21 ft/sec, and $\frac{dy}{dt}(0) =$ ______ $\sin 45° \approx$ ______ ft/sec.

---

15. $e^t\vec{i} - e^{-t}\vec{j}$, $\vec{i} - \vec{j}$, $-\vec{i}$, $e^t - t$, $\vec{i} + \vec{j}$, $e^{-t} - 2$

16. c_2, $-\frac{1}{2}gt^2$, seconds

17. position coordinates, velocity components

The parametric equations for the motion are $x = c_1t + c_2$ and $y = -\frac{1}{2}gt^2 + c_3t + c_4$. From the initial conditions, we find $c_2 = 0$, $c_1 =$ ______, $c_4 =$ ______, and $c_3 = 21.21$.
To find the horizontal range R, we set $y = -\frac{1}{2}gt^2 + 21.21t + 3$ equal to ______ and solve for t: using $g = 32$ ft/sec²,

$$t \approx \frac{-21.21 \pm \sqrt{(21.21)^2 + \_\_\_\_\_\_}}{-32} \approx 1.45 \text{ sec}$$

(since t must be nonnegative we take the negative square root). Then, R = ______ · (1.45), the value of ______ when t = 1.45. Hence, R ≈ ______ ft. Since R < 35 ft, the ball ______ reach the building.

11.3 DIRECTED DISTANCE AND THE UNIT TANGENT VECTOR $\vec{T}$

OBJECTIVE A: Given the coordinates for a curve in space in terms of some parameter t, find the length of the curve for a specified interval $a \le t \le b$.

19. Suppose the curve is given by $x = \frac{1}{3}(1 + t)^{3/2}$, $y = \frac{1}{3}(1 - t)^{3/2}$ and $z = \frac{1}{2}t$. To find the length of the curve for $-1 \le t \le 1$, calculate

$$\frac{dx}{dt} = \_\_\_\_\_\_, \quad \frac{dy}{dt} = \_\_\_\_\_\_, \quad \frac{dz}{dt} = \frac{1}{2}.$$

Then, $$\frac{ds}{dt} = \sqrt{\left(\frac{dx}{dt}\right)^2 + \left(\frac{dy}{dt}\right)^2 + \left(\frac{dz}{dt}\right)^2}$$
$$= \sqrt{\_\_\_\_\_\_ + \frac{1}{4}} = \_\_\_\_\_\_ .$$

The length of the given curve is therefore

$$s = \int_{-1}^{1} \left(\frac{ds}{dt}\right) dt = \frac{1}{2}\sqrt{3} \int_{-1}^{1} \_\_\_\_\_\_ \, dt = \_\_\_\_\_\_ .$$

OBJECTIVE B: Given the position vector for the motion of a particle, find the unit tangent vector $\vec{T}$ to the curve at any point of the curve.

20. Suppose the position vector of the motion in the xy-plane is given by $\vec{r} = \ln t\,\vec{i} + t^2\vec{j}$ for $t > 0$. Then

---

18. 0, 3, 45°, 30, 21.21, 21.21, 3, zero, 192, 21.21, x, 30.75, does not

19. $\frac{1}{2}(1 + t)^{1/2}$, $-\frac{1}{2}(1 - t)^{1/2}$, $\frac{1}{4}(1 + t) + \frac{1}{4}(1 - t)$, $\frac{1}{2}\sqrt{3}$, 1, $\sqrt{3}$

$\vec{v} = \frac{d\vec{r}}{dt} =$ ____________; $|\vec{v}| = \sqrt{\qquad\qquad} = \frac{1}{t}\sqrt{\qquad\qquad}$;

$\vec{T} = \frac{\vec{v}}{|\vec{v}|} = \left(1 + 4t^4\right)^{-1/2}\vec{i} +$ ________________ $\vec{j}$.

21. Consider the motion in space described by the position vector $\vec{r} = \tan t\,\vec{i} + \vec{j} + \sec t\,\vec{k}$, for $-\frac{\pi}{2} < t < \frac{\pi}{2}$. Then,

$\vec{v} = \frac{d\vec{r}}{dt} =$ ________________________;

$|\vec{v}| = \sqrt{\sec^4 t + \qquad\qquad}$

$= |\sec t|\sqrt{\qquad\qquad} = (\sec t)\sqrt{2\sec^2 t - 1}$;

$\vec{T} = \frac{\vec{v}}{|\vec{v}|} =$ ________________________________.

22. Suppose the tangent vector to a curve in the xy-plane, having position vector $\vec{r}(t)$, is everywhere perpendicular to some nonzero constant vector $\vec{a}$. Then,

$$\frac{d\vec{r}}{dt} = f(t)\vec{u},$$

where $\vec{u}$ is a unit vector perpendicular to $\vec{a}$. Let $g(t)$ be an indefinite integral of f, so that $\frac{d}{dt}g(t) =$ _____. Then,

$$\frac{d}{dt}[\vec{r}(t) - g(t)\vec{u}] = \text{\_\_\_\_\_\_\_\_\_\_} = \vec{0}.$$

It follows that $\vec{r}(t) - g(t)\vec{u}$ is a constant vector $\vec{c}$, so that $\vec{r}(t) =$ __________. Therefore, the curve must lie along the line $\vec{c} + s\vec{u}$, where $s = g(t)$. Thus, if the tangent vector to a curve is everywhere perpendicular to a constant nonzero vector $\vec{a}$, then the curve runs along a straight line perpendicular to $\vec{a}$.

11.4 CURVATURE, TORSION, AND THE FRENET FRAME

OBJECTIVE A: Given a curve in the xy-plane, find the curvature at any point on the curve.

23. If $\vec{r} = x\vec{i} + y\vec{j}$, where the scalar components x and y are differentiable functions of t, then the curvature κ may be computed according to the formula

---

20. $\frac{1}{t}\vec{i} + 2t\vec{j}$, $\frac{1}{t^2} + 4t^2$, $1 + 4t^4$, $2t^2\left(1 + 4t^4\right)^{-1/2}$

21. $\sec^2 t\,\vec{i} + \sec t\tan t\,\vec{k}$, $\sec^2 t\tan^2 t$, $\sec^2 t + \tan^2 t$, $\sec t(2\sec^2 t - 1)^{-1/2}\vec{i} + \tan t(2\sec^2 t - 1)^{-1/2}\vec{k}$

22. $f(t)$, $\frac{d\vec{r}}{dt} - f(t)\vec{u}$, $\vec{c} + g(t)\vec{u}$

$$\kappa = \frac{\underline{\hspace{3cm}}}{|\vec{v}|^3} = \frac{|\dot{x}\ddot{y} - \ddot{x}\dot{y}|}{\left(\dot{x}^2 + \dot{y}^2\right)^{3/2}} .$$

Note that κ is a scalar quantity, and we assume that the velocity vector $\vec{v}$ is not __________.

24. Suppose a curve is given parametrically by $x = t$ and $y = \frac{1}{3}t^3$. Then, $\dot{x} =$ _____, $\dot{y} =$ _____, $\ddot{x} =$ _____, $\ddot{y} =$ _____.
Next calculate

$$\vec{v} \times \vec{a} = \underline{\hspace{4cm}}\vec{k} = 2t\vec{k} .$$

Hence,

$$\kappa = \frac{|2t|}{\underline{\hspace{2cm}}} .$$

25. Given the curve $y = \frac{1}{x}$, $x \neq 0$, first parameterize it in the form $x = t$ and $y = \frac{1}{t}$, $t \neq 0$. The position vector is $\vec{r} =$ ______________. Then $\vec{v} =$ ______________ and $\vec{a} = -\frac{2}{t^3}\vec{j}$. Thus,

$$\vec{v} \times \vec{a} = \begin{vmatrix} \vec{i} & \vec{j} & \vec{k} \\ 1 & -1/t^2 & 0 \\ 0 & -2/t^3 & 0 \end{vmatrix}$$

Hence the curvature is

$$\kappa = \frac{|2/t^3|}{[\underline{\hspace{3cm}}]^{3/2}} = \underline{\hspace{5cm}} .$$

OBJECTIVE B: Given a curve in the xy-plane, find an equation of the circle of curvature at a specified point.

26. Let us find an equation of the osculating circle to $y = \sin x$ at the point $\left(\frac{\pi}{2}, 1\right)$. First we parameterize the curve: $\vec{r} = t\vec{i} +$ _______$\vec{j}$. Then the velocity and acceleration vectors are $\vec{v} = \vec{i} + \cos t\vec{j}$ and $\vec{a} =$ __________. Thus,

---

23. $|\vec{v} \times \vec{a}|$, zero

24. 1, t^2, 0, 2t, $|\dot{x}\ddot{y} - \ddot{x}\dot{y}|$, $\left(1 + t^4\right)^{3/2}$

25. $t\vec{i} + \frac{1}{t}\vec{j}$, $\vec{i} - \frac{1}{t^2}\vec{j}$, $-\frac{2}{t^3}\vec{k}$, $1 + \frac{1}{t^4}$, $\frac{|2x^3|}{\left(1 + x^4\right)^{3/2}}$ since $t = x$

$$\vec{v} \times \vec{a} = \begin{vmatrix} \vec{i} & \vec{j} & \vec{k} \\ 1 & \cos t & 0 \\ 0 & -\sin t & 0 \end{vmatrix} = \underline{\hspace{3cm}} .$$

The curvature is

$$\kappa = \frac{|\sin t|}{[\underline{\hspace{3cm}}]^{3/2}}$$

so that at $t = \frac{\pi}{2}$, $\kappa =$ ______. The radius of curvature is $\rho = \frac{1}{\kappa} =$ ______ which is the radius of the osculating circle. The tangent to $y = \sin x$ when $x = \frac{\pi}{2}$ is horizontal, so the normal is in the __________ direction. Therefore, the center of the osculating circle is the point ________. An equation of the circle is given by

____________________ .

OBJECTIVE C: Given the coordinates of a curve in space as differentiable functions of t, find the curvature at any point using the formula $\kappa = \frac{|\vec{v} \times \vec{a}|}{|\vec{v}|^3}$.

27. Consider the space curve with position described by $\vec{r} = (t + 1)\vec{i} - t^2\vec{j} + (1 - 2t)\vec{k}$. To calculate the curvature κ at any point, we find $\vec{v} =$ _______________ and $\vec{a} =$ _______. Hence,

$$\vec{v} \times \vec{a} = \begin{vmatrix} \vec{i} & \vec{j} & \vec{k} \\ 1 & -2t & -2 \\ 0 & -2 & 0 \end{vmatrix} = \underline{\hspace{3cm}}, \text{ and}$$

$|\vec{v} \times \vec{a}| = \sqrt{\underline{\hspace{2.5cm}}} =$ _______. Also, $|\vec{v}| =$ __________.

Therefore, $\kappa = \frac{|\vec{v} \times \vec{a}|}{\underline{\hspace{1.5cm}}} =$ ____________ gives the curvature for any value of t. In particular, for $t = 0$, $\kappa =$ __________.

OBJECTIVE D: Given the coordinates of a curve in space as differentiable functions of t, find the torsion τ using Formula 16 in this section of the Thomas/Finney text.

---

26. $\sin t$, $-\sin t\vec{j}$, $-\sin t\vec{k}$, $(1 + \cos^2 t)$, 1, 1, vertical, $\left(\frac{\pi}{2}, 0\right)$, $\left(x - \frac{\pi}{2}\right)^2 + y^2 = 1$

27. $\vec{i} - 2t\vec{j} - 2\vec{k}$, $-2\vec{j}$, $-4\vec{i} - 2\vec{k}$, $16 + 4$, $2\sqrt{5}$, $\sqrt{5 + 4t^2}$, $|\vec{v}|^3$, $\frac{2\sqrt{5}}{\left(5 + 4t^2\right)^{3/2}}$, $\frac{2}{5}$

28. For the curve $\vec{r} = (t + 1)\vec{i} - t^2\vec{j} + (1 - 2t)\vec{k}$ in Problem 27, we calculate the determinant

$$\begin{vmatrix} \dot{x} & \dot{y} & \dot{z} \\ \ddot{x} & \ddot{y} & \ddot{z} \\ \dddot{x} & \dddot{y} & \dddot{z} \end{vmatrix} = \begin{vmatrix} \_\_ & \_\_ & \_\_ \\ \_\_ & \_\_ & \_\_ \\ 0 & 0 & 0 \end{vmatrix} = \_\_\_\_ .$$

Therefore, the torsion $\tau = 0$ so the moving particle tends to remain in the osculating plane as it travels along the curve.

OBJECTIVE E: Given the coordinates for a curve in terms of some parameter t, find the unit tangent vector $\vec{T}$, the principal normal vector $\vec{N}$, the curvature κ, the unit binormal vector $\vec{B}$, and the torsion τ.

29. Suppose the position vector of the curve is given by

$\vec{r} = 2t\vec{i} + t^2\vec{j} + \frac{1}{3}t^3\vec{k}$. Then $\vec{v} = \frac{d\vec{r}}{dt} = 2\vec{i} + 2t\vec{j} + \_\_\_\_\vec{k}$ and

$$|\vec{v}| = \sqrt{\_\_\_\_\_\_\_\_\_\_} = \sqrt{\left(2 + t^2\right)^2} = 2 + t^2 ,$$

$$\vec{T} = \frac{\vec{v}}{|\vec{v}|} = \frac{2}{2 + t^2}\vec{i} + \_\_\_\_\_\_\_\_\vec{j} + \frac{t^2}{2 + t^2}\vec{k} .$$

Differentiation of $\vec{T}$ with respect to t gives

$$\frac{d\vec{T}}{dt} = -\frac{4t}{\left(2 + t^2\right)^2}\vec{i} + \_\_\_\_\_\_\_\_\vec{j} + \frac{4t}{\left(2 + t^2\right)^2}\vec{k}$$

$$= \frac{2}{\left(2 + t^2\right)^2}\left[\_\_\_\_\_\_\_\_\_\_\_\_\_\_\_\_\right] .$$

By the rule $\frac{ds}{dt} = |\vec{v}|$ and the chain rule,

$$\frac{d\vec{T}}{ds} = \frac{d\vec{T}/dt}{ds/dt} = \_\_\_\_\_\_\_\_ \left[-2t\vec{i} + (2 - t^2)\vec{j} + 2t\vec{k}\right] ;$$

$$\kappa = \left|\frac{d\vec{T}}{ds}\right| = \frac{2}{\left(2 + t^2\right)^3}\sqrt{\_\_\_\_\_\_\_\_\_\_\_\_\_\_\_\_} = \frac{2}{\left(2 + t^2\right)^2} .$$

Then, $$\vec{N} = \frac{d\vec{T}/ds}{|d\vec{T}/ds|} = -\frac{2t}{2 + t^2}\vec{i} + \_\_\_\_\_\_\_\_\vec{j} + \_\_\_\_\_\_\_\_\vec{k} .$$

Finally, $\vec{B} = \vec{T} \times \vec{N}$ gives

$$\vec{B} = \frac{t^2}{2 + t^2}\vec{i} + \_\_\_\_\_\_\_\_\vec{j} + \frac{2}{2 + t^2}\vec{k} .$$

---

28. $\begin{vmatrix} 1 & -2t & -2 \\ 0 & -2 & 0 \\ 0 & 0 & 0 \end{vmatrix}$, 0

29. t^2, $4 + 4t^2 + t^4$, $\frac{2t}{2 + t^2}$, $\frac{2(2 - t^2)}{\left(2 + t^2\right)^2}$, $-2t\vec{i} + (2 - t^2)\vec{j} + 2t\vec{k}$, $\frac{2}{\left(2 + t^2\right)^3}$,

$4t^2 + \left(2 - t^2\right)^2 + 4t^2$, $\frac{2 - t^2}{2 + t^2}$, $\frac{2t}{2 + t^2}$, $\frac{-2t}{2 + t^2}$

30. For the curve in Problem 29,

$$\begin{vmatrix} \dot{x} & \dot{y} & \dot{z} \\ \ddot{x} & \ddot{y} & \ddot{z} \\ \dddot{x} & \dddot{y} & \dddot{z} \end{vmatrix} =$$

$$\begin{vmatrix} \_\_\_ & \_\_\_ & \_\_\_ \\ \_\_\_ & \_\_\_ & \_\_\_ \\ \_\_\_ & \_\_\_ & \_\_\_ \end{vmatrix} = \_\_\_\_\_\_\_\_\_\_ .$$

Also,

$$\vec{v} \times \vec{a} = \begin{vmatrix} \vec{i} & \vec{j} & \vec{k} \\ 2 & 2t & t^2 \\ 0 & 2 & 2t \end{vmatrix} = \_\_\_\_\_\_\_\_\_\_\_\_\_\_\_\_ .$$

Therefore, the torsion is

$$\tau = \frac{8}{\_\_\_\_\_\_\_\_\_\_} .$$

OBJECTIVE F: Given the position vector for the motion of a particle, find the velocity and acceleration vectors, the speed $\frac{ds}{dt}$, and the tangential and normal components of acceleration.

31. Consider the path described by $\vec{r} = t\vec{i} + \sin t\vec{j}$. Then,

$\vec{v} = \frac{d\vec{r}}{dt} = \_\_\_\_\_\_\_\_\_\_$, the velocity vector;

$\vec{a} = \frac{d\vec{v}}{dt} = \_\_\_\_\_\_\_\_\_\_$, the acceleration vector;

$\frac{ds}{dt} = |\vec{v}| = \_\_\_\_\_\_\_\_\_\_$, the speed;

$\frac{d^2s}{dt^2} = a_T = \frac{\_\_\_\_\_\_\_\_\_\_}{\sqrt{1 + \cos^2 t}}$, the tangential component of acceleration;

---

30. $\begin{vmatrix} 2 & 2t & t^2 \\ 0 & 2 & 2t \\ 0 & 0 & 2 \end{vmatrix}$, 8, $2t^2\vec{i} - 4t\vec{j} + 4\vec{k}$, $4t^4 + 16t^2 + 16$

and

$$a_N = \sqrt{|\vec{a}|^2 - \underline{\hspace{2cm}}} = \sqrt{\sin^2 t - \underline{\hspace{3cm}}}$$

$$= \sqrt{\frac{\underline{\hspace{1.5cm}}}{1 + \cos^2 t}}, \quad \text{or} \quad a_N = \frac{|\sin t|}{\sqrt{1 + \cos^2 t}},$$ the normal component of acceleration.

32. For the path given by $\vec{r} = 3\vec{i} + t^2\vec{j} + t^3\vec{k}$, $t \geq 0$,

$\vec{v} = \frac{d\vec{r}}{dt} =$ ____________, the velocity vector;

$\vec{a} = \frac{d\vec{v}}{dt} =$ ____________, the acceleration vector;

$\frac{ds}{dt} = |\vec{v}| =$ ____________, the speed;

$\frac{d^2s}{dt^2} = \sqrt{4 + 9t^2} + \frac{\underline{\hspace{2cm}}}{\sqrt{4 + 9t^2}} = \frac{\underline{\hspace{1.5cm}}}{\sqrt{4 + 9t^2}}$, the tangential component of acceleration; and

$$a_N = \sqrt{\underline{\hspace{1.5cm}} - a_T^2} = \sqrt{4 + 36t^2 - \frac{\left(4 + 18t^2\right)^2}{4 + 9t^2}}$$

$$= \frac{\sqrt{\left(4 + 36t^2\right)\underline{\hspace{1.5cm}} - \left(4 + 18t^2\right)^2}}{\sqrt{4 + 9t^2}} = \frac{\underline{\hspace{1.5cm}}}{\sqrt{4 + 9t^2}},$$ the normal component of acceleration.

Remark: If $t < 0$, then $|\vec{v}| = -t\sqrt{4 + 9t^2}$.

11.5 PLANETARY MOTION AND SATELLITES

OBJECTIVE: Given a curve $r = f(\theta)$ in the plane in polar coordinates and the rate $\frac{d\theta}{dt}$, or given the polar coordinates r and θ as functions of the parameter t, find the velocity and acceleration vectors in terms of $\vec{u}_r$ and $\vec{u}_\theta$.

33. In terms of the vectors $\vec{u}_r$ and $\vec{u}_\theta$, $\vec{v} =$ _____ $\vec{u}_r$ + ______ $\vec{u}_\theta$ and $\vec{a} =$ [________________]$\vec{u}_r$ + [__________________]$\vec{u}_\theta$ give the velocity and acceleration vectors, respectively, of the moving particle in polar coordinates.

---

31. $\vec{i} + \cos t\vec{j}$, $-\sin t\vec{j}$, $\sqrt{1 + \cos^2 t}$, $-\sin t \cos t$, $a_T{}^2$, $\frac{\sin^2 t + \cos^2 t}{1 + \cos^2 t}$, $\sin^2 t$

32. $2t\vec{j} + 3t^2\vec{k}$, $2\vec{j} + 6t\vec{k}$, $t\sqrt{4 + 9t^2}$, $9t^2$, $4 + 18t^2$, $|\vec{a}|^2$, $4 + 9t^2$, $6t$

33. $\frac{dr}{dt}$, $r\frac{d\theta}{dt}$, $\frac{d^2r}{dt^2} - r\left(\frac{d\theta}{dt}\right)^2$, $r\frac{d^2\theta}{dt^2} + 2\frac{dr}{dt}\frac{d\theta}{dt}$

34. Suppose a particle moves on the cardioid $r = a(1 + \cos\theta)$ and that the radius vector turns counterclockwise at the constant rate $\frac{d\theta}{dt} = \frac{5}{a\sqrt{3}}$ rad/sec. Let us find the polar form of the velocity and acceleration vectors when $\theta = \frac{\pi}{3}$. Now,

$$\frac{dr}{dt} = \frac{dr}{d\theta} \cdot \frac{d\theta}{dt} = \underline{\qquad\qquad} \cdot \frac{5}{a\sqrt{3}} = \underline{\qquad\qquad\qquad} \text{ and}$$

$r\frac{d\theta}{dt} = \underline{\qquad\qquad\qquad}$. Evaluation of these components at $\theta = \frac{\pi}{3}$ gives

$$\vec{v} = \underline{\qquad} \vec{u}_r + \underline{\qquad\quad} \vec{u}_\theta, \text{ the velocity vector.}$$

Next,

$$\frac{d^2r}{dt^2} = \frac{d\dot{r}}{d\theta}\frac{d\theta}{dt} = \underline{\qquad\qquad} \cdot \frac{5}{a\sqrt{3}} = \underline{\qquad\qquad}$$

so that

$$\frac{d^2r}{dt^2} - r\left(\frac{d\theta}{dt}\right)^2 = -\frac{25}{6a} - \left(\underline{\qquad}\right)\frac{25}{3a^2} = \underline{\qquad\qquad} \text{ when } \theta = \frac{\pi}{3}.$$

Also for $\theta = \frac{\pi}{3}$,

$$r\frac{d^2\theta}{dt^2} + 2\frac{dr}{dt}\frac{d\theta}{dt} = \frac{3a}{2}(0) + 2\left(\underline{\qquad}\right)\frac{5}{a\sqrt{3}} = \underline{\qquad\qquad}.$$

Therefore,

$$\vec{a} = [\underline{\qquad\quad}]\vec{u}_r + [\underline{\qquad\quad}]\vec{u}_\theta, \text{ the acceleration.}$$

35. Consider a particle moving along the curve defined parametrically by $r = e^t$ and $\theta = t^2$. Then,

$$\frac{dr}{dt} = \underline{\qquad\quad}, \quad \frac{d\theta}{dt} = \underline{\qquad\quad}; \quad \frac{d^2r}{dt^2} = \underline{\qquad\quad}, \quad \frac{d^2\theta}{dt^2} = \underline{\qquad\quad}.$$

The velocity at any time t is given by

$$\vec{v} = \underline{\qquad\qquad} \vec{u}_r + \underline{\qquad\qquad} \vec{u}_\theta;$$

and the acceleration is given by

$$a = [e^t - \underline{\qquad\qquad}]\vec{u}_r + [2e^t + \underline{\qquad\qquad}]\vec{u}_\theta$$
$$= \underline{\qquad} \vec{u}_r + \underline{\qquad\qquad\qquad\qquad} \vec{u}_\theta.$$

---

34. $-a\sin\theta$, $-\frac{5}{\sqrt{3}}\sin\theta$, $\frac{5}{\sqrt{3}}(1 + \cos\theta)$, $-\frac{5}{2}$, $\frac{5\sqrt{3}}{2}$, $-\frac{5}{\sqrt{3}}\cos\theta$, $-\frac{25}{3a}\cos\theta$, $\frac{3a}{2}$, $-\frac{50}{3a}$, $-\frac{5}{2}$, $\frac{-25}{a\sqrt{3}}$, $-\frac{50}{3a}$, $\frac{-25}{a\sqrt{3}}$

35. e^t, $2t$, e^t, 2, e^t, $2te^t$, $4t^2e^t$, $4te^t$, $e^t\left(1 - 4t^2\right)$, $2e^t(1 + 2t)$

CHAPTER 11 SELF-TEST

1. Find the first and second derivatives $\vec{f}'(t)$ and $\vec{f}''(t)$ of the following vector functions.
   (a) $\vec{f}(t) = (\ln t)\vec{i} - t^{-2}\vec{j} + e^{t^2}\vec{k}, \quad t > 0$
   (b) $\vec{f}(t) = (t \sin t)\vec{i} + (\tan^{-1} t)\vec{j} + e^{-t^2}\vec{k}$

2. Find the velocity and acceleration vectors, and the speed of a particle moving along a curve according to the position vector given as a function of time.
   (a) $\vec{r} = (3t^2 - 5)\vec{i} + (\ln t)\vec{j}, \quad t > 0$
   (b) $\vec{r} = e^{-2t}\vec{i} + 5 \cos 3t\vec{j} + 5 \sin 3t\vec{k}$

3. Find the cosine of the angle between the velocity and acceleration vectors at any time t in Problem 2(b).

4. A cannon whose muzzle is tilted at an angle of elevation of $30°$ shoots a ball with an initial velocity of 1200 m/sec.
   (a) Find parametric equations describing the motion of the cannonball.
   (b) How far from the cannon does the ball land, and what is its velocity and speed at the time of impact with the earth?
   (c) How high does the ball get and what is the total time the ball spends in the air?
   Assume that the mouth of the cannon is at ground level and that gravity is the only force acting on the cannonball.

5. Find the unit tangent vector, the principal normal, the curvature, and the length of the curve over the interval $1 \le t \le 2$, for the plane curve
$$\vec{r} = (2 \ln t)\vec{i} - \left(\frac{1}{t} + t\right)\vec{j} .$$

6. Find an equation of the osculating circle when $t = 1$ for the curve in Problem 5.

7. Find the unit tangent vector $\vec{T}$, the principal normal vector $\vec{N}$, the curvature κ, and the unit binormal vector $\vec{B}$ for the space curve given by
$$\vec{r} = (t + 1)\vec{i} - t^2\vec{j} + (1 - 2t)\vec{k} .$$

8. Establish the result
$$\frac{d}{dt}|\vec{u}| = \frac{\vec{u} \cdot \vec{u}'}{|\vec{u}|}$$
where $\vec{u}$ is a differentiable vector function of t for which $|\vec{u}|$ is never zero. Here $\vec{u}'$ means $\frac{d\vec{u}}{dt}$.

9. Find the velocity and acceleration vectors, the speed $\frac{ds}{dt}$, and the tangential and normal components of acceleration for the motion described by

$$\vec{r} = t\vec{i} + (\ln t)\vec{j}, \quad t > 0$$

10. Find the curvature and torsion of the path

$$\vec{r} = e^t \cos t\,\vec{i} + e^t \sin t\,\vec{j} + e^t\vec{k}$$

when $t = 0$.

11. A particle moves counterclockwise on the circle $r = b \cos \theta$, $b > 0$, with constant speed v_0. Find the acceleration vector in terms of $\vec{u}_r$ and $\vec{u}_\theta$.

SOLUTIONS TO CHAPTER 11 SELF-TEST

1. (a) $\vec{f}'(t) = t^{-1}\vec{i} + 2t^{-3}\vec{j} + 2te^{t^2}\vec{k}$

$\vec{f}''(t) = -t^{-2}\vec{i} - 6t^{-4}\vec{j} + 2e^{t^2}(1 + 2t^2)\vec{k}$

(b) $\vec{f}'(t) = (\sin t + t\cos t)\vec{i} + \frac{1}{1 + t^2}\vec{j} - 2te^{-t^2}\vec{k}$

$\vec{f}''(t) = (2\cos t - t\sin t)\vec{i} + \frac{-2t}{(1 + t^2)^2}\vec{j} + 2e^{-t^2}(2t^2 - 1)\vec{k}$

2. (a) $\vec{v} = \frac{d\vec{r}}{dt} = 6t\vec{i} + t^{-1}\vec{j}$, velocity

$\vec{a} = \frac{d\vec{v}}{dt} = 6\vec{i} - t^{-2}\vec{j}$, acceleration

$\frac{ds}{dt} = |\vec{v}| = \sqrt{36t^2 + t^{-2}}$, speed

(b) $\vec{v} = -2e^{-2t}\vec{i} - 15\sin 3t\vec{j} + 15\cos 3t\vec{k}$, velocity

$\vec{a} = \frac{d\vec{v}}{dt} = 4e^{-2t}\vec{i} - 45\cos 3t\vec{j} - 45\sin 3t\vec{k}$, acceleration

$\frac{ds}{dt} = |\vec{v}| = \sqrt{4e^{-4t} + 225}$, speed

3. $\cos\theta = \frac{\vec{a}\cdot\vec{v}}{|\vec{a}||\vec{v}|}$; $\vec{a}\cdot\vec{v} = -8e^{-4t}$ and $|\vec{a}| = \sqrt{16e^{-4t} + 2025}$.

Therefore, $\cos\theta = \dfrac{-8e^{-4t}}{\sqrt{4e^{-4t} + 225}\cdot\sqrt{16e^{-4t} + 2025}}$.

4. (a) $\frac{d^2x}{dt^2} = 0$ m/sec^2, $\frac{dx}{dt} = c_1$ m/sec, $x = c_1t + c_2$ m,

$\frac{d^2y}{dt^2} = -g$ m/sec^2, $\frac{dy}{dt} = -gt + c_3$ m/sec,

$y = -\frac{1}{2}gt^2 + c_3t + c_4$ m. From the initial conditions, $t = 0$, $x = 0$, $y = 0$, $\frac{dx}{dt}(0) = v_0\cos 30^\circ = 600\sqrt{3}$ and $\frac{dy}{dt}(0) = v_0\sin 30^\circ = 600$, we find $c_1 = 600\sqrt{3}$, $c_2 = 0$, $c_3 = 600$, and $c_4 = 0$. Thus,

$$x = 600\sqrt{3}t \quad\text{and}\quad y = -\tfrac{1}{2}gt^2 + 600t$$

are parametric equations for the motion. Here, $g \approx 9.81$ m/sec^2.

(b) The maximum range occurs when $y = 0$ or $t = \frac{2\cdot 600}{g}$ ≈ 122.3 sec. The range is then $R = 600\sqrt{3}(\frac{1200}{g})$ $\approx 127{,}123$ m $= 1{,}271.23$ km. The velocity at any time is the vector $\vec{v} = \frac{dx}{dt}\vec{i} + \frac{dy}{dt}\vec{j}$. When $t = \frac{1200}{g}$, we find

$$\vec{v} = 600\sqrt{3}\vec{i} + (600 - g\cdot\tfrac{1200}{g})\vec{j} = 600(\sqrt{3}\vec{i} - \vec{j}),$$

as the velocity of impact. Then, $|\vec{v}| = 600\sqrt{4} \approx 1200$ m/sec is the speed on impact with the earth.

(c) The maximum height of the cannonball occurs when $\frac{dy}{dt} = 0$ or $t_m = \frac{600}{g}$; then

$$h = -\frac{1}{2}g\left(\frac{600}{g}\right)^2 + 600\left(\frac{600}{g}\right) \approx 183.49 \text{ km}$$

is the maximum height attained. Finally, the ball remains in the air

$$2t_m = 2\left(\frac{600}{g}\right) \approx 122.3 \text{ sec} .$$

5. $\vec{v} = \frac{d\vec{r}}{dt} = 2t^{-1}\vec{i} + \frac{1 - t^2}{t^2}\vec{j}$ so that

$$|\vec{v}| = \sqrt{\frac{4}{t^2} + \frac{1 - 2t^2 + t^4}{t^4}} = \frac{t^2 + 1}{t^2} .$$

Thus the unit tangent vector is

$$\vec{T} = \frac{\vec{v}}{|\vec{v}|} = \frac{2t}{1 + t^2}\vec{i} + \frac{1 - t^2}{1 + t^2}\vec{j}$$

and the principal normal is

$$\vec{N} = -\frac{1 - t^2}{1 + t^2}\vec{i} + \frac{2t}{1 + t^2}\vec{j}.$$

The length of the curve is given by the integral

$$s = \int_1^2 |\vec{v}|dt = \int_1^2 \left(1 + t^{-2}\right)dt = t - \frac{1}{t}\Big|_1^2 = \frac{3}{2}.$$

To calculate the curvature,

$$\dot{x} = \frac{2}{t}, \quad \dot{y} = \frac{1}{t^2} - 1, \quad \ddot{x} = -\frac{2}{t^2}, \quad \ddot{y} = -\frac{2}{t^3}$$

gives

$$\kappa = \frac{|\dot{x}\ddot{y} - \dot{y}\ddot{x}|}{|\vec{v}|^3} = \frac{|-4t^{-4} + 2t^{-4} - 2t^{-2}|}{\left(t^2 + 1\right)^3 t^{-6}} = \frac{2t^2}{\left(t^2 + 1\right)^2} .$$

6. From our calculation in the solution to Problem 5,

$\rho = \frac{1}{\kappa} = \frac{\left(t^2 + 1\right)^2}{2t^2}$, so $\rho = 2$ is the radius of curvature when $t = 1$. Also, $\vec{N} = -\frac{1 - t^2}{1 + t^2}\vec{i} + \frac{2t}{1 + t^2}\vec{j}$ so that $\vec{N} = \vec{j}$, and $\vec{r} = -2\vec{j}$ is the position of the particle at $t = 1$; i.e., the particle is located at the point $(0,-2)$. The center is located $\rho = 2$ units from the position point $(0,-2)$ in the direction $\vec{N} = \vec{j}$; thus, the center of the osculating circle is $(0,0)$. Therefore,

$$x^2 + y^2 = 4$$

is an equation of the osculating circle when $t = 1$.

7. $\vec{v} = \frac{d\vec{r}}{dt} = \vec{i} - 2t\vec{j} - 2\vec{k}, \quad |\vec{v}| = \frac{ds}{dt} = \sqrt{5 + 4t^2}.$ Thus,

$\vec{T} = \frac{\vec{v}}{|\vec{v}|} = \left(5 + 4t^2\right)^{-1/2}(\vec{i} - 2t\vec{j} - 2\vec{k}).$

$$\frac{d\vec{T}}{dt} = -\frac{1}{2}\left(5 + 4t^2\right)^{-3/2} 8t[\vec{i} - 2t\vec{j} - 2\vec{k}] + \left(5 + 4t^2\right)^{-1/2}(-2\vec{j})$$

$$= 2\left(5 + 4t^2\right)^{-3/2}[-2t\vec{i} - 5\vec{j} + 4t\vec{k}];$$

$$\frac{d\vec{T}}{ds} = \frac{d\vec{T}/dt}{ds/dt} = 2\left(5 + 4t^2\right)^{-2}[-2t\vec{i} - 5\vec{j} + 4t\vec{k}];$$

$$\kappa = \left|\frac{d\vec{T}}{ds}\right| = 2\left(5 + 4t^2\right)^{-2}\sqrt{20t^2 + 25} = 2\sqrt{5}\left(5 + 4t^2\right)^{-3/2};$$

$$\vec{N} = \frac{1}{\kappa}\frac{d\vec{T}}{ds} = \left(5 + 4t^2\right)^{-1/2}[-\frac{2t}{\sqrt{5}}\vec{i} + \sqrt{5}\vec{j} + \frac{4t}{\sqrt{5}}\vec{k}]$$

$$\vec{B} = \vec{T} \times \vec{N} = -\frac{2}{\sqrt{5}}\vec{i} - \frac{1}{\sqrt{5}}\vec{k}.$$

8. Now, $|\vec{u}| = \sqrt{\vec{u} \cdot \vec{u}}$ so that

$$\frac{d}{dt}|\vec{u}| = \frac{d}{dt}\sqrt{\vec{u} \cdot \vec{u}} = \frac{1}{2\sqrt{\vec{u} \cdot \vec{u}}}\frac{d}{dt}\left(\vec{u} \cdot \vec{u}\right) = \frac{\vec{u}' \cdot \vec{u} + \vec{u} \cdot \vec{u}'}{2\sqrt{\vec{u} \cdot \vec{u}}} = \frac{\vec{u} \cdot \vec{u}'}{|\vec{u}|},$$

as claimed.

9. $\vec{v} = \frac{d\vec{r}}{dt} = \vec{i} + t^{-1}\vec{j}$, velocity vector;

$\vec{a} = \frac{d\vec{v}}{dt} = -t^{-2}\vec{j}$, acceleration vector;

$|\vec{v}| = \frac{ds}{dt} = \left(1 + t^{-2}\right)^{1/2} = \frac{\sqrt{1 + t^2}}{t}$, speed;

$\frac{d^2s}{dt^2} = -t^{-2}\sqrt{1 + t^2} + t^{-1} \cdot \frac{t}{\sqrt{1 + t^2}}$ or,

$a_T = \frac{-1}{t^2\sqrt{1 + t^2}}$, tangential component of acceleration

$$a_N = \sqrt{|\vec{a}|^2 - a_T^{\,2}} = \sqrt{\frac{1}{t^4} - \frac{1}{t^4(1 + t^2)}}$$

$= \sqrt{\frac{t^2}{t^4(1 + t^2)}} = \frac{1}{t\sqrt{1 + t^2}}$, normal component of acceleration

10. $\vec{v} = e^t(\cos t - \sin t)\vec{i} + e^t(\cos t + \sin t)\vec{j} + e^t\vec{k}$ and
$\vec{a} = -2e^t \sin t\vec{i} + 2e^t \cos t\vec{j} + e^t\vec{k}$
Thus, when $t = 0$, $\vec{v}(0) = \vec{i} + \vec{j} + \vec{k}$ and $\vec{a}(0) = 2\vec{j} + \vec{k}$. Then,

$$\vec{v}(0) \times \vec{a}(0) = \begin{vmatrix} \vec{i} & \vec{j} & \vec{k} \\ 1 & 1 & 1 \\ 0 & 2 & 1 \end{vmatrix} = -\vec{i} - \vec{j} + 2\vec{k}$$

and $|\vec{v}(0) \times \vec{a}(0)| = \sqrt{6}$, $|\vec{v}(0)| = \sqrt{3}$. Therefore, the curvature is given by

$$\kappa = \frac{|\vec{v}(0) \times \vec{a}(0)|}{|\vec{v}(0)|^3} = \frac{\sqrt{6}}{3\sqrt{3}} = \frac{\sqrt{2}}{3}.$$

Using formula (16) on page 801 of Finney/Thomas, the torsion is given by

$$\tau = \pm \frac{\begin{vmatrix} e^t(\cos t - \sin t) & e^t(\sin t + \cos t) & e^t \\ -2e^t \sin t & 2e^t \cos t & e^t \\ -2e^t(\sin t + \cos t) & 2e^t(\cos t - \sin t) & e^t \end{vmatrix}}{|\vec{v}(0) \times \vec{a}(0)|^2}$$

evaluated at $t = 0$, or

$$\tau = \frac{\begin{vmatrix} 1 & 1 & 1 \\ 0 & 2 & 1 \\ -2 & 2 & 1 \end{vmatrix}}{\left(\sqrt{6}\right)^2} = \frac{1}{3} \quad \text{when} \quad t = 0.$$

11. $\frac{dr}{dt} = -b \sin\theta \frac{d\theta}{dt}$ and $r\frac{d\theta}{dt} = b\cos\theta \frac{d\theta}{dt}$.

Since $\vec{v} = \frac{dr}{dt}\vec{u}_r + r\frac{d\theta}{dt}\vec{u}_\theta$, we have

$$|\vec{v}| = \vec{v}_0 = \sqrt{b^2 \sin^2\theta + b^2 \cos^2\theta}\left|\frac{d\theta}{dt}\right| = b\frac{d\theta}{dt},$$

since $b > 0$ and the particle is moving counterclockwise.

Therefore, $\frac{d\theta}{dt} = \frac{\vec{v}_0}{b}$ is constant. Next,

$$\frac{d^2r}{dt^2} = \frac{d\dot{r}}{d\theta}\frac{d\theta}{dt} = -b\cos\theta\left(\frac{d\theta}{dt}\right)^2 = -\frac{\vec{v}_0^{\,2}}{b}\cos\theta$$

so

$$\frac{d^2r}{dt^2} - r\left(\frac{d\theta}{dt}\right)^2 = -\frac{\vec{v}_0^{\,2}}{b}\cos\theta - (b\cos\theta)\left(\frac{\vec{v}_0}{b}\right)^2$$

$$= -\frac{2\vec{v}_0^{\,2}}{b}\cos\theta, \quad \vec{u}_r\text{-component of } \vec{a};$$

Now $\frac{d^2\theta}{dt^2} = 0$, and we find

$$2\frac{dr}{dt}\frac{d\theta}{dt} = -2b\sin\theta\left(\frac{d\theta}{dt}\right)^2 = -\frac{2\vec{v}_0^{\,2}}{b}\sin\theta, \quad \vec{u}_\theta\text{-component of } \vec{a}.$$

Hence, the acceleration vector is given by

$$\vec{a} = \left(-\frac{2\vec{v}_0^{\,2}}{b}\cos\theta\right)\vec{u}_r + \left(-\frac{2\vec{v}_0^{\,2}}{b}\sin\theta\right)\vec{u}_\theta.$$

CHAPTER 12 FUNCTIONS OF TWO OR MORE VARIABLES AND THEIR DERIVATIVES

12.1 FUNCTIONS OF TWO OR MORE INDEPENDENT VARIABLES

OBJECTIVE A: Given a function $w = f(x,y)$, find its domain and range.

1. For the function $w = \sqrt{x^2 - y^2}$, in order that w be a real number, the expression $x^2 - y^2$ must be ____________ or, $x^2 \geq$ ________. Equivalently, $|x| \geq$ __________. Sketch a graph of the domain set in the coordinate system at the right.

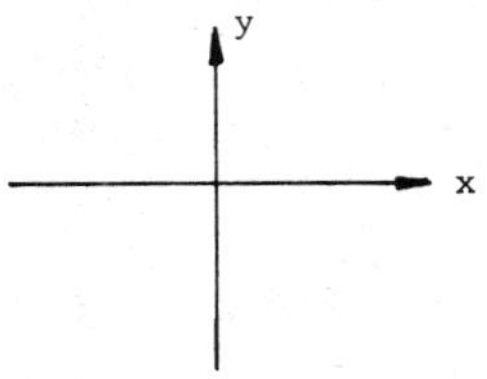

Since $y = 0$ gives $w = \sqrt{x^2}$, the range of f is the set of values ______________________________.

2. Consider the function $w = \frac{x}{y}e^{-x^2}$. Now $\frac{x}{y}$ is a real number for any value of x and any value of $y \neq$ ______. Also, e^{-x^2} is a real number for x satisfying __________. Therefore, w is a real number except when _______; that is, the domain of w contains all points in the xy-plane except the __________.

OBJECTIVE B: Given a function $w = f(x,y)$, represent the function
(a) by sketching a surface in space, and
(b) by drawing an assortment of level curves in the plane.

3. Let $f(x,y) = 4x^2 + 9y^2$. The equation $w = 4x^2 + 9y^2$ describes an elliptic ___________ in xyw-space. The section cut out from the surface by the yw-plane is $x = 0$, _________ which is a parabola with vertex at the origin, opening upward. When

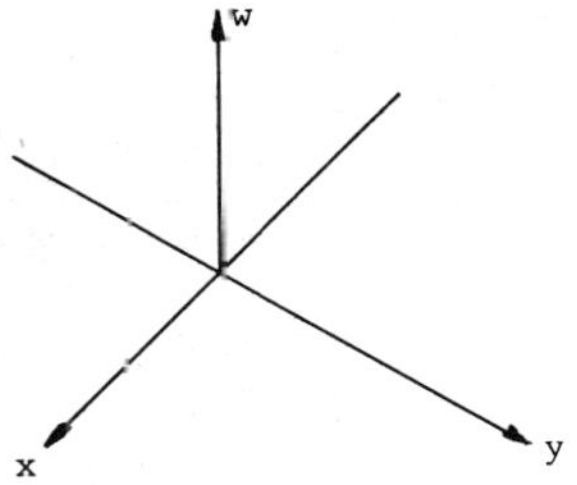

---

1. nonnegative, y^2, $|y|$, shaded portion in figure gives (x,y) points where $|x| \geq |y|$, $w \geq 0$

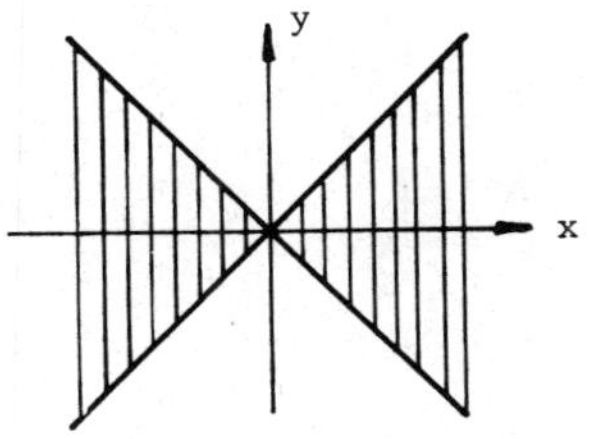

2. 0, $-\infty < x < \infty$, $y = 0$, x-axis

$y = 0$, ________ is also a parabola opening upward. Sketch the graph of the surface.

4. A level curve for the constant $c > 0$, and function in Problem 3, is given by the equation

$$c = \_\_\_\_\_\_\_\_\_\_ .$$

For a fixed value of c, the level curve is an ________ in the xy-plane. If $c = 0$ the level curve consists of a single point, namely the origin.

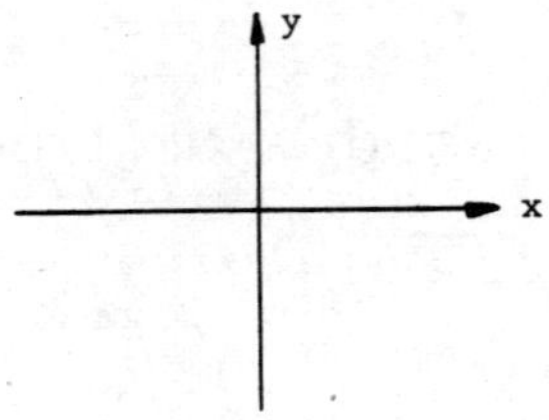

OBJECTIVE C: Find an equation for a level surface of a given function $f(x,y,z)$ that passes through a specified point (x_0, y_0, z_0).

5. For the function $f(x,y,z) = \sin(x + y^2 - 2z)$ and the point $(-1, 1, -\frac{\pi}{4})$, first find the value of the function at the point:

$$f(-1, 1, -\tfrac{\pi}{4}) = \sin(\_\_\_\_\_\_\_\_) = \_\_\_\_\_\_\_\_ .$$

Then an equation for a level surface of f passing through the point is

________________________ .

12.2 LIMITS AND CONTINUITY

OBJECTIVE A: Given an elementary function of two variables x and y, find its limit as (x,y) approches the point (x_0, y_0), if the limit exists.

6. $$\lim_{(x,y)\to(0,0)} \frac{e^x + e^{-y}}{xy + 1} = \frac{1 + \_\_\_\_}{0 + 1} = \_\_\_\_\_\_\_\_ .$$

7. $$\lim_{(x,y)\to(3,3)} \tan^{-1}\frac{y}{x} = \tan^{-1}\frac{3}{\_\_\_\_} = \tan^{-1}\_\_\_\_ = \_\_\_\_\_\_ .$$

---

3. paraboloid, $w = 9y^2$, $w = 4x^2$

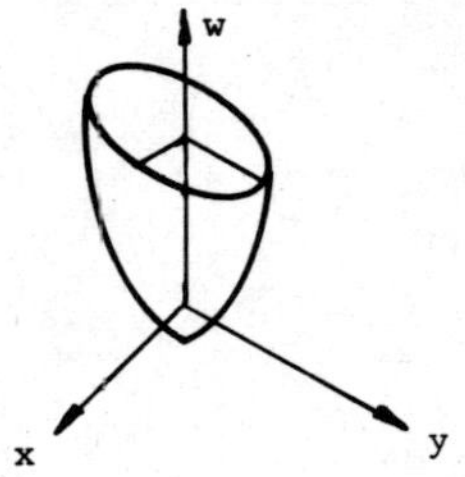

4. $4x^2 + 9y^2$, ellipse

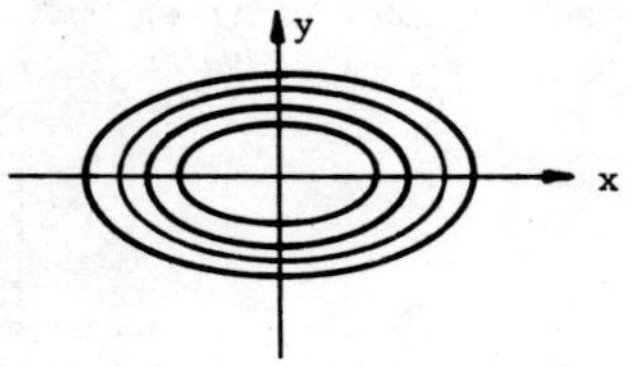

5. $-1 + 1 + \frac{\pi}{2}$, 1, $\sin(x + y^2 - 2z) = 1$

6. 1, 2

7. 3, 1, $\frac{\pi}{4}$

8. In order for $f(x,y)$ to have a limit as $(x,y) \to (x_0,y_0)$, the limits along <u>all</u> paths of approach have to _______.

OBJECTIVE B: Determine the points in the xy-plane at which a given function $f(x,y)$ is continuous.

9. A function $f(x,y)$ is continuous at (x_0,y_0) in the plane if

(1) f is __________ at (x_0,y_0),

(2) $\lim_{(x,y)\to(x_0,y_0)} f(x,y)$ ______________,

(3) $\lim_{(x,y)\to(x_0,y_0)} f(x,y) =$ __________.

10. The function $f(x,y) = \cos(x - y)$ is defined at every point in the plane. Moreover,

$$\lim_{(x,y)\to(x_0,y_0)} \cos(x - y) = \text{\_\_\_\_\_\_\_\_\_\_\_\_\_\_}$$

and

$$f(x_0,y_0) = \text{\_\_\_\_\_\_\_\_\_\_\_\_\_\_\_\_}.$$

We conclude that $\cos(x - y)$ is continuous at every point in the plane.

11. The function $f(x,y) = \frac{x^2 - xy}{x - y}$ is defined and continuous at all points in the plane except along the line __________. However, for any point (a,a) in the plane,

$$\lim_{(x,y)\to(a,a)} \frac{x^2 - xy}{x - y} = \lim_{(x,y)\to(a,a)} \frac{x(x - y)}{x - y}$$

$$= \lim_{(x,y)\to(a,a)} \text{\_\_\_\_\_\_}, \quad \text{provided } x \neq y$$

$$= \text{\_\_\_\_\_\_\_\_}.$$

Therefore, the limit of $f(x,y)$ <u>does exist</u> for every point in the plane. Nevertheless, since $f(x,y)$ fails to be defined when $x = y$, the function is discontinuous at every point (a,a) along the line $x = y$.

12.3 PARTIAL DERIVATIVES

OBJECTIVE A: Given an equation of a real-valued function of several variables, find the partial derivatives with respect to each variable.

---

8. agree

9. defined, exists, $f(x_0,y_0)$

10. $\cos(x_0 - y_0)$, $\cos(x_0 - y_0)$

11. $y = x$, x, a

12. $f(x,y) = xe^{-y} + y \cos x$
$f_x(x,y) = e^{-y} +$ __________ and $f_y(x,y) =$ ________ $+ \cos x$.

13. $w = xye^{-y^2/2}$
$\frac{\partial w}{\partial x} =$ __________ and $\frac{\partial w}{\partial y} = xe^{-y^2/2} -$ __________.

14. $g(x,y,z) = \frac{z}{y} + \tan(xy - 1)$
$g_x(x,y,z) =$ __________,
$g_y(x,y,z) =$ ________ $+ x \sec^2(xy - 1)$, and $g_z(x,y,z) =$ ________.

15. $h(x,y,z,w,\lambda,\mu) = (x - w)^2 + (y - z)^2 - \lambda(y - x - 1) - \mu(w - z^2)$
$h_x(x,y,z,w,\lambda,\mu) = 2(x - w) +$ ________,
$h_y(x,y,z,w,\lambda,\mu) =$ ________ $- \lambda$,
$h_z(x,y,z,w,\lambda,\mu) = -2(y - z) +$ ________,
$h_w(x,y,z,w,\lambda,\mu) =$ ________ $- \mu$,
$h_\lambda(x,y,z,w,\lambda,\mu) =$ ________, and
$h_\mu(x,y,z,w,\lambda,\mu) =$ ________.

OBJECTIVE B: Given a function of several independent variables, calculate all partial derivatives of the second-order.

16. For the function $f(x,y) = xe^{-y} + y \cos x$ we found in Problem 12 above that,

$$f_x = e^{-y} - y \sin x \quad \text{and} \quad f_y = -xe^{-y} + \cos x.$$

Hence, the second-order partials are given by

$f_{xx} = \frac{\partial}{\partial x}(f_x) =$ __________, $f_{xy} = \frac{\partial}{\partial y}(f_x) =$ __________,

$f_{yx} =$ __________ $= -e^{-y} - \sin x$, $f_{yy} =$ __________ $=$ __________.

17. Let $g(x,y,z) = x^3y + xyz + 3yz^2$. Then,
$g_x = 3x^2y + yz$, $g_y =$ __________, $g_z = xy + 6yz$.
The second-order partials are given by
$g_{xx} =$ ________, $g_{xy} =$ ________, $g_{xz} = y$,
$g_{yx} = 3x^2 + z$, $g_{yy} =$ ________, $g_{yz} =$ ________,
$g_{zx} =$ ________, $g_{zy} = x + 6z$, $g_{zz} =$ ________.
Note that the various mixed derivatives are equal: $g_{xy} = g_{yx}$, $g_{xz} = g_{zx}$, and $g_{yz} = g_{zy}$.

---

12. $-y \sin x$, $-xe^{-y}$ 13. $ye^{-y^2/2}$, $xy^2e^{-y^2/2}$ 14. $y \sec^2(xy - 1)$, $-\frac{z}{y^2}$, $\frac{1}{y}$

15. λ, $2(y - z)$, $2z\mu$, $-2(x - w)$, $-y + x + 1$, $-w + z^2$

16. $-y \cos x$, $-e^{-y} - \sin x$, $\frac{\partial}{\partial x}(f_y)$, $\frac{\partial}{\partial y}(f_y)$, xe^{-y}

17. $x^3 + xz + 3z^2$, $6xy$, $3x^2 + z$, 0, $x + 6z$, y, $6y$

18. The Mixed Derivative Theorem guarantees the equality

____

provided $f(x,y)$ and its partial derivatives ______, ______, ______, ______ are all defined throughout an __________ region containing the point (a,b) and are all ______________ at (a,b).

12.4 DIFFERENTIABILITY, LINEARIZATION, AND DIFFERENTIALS

19. A function $f(x,y)$ is differentiable at (x_0, y_0) if the partial derivatives __________ and __________ exist, and the following equation holds for f at (x_0, y_0):

$f(x_0+\Delta x, y_0+\Delta y) - f(x_0, y_0)$

$= $ ______________________________________ ,

where $\epsilon_1,\ \epsilon_2 \to 0$ as ________________ .

20. If a function $f(x,y)$ is differentiable at (x_0, y_0), then it is ____________________ at (x_0, y_0).

OBJECTIVE A: Given a function $f(x,y)$, find the standard linear approximation to it near a specified point.

21. Given the function $f(x,y)$ the linearization of it at the point (x_0, y_0) is

$L(x,y) = $ ____________________________________.

The right side of the previous equation represents the __________ that is tangent to the surface $w = f(x,y)$ at the point (x_0, y_0).

22. For the surface $f(x,y) = 3xy + ye^x - x\sin y$ we have $f_x(x,y) = $ __________________ and $f_y(x,y) = 3x + e^x - x\cos y$. Hence, near the point $(0, \frac{\pi}{2})$ the surface $w = f(x,y)$ can be approximated linearly by the tangent plane

$L(x,y) = $ ____ + __________ $(x - 0) + (1)$________ = ______________.

---

18. $f_{xy}(a,b) = f_{yx}(a,b)$, f_x, f_y, f_{xy}, f_{yx}, open, continuous

19. $f_x(x_0, y_0)$, $f_y(x_0, y_0)$, $f_x(x_0, y_0)\Delta x + f_y(x_0, y_0)\Delta y + \epsilon_1 \Delta x + \epsilon_2 \Delta y$, $\Delta x,\ \Delta y \to 0$

20. continuous

21. $f(x_0, y_0) + f_x(x_0, y_0)(x - x_0) + f_y(x_0, y_0)(y - y_0)$, plane

22. $3y + ye^x - \sin y$, $\frac{\pi}{2}$, $(2\pi - 1)$, $y - \frac{\pi}{2}$, $(2\pi - 1)x + y$

OBJECTIVE B: Given a surface $w = f(x,y)$, find the change df along the plane tangent to the surface at some given point (x_0, y_0, w_0) for specified increments Δx and Δy.

23. Consider the surface $w = f(x,y) = y\cos(x + y)$. For the point $(\frac{\pi}{2}, \frac{\pi}{2}, \_\_\_)$, the change along the tangent plane is given by

$$df = \Delta L = f_x(\tfrac{\pi}{2}, \tfrac{\pi}{2})\Delta x + \_\_\_\_\_\_\_\_ .$$

Now, $\frac{\partial f}{\partial x} = \_\_\_\_\_\_\_\_$ and $\frac{\partial f}{\partial y} = \_\_\_\_\_\_\_\_$. Thus, $f_x(\frac{\pi}{2}, \frac{\pi}{2}) = 0$ and $f_y(\frac{\pi}{2}, \frac{\pi}{2}) = \_\_\_\_$. For the increments $\Delta x = -0.1$ and $\Delta y = 0.05$ we have $df = \Delta L = \_\_\_\_\_\_$ as the change along the tangent plane. On the other hand, the actual change along the surface itself is

$$\Delta f = f(\tfrac{\pi}{2} - 0.1, \tfrac{\pi}{2} + 0.05) - f(\tfrac{\pi}{2}, \tfrac{\pi}{2})$$

$$\approx f(1.471, 1.621) + \_\_\_\_ \approx \_\_\_\_\_\_ \cos(3.092) + 1.571$$

$$\approx 1.621(-0.999) + 1.571 \approx -0.048$$

with the calculations done on a calculator.

OBJECTIVE C: Use Equation (10) in the text to find an upper bound for the magnitude $|E|$ of the error in the approximation $f(x,y) \approx L(x,y)$ over a specified rectangle R.

24. For the surface $f(x,y) = 3xy + ye^x - x\sin y$ in Problem 22 above, we found the approximation $L(x,y) = (2\pi - 1)x + y$ near the point $(0, \frac{\pi}{2})$. Calculation of the second partials yields $f_{xx} = ye^x$, $f_{yy} = \_\_\_\_\_\_\_\_$, and $f_{xy} = \_\_\_\_\_\_\_\_$. For the rectangle $|x| \le 0.1$ and $\left|y - \frac{\pi}{2}\right| \le \frac{\pi}{2}$ we have the following bounds:

$$|f_{xx}| = |y||e^x| \le \_\_\_\_\_\_ \approx 3.48,$$

$$|f_{yy}| = |x||\sin y| \le \_\_\_\_\_, \text{ and}$$

$$|f_{xy}| \le 3 + e^x + |\cos y| \le 3 + 1.2 + \_\_\_\_ \approx \_\_\_\_ .$$

A common upper bound for these second partials on R is $M = 6$ (or any number larger than $\_\_\_\_\_\_$). With $(x_0, y_0) = (0, \frac{\pi}{2})$ we then know that, throughout R,

$$|E(x,y)| \le \_\_\_\_\_\_ \left(|x| + \left|y - \tfrac{\pi}{2}\right|\right)^2 .$$

---

23. $-\frac{\pi}{2}$, $f_y(\frac{\pi}{2}, \frac{\pi}{2})\Delta y$, $-y\sin(x + y)$, $\cos(x + y) - y\sin(x + y)$, -1, -0.05, $\frac{\pi}{2}$, 1.621

24. $x\sin y$, $3 + e^x - \cos y$, $\pi e^{0.1}$, 0.1, 1, 5.2, 5.2, 3

OBJECTIVE D: Use the approximation

$$\Delta f = f(x,y) - f(x_0,y_0) \approx \underbrace{f_x(x_0,y_0)\Delta x + f_y(x_0,y_0)\Delta y}_{df}$$

to discuss the sensitivity of $f(x,y)$ to small changes in x and y near a given point (x_0,y_0).

25. The surface area of a cone of radius r and height h is given by the formula

$$S = \pi r\sqrt{r^2 + h^2} .$$

To calculate ΔL, we determine

$\frac{\partial S}{\partial r} = \pi\sqrt{r^2 + h^2} +$ ______________, and $\frac{\partial S}{\partial h} =$ ______________.

Therefore, near the point $(r_0,h_0) = (3,4)$,

$$\Delta S \approx dS = \frac{\partial S}{\partial r}(r_0,h_0)\Delta r + \frac{\partial S}{\partial h}(r_0,h_0)\Delta h = \_\_\_\_ \Delta r + \_\_\_\_ \Delta h.$$

Hence, a one-unit change in r will change S by about $\frac{34\pi}{5}$ units. A one-unit change in h will change S by about _____ units. The surface area of a cone of radius 3 and height 4 is nearly ______ times more sensitive to a small change in r than it is to a change of the same size in h.

12.5 THE CHAIN RULE

OBJECTIVE A: Let w be a differentiable function of the variables $x,y,z,\ldots,v$ and let these in turn be differentiable functions of a second set of variables $p,q,r,\ldots,t$. Calculate the derivative of w with respect to any one of the variables in the second set by use of the chain rule for partial derivatives.

26. To express $\frac{dw}{dt}$ as a function of t if $w = x^2 - xy$ and $x = e^t$, $y = \ln t$ we first differentiate w with respect to each of the variables x,y in the first set (intermediate variables):

$\frac{\partial w}{\partial x} =$ ____________ and $\frac{\partial w}{\partial y} =$ ____________.

Next, we differentiate each of the variables x,y with respect to the one variable t of the second set (independent variables):

---

25. $\frac{\pi r^2}{\sqrt{r^2 + h^2}}$, $\frac{\pi rh}{\sqrt{r^2 + h^2}}$, $\frac{34\pi}{5}$, $\frac{12\pi}{5}$, $\frac{12\pi}{5}$, three

$$\frac{dx}{dt} = \_\_\_\_\_\_\_\_ \quad \text{and} \quad \frac{dy}{dt} = \_\_\_\_\_\_\_\_ .$$

Then we form the products of corresponding derivatives, add these products together, and substitute as follows:

$$\frac{dw}{dt} = \frac{\partial w}{\partial x}\frac{dx}{dt} + \_\_\_\_\_\_\_\_ = (2x - y)e^t + \_\_\_\_\_\_\_\_$$
$$= (2e^t - \ln t)e^t - \_\_\_\_\_\_\_\_ .$$

27. To express $\frac{\partial w}{\partial u}$ and $\frac{\partial w}{\partial v}$ as functions of u and v if $w = x^y + z$ and $x = 1 + u^2$, $y = e^v$, $z = uv$ we first differentiate w with respect to each of the variables x,y,z in the first set (intermediate variables):

$$\frac{\partial w}{\partial x} = \_\_\_\_\_\_\_\_, \quad \frac{\partial w}{\partial y} = \_\_\_\_\_\_\_\_, \quad \frac{\partial w}{\partial z} = \_\_\_\_\_\_\_\_ .$$

Next, we differentiate each of those variables with respect to the first variable u of the second set (independent variables):

$$\frac{\partial x}{\partial u} = \_\_\_\_\_\_, \quad \frac{\partial y}{\partial u} = 0, \quad \frac{\partial z}{\partial u} = \_\_\_\_\_\_ .$$

Then

$$\frac{\partial w}{\partial u} = \frac{\partial w}{\partial x}\frac{\partial x}{\partial u} + \frac{\partial w}{\partial y}\frac{\partial y}{\partial u} + \_\_\_\_\_\_\_\_\_\_$$
$$= (yx^{y-1})(2u) + (x^y \ln x)(0) + \_\_\_\_\_\_ = e^v(1 + u^2)^{e^v-1}(2u) + v.$$

To calculate $\frac{\partial w}{\partial v}$ we differentiate each of the variables x,y,z in the first set with respect to the second variable v of the second set (independent variables):

$$\frac{\partial x}{\partial v} = 0, \quad \frac{\partial y}{\partial v} = \_\_\_\_\_\_\_\_, \quad \frac{\partial z}{\partial v} = \_\_\_\_\_\_\_\_ .$$

Then,

$$\frac{\partial w}{\partial v} = \frac{\partial w}{\partial x}\frac{\partial x}{\partial v} + \_\_\_\_\_\_\_\_\_\_$$
$$= (yx^{y-1})(0) + \_\_\_\_\_\_\_\_\_\_ + (1)(u) = \_\_\_\_\_\_\_\_\_\_\_\_\_\_ .$$

28. Suppose that $w = f\left(\frac{y}{x}\right)$ for a differentiable function f. Show that $\frac{\partial w}{\partial x} = -\frac{y}{x^2} f'\left(\frac{y}{x}\right)$ and $\frac{\partial w}{\partial y} = \frac{1}{x} f'\left(\frac{y}{x}\right)$.

<u>Solution</u>. Let $w = f(u)$ where $u = \frac{y}{x}$. To find the partial derivatives of w, we first differentiate w with respect to

---

26. $2x - y$, $-x$, e^t, $\frac{1}{t}$, $\frac{\partial w}{\partial y}\frac{dy}{dt}$, $(-x)\frac{1}{t}$, $\frac{1}{t}e^t$

27. yx^{y-1}, $x^y \ln x$, 1, 2u, v, $\frac{\partial w}{\partial z}\frac{\partial z}{\partial u}$, 1(v), e^v, u, $\frac{\partial w}{\partial y}\frac{\partial y}{\partial v} + \frac{\partial w}{\partial z}\frac{\partial z}{\partial v}$, $(x^y \ln x)e^v$, $(1 + u^2)^{e^v} \ln(1 + u^2)e^v + u$

the single variable u of the first set: $\frac{dw}{du} = f'(u)$. To find $\frac{\partial w}{\partial x}$ we next calculate the derivative of the variable u from the first set with respect to the first variable x of the second set: $\frac{\partial u}{\partial x} =$ ________. Then the chain rule gives

$$\frac{\partial w}{\partial x} = \frac{dw}{du}\frac{\partial u}{\partial x} = \text{\_\_\_\_\_\_\_\_\_\_\_\_\_\_\_\_} \quad \text{as claimed.}$$

To find $\frac{\partial w}{\partial y}$ we calculate the derivative of the variable u from the first set with respect to the second variable y of the second set: $\frac{\partial u}{\partial y} =$ ______. Then the chain rule gives

$$\frac{\partial w}{\partial y} = \text{\_\_\_\_\_\_\_\_\_\_\_\_} = \text{\_\_\_\_\_\_\_\_\_\_\_\_}.$$

29. A point moves on the surface $w = x^3 + 2xy^2$ with x increasing at the rate of 4 cm/sec and y increasing at 6 cm/sec. At what rate is $\frac{\partial w}{\partial x}$ changing at the moment when $x = 2$ cm and $y = 5$ cm?

<u>Solution</u>. Let $u = \frac{\partial w}{\partial x} =$ __________. We want to calculate $\frac{du}{dt}$. Now, by the chain rule,

$$\frac{du}{dt} = \text{\_\_\_\_\_\_\_\_\_\_\_\_\_\_} = (6x)\frac{dx}{dt} + \text{\_\_\_\_\_\_\_\_\_\_\_\_}.$$

At the specified moment,

$$\frac{du}{dt} = (12)(4) + \text{\_\_\_\_\_\_\_\_\_\_\_\_} = \text{\_\_\_\_\_\_\_\_\_\_\_\_} \ \text{cm}^2/\text{sec}.$$

OBJECTIVE B: Assuming a given equation $F(x,y,z) = 0$ determines z as a differentiable function of x and y, calculate the partial derivatives $\frac{\partial z}{\partial x}$ and $\frac{\partial z}{\partial y}$ at points where $F_z \neq 0$.

30. Consider the equation $xz^2 + xy - y^3 = 0$. Denote the left side in functional notation by $F(x,y,z)$. Then

$$F_x = \text{\_\_\_\_\_\_\_\_}, \quad F_y = \text{\_\_\_\_\_\_\_\_}, \quad \text{and} \quad F_z = \text{\_\_\_\_\_\_\_\_}.$$

Thus, at all points where $2xz^2 \neq 0$,

$$\frac{\partial z}{\partial x} = \frac{\text{\_\_\_\_}}{2xz^2} \quad \text{and} \quad \frac{\partial z}{\partial y} = \frac{\text{\_\_\_\_}}{2xz^2}.$$

---

28. $-\frac{y}{x^2}$, $f'(u)\left(-\frac{y}{x^2}\right)$, $\frac{1}{x}$, $\frac{dw}{du}\frac{\partial u}{\partial y}$, $f'(u)\left(\frac{1}{x}\right)$

29. $3x^2 + 2y^2$, $\frac{\partial u}{\partial x}\frac{dx}{dt} + \frac{\partial u}{\partial y}\frac{dy}{dt}$, $(4y)\frac{dy}{dt}$, $(20)(6)$, 168

30. y, $x - 3y^2$, $2xz^2$, $-y$, $-(x - 3y^2)$

12.6 PARTIAL DERIVATIVES WITH CONSTRAINED VARIABLES

OBJECTIVE: Given a function $w = f(x,y,z)$ and an equation $g(x,y,z) = 0$, determine partial derivatives of w when the independent variables are specified.

31. If $w = x^2 - y + z$ and $x + 2y - z = 0$, find $\left(\frac{\partial w}{\partial y}\right)_z$.

Solution. The notation $\left(\frac{\partial w}{\partial y}\right)_z$ means that the variables ______ and ______ are independent. Thus, from the equation $x + 2y - z = 0$ we find $x =$ ________. Substitution of this value of x into the expression for w gives

$$w = (z - 2y)^2 - y + z = \underline{\qquad\qquad\qquad\qquad}.$$

Therefore,

$$\left(\frac{\partial w}{\partial y}\right)_z = \underline{\qquad\qquad\qquad}.$$

32. If $w = x^2 - y + z$ and $x^3 - 2xy - z = 0$, find $\left(\frac{dw}{dy}\right)_z$.

Solution. This problem is similar to the previous one except that it is not convenient to eliminate x in the expression for w. Thus we differentiate each equation implicitly with respect to y, treating y and z as independent variables and ______ and ______ as dependent variables. This gives

$$\frac{\partial w}{\partial y} = 2x\,\frac{\partial x}{\partial y} - \underline{\qquad\qquad}$$

and

$$\underline{\qquad\qquad} - 2x - 2\,\frac{\partial x}{\partial y}\,y - 0 = 0\ .$$

Solving for $\frac{\partial x}{\partial y}$ in the second equation gives

$$\frac{\partial x}{\partial y} = \underline{\qquad\qquad\qquad}\ .$$

Substitution into the equation for $\frac{\partial w}{\partial y}$ then yields

$$\left(\frac{\partial w}{\partial y}\right)_z = \frac{4x^2}{3x^2 - 2y} - 1$$

$$= \underline{\qquad\qquad\qquad}\ .$$

12.7 DIRECTIONAL DERIVATIVES, GRADIENT VECTORS, AND TANGENT PLANES

OBJECTIVE A: Given a function $w = f(x,y,z)$, find the gradient vector at a specified point $P_0(x_0,y_0,z_0)$.

---

31. y, z, $z - 2y$, $z^2 - 4yz + 4y^2 - y + z$, $-4z + 8y - 1$

32. w, x, 1, $3x^2\,\frac{\partial x}{\partial y}$, $\frac{2x}{3x^2 - 2y}$, $\frac{x^2 + 2y}{3x^2 - 2y}$

33. For the function $f(x,y,z) = y \ln x^2 + x \cos z$ and the point $P_0(-1,2,\frac{\pi}{2})$, the gradient vector is obtained by calculating the partial derivatives of f at P_0:

$f_x =$ ________$|_0 = -4$, $f_y = \ln x^2|_0 =$ ________,

$f_z =$ ________$|_0 =$ ________. Thus, $\vec{\nabla} f =$ ____________.

OBJECTIVE B: Given a function f of two or three variables, find the directional derivative of f at a given point, and in the direction of a given vector $\vec{A}$.

34. Let us find the directional derivative of $f = e^{x \tan y}$ at the point $(1,\frac{\pi}{4})$, and in the direction $\vec{A} = \frac{1}{e}\vec{i} + \frac{2}{e}\vec{j}$. Now,

$$\frac{\partial f}{\partial x} = \text{\_\_\_\_\_\_\_\_\_\_\_\_} \quad \text{and} \quad \frac{\partial f}{\partial y} = \text{\_\_\_\_\_\_\_\_\_\_\_\_}.$$

Thus, we obtain the gradient vector

$$\vec{\nabla} f = f_x\left(1,\frac{\pi}{4}\right)\vec{i} + f_y\left(1,\frac{\pi}{4}\right)\vec{j} = \text{\_\_\_\_\_\_\_\_\_\_}.$$

Next, $|\vec{A}| =$ ________, and hence a unit vector in the direction of $\vec{A}$ is given by

$$\vec{u} = \frac{\vec{A}}{|\vec{A}|} = \text{\_\_\_\_\_\_\_\_\_\_}.$$

The derivative of f in the direction $\vec{A}$ can now be calculated from the vectors $\vec{u}$ and grad f as

$$\vec{u} \cdot \vec{\nabla} f = \frac{1}{\sqrt{5}}(\text{\_\_\_\_\_\_}) + \text{\_\_\_\_\_\_}(2e) = \text{\_\_\_\_\_\_\_\_}.$$

35. Consider the function $f = x^2 + 5y \sin z$. To find the directional derivative of f at the point $P_0(1,1,\frac{\pi}{2})$ in the direction from P_0 toward the point $P_1(4,5,\frac{\pi}{2})$, we first calculate the partial derivatives of f at P_0. Thus,

$f_x =$ ______$|_{(1,1,\pi/2)} =$ ________, $f_y = 5 \sin z|_{(1,1,\pi/2)} =$ ________,
$f_z =$ ____________$|_{(1,1,\pi/2)} = 0$.

Therefore, the gradient of f at $(1,1,\frac{\pi}{2})$ is

$$\vec{\nabla} f = \text{\_\_\_\_\_\_\_\_\_\_\_\_}.$$

The vector $\vec{A} = \vec{P_0P_1} = 3\vec{i} + 4\vec{j} + 0\vec{k}$ has magnitude

---

33. $\frac{2y}{x} + \cos z$, 0, $-x \sin z$, 1, $-4\vec{i} + 0\vec{j} + \vec{k}$

34. $\tan y\, e^{x \tan y}$, $x \sec^2 y\, e^{x \tan y}$, $e\vec{i} + 2e\vec{j}$, $\frac{\sqrt{5}}{e}$, $\frac{1}{\sqrt{5}}\vec{i} + \frac{2}{\sqrt{5}}\vec{j}$, e, $\frac{2}{\sqrt{5}}$, $\sqrt{5}\,e$

$$|\vec{A}| = \sqrt{\_\_\_\_\_\_\_\_\_\_} = \_\_\_\_\_\_ .$$

Thus, the direction of $\vec{A}$ is

$$\vec{u} = \frac{\vec{A}}{|\vec{A}|} = \_\_\_\_\_\_\_\_\_\_\_\_ .$$

The derivative of f in the direction $\vec{A}$ is

$$\vec{u} \cdot \vec{\nabla} f = \tfrac{3}{5}(\_\_\_\_\_) + \_\_\_\_\_\_ (5) + 0(0) = \_\_\_\_\_\_\_ .$$

OBJECTIVE C: Given a function f of two or three variables, determine the direction one should travel, starting from a given point P_0, to obtain the most rapid rate of increase or decrease (whichever is specified) of the function.

36. The function $w = f(x,y,z)$ changes most rapidly from the point $P_0(x_0,y_0,z_0)$ in the direction of the vector _______. Moreover, the directional derivative in this direction equals the ___________ of the gradient vector. In this case the gradient vector lies in 3-space, which contains the domain of the function f.

37. In which direction should one travel, starting from the point $P_0(1, 1, \frac{\pi}{2})$, in order to obtain the most rapid rate of decrease of the function $f = x^2 + 5y \sin z$? What is the instantaneous rate of change of f per unit of distance in this direction?

Solution. In Problem 35 we calculated $\vec{\nabla} f(P_0) = \_\_\_\_\_\_\_\_\_\_$. Since the directional derivative of f in the direction $\vec{u}$ is given by

$$\vec{u} \cdot \vec{\nabla} f = |\vec{\nabla} f| \cos \theta ,$$

where θ is the angle between the unit vector $\vec{u}$ and the vector ______, the value of the directional derivative is smallest when $\cos \theta = \_\_\_\_\_\_$ or $\theta = \_\_\_\_\_\_$. Thus, $\vec{u} = \_\_\_\_\_\_\_\_\_\_\_\_\_\_\_\_$. The value of the directional derivative in this direction is

$$\vec{u} \cdot \vec{\nabla} f = \_\_\_\_\_\_\_\_ .$$

This value is the negative of the magnitude of the gradient.

38. The function $w = f(x,y)$ changes most rapidly from the point $P_0(x_0,y_0)$ in the direction of the gradient vector

$$\vec{\nabla} f = \_\_\_\_\_\_\_\_\_\_\_\_\_\_\_\_$$

in the xy-plane (which contains the domain of the function).

---

35. $2x$, 2, 5, $5y \cos z$, $2\vec{i} + 5\vec{j} + 0\vec{k}$, $3^2 + 4^2 + 0^2$, 5, $\frac{3}{5}\vec{i} + \frac{4}{5}\vec{j} + 0\vec{k}$, 2, $\frac{4}{5}$, $\frac{26}{5}$

36. $\vec{\nabla} f$, magnitude

37. $2\vec{i} + 5\vec{j} + 0\vec{k}$, $\vec{\nabla} f$, -1, π, $-\frac{2}{\sqrt{29}}\vec{i} - \frac{5}{\sqrt{29}}\vec{j} + 0\vec{k}$, $-\sqrt{29}$

The directional derivative in this direction equals the magnitude of the vector ______.

39. Consider the function $f = x^y$. At the point $P_0(e,0)$ the partial derivatives of f are

$$f_x = \_\_\_\_\_\_\big|_{(e,0)} = \_\_\_\_\_\_, \quad f_y = \_\_\_\_\_\_\big|_{(e,0)} = \_\_\_\_\_\_$$

so that $\vec{\nabla} f =$ ______. The maximum value of the directional derivative at P_0 occurs in the direction $\vec{u} =$ ______, and this value equals $|\vec{\nabla} f| =$ ______.

Remark. Notice that the gradient vector for a function of two variables lies in the xy-plane, whereas for a function of three variables it lies in space.

OBJECTIVE D: Find the plane which is tangent to the level surface $f(x,y,z) = \text{constant}$ at a specified point $P_0(x_0,y_0,z_0)$.

40. The gradient vector $\vec{\nabla} f(P_0)$ is ______ to the level surface

$$f(x,y,z) = \text{constant}$$

at the point $P_0(x_0,y_0,z_0)$ on the surface.

41. Consider the surface $z = e^{3x} \sin 3y + 2$. Let

$$w = f(x,y,z) = e^{3x} \sin 3y - z$$

so the equation of the surface has the form

$$f(x,y,z) = \text{constant}.$$

In this case the constant is equal to ______. The point $P_0(0, \frac{\pi}{6}, 3)$ lies on the surface and the vector

$$\vec{\nabla} f(P_0) = \left(f_x \vec{i} + f_y \vec{j} + f_z \vec{k}\right)_0$$

$$= \left(3e^{3x} \sin 3y \vec{i} + \_\_\_\_\_\_\_\_ \vec{j} - \vec{k}\right)_0$$

$$= \_\_\_\_\_\_\_\_$$

is normal to the surface at P_0. Thus, an equation of the tangent plane to the surface at P_0 is

$$\_\_\_\_ (x - 0) + 0(\_\_\_\_\_) + \_\_\_\_ (z - 3) = 0, \quad \text{or} \quad z = \_\_\_\_\_\_.$$

---

38. $f_x(x_0,y_0)\vec{i} + f_y(x_0,y_0)\vec{j}$, $\vec{\nabla} f$

39. yx^{y-1}, 0, $x^y \ln x$, 1, $0\vec{i} + 1\vec{j}$, $\vec{j}$, 1

40. normal

41. -2, $3e^{3x} \cos 3y$, $3\vec{i} + 0\vec{j} - \vec{k}$, 3, $y - \frac{\pi}{6}$, -1, $3(x + 1)$

42. Since the gradient vector $3\vec{i} + 0\vec{j} - \vec{k}$ is normal to the surface in Problem 41 at the point $P_0(0, \frac{\pi}{6}, 3)$, equations of the normal to the surface at P_0 are

$$x = 0 + 3t, \quad y = \_\_\_\_\_\_\_\_, \quad \text{and} \quad z = \_\_\_\_\_\_\_\_ .$$

These equations also may be written in the form $\frac{x}{3} = \_\_\_\_\_\_\_\_$, $y = \_\_\_\_\_\_\_\_$.

OBJECTIVE E: Given a surface $w = f(x,y)$, find an equation of the tangent plane to the surface at a specified point P_0, if the tangent plane exists.

43. The point $P_0(1,-2,3)$ lies on the surface $w = \sqrt{3x^2 - xy + y^2}$. To find an equation of the tangent plane, calculate

$$f_x(1,-2) = \frac{1}{2}(6x - y)\left(3x^2 - xy + y\right)\Big|_{(1,-2)} = \_\_\_\_\_\_\_\_ ;$$

$$f_y(1,-2) = \_\_\_\_\_\_\_\_\_\_\_\_\_\_\_\_\Big|_{(1,-2)} = -\frac{5}{6};$$

Therefore, an equation of the tangent plane is

$$\frac{4}{3}(x - 1) + \_\_\_\_\_ (y + 2) + \_\_\_\_\_ (w - 3) = 0$$

or,

$$8x - 5y - 6w = \_\_\_\_\_\_\_\_ .$$

OBJECTIVE F: Given a surface $w = f(x,y)$, find the normal line (if it exists) to the surface at a specified point P_0.

44. For the surface and point in Problem 41 above, for a normal vector $\vec{N}$ to the surface P_0 we may take $\vec{N} = 8\vec{i} + \_\_\_\_\_\_\_\_$. Thus, equations for the normal line are given by

$$x = \_\_\_\_\_ + 8t, \quad y = -2 - \_\_\_\_\_\_, \quad w = \_\_\_\_\_\_ .$$

Alternatively, the normal line is

$$\frac{x - 1}{8} = \frac{y + 2}{\_\_\_\_\_} = \_\_\_\_\_\_\_\_ .$$

OBJECTIVE G: Given two surfaces $f(x,y,z) = \text{constant}$ and $g(x,y,z) = \text{constant}$, find parametric equations for the line tangent to the curve C of intersection of the surfaces at a specified point $P_0(x_0,y_0,z_0)$ on C.

---

42. $\frac{\pi}{6} - 0t$, $3 - t$, $\frac{z - 3}{-1}$, $\frac{\pi}{6}$

43. $\frac{4}{3}$, $\frac{1}{2}(2y - x)\left(3x^2 - xy + y^2\right)^{-1/2}$, $-\frac{5}{6}$, -1, 0

44. $-5\vec{j} - 6\vec{k}$, 1, $5t$, $3 - 6t$, -5, $\frac{w - 3}{-6}$

45. Consider the surfaces $f(x,y,z) = x^2 + y - z = 1$ and $g(x,y,z) = x + y + z = 3$. The point $(1,1,1)$ lies on the curve of intersection of the two surfaces. The tangent line is ____________ to both $\vec{\nabla}f$ and $\vec{\nabla}g$ at $(1,1,1)$. The vector $\vec{v}$ = ____________ will therefore be parallel to the line. Now,

$$\vec{\nabla}f(1,1,1) = (2x\vec{i} + \vec{j} - \vec{k})_{(1,1,1)} = \_\_\_\_\_\_\_\_\_\_$$

and

$$\vec{\nabla}g(1,1,1) = (\_\_\_\_\_\_\_\_\_\_)_{(1,1,1)} = \_\_\_\_\_\_\_\_\_\_ .$$

Hence,

$$\vec{v} = (\vec{i} + \vec{j} - \vec{k}) \times (\vec{i} + \vec{j} + \vec{k}) = \_\_\_\_\_\_\_\_\_\_ .$$

The tangent line is

$$x = 1 + 2t, \quad y = \_\_\_\_\_\_\_\_, \quad z = \_\_\_\_\_\_\_\_ .$$

12.8 MAXIMA, MINIMA, AND SADDLE POINTS

OBJECTIVE A: Given the surface $z = f(x,y)$ defined by a function f which has continuous partial derivatives over some region R, examine the surface for local extrema. Use the second derivative test to classify the relative extrema as a local maximum, local minimum, or saddle point.

46. A necessary condition that must be satisfied if $z = f(x,y)$ has a maximum (or minimum) value occurring at the point (a,b) that is not on the boundary of the region R is that ______________________.

47. Assume (a,b) is an interior point of the region R. Suppose $f_x(a,b) = f_y(a,b) = 0$ and $f_{xx}(a,b) \neq 0$. Then at (a,b) the function $f(x,y)$ has:
   (i) A local minimum if ______________.
   (ii) A local maximum if ______________.
   (iii) A saddle point if ______________.
   (iv) The test is inconclusive if ______________.

48. Consider the function $f(x,y) = x^2 - xy + y^3 - x$. We set

$$\frac{\partial f}{\partial x} = 2x - y - 1 = 0 \quad \text{and} \quad \frac{\partial f}{\partial y} = \_\_\_\_\_\_\_\_\_\_ = 0 .$$

The first equation is equivalent to $y = 2x - 1$, and substitution of this into the second equation gives

---

45. perpendicular, $\vec{\nabla}f \times \vec{\nabla}g$, $\vec{i} + \vec{j} - \vec{k}$, $\vec{i} + \vec{j} + \vec{k}$, $\vec{i} + \vec{j} + \vec{k}$, $2\vec{i} - 2\vec{j}$, $1 - 2t$, 1

46. $\frac{\partial f}{\partial x} = 0$ and $\frac{\partial f}{\partial y} = 0$ at (a,b)

47. $f_{xx} > 0$ and $f_{xx}f_{yy} - f_{xy}^2 > 0$ at (a,b), $f_{xx} < 0$ and $f_{xx}f_{yy} - f_{xy}^2 > 0$ at (a,b), $f_{xx}f_{yy} - f_{xy}^2 < 0$ at (a,b), $f_{xx}f_{yy} - f_{xy}^2 = 0$ at (a,b)

$-x + 3(2x - 1)^2 = 0$, or $12x^2 - 13x + 13 = 0$. Thus, $x = \frac{1}{3}$ or $x = \frac{3}{4}$. It follows that the points ________ and ________ are critical points where f_x and f_y are simultaneously 0. Next we find, f_{xx} = ____, f_{xy} = ____, and $f_{yy} = 6y$. Let us test the critical point $(\frac{1}{3}, -\frac{1}{3})$. If $f_{xx}(\frac{1}{3}, -\frac{1}{3})$ = ____, $f_{xy}(\frac{1}{3}, -\frac{1}{3})$ = ____, and $f_{yy}(\frac{1}{3}, -\frac{1}{3})$ = ____, then $f_{xx}f_{yy} - f_{xy}^2 = -5$. We conclude that the surface has a ____________ at $(\frac{1}{3}, -\frac{1}{3})$. To test the point $(\frac{3}{4}, \frac{1}{2})$, we have $f_{xx}(\frac{3}{4}, \frac{1}{2}) = 2$, $f_{xy}(\frac{3}{4}, \frac{1}{2})$ = ____, $f_{yy}(\frac{3}{4}, \frac{1}{2}) = 3$. Then, $f_{xx}f_{yy} - f_{xy}^2$ = ______ and $f_{xx} > 0$. We conclude that the surface has a ________________ at $(\frac{3}{4}, \frac{1}{2})$.

49. For the function $f(x,y) = x^3 - 3x^2y^2 + y^4$, we find

$$\frac{\partial f}{\partial x} = \underline{\qquad\qquad} = 3x(\underline{\qquad\qquad}) \text{ and}$$

$$\frac{\partial f}{\partial y} = \underline{\qquad\qquad} = 2y(\underline{\qquad\qquad}).$$

From $\frac{\partial f}{\partial x} = 0$ and $\frac{\partial f}{\partial y} = 0$, $x = 0$ if and only if $y = 0$ also. Hence ____________ is one critical point. If $x \neq 0$, then $\frac{\partial f}{\partial x} = 3x(x - 2y^2) = 0$ demands $x = 2y^2$. Since $y \neq 0$, $2y(2y^2 - 3x^2) = 0$ gives $2y^2 - 3x^2 = 0$, and substitution of $x = 2y^2$ into this last equation gives __________ = 0 or, $x(1 - 3x) = 0$. It follows that x = ____. From $x = 2y^2$ we find that $\left(\frac{1}{3}, \frac{1}{\sqrt{6}}\right)$ and __________ are also critical points of f. Next we test these critical points. First, we compute the second partial derivatives: $f_{xx} = 6(x - y^2)$, f_{xy} = __________, and $f_{yy} = 6(2y^2 - x^2)$.

(a) The critical point $(0,0)$:

$f_{xx}(0,0) = 0$, $f_{xy}(0,0) = 0$, and $f_{yy}(0,0) = 0$. Therefore, the second derivative test yields <u>no information</u> concerning the surface at the point $(0,0)$. However, a little further analysis shows that the surface has a saddle point at $(0,0)$.

(b) The critical point $\left(\frac{1}{3}, \frac{1}{\sqrt{6}}\right)$:

$f_{xx}\left(\frac{1}{3}, \frac{1}{\sqrt{6}}\right)$ = ________, $f_{xy}\left(\frac{1}{3}, \frac{1}{\sqrt{6}}\right)$ = ________, and $f_{yy}\left(\frac{1}{3}, \frac{1}{\sqrt{6}}\right) = \frac{4}{3}$. Then, $f_{xx}f_{yy} - f_{xy}^2$ = ______ and we conclude that the surface has a ____________ at $\left(\frac{1}{3}, \frac{1}{\sqrt{6}}\right)$.

---

48. $-x + 3y^2$, $(\frac{1}{3}, -\frac{1}{3})$, $(\frac{3}{4}, \frac{1}{2})$, 2, -1, 2, -1, -2, saddle point, -1, 5, local minimum

(c) The critical point $\left(\frac{1}{3}, -\frac{1}{\sqrt{6}}\right)$:

$f_{xx}\left(\frac{1}{3}, -\frac{1}{\sqrt{6}}\right) = 1$, $f_{xy}\left(\frac{1}{3}, -\frac{1}{\sqrt{6}}\right) = \frac{4}{\sqrt{6}}$, and $f_{yy}\left(\frac{1}{3}, -\frac{1}{\sqrt{6}}\right) =$ ________.

Thus, $f_{xx}f_{yy} - f_{xy}^2 =$ ________ and we conclude that the surface has a ______________ at $\left(\frac{1}{3}, -\frac{1}{\sqrt{6}}\right)$.

OBJECTIVE B: Find the absolute maxima and minima of a given function $f(x,y)$ over a specified domain.

50. Consider the function $f(x,y) = x^3 - xy + y^2$ on the closed triangular plate bounded by the lines $x = 0$, $y = 1$, $y = x$ in the first quadrant. First we consider the interior points of the region. For these we set

$$f_x = \_\_\_\_\_\_\_\_ = 0$$

$$f_y = \_\_\_\_\_\_\_\_ = 0.$$

Thus, the second equation gives $x = 2y$ and substitution into the first equation yields $12y^2 - y = 0$. Then, $y = 0$ or $y =$ ________. Hence the critical points are __________ and __________. However, the point __________ lies outside of the region so it will not be considered.

Next we consider the boundary of the triangular region.

(i) $x = 0$: $f(0,y) = y^2$ may be regarded as a function of y on the closed interval $0 \le y \le 1$. Its minimum occurs at $y = 0$ where $f(0,0) = 0$ and its maximum occurs at $y =$ __________ where $f(0,1) =$ __________.

(ii) $y = 1$: $f(x,1) =$ ____________ may be regarded as a function of x on the closed interval $0 \le x \le 1$. Its derivative is $3x^2 - 1$, which is zero when $x =$ ________ in the interval. We now determine the value of $f(x,1)$ at this point and the endpoints of the interval:

$f(\frac{1}{\sqrt{3}}, 1) =$ ______________, $f(0,1) =$ _____, $f(1,1) =$ _____.

(iii) $y = x$: $f(x,x) =$ _____ may be regarded as a function of x on the closed interval $0 \le x \le 1$. Its derivative is $3x^2$, which is positive over the interval, so the function is increasing. Thus the minimum value occurs at the endpoint ________ and the maximum value occurs at ________.

---

49. $3x^2 - 6xy^2$, $x - 2y^2$, $4y^3 - 6x^2y$, $2y^2 - 3x^2$, $(0,0)$, $x - 3x^2$, $\frac{1}{3}$, $\left(\frac{1}{3}, -\frac{1}{\sqrt{6}}\right)$, $-12xy$, 1, $-\frac{4}{\sqrt{6}}$, $-\frac{4}{3}$, saddle point, $\frac{4}{3}$, $-\frac{4}{3}$, saddle point

Putting all of this information together, we find that the function has an absolute maximum value of 1 occurring at (0,1) and (1,1) and an absolute minimum value of ____ occurring at ______.

12.9 LAGRANGE MULTIPLIERS

OBJECTIVE: Using the method of Lagrange multipliers, solve extremal problems for functions of several independent variables subject to one constraint equation.

51. To determine the minimum distance from the origin to the hyperbola $xy = 1$, we would want to minimize the function

$$f(x,y) = x^2 + y^2$$

subject to the constraint

$$g(x,y) = xy - 1 = 0.$$

We let $H(x,y,\lambda) = x^2 + y^2 - \lambda(xy - 1)$. Then, $H_x =$ ________ $= 0$, $H_y = 2y - \lambda x = 0$, $H_\lambda =$ ________ $= 0$. From the first two of these equations we obtain $x = \frac{1}{2}\lambda y$ and $y =$ ________, and subsequent substitution into the last equation $xy = 1$ gives ________ $= 1$. Since $xy = 1$ this yields $\lambda^2 = 4$ or, $\lambda = \pm 2$. Now, $0 = xy - 1 = x\left(\frac{1}{2}\lambda x\right) - 1 = \frac{\lambda x^2}{2} - 1$ implies $x^2 = \frac{2}{\lambda}$. Thus, λ cannot be negative for real x. Hence, $\lambda =$ ____. Then $x^2 = \frac{2}{\lambda} = 1$ or $x = \pm 1$. Since $xy = 1$ this provides the points (1,1) and ________. From the geometry of the problem it is clear that there is a minimum distance from the origin to the hypberbola, and it has the value

$$D = \sqrt{f(1,1)} = \sqrt{f(-1,-1)} = \_\_\_\_.$$

Notice that there is no maximum distance.

52. Determine the radius r and the height h of the cylinder of maximum surface area which can be inscribed in a sphere of radius a.

<u>Solution</u>. We want to maximize the surface area $f(r,h) = 2\pi rh$ of the inscribed cylinder subject to the constraint

$$r^2 + \left(\frac{h}{2}\right)^2 = a^2$$

---

50. $3x^2 - y$, $-x + 2y$, $\frac{1}{12}$, (0,0), $(\frac{1}{6},\frac{1}{12})$, $(\frac{1}{6},\frac{1}{12})$, 1, 1, $x^3 - x + 1$, $\frac{1}{\sqrt{3}}$, $\left(1 - \frac{2}{3\sqrt{3}}\right)$, 1, 1, x^3, (0,0), (1,1), 0, (0,0)

51. $2x - \lambda y$, $-xy + 1$, $\frac{1}{2}\lambda x$, $\frac{1}{4}\lambda^2 xy$, 2, (-1,-1), $\sqrt{2}$

as in the figure at the right. Assume that both $r > 0$ and $h > 0$ so we do have an inscribed cylinder. Let

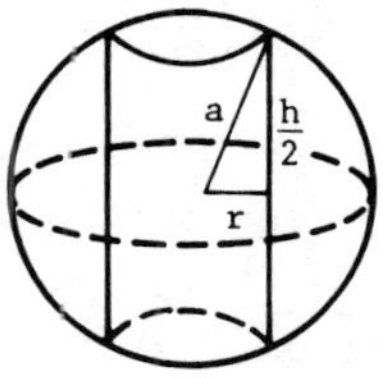

$$H(r,h,\lambda) = 2\pi rh - \lambda\left(r^2 + \frac{h^2}{4} - a^2\right).$$

Then,

$H_r =$ ______________ $= 0$,

$H_h = 2\pi r - \frac{1}{2}h\lambda = 0$, and

$H_\lambda =$ ______________ $= 0$. If $\lambda = 0$, the equations $H_r = H_h = 0$ would require both $r = 0$ and $h = 0$, contrary to the assumption that we do have an inscribed cylinder. Thus, neither r, h, nor λ is zero. Also, from the equations $H_r = 0$ and $H_h = 0$, $\lambda r = \pi h$ and $\lambda h = 4\pi r$. Division of these last equations gives

$$\frac{\lambda r}{\lambda h} = \frac{\pi h}{\_\_\_\_} \quad \text{or,} \quad 4r^2 = \_\_\_\_\_\_\_\_\_\_ .$$

Substitution into the constraint equation then yields $r^2 +$ ________ $= a^2$ or, $r =$ __________ (since $r > 0$). Then, $h = 2r =$ __________. The geometric nature of the problem ensures that the point $(r,h) = \left(\frac{a}{\sqrt{2}}, \sqrt{2}a\right)$ yields a maximum surface area

$$f\left(\frac{a}{\sqrt{2}}, \sqrt{2}a\right) = \_\_\_\_\_\_\_\_\_\_ .$$

53. To maximize the function $f(x,y,z) = x^2 + 2y - z^2$ subject to the two constraints $2x - y = 0$ and $y + z = 0$, form the function

$$H(x,y,z,\lambda,\mu) = x^2 + 2y - z^2 - \lambda(2x - y) - \mu(y + z).$$

Then,

$$H_\lambda = -2x + y = 0, \quad \text{and} \quad H_\mu = -y - z = 0 .$$

From $H_x = 0$ we have $x =$ ________. Substitution into $H_\lambda = 0$ and $H_\mu = 0$ gives $y = 2x =$ ________ and $z = -y =$ ________. Substitution of this expression for z into the equation $H_z = 0$ gives $\mu =$ ________. Thus, the equation for $H_y = 0$ becomes

$$2 + \lambda - \mu = 2 + \lambda - \_\_\_\_\_\_ = 0 \quad \text{or,} \quad \lambda = \_\_\_\_\_\_\_\_ .$$

Then, this value of λ gives

$$x = \frac{2}{3}, \quad y = \_\_\_\_\_, \quad z = \_\_\_\_\_, \quad \text{and} \quad \mu = \_\_\_\_\_ .$$

Therefore, the point $P_0(\frac{2}{3}, \frac{4}{3}, -\frac{4}{3})$ gives $f(\frac{2}{3}, \frac{4}{3}, -\frac{4}{3}) =$ ________. This is a <u>maximum</u> value for f because when $x = y/2$ and $z = -y$ from the constraint equations are substituted into $f(x,y,z)$ we find,

$$F(y) = \frac{y^2}{4} + 2y - y^2 = 2y - \frac{3}{4}y^2 \quad \text{and} \quad F''(y) < 0 .$$

---

52. $2\pi h - 2r\lambda$, $-r^2 - \frac{h^2}{4} + a^2$, $4\pi r$, h^2, r^2, $\frac{a}{\sqrt{2}}$, $\sqrt{2}a$, $2\pi a^2$

Thus, f does not have ________ value subject to the constraints.

12.10 TAYLOR'S FORMULA, SECOND DERIVATIVES, AND ERROR ESTIMATES

OBJECTIVE A: Know the second derivative test for $f(x,y)$ at a point (a,b) interior to a region R at which f_x and f_y are zero. Assume the first and second partial derivatives of $f(x,y)$ are continuous throughout R.

54. f has a local maximum at (a,b) if ________ and ________________ at (a,b).

55. f has a local minimum at (a,b) if ________ and ________________ at (a,b).

56. f has a saddle point at (a,b) if ________________ at (a,b).

57. The test is inconclusive if ________________ at (a,b).

OBJECTIVE B: Know the error estimate for the standard linear approximation of $f(x,y)$.

58. Assume that $f(x,y)$ and its first and second order partial derivatives are continuous throughout a rectangle R centered at the point (x_0,y_0). Then the absolute value $|E|$ of the difference between f and its linearization at a point (x_0,y_0) in R satisfies the inequality

$$|E| \le \underline{\hspace{6cm}} .$$

Here the number B is an upper bound for ________, ________, and ________ on R.

OBJECTIVE C: Use Taylor's formula to find a quadratic approximation to $f(x,y)$ near the origin. Assume appropriate continuity conditions on the partial derivatives through order 3.

59. According to Taylor's formula (17) in the text, a quadratic approximation to $f(x,y)$ is given by

$$f(x,y) \approx \underline{\hspace{8cm}} ,$$

---

53. $2x - 2\lambda$, $2 + \lambda - \mu$, $-2z - \mu = 0$, λ, 2λ, -2λ, 4λ, 4λ, $\frac{2}{3}$, $\frac{4}{3}$, $-\frac{4}{3}$, $\frac{8}{3}$, $\frac{4}{3}$, minimum

54. $f_{xx} < 0$ and $f_{xx}f_{yy} - f_{xy}^2 > 0$ 55. $f_{xx} > 0$ and $f_{xx}f_{yy} - f_{xy}^2 > 0$ 56. $f_{xx}f_{yy} - f_{xy}^2 < 0$

57. $f_{xx}f_{yy} - f_{xy}^2 = 0$ 58. $\frac{1}{2}B(|x - x_0| + |y - y_0|)^2$, $|f_{xx}|$, $|f_{xy}|$, $|f_{yy}|$

where all the first and second partial derivatives are to be evaluated at ______________.

60. To find a quadratic polynomial that approximates

$$f(x,y) = xe^y$$

near the origin we first calculate all first and second partial derivatives:

$$f_x = e^y,$$
$$f_y = \_\_\_\_\_\_,$$
$$f_{xx} = \_\_\_\_\_\_,$$
$$f_{xy} = \_\_\_\_\_\_,$$
$$f_{yy} = xe^y.$$

Then,

$$f(0,0) = 0,$$
$$f_x(0,0) = 1,$$
$$f_y(0,0) = \_\_\_\_\_\_,$$
$$f_{xx}(0,0) = \_\_\_\_\_\_,$$
$$f_{xy}(0,0) = \_\_\_\_\_\_,$$
$$f_{yy}(0,0) = \_\_\_\_\_\_.$$

A quadratic approximation is

$$xe^y \approx \_\_\_\_\_\_\_\_\_\_\_\_.$$

OBJECTIVE D: Suppose $w = f(x,y)$ is a twice-differentiable function of x and y, and $x = x(t)$, $y = y(t)$ are twice-differentiable functions of t. Calculate $\frac{d^2w}{dt^2}$.

61. Find $\frac{d^2w}{dt^2}$ if $w = f(x,y)$, $x = t^2$, $y = \cos t$.

Solution. From the chain rule,

$$\frac{dw}{dt} = f_x \frac{dx}{dt} + f_y \frac{dy}{dt} = \_\_\_\_\_\_\_\_\_\_\_\_ .$$

Therefore,

$$\frac{d^2w}{dt^2} = \frac{d}{dt}(2tf_x) + \frac{d}{dt}(-\sin t \cdot f_y)$$
$$= 2f_x + 2t\frac{d}{dt}(f_x) - (\cos t)f_y - (\sin t)\frac{d}{dt}(\_\_\_\_\_\_).$$

Applying the chain rule again,

---

59. $f(0,0) + xf_x + yf_y + \frac{1}{2!}(x^2f_{xx} + 2xyf_{xy} + y^2f_{yy})$, the origin

60. xe^y, 0, e^y, 0, 0, 1, 0, $x + xy$

$$\frac{d}{dt}(f_x) = f_{xx}\frac{dx}{dt} + \underline{\hspace{3cm}}$$
$$= \underline{\hspace{3cm}} + (-\sin t)f_{xy},$$
$$\frac{d}{dt}(f_y) = \underline{\hspace{4cm}} + f_{yy}\frac{dy}{dt}$$
$$= 2tf_{yx} + (-\sin t)f_{yy}.$$

Substituting these expressions into the formula for $\frac{d^2w}{dt^2}$ gives

$$\frac{d^2w}{dt^2} = 2f_x + 2t\frac{d}{dt}(f_x) - (\cos t)f_y - (\sin t)\frac{d}{dt}(f_y)$$
$$= 2f_x + 2t[\underline{\hspace{6cm}}]$$
$$- (\cos t)f_y - (\sin t)[\underline{\hspace{7cm}}]$$
$$= 2f_x - (\cos t)f_y + 2t^2 f_{xx}$$
$$- (\underline{\hspace{2.5cm}})f_{xy} + (\sin^2 t)f_{yy}.$$

OBJECTIVE E: Suppose $w = f(u,v)$ where $f(u,v)$ is a twice-differentiable function of u and v, and $u = u(x,y)$, $v = v(x,y)$ are twice-differentiable functions of x and y. Calculate the second-order partials w_{xx}, w_{xy}, w_{yx}, and w_{yy}.

62. Consider $w = f(u)$, where $u = x \cos y$. Then,

$$w_x = \frac{dw}{du}\frac{\partial u}{\partial x} = \underline{\hspace{4cm}},$$

$$w_y = \frac{dw}{du}\frac{\partial u}{\partial y} = \underline{\hspace{4cm}},$$

$$w_{xx} = \frac{\partial}{\partial x}(w_x) = f''(u)\frac{\partial u}{\partial x}\cos y = \underline{\hspace{4cm}},$$

$$w_{xy} = \frac{\partial}{\partial y}(w_x) = f''(u)\frac{\partial u}{\partial y}\cos y + (\underline{\hspace{4cm}})$$
$$= \underline{\hspace{8cm}},$$

$$w_{yx} = \frac{\partial}{\partial x}(w_y) = -f'(u)\sin y + (\underline{\hspace{5cm}})$$
$$= \underline{\hspace{8cm}},$$

$$w_{yy} = \frac{\partial}{\partial y}(w_y) = \underline{\hspace{8cm}}$$
$$= x^2 f''(u)\sin^2 y - xf'(u)\cos y.$$

---

61. $2tf_x - (\sin t)f_y$, f_y, $f_{xy}\frac{dy}{dt}$, $2tf_{xx}$, $f_{yx}\frac{dx}{dt}$, $2tf_{xx} - (\sin t)f_{xy}$, $2tf_{yx} + (-\sin t)f_{yy}$, $4t \sin t$

62. $f'(u)\cos y$, $-xf'(u)\sin y$, $f''(u)\cos^2 y$, $f'(u)(-\sin y)$, $-xf''(u)\sin y \cos y - f'(u)\sin y$, $-xf''(u)\frac{\partial u}{\partial x}\sin y$, $-f'(u)\sin y - xf''(u)\cos y \sin y$, $-xf''(u)\frac{\partial u}{\partial y}\sin y - xf'(u)\cos y$

CHAPTER 12 SELF-TEST

1. Determine, if possible, the following limits. If the limit exists, say what it is; if it does not exist, say why not.

   (a) $\lim\limits_{(x,y)\to(-1,1)} \dfrac{4x^2 - 2y + 3}{x^2 - y^2 - 1}$ (b) $\lim\limits_{(x,y)\to(0,0)} \dfrac{y^2}{x^2 + y^2}$

   (c) $\lim\limits_{(x,y)\to(0,0)} \dfrac{x - x \cos y}{2y \sin x}$

2. (a) Sketch the surface $w = f(x,y) = x^2 - 2$ in space.
   (b) Sketch the level curves of the function $f(x,y) = y - x^2 + x$ for $w = 0$, $w = 2$, and $w = -2$.
   (c) Find the largest possible xy-domain on which $w = \ln \frac{x}{y}$ is a real variable.

3. Find all first- and second-order partial derivatives.
   (a) $w = 3e^{2x} \cos y$ (b) $f(x,y,z) = zx^y$, $x > 0$

4. Find the normal line to the surface $f(x,y) = e^x \sin y$ at the point $P_0(1, \frac{\pi}{2}, e)$.

5. Find an equation of the tangent plane to the hyperboloid $4x^2 - 9y^2 - 9z^2 - 36 = 0$ at $P_0(3\sqrt{3}, 2, 2)$.

6. (a) Find the directional derivative of the function $f = z \tan^{-1} \frac{x}{y}$ at the point $P_0(1,1,2)$, and in the direction $\vec{A} = -6\vec{i} + 2\vec{j} - 3\vec{k}$.
   (b) What is the maximum value of the directional derivatives of f at P_0, and the direction of the maximum rate of change?

7. Find the indicated derivatives using the chain rule.
   (a) $\frac{dw}{dt}$, for $w = t^2 + x \sin y$, $x = \frac{1}{t}$, $y = \tan^{1} t$
   (b) $\frac{\partial^2 w}{\partial v^2}$, for $w = \sin(4x + 5y)$, $x = u + v$, $y = u - v$

8. If $w = x + f(xy)$, where f is a differentiable function, show that $x \frac{\partial w}{\partial x} - y \frac{\partial w}{\partial y} = x$.

9. If $w = xy + z^2 + t$ and $x - y + z = t$, find $\left(\frac{\partial w}{\partial t}\right)_{x,y}$.

10. Test the surface $z = xy^2 - 2xy + 2x^2 - 15x$ for maxima, minima, and saddle points.

11. Find the maximum value of $w = xyz$ among all points lying on the intersection of the planes $x + y + z = 40$ and $x + y - z = 0$.

12. Find the absolute maximum and absolute minimum of $f(x,y) = 48xy - 32x^3 - 24y^2$ in the region bounded by the square $0 \le x \le 1$ and $0 \le y \le 1$.

13. Find the change along the plane tangent to the surface $f(x,y) = \frac{x - y}{x + y}$ at $P_0(-1,2,-3)$, when $\Delta x = -0.1$ and $\Delta y = 0.02$. Compare this value with the increment Δf.

14. Find a linear approximation to the function $f(x,y) = xye^{x+y}$ near the point $(\frac{1}{2},-\frac{1}{2})$.

15. Estimate the change in the volume

$$V = \frac{1}{3}\pi h(R^2 + Rr + r^2)$$

of the frustrum of a cone if the upper radius r is decreased from 4 to 3.8 cm, the base radius R is increased from 6 to 6.1 cm, and the height is increased from 8 to 8.3 cm.

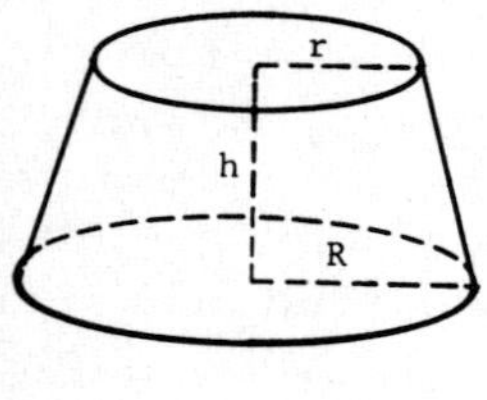

16. Find a quadratic approximation to the function $f(x,y) = \frac{1}{1 - x} + e^y$ near the origin.

17. Suppose that the production of a certain commodity depends on two inputs, say A and B. The amounts of these are given by 100x and 100y, whose prices per unit are, respectively, \$4 and \$1. The amount of output is given by 100z, the price per unit of which is \$9. Furthermore, the production function is given by

$$f(x,y) = 5 - \frac{1}{x} - \frac{1}{y}.$$

Determine the greatest profit.

SOLUTIONS TO CHAPTER 12 SELF-TEST

1. (a) $\lim_{(x,y)\to(-1,1)} \frac{4x^2 - 2y + 3}{x^2 - y^2 - 1} = \frac{4(-1)^2 - 2(1) + 3}{(-1)^2 - (1)^2 - 1} = \frac{5}{-1} = -5.$

(b) Along the line $y = x$, $f(x,y) = f(x,x) = \frac{x^2}{x^2 + x^2} = \frac{1}{2}$, $x \neq 0$.

Along the line $y = 2x$, $f(x,y) = f(x,2x) = \frac{4x^2}{x^2 + 4x^2} = \frac{4}{5}$, $x \neq 0$.
Therefore, the limits along different paths do not agree so we conclude that f has no limit as $(x,y) \to (0,0)$.

(c) $\lim_{(x,y)\to(0,0)} \frac{x - x\cos y}{2y \sin x} = \lim_{(x,y)\to(0,0)} \frac{x(1 - \cos y)}{2 \sin x \cdot y}$

$= \lim_{x\to 0} \frac{x}{2 \sin x} \cdot \lim_{y\to 0} \frac{1 - \cos y}{y} = \frac{1}{2} \cdot 0 = 0.$

2. (a) For every value of y, f is the parabola

$f(x,y) = x^2 - 2$.

The graph of this cylinder is sketched at the right.

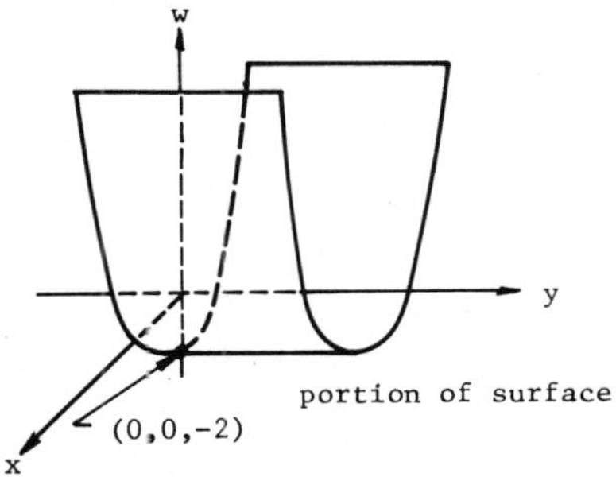

(b) For any fixed $w = c$,
$y - x^2 + x = c$ or,
$y - c = x^2 - x$ gives
$y - \left(c - \frac{1}{4}\right) = \left(x - \frac{1}{2}\right)^2$,
which is a parabola. The level curves $w = 0, 2, -2$ are sketched at the right.

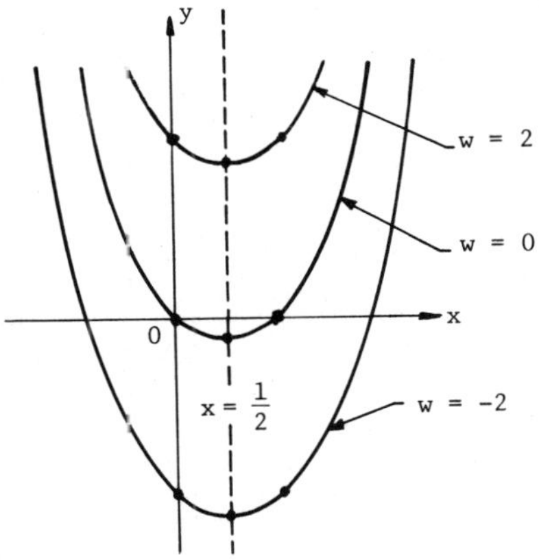

(c) For $w = \ln \frac{x}{y}$ to be real-valued it is necessary that $y \neq 0$ and that $\frac{x}{y} > 0$. Therefore, the domain is the set of points (x,y) where x and y are both positive, or both negative (i.e., the first and third quadrants of the xy-plane excluding the axes).

3. (a) $\frac{\partial w}{\partial x} = 6e^{2x} \cos y$, $\frac{\partial w}{\partial y} = -3e^{2x} \sin y$, $\frac{\partial^2 w}{\partial x \partial y} = \frac{\partial^2 w}{\partial y \partial x} = -6e^{2x} \sin y$,

$\frac{\partial^2 w}{\partial x^2} = 12e^{2x} \cos y$, $\frac{\partial^2 w}{\partial y^2} = -3e^{2x} \cos y$

(b) $f_x = yzx^{y-1}$, $f_y = zx^y \ln x$, $f_z = x^y$, $f_{xx} = y(y - 1)zx^{y-2}$,

$f_{xy} = zx^{y-1} + yzx^{y-1} \ln x$, $f_{xz} = yx^{y-1}$, $f_{yx} = zx^{y-1} + yzx^{y-1} \ln x$,

$f_{yy} = zx^y(\ln x)^2$, $f_{yz} = x^y \ln x$, $f_{zx} = yx^{y-1}$, $f_{zy} = x^y \ln x$,

$f_{zz} = 0$

4. Notice that the point P_0 does lie on the surface since its coordinates satisfy the equation $w = e^x \sin y$. Next,

$f_x\left(1, \frac{\pi}{2}\right) = e^x \sin y\Big|_{\left(1,\frac{\pi}{2}\right)} = e$, and $f_y\left(1, \frac{\pi}{2}\right) = e^x \cos y\Big|_{\left(1,\frac{\pi}{2}\right)} = 0$.

Thus, the vector $\vec{N} = e\vec{i} + 0\vec{j} - \vec{k}$ is normal to the surface at P_0. The normal line can be represented parametrically by

$$x = 1 + et, \quad y = \frac{\pi}{2}, \quad z = e - t.$$

5. Let $g(x,y,z) = 4x^2 - 9y^2 - 9z^2$. Notice that P_0 does lie on the given surface since $g(3\sqrt{3},2,2) = 36$. Next,

$g_x(3\sqrt{3}, 2, 2) = 8x|_{P_0} = 24\sqrt{3}$,

$g_y(3\sqrt{3}, 2, 2) = -18y|_{P_0} = -36$,

$g_z(3\sqrt{3}, 2, 2) = -18z|_{P_0} = -36$.

The vector grad $g(P_0) = 24\sqrt{3}\vec{i} - 36\vec{j} - 36\vec{k}$ is normal to the surface at P_0. Hence,

$$24\sqrt{3}(x - 3\sqrt{3}) - 36(y - 2) - 36(z - 2) = 0$$

or,

$$2\sqrt{3}x - 3y - 3z = 6$$

is an equation of the tangent plane.

6. (a) $f_x = z \cdot \frac{1}{1 + (x/y)^2} \cdot \frac{1}{y} = \frac{zy}{x^2 + y^2}$,

$f_y = z \cdot \frac{1}{1 + (x/y)^2} \cdot \left(\frac{-x}{y^2}\right) = \frac{-zx}{x^2 + y^2}$,

and

$$f_z = \tan^{-1}\frac{x}{y}$$

Then, $\vec{\nabla} f(P_0) = f_x(1,1,2)\vec{i} + f_y(1,1,2)\vec{j} + f_z(1,1,2)\vec{k}$
$= \vec{i} - \vec{j} + \frac{\pi}{4}\vec{k}.$

A unit vector in the direction of $\vec{A}$ is

$$\vec{u} = \frac{\vec{A}}{|\vec{A}|} = \frac{\vec{A}}{\sqrt{36 + 4 + 9}} = -\frac{6}{7}\vec{i} + \frac{2}{7}\vec{j} - \frac{3}{7}\vec{k}\ .$$

Thus, the directional derivative of f in the direction $\vec{A}$ at P_0 is

$$\vec{\nabla} f \cdot \vec{u} = -\frac{6}{7} - \frac{2}{7} - \frac{3\pi}{28} = -\frac{32 + 3\pi}{28} \approx -1.48.$$

(b) The direction of the maximum rate of change is in the direction of the gradient, $\vec{\nabla} f$. The value of the directional derivative in that direction is

$$|\vec{\nabla} f| = \sqrt{1 + 1 + \left(\frac{\pi}{4}\right)^2} = \frac{1}{4}\sqrt{32 + \pi^2} \approx 1.62.$$

7. (a) Let $z = t$ so that $w = z^2 + x \sin y$. Then,

$$\frac{dw}{dt} = \frac{\partial w}{\partial x}\frac{dx}{dt} + \frac{\partial w}{\partial y}\frac{dy}{dt} + \frac{\partial w}{\partial z}\frac{dz}{dt}$$
$$= (\sin y)\left(-t^{-2}\right) + (x \cos y)\left(\frac{1}{1 + t^2}\right) + (2z)(1)$$
$$= -t^{-2}\sin(\tan^{-1} t) + \frac{1}{t(1 + t^2)}\cos(\tan^{-1} t) + 2t.$$

(b) $\frac{\partial w}{\partial v} = \frac{\partial w}{\partial x}\frac{\partial x}{\partial v} + \frac{\partial w}{\partial y}\frac{\partial y}{\partial v} = 4\cos(4x + 5y) - 5\cos(4x + 5y)$

Then, setting $r = \frac{\partial w}{\partial v} = -\cos(4x + 5y)$,

$$\frac{\partial^2 w}{\partial v^2} = \frac{\partial}{\partial v}\left(\frac{\partial w}{\partial v}\right) = \frac{\partial r}{\partial v} = \frac{\partial r}{\partial x}\frac{\partial x}{\partial v} + \frac{\partial r}{\partial y}\frac{\partial y}{\partial v}$$
$$= 4\sin(4x + 5y) - 5\sin(4x + 5y) = -\sin(4x + 5y)$$
$$= -\sin(9u - v).$$

8. Let $u = xy$, so that $w = x + f(u)$. Then,

$$\frac{\partial w}{\partial x} = 1 + f'(u)\frac{\partial u}{\partial x} = 1 + yf'(xy), \quad \text{and}$$
$$\frac{\partial w}{\partial y} = f'(u)\frac{\partial u}{\partial y} = xf'(xy).$$

Therefore,

$$x\frac{\partial w}{\partial x} - y\frac{\partial w}{\partial y} = x\left(1 + yf'(xy)\right) = y\left(xf'(xy)\right) = x, \quad \text{as claimed.}$$

9. There are 5 unknowns w,x,y,z,t and 2 equations given in the problem. We are given that x,y,t are independent and w,z are dependent. An arrow diagram shows how the variables are related:

$$\begin{pmatrix} x \\ y \\ t \end{pmatrix} \rightarrow \begin{pmatrix} x \\ y \\ z \\ t \end{pmatrix} \rightarrow w$$

To find $\frac{\partial w}{\partial t}$ in this situation:

$$\frac{\partial w}{\partial t} = \frac{\partial w}{\partial x}\frac{\partial x}{\partial t} + \frac{\partial w}{\partial y}\frac{\partial y}{\partial t} + \frac{\partial w}{\partial z}\frac{\partial z}{\partial t} + \frac{\partial w}{\partial t}\frac{\partial t}{\partial t} .$$

Using the formula for w,

$$w = xy + z^2 + t,$$

$$\frac{\partial w}{\partial t} = y\frac{\partial x}{\partial t} + x\frac{\partial y}{\partial t} + 2z\frac{\partial z}{\partial t} + (1)\frac{\partial t}{\partial t} .$$

Now the variables x, y, and t are independent and we can solve for z in terms of them from the second equation given in the problem:

$$z = t - x + y .$$

Thus,

$$\frac{\partial x}{\partial t} = 0, \quad \frac{\partial y}{\partial t} = 0, \quad \frac{\partial z}{\partial t} = 1, \quad \frac{\partial t}{\partial t} = 1 .$$

Substitution into the expression for $\frac{\partial w}{\partial t}$ gives the desired result:

$$\begin{aligned} \left(\frac{\partial w}{\partial t}\right)_{x,y} &= y \cdot 0 + x \cdot 0 + 2z(1) + (1)(1) \\ &= 2z + 1 \\ &= 2(t - x + y) + 1, \end{aligned}$$ in terms of the independent variables.

10. Let $f(x,y) = xy^2 - 2xy + 2x^2 - 15x$. Then $f_x = y^2 - 2y + 4x - 15$ and $f_y = 2xy - 2x$. Thus, $f_y = 2x(y - 1) = 0$, if $x = 0$ or $y = 1$. If $f_x = 0$ and $x = 0$, then $y^2 - 2y - 15 = 0$, or $(y - 5)(y + 3) = 0$. thus, $(0,5)$ and $(0,-3)$ are critical points. If $f_x = 0$ and $y = 1$, then $1 - 2 + 4x - 15 = 0$, or $x = 4$. Thus, $(4,1)$ is a critical point. We test these critical points with $f_{xx} = 4$, $f_{xy} = 2y - 2$, and $f_{yy} = 2x$.

At $(0,-3)$: Let $A = f_{xx}(0,-3) = 4$, $B = f_{xy}(0,-3) = -8$, and $C = f_{yy}(0,-3) = 0$. Then, $AC - B^2 = -64 < 0$, so the surface has a saddle point at $(0,-3)$.

At $(0,5)$: Let $A = f_{xx}(0,5) = 4$, $B = f_{xy}(0,5) = 8$, and $C = f_{yy}(0,5) = 0$. Then $AC - B^2 = -64 < 0$, so again the surface has a saddle point at $(0,5)$.

At $(4,1)$: Let $A = f_{xx}(4,1) = 4$, $B = f_{xy}(4,1) = 0$, and $C = f_{yy}(4,1) = 8$. Then, $AC - B^2 = 32 > 0$ and $A > 0$, so the surface has a relative minimum at $(4,1)$.

11. Form the function

$$H(x,y,z,\lambda,\mu) = xyz - \lambda(x + y + z - 40) - \mu(x + y - z) .$$

Setting $H_x = H_y = H_z = H_\lambda = H_\mu = 0$ gives the equations

$yz - \lambda - \mu = 0$ (1) $\qquad xz - \lambda - \mu = 0$ (2)

$xy - \lambda + \mu = 0$ (3) $\qquad -x - y - z + 40 = 0$ (4)

$-x - y + z = 0$ (5)

Subtracting equation (4) from (5) gives $2z - 40 = 0$ or $z = 20$. Substitution into (1) and (2) yields

$$\left.\begin{aligned} 20y &= \lambda + \mu \\ 20x &= \lambda + \mu \end{aligned}\right\} \quad \text{Thus, } x = y .$$

Substitution into (5) gives $-2x + 20 = 0$ or $x = 10$ and $y = 10$. Thus, $(10,10,20)$ is the unique extremal point subject to the two constraints. Thus, $w = 10 \cdot 10 \cdot 20 = 2000$ is the maximum value.

To see that this is a maximum, note that the intersection of the two planes defined by the constraint equations is the line $x + y = 20$, $z = 20$. That is, we can think of maximizing $w = 20xy$ for points on the line $x + y = 20$. For $y > 20$ or $x > 20$, the line passes into the second or fourth quadrants, respectively, whence $w = 20xy$ would be negative. Thus, there can be no minimum. The maximum occurs precisely when $x = y = 10$ along that line.

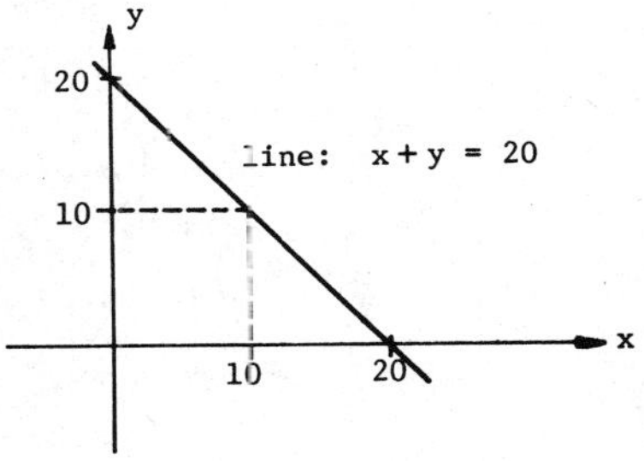

12. We first consider the points interior to the square:

$$\left.\begin{aligned} \frac{\partial f}{\partial x} &= 48y - 96x^2 = 0 \\ \frac{\partial f}{\partial y} &= 48x - 48y = 0 \end{aligned}\right\} \text{ Solving simultaneously, } \quad y = x \text{ and } 48x - 96x^2 = 0 \text{ or } x = 0, \ x = \tfrac{1}{2}.$$

Thus, $(0,0)$ and $(\frac{1}{2},\frac{1}{2})$ are critical points (one of which occurs on the boundary of the specified region). Next,

$$f(0,0) = 0 \quad \text{and} \quad f(\tfrac{1}{2},\tfrac{1}{2}) = \frac{48}{4} - \frac{32}{8} - \frac{24}{4} = 2 .$$

We consider the four boundaries of the region:

(a) $f(x,0) = -32x^3$ has a minimum value of -32 when $x = 1$ and a maximum value of 0 when $x = 0$.

(b) $f(1,y) = 48y - 32 - 24y^2$. Now,

$$\frac{d}{dy}(48y - 32 - 24y^2) = 48 - 48y = 0 \quad \text{implies} \quad y = 1.$$

When $y = 1$ we have $f(1,1) = -8$ which is a relative maximum for $f(1,y)$. The minimum value is $f(1,0) = -32$.

(c) $f(x,1) = 48x - 32x^3 - 24$. Here,

$$\frac{d}{dx}(48x - 32x^3 - 24) = 48 - 96x^2 = 0 \quad \text{implies} \quad x = \pm\frac{\sqrt{2}}{2}.$$

We must have $x \geq 0$ so we pick $x = \frac{\sqrt{2}}{2}$. Then,

$f\left(\frac{\sqrt{2}}{2},1\right) = 16\sqrt{2} - 24$ is a relative maximum. Moreover, $f(0,1) = -24$ is the absolute minimum on this boundary.

(d) $f(0,y) = -24y^2$ which has a minimum value of -24 when $y = 1$ and a maximum value of 0 when $y = 0$.

Putting all of this together yields $-32 = f(1,0)$ as the absolute minimum and $2 = f(\frac{1}{2},\frac{1}{2})$ as the absolute maximum.

13. $\Delta T = \frac{\partial w}{\partial x}\,\Delta x + \frac{\partial w}{\partial y}\,\Delta y = \frac{2y}{(x + y)^2}\,\Delta x - \frac{2x}{(x + y)^2}\,\Delta y$

Thus for the point $(x_0,y_0) = (-1,2)$, $\Delta x = -0.1$ and $\Delta y = 0.02$, we find

$$\Delta T = \tfrac{4}{1}(-0.1) + \tfrac{2}{1}(0.02) = -0.36\ .$$

On the other hand, the increment giving the change along the surface $w = f(x,y)$ itself is

$$\Delta f = f(-1.1,2.02) - f(-1,2) = \frac{-1.1 - 2.02}{-1.1 + 2.02} - \frac{-1 - 2}{-1 + 2}$$
$$= \frac{-3.12}{0.92} + \frac{3}{1} = -0.39.$$

14. Calculating the partial derivatives

$$f_x(1,-1) = ye^{x+y} + xye^{x+y}\Big|_{\left(\frac{1}{2},-\frac{1}{2}\right)} = -\tfrac{1}{2} - \tfrac{1}{4} = -\tfrac{3}{4}, \quad \text{and}$$

$$f_y(1,-1) = xe^{x+y} + xye^{x+y}\Big|_{\left(\frac{1}{2},-\frac{1}{2}\right)} = \tfrac{1}{2} - \tfrac{1}{4} = \tfrac{1}{4}\ .$$

Thus, a linear approximation near $\left(\frac{1}{2},-\frac{1}{2}\right)$ is given by

$$T(x,y) = f\left(\tfrac{1}{2},-\tfrac{1}{2}\right) + f_x\left(\tfrac{1}{2},-\tfrac{1}{2}\right)\left(x - \tfrac{1}{2}\right) + f_y\left(\tfrac{1}{2},-\tfrac{1}{2}\right)\left(y + \tfrac{1}{2}\right)$$
$$= -\tfrac{1}{4} + \left(-\tfrac{3}{4}\right)\left(x - \tfrac{1}{2}\right) + \tfrac{1}{4}\left(y + \tfrac{1}{2}\right), \quad \text{or} \quad T(x,y) = \tfrac{1}{4}(1 - 3x + y).$$

15. $\Delta V \approx \frac{\partial V}{\partial r}\,\Delta r + \frac{\partial V}{\partial R}\,\Delta R + \frac{\partial V}{\partial h}\,\Delta h$

$$= \tfrac{1}{3}\pi h(R + 2r)\Delta r + \tfrac{1}{3}\pi h(2R + r)\Delta R + \tfrac{1}{3}\pi(R^2 + Rr + r^2)\Delta h.$$

At $r = 4$, $R = 6$, $h = 8$, $\Delta r = -0.2$, $\Delta R = 0.1$, and $\Delta h = 0.3$, we find

$$\Delta V \approx \left(\tfrac{112\pi}{3}\right)(-0.2) + \left(\tfrac{128\pi}{3}\right)(0.1) + \left(\tfrac{76\pi}{3}\right)(0.3) = 4.4\pi.$$

The volume increases by about $4.4\pi \approx 13.8$ cubic centimeters.

16. $f(0,0) = \frac{1}{1 - x} + e^y\Big|_{(0,0)} = 2,$ $f_x(0,0) = \frac{1}{(1 - x)^2}\Big|_{(0,0)} = 1$

$f_y(0,0) = e^y\Big|_{(0,0)} = 1,$ $f_{xx}(0,0) = \frac{2}{(1 - x)^3}\Big|_{(0,0)} = 2$

$f_{xy}(0,0) = 0,$ $f_{yy}(0,0) = e^y\Big|_{(0,0)} = 1 .$

Thus,

$$\frac{1}{1 - x} + e^y \approx 2 + (x\cdot 1 + y\cdot 1) + \tfrac{1}{2}(x^2\cdot 2 + 2xy\cdot 0 + y^2\cdot 1)$$
$$= 2 + x + y + x^2 + \tfrac{1}{2}y^2 .$$

<u>Note</u>: From your study of the Maclaurin series in Section 8.7, the second degree Taylor polynomials of e^y and $\frac{1}{1 - x}$ near the origin are

$$e^y \approx 1 + y + \tfrac{1}{2}y^2$$

and

$$\frac{1}{1 - x} \approx 1 + x + x^2 .$$

17. We wish to maximize the profit function

$$P(x,y,z) = 9(100z) - 4(100x) - 100y$$

subject to the constraint given by the equation $z = 5 - \frac{1}{x} - \frac{1}{y}$. Thus, let

$$h(x,y,z,\lambda) = 900z - 400x - 100y - \lambda\left(\tfrac{1}{x} + \tfrac{1}{y} + z - 5\right) .$$

Setting $h_x = h_y = h_z = h_\lambda = 0$ gives the equations

$$-400 + \frac{\lambda}{x^2} = 0$$
$$-100 + \frac{\lambda}{y^2} = 0$$
$$900 - \lambda = 0$$
$$-\tfrac{1}{x} - \tfrac{1}{y} - z + 5 = 0$$

Solving simultaneously, $\lambda = 900$, $x^2 = \frac{900}{400}$ and $y^2 = \frac{900}{100}$. Thus, $x = \frac{3}{2}$, $y = 3$, and from the last equation, $z = 4$ (all variables must be positive here). Therefore,

$$P\left(\tfrac{3}{2}, 3, 4\right) = 900 \cdot 4 - 400 \cdot \tfrac{3}{2} - 100 \cdot 3 = 2700.$$

Because x and y are both in the interval $(0, \infty)$, and P is a negative number when x and y are either close to zero or very large, we conclude that this corresponds to a <u>maximum profit</u> of \$2700.

CHAPTER 13 MULTIPLE INTEGRALS

13.1 DOUBLE INTEGRALS

OBJECTIVE A: Evaluate a given (double) iterated integral, and sketch the region over which the integration extends.

1. $\int_0^1 \int_{x^3}^{x^2} xy \, dy \, dx$

$= \int_0^1 [\_\_\_\_\_\_\_\_]_{y=x^3}^{y=x^2} \, dx$

$= \int_0^1 \left(\frac{1}{2}x^5 - \_\_\_\_\_\_\_\_\right) dx$

$= \frac{1}{12}x^6 - \_\_\_\_\_\_\_\_]_{x=0}^{x=1}$

$= \frac{1}{12} - \_\_\_\_\_\_\_\_ = \_\_\_\_\_\_\_\_.$

Sketch the region of integration in the coordinate system provided.

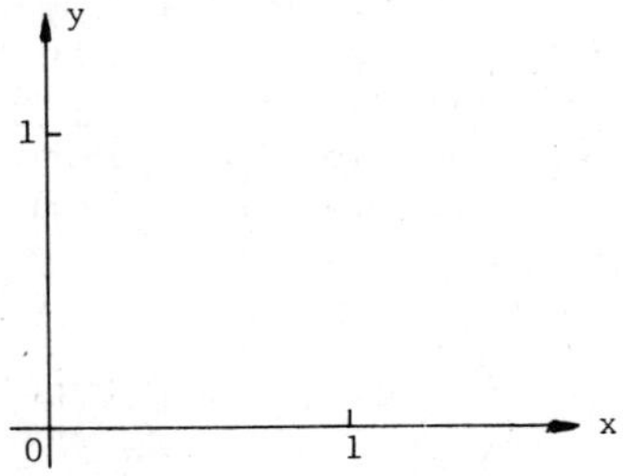

2. $\int_0^{\pi} \int_0^{y^2} \sin \frac{x}{y} \, dx \, dy$

$= \int_0^{\pi} [\_\_\_\_\_\_\_\_]_{x=0}^{x=y^2}$

$= \int_0^{\pi} (-y \cos y + \_\_\_\_\_) \, dy$

$= \left(-y \sin y]_{y=0}^{y=\pi} + \int_0^{\pi} \sin y \, dy\right)$

$+ \_\_\_\_\_\_\_\_]_{y=0}^{y=\pi}$

$= 0 + (\_\_\_\_\_)]_{y=0}^{y=\pi} + \frac{\pi^2}{2} = \_\_\_\_\_\_\_\_ \approx 6.93.$

Sketch the region of integration.

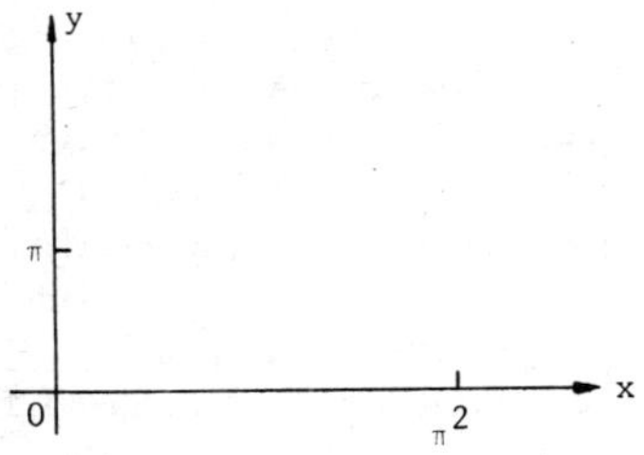

---

1. $\frac{1}{2}xy^2$, $\frac{1}{2}x^7$, $\frac{1}{16}x^8$, $\frac{1}{16}$, $\frac{1}{48}$

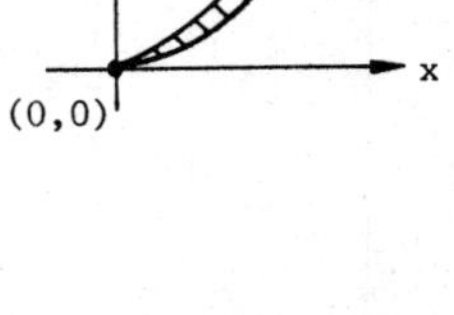

2. $-y \cos \frac{x}{y}$, y, $\frac{1}{2}y^2$, $-\cos y$, $\frac{\pi^2}{2} + 2$

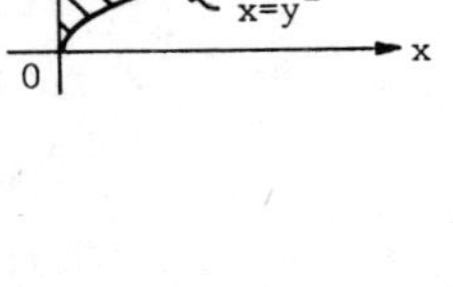

OBJECTIVE B: Given a (double) iterated integral, write an equivalent double iterated integral with the order of integration reversed. Sketch the region over which the integration takes place and evaluate the new integral.

3. $\int_0^2 \int_y^2 e^{x^2}\, dx\, dy$

First sketch the region of integration in the coordinate system at the right: as y varies from $y = 0$ to $y = 2$, x varies from ________________.
Reversing the order of integration: as x varies from $x = 0$ to $x = 2$, y varies from ________________.
Thus,

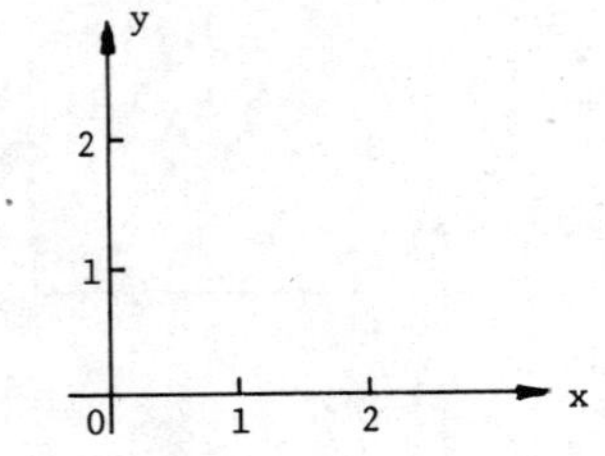

$$\int_0^2 \int_y^2 e^{x^2}\, dx\, dy = \int_{\_\_}^{\_\_} \int_{\_\_}^{\_\_} e^{x^2}\, dy\, dx$$

$$= \int_0^2 \underline{\qquad\qquad}\Big]_{y=0}^{y=x} dx = \int_0^2 \underline{\qquad\qquad}\, dx$$

$$= \underline{\qquad\qquad}\Big]_{x=0}^{x=2} = \underline{\qquad\qquad\qquad} \approx 26.80.$$

4. $\int_0^2 \int_y^{6-y^2} 2xy^2\, dx\, dy$

First sketch the region of integration in the coordinate system at the right: as y varies from $y = 0$ to $y = 2$, x varies from ____________________.
Reversing the order of integration, as x varies from $x = 0$ to $x = 2$, y varies from ________________; but as x varies from $x = 2$ to $x = 6$, y varies from ________________.
Thus, the iterated integral becomes the sum of two iterated integrals when the order of integration is reversed:

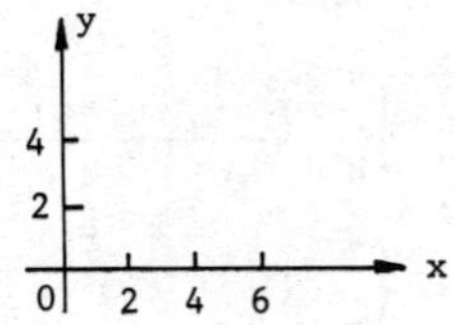

---

3. $x = y$ to $x = 2$, $y = 0$ to $y = x$,

$\int_0^2 \int_0^x$, ye^{x^2}, xe^{x^2}, $\frac{1}{2}e^{x^2}$,

$\frac{1}{2}\left(e^4 - 1\right)$

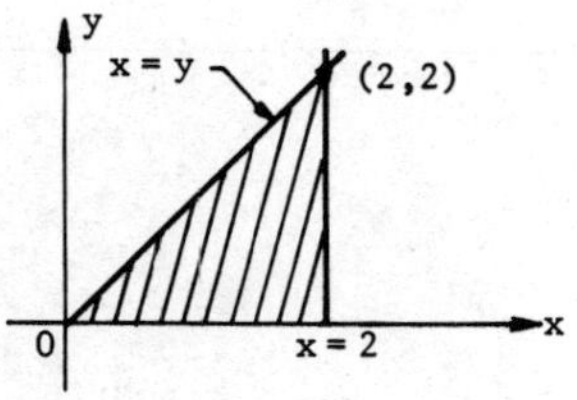

$$\int_0^2 \int_y^{6-y^2} 2xy^2 \, dx \, dy = \int_{\_\_}^{\_\_} \int_{\_\_}^{\_\_} 2xy^2 \, dy \, dx + \int_{\_\_}^{\_\_} \int_{\_\_}^{\_\_} 2xy^2 \, dy \, dx$$

$$= \int_0^2 \_\_\_\_\_\_ \Big]_{y=0}^{y=x} dx + \int_2^6 \frac{2}{3}xy^3\Big]_{\_\_}^{\_\_} dx$$

$$= \int_0^2 \frac{2}{3}x^4 \, dx + \int_2^6 \frac{2}{3}x(6 - x)^{3/2} \, dx$$

$$= \_\_\_\_\_\_ \Big]_{x=0}^{x=2} + \int_4^0 -\frac{2}{3}(6 - u)u^{3/2} \, du$$

(where $u = 6 - x$)

$$= \_\_\_\_\_\_ - \frac{2}{3}\left(\frac{12}{5}u^{5/2} - \frac{2}{7}u^{7/2}\right)\Big]_{u=4}^{u=0} \approx 31.09.$$

OBJECTIVE C: Find the volume of a solid whose base is a specified region A in the xy-plane, and whose top is a given surface $z = f(x,y)$.

5. The base of a solid is the region in the xy-plane that is bounded by the ellipse $x^2 + 9y^2 = 36$ for $y \le 0$. Sketch this region in the coordinate system at the right. The top of the solid is the plane $z = -y$. Thus, the volume of the solid is computed as the following double integral:

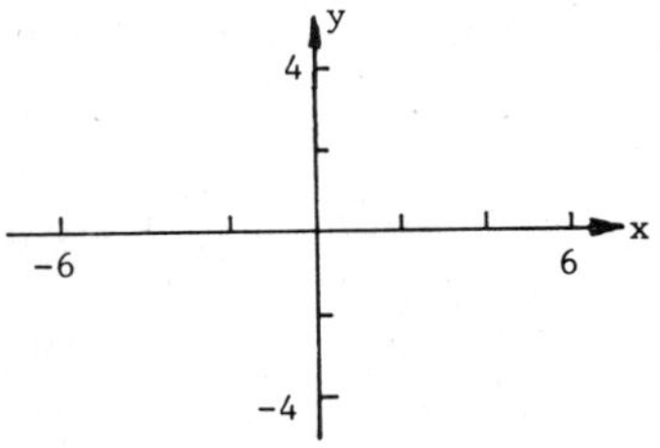

$$V = \int_{\_\_}^{\_\_} \int_{\_\_}^{\_\_} -y \, dy \, dx = \int_{-6}^{6} \_\_\_\_\_\_ \Big]_{y=\_\_}^{y=\_\_} dx$$

$$= \frac{1}{2}\int_{-6}^{6} \_\_\_\_\_\_ \, dx = \frac{1}{18}(\_\_\_\_\_\_)\Big]_{x=-6}^{x=6} = \_\_\_\_\_\_ .$$

---

4. $x = y$ to $x = 6 - y^2$, $y = 0$ to $y = x$,
$y = 0$ to $y = \sqrt{6 - x}$,
$\int_0^2 \int_0^x + \int_2^6 \int_0^{\sqrt{6-x}}$, $\frac{2}{3}xy^3$,
$\Big]_{y=0}^{y=\sqrt{6-x}}$, $\frac{2}{15}x^5$, $\frac{64}{15}$

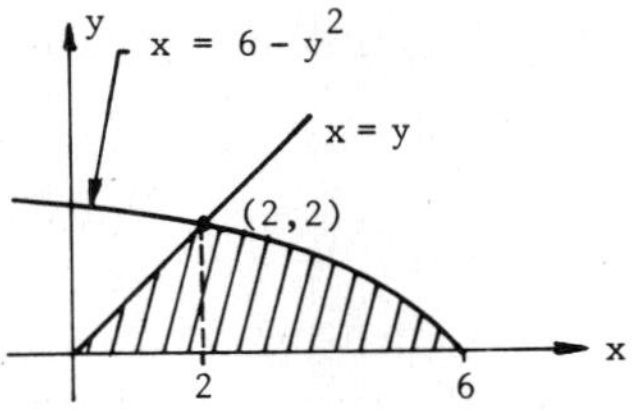

5. $\int_{-6}^{6} \int_{-\frac{1}{3}\sqrt{36-x^2}}^{0}$,
$-\frac{1}{2}y^2\Big]_{y=-\frac{1}{3}\sqrt{36-x^2}}^{y=0}$,
$\frac{1}{9}(36 - x^2)$, $36x - \frac{1}{3}x^3$, 16

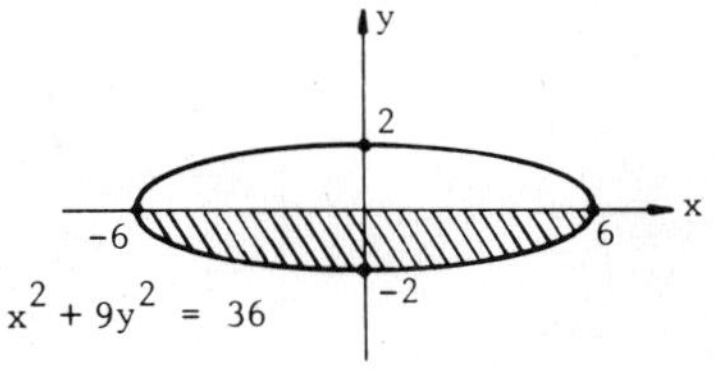

13.2 AREAS, MOMENTS, AND CENTERS OF MASS

OBJECTIVE A: For a specified region R in the xy-plane
(a) sketch the region R;
(b) label each bounding curve of the region with its equation, and find the coordinates of the boundary points where the curves intersect; and
(c) find the area of the region by evaluating an appropriate (double) iterated integral.

6. Let us find the area of the region R in the xy-plane bounded by the circle $x^2 + y^2 = 16$ and the parabola $y^2 = 6x$. First sketch the region R and label the bounding curves in the coordinate system at the right. Notice that we seek the area <u>inside</u> both curves because x must be positive in order that $y^2 = 6x$ hold for real numbers. Next we calculate the points of intersection of the circle and parabola. Substituting $y^2 = 6x$ into the equation for the circle gives

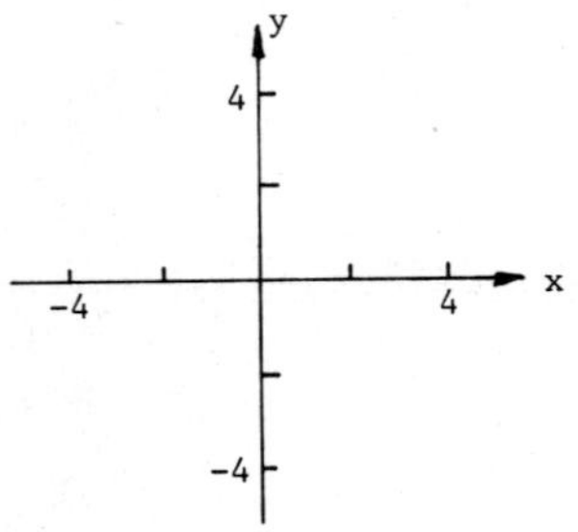

________ = 16 or, (x + 8)(________) = 0. Thus, x = _______ since x cannot be negative. Then $y^2 = 6x$ = _______. This yields the two points ___________ and ___________ as the boundary points where the two curves intersect. We now want to decide what order of integration we should choose. We see that <u>vertical</u> strips sometimes go from the lower branch of the parabola to the upper branch (if $0 \le x \le 2$), but sometimes from the lower semi-circle to the upper semi-circle (if $2 \le x \le 4$). Thus, integration in the order of first y and then x requires that the area be taken in two separate pieces.

On the other hand, <u>horizontal</u> strips always go from the parabola as the left boundary over to the circle on the right, and the area is given by the integral

$$A = \int_{\_\_\_}^{\_\_\_} \int_{\_\_\_}^{\_\_\_\_\_} dx\, dy \; .$$

---

6. $x^2 + 6x$, $x - 2$, 2, 12, $(2, -2\sqrt{3})$

$(2, 2\sqrt{3})$, $\int_{-2\sqrt{3}}^{2\sqrt{3}}$, $\int_{y^2/6}^{\sqrt{16 - y^2}}$

$\sqrt{16 - y^2} - \frac{1}{6}y^2$

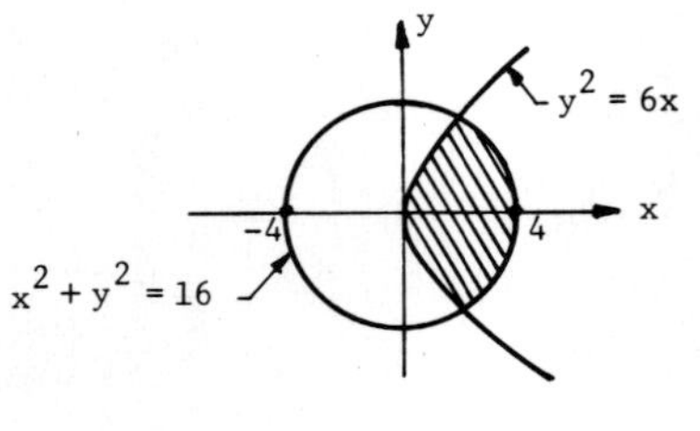

Evaluation of this integral gives the result

$$A = \int_{-2\sqrt{3}}^{2\sqrt{3}} (\underline{\hspace{6em}})\, dy$$

$$= \tfrac{1}{2}\left(y\sqrt{16 - y^2} + 16 \sin^{-1} \tfrac{y}{4}\right) - \tfrac{1}{18} y^3 \Big]_{y=-2\sqrt{3}}^{y=2\sqrt{3}}$$

$$= \frac{4\sqrt{3}}{3} + 8 \sin^{-1} \frac{\sqrt{3}}{2} - 8 \sin^{-1}\left(-\frac{\sqrt{3}}{2}\right)$$

$$= \frac{4\sqrt{3}}{3} + 8\left(\frac{\pi}{3}\right) - 8\left(-\frac{\pi}{3}\right) = \frac{4\sqrt{3} + 16\pi}{3} \approx 19.06.$$

7. Find the area of the region in the first quadrant that is bounded by the curves $x + y = 4$ and $y = \frac{3}{x}$.

Solution. Sketch the region in the coordinate system at the right, and label the bounding curves. To calculate the points of intersection of the line and the hyperbola, substitute $y = 4 - x$ into $xy = 3$ which gives the result ______________, or $(x - 3)(\underline{\hspace{3em}}) = 0$. This yields the two points $(3,1)$ and _______ as the boundary points where the two curves intersect. In this example, either order of integration leads to a single double integral giving the area. If we use horizontal strips, the area is given by

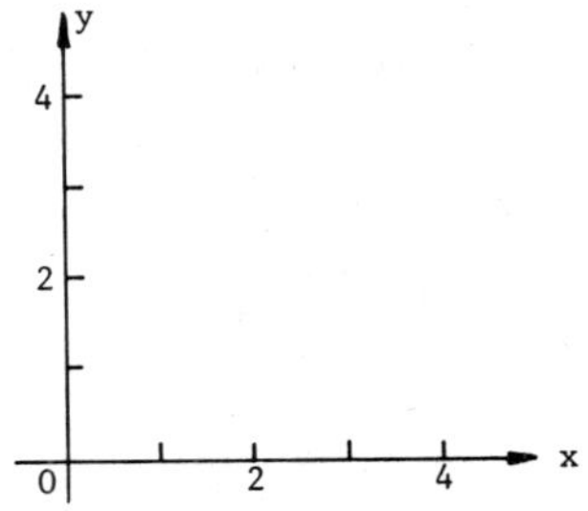

$$A = \int_{\_\_}^{\_\_} \int_{\_\_}^{\_\_} dx\, dy .$$

On the other hand, using vertical strips the area is given by

$$A = \int_{\_\_}^{\_\_} \int_{\_\_}^{\_\_} dy\, dx .$$

Evaluation of either integral (we take the latter) gives

$$A = \int_1^3 (\underline{\hspace{6em}})\, dx$$

$$= 4x - \tfrac{1}{2}x^2 - 3 \ln x\Big]_{x=1}^{x=3} = 4 - 3 \ln 3 \approx 0.704.$$

---

7. $x(4 - x) = 3$, $x - 1$, $(1,3)$,

$$\int_1^3 \int_{3/y}^{4-y} dx\, dy, \quad \int_1^3 \int_{3/x}^{4-x} dy\, dx,$$

$4 - x - \frac{3}{x}$

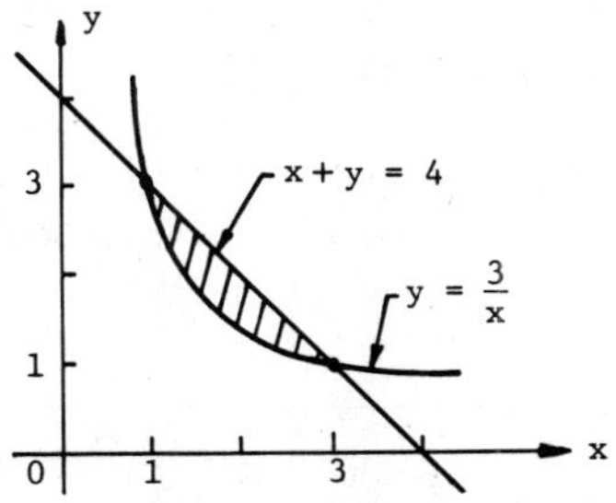

OBJECTIVE B: Given a plane region R in the xy-plane, find its center of mass.

8. Consider the region R in the xy-plane bounded by the curves $y^2 = x$ and $y = x$. The region R is sketched in the figure at the right. To find the center of mass we assume the region has constant uniform density $\delta(x,y) \equiv c$. First, calculate the mass of the region. This is given by the double integral,

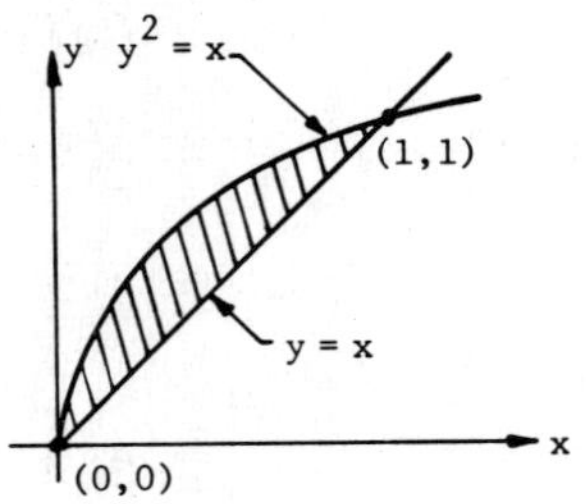

$$M = \iint \delta(x,y)\, dA = \int_{\_\_\_}^{\_\_\_} \int_{\_\_\_}^{\_\_\_} c\, dy\, dx$$

$$= \int_0^1 \underline{\qquad\qquad} dx = c\left(\tfrac{2}{3}x^{3/2} - \tfrac{1}{2}x^2\right)\Big]_{x=0}^{x=1} = \underline{\qquad\qquad}.$$

Next, calculate the moment of the mass with respect to the x-axis,

$$M_x = \iint \underline{\qquad\qquad} = \int_0^1 \int_x^{\sqrt{x}} cy\, dy\, dx$$

$$= \frac{c}{2}\int_0^1 \underline{\qquad\qquad}\Big]_{y=x}^{y=\sqrt{x}} dx = \frac{c}{2}\int_0^1 (x - x^2)\, dx$$

$$= \frac{c}{2}\left(\tfrac{1}{2}x^2 - \tfrac{1}{3}x^3\right)\Big]_{x=0}^{x=1} = \underline{\qquad\qquad}.$$

The moment of the mass with respect to the y-axis is,

$$M_y = \iint x\delta(x,y)\, dA = \int_{\_\_\_}^{\_\_\_} \int_{\_\_\_}^{\_\_\_} cx\, dy\, dx$$

$$= c\int_0^1 x(\sqrt{x} - x)\, dx = c(\underline{\qquad\qquad})\Big]_{x=0}^{x=1} = \underline{\qquad\qquad}.$$

We then obtain the coordinates of the center of mass,

$$\bar{x} = \frac{M_y}{M} = \underline{\qquad\qquad} \quad \text{and} \quad \bar{y} = \frac{M_x}{M} = \underline{\qquad\qquad}.$$

OBJECTIVE C: Given a plane region R in the xy-plane, find its moments of inertia about various axes.

9. Find the moments of inertia about the x-axis and about the y-axis for the plane region bounded by the parabola $y = kx^2$, $k > 0$, and the line $y = b$, $b > 0$.

Solution. A sketch of the region is given in the figure on the next page. The x-coordinates of the points of intersection of the line $y = b$ and the parabola $y = kx^2$ are $x = -\sqrt{b/k}$ and $x = \underline{\qquad\qquad}$.

---

8. $\int_0^1 \int_x^{\sqrt{x}}$, $c(\sqrt{x} - x)$, $\frac{c}{6}$, $y\,\delta(x,y)\,dA$, y^2, $\frac{c}{12}$, $\int_0^1 \int_x^{\sqrt{x}}$, $\frac{2}{5}x^{5/2} - \frac{1}{3}x^3$, $\frac{c}{15}$, $\frac{2}{5}$, $\frac{1}{2}$

We assume that the region is of constant uniform density $\delta(x,y) \equiv 1$. Then the moment of inertia about the x-axis is given by

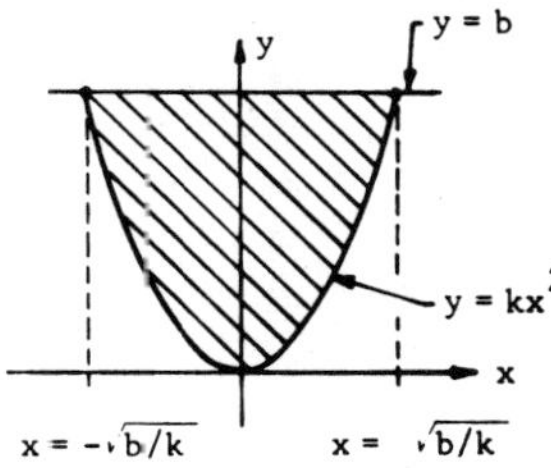

$$I_x = \iint y^2 \delta(x,y)\, dA$$

$$= \int_{\_\_\_}^{\_\_\_} \int_{\_\_\_}^{\_\_\_} y^2\, dx\, dy$$

$$= \frac{2}{\sqrt{k}} \int_0^b \underline{\qquad\qquad}\, dy = \underline{\qquad\qquad}\ .$$

The moment of inertia about the y-axis is

$$I_y = \iint \underline{\qquad\qquad\qquad} = \int_0^b \int_{-\sqrt{y/k}}^{\sqrt{y/k}} x^2\, dx\, dy$$

$$= \frac{2}{3k^{3/2}} \int_0^b \underline{\qquad\qquad}\, dy = \underline{\qquad\qquad}\ .$$

If we calculate the mass of the plane region,

$$M = \iint \delta(x,y)\, dA = \int_0^b \int_{-\sqrt{y/k}}^{\sqrt{y/k}} dx\, dy = 2\int_0^b \sqrt{y/k}\, dy = \frac{4b^{3/2}}{4\sqrt{k}}\ ,$$

then we can express the moments of inertia in terms of the mass as follows:

$$I_x = \frac{3b^2}{7} M \quad \text{and} \quad I_y = \underline{\qquad\qquad}\ .$$

13.3 DOUBLE INTEGRALS IN POLAR FORM

OBJECTIVE A: Given a (double) iterated integral in Cartesian coordinates, change it to an equivalent double integral in polar coordinates and then evaluate the polar integral.

10. $\displaystyle\int_0^{a/\sqrt{2}} \int_y^{\sqrt{a^2-y^2}} \sin(x^2 + y^2)\, dx\, dy$

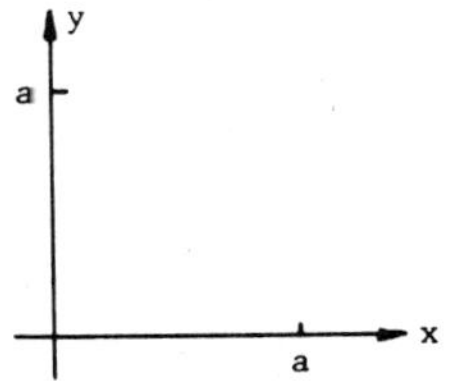

First sketch the region of integration in the coordinate system at the right. In converting the integral to polar coordinates we need to find the polar limits of integration for the region. We see that θ varies from θ = ______ to $\theta = \frac{\pi}{4}$ radians, and r varies from r = 0 to r = ______ units. Thus, the integral becomes

---

9. $\sqrt{b/k}$, $\displaystyle\int_0^b \int_{-\sqrt{y/k}}^{\sqrt{y/k}}$, $y^{5/2}$, $\dfrac{4b^{7/2}}{7\sqrt{k}}$, $x^2\delta(x,y)\, dA$, $y^{3/2}$, $\dfrac{4b^{5/2}}{15k^{3/2}}$, $\dfrac{b}{5k} M$

<u>In Cartesian coordinates</u> <u>In polar coordinates</u>

$$\int_0^{a/\sqrt{2}} \int_y^{\sqrt{a^2-y^2}} \sin(x^2 + y^2)\,dx\,dy = \int_{\_\_\_}^{\pi/4} \int_0^{\_\_\_} \_\_\_\_\_\_\_\_\_\_ \,dr\,d\theta$$

$$= \int_0^{\pi/4} \Big[\_\_\_\_\_\_\_\_\_\_\Big]_{r=0}^{r=a} d\theta$$

$$= \int_0^{\pi/4} \left(\frac{1}{2} - \frac{1}{2}\cos a^2\right) d\theta$$

$$= \_\_\_\_\_\_\_\_\_\_\_\_\_\_ .$$

11. $\displaystyle\int_0^1 \int_{\sqrt{1-x^2}}^{\sqrt{2-x^2}} \frac{1}{\sqrt{x^2 + y^2}}\,dy\,dx$

A sketch of the region of integration is shown at the right. Notice that the line $y = x$ intersects the circle $x^2 + y^2 = 2$ at the point $(1,1)$. Let us find the polar limits of integration for this region. The region can be described as the union of two regions: as θ varies from $\theta = 0$ to $\theta = \frac{\pi}{4}$, r varies from $r = \_\_\_\_\_\_$ (on the circle $x^2 + y^2 = 1$) to the line $x = 1$ or $r \sec \theta$ (since $x = r \cos \theta = 1$); as θ varies from $\theta = \frac{\pi}{4}$ to $\theta = \frac{\pi}{2}$, r varies from $\_\_\_\_\_\_\_\_\_\_$ (from the circle $x^2 + y^2 = 1$ to the circle $x^2 + y^2 = 2$). Therefore, the integral becomes

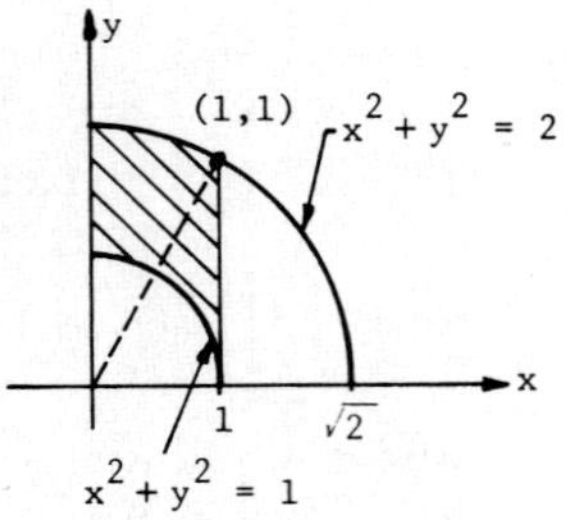

<u>In Cartesian coordinates</u>

$$\int_0^1 \int_{\sqrt{1-x^2}}^{\sqrt{2-x^2}} \frac{1}{\sqrt{x^2 + y^2}}\,dy\,dx$$

<u>In polar coordinates</u>

$$= \int_0^{\pi/4} \int_{\_\_\_}^{\_\_\_} \left(\frac{1}{r}\right) r\,dr\,d\theta + \int_{\_\_\_}^{\_\_\_} \int_{\_\_\_}^{\_\_\_} \left(\frac{1}{r}\right) dr\,d\theta$$

---

10. 0, a, $\displaystyle\int_0^{\pi/4} \int_0^a \sin(r^2)\,r\,dr\,d\theta$,

$-\frac{1}{2}\cos(r^2)$, $\frac{\pi}{4}\left(\frac{1}{2} - \frac{1}{2}\cos a^2\right)$

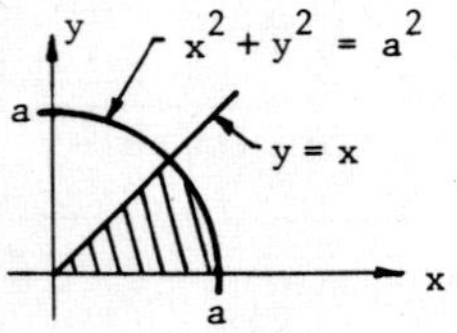

$$= \int_0^{\pi/4} (\_\_\_\_\_\_\_\_\_\_)\, d\theta + \int_{\pi/4}^{\pi/2} (\sqrt{2} - 1)\, d\theta$$

$$= \ln|\sec\theta + \tan\theta| - \theta\Big]_{\theta=0}^{\theta=\pi/4} + \_\_\_\_\_\_\_\_\_\_\Big]_{\theta=\pi/4}^{\theta=\pi/2}$$

$$= \left(\ln\left|\sec\frac{\pi}{4} + \tan\frac{\pi}{4}\right| - \frac{\pi}{4} - 0\right) + \_\_\_\_\_\_\_\_\_\_$$

$$= \ln\left(\sqrt{2} + 1\right) + \frac{\pi}{4}\left(\sqrt{2} - 2\right) \approx 0.42.$$

OBJECTIVE B: In an applied problem involving double integration (e.g., finding an area, volume, center of mass or moment of inertia), express the double integral in polar coordinates (when appropriate, to make the integrations easier), and then evaluate the integral thus obtained.

12. Let us find the area of one petal of the rose $r = a \sin 3\theta$ sketched in the figure at the right. The petal in the first quadrant is traced out as θ varies from $\theta = 0$ to $\theta = \frac{\pi}{3}$: r starts at $r = 0$, reaches its maximum value $r = a$ when $\theta =$ ________, and returns to $r = 0$ when $\theta = \frac{\pi}{3}$. Thus, as θ varies from $\theta = 0$ to $\theta = \frac{\pi}{3}$, r varies from ____________. The area of the petal is given in terms of polar coordinates by

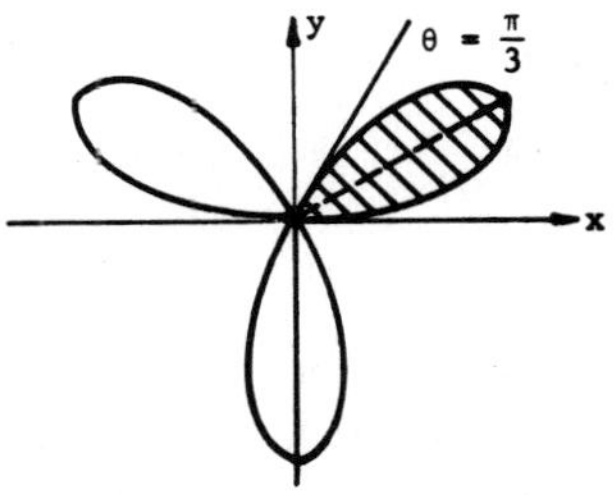

$$A = \iint dA = \int_{\_\_}^{\_\_} \int_{\_\_}^{\_\_} r\, dr\, d\theta$$

$$= \int_0^{\pi/3} \_\_\_\_\_\_\_\_\Big]_{r=0}^{r=a\sin\theta} d\theta = \int_0^{\pi/3} \_\_\_\_\_\_\_\_\_\_\_\_ \, d\theta$$

$$= \frac{a^2}{4}\int_0^{\pi/3} (1 - \cos 6\theta)\, d\theta = \frac{a^2}{4}\Big[\_\_\_\_\_\_\_\_\_\_\Big]_{\theta=0}^{\theta=\pi/3} = \_\_\_\_\_\_\_\_ .$$

---

11. 1, $r = 1$ to $r = \sqrt{2}$, $\int_0^{\pi/4}\int_1^{\sec\theta} + \int_{\pi/4}^{\pi/2}\int_1^{\sqrt{2}}$, $\sec\theta - 1$, $(\sqrt{2} - 1)\theta$, $\frac{\pi}{4}(\sqrt{2} - 1)$

12. $\frac{\pi}{6}$, $r = 0$ to $r = a \sin 3\theta$ (the boundary of the petal), $\int_0^{\pi/3}\int_0^{a\sin 3\theta}$, $\frac{1}{2}r^2$, $\frac{1}{2}a^2\sin^2 3\theta$, $\theta - \frac{1}{6}\sin 6\theta$, $\frac{\pi a^2}{12}$

13. Let us find the center of mass of the semi-circular region bounded by the x-axis and the curve $y = \sqrt{a^2 - x^2}$, when the density of the region is proportional to the square of its distance from the center of the semi-circular arc: $\delta(x,y) = k(x^2 + y^2)$ for some proportionality constant k. The region is sketched in the figure at the right. In terms of polar coordinates, the mass of the region is given by

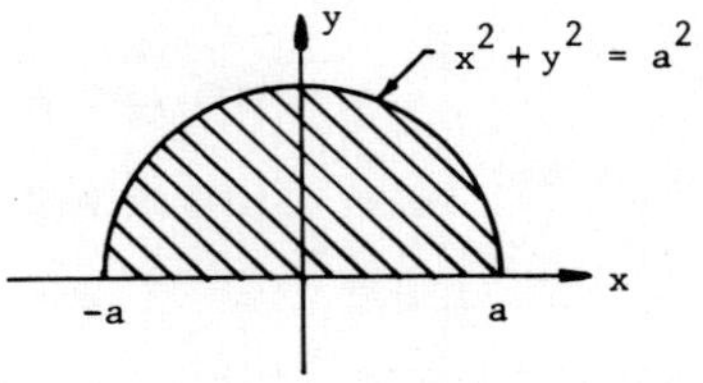

$$M = \iint \delta(x,y)\, dA = \int_{\_\_}^{\_\_} \int_{\_\_}^{\_\_} kr^2 \cdot r\, dr\, d\theta$$

$$= \int_0^{\pi} \frac{k}{4} r^4 \Big]_{r=0}^{r=a} d\theta = \underline{\hspace{3cm}} .$$

The moment of the mass with respect to the x-axis in terms of polar coordinates is

$$M_x = \iint y\delta(x,y)\, dA = \int_0^{\pi} \int_0^{a} \underline{\hspace{3cm}} \cdot r\, dr\, d\theta$$

$$= \int_0^{\pi} \underline{\hspace{3cm}}\, d\theta = \frac{2ka^5}{5} .$$

From the symmetry of the plate and its density function across the y-axis, it is clear that M_y is zero. (This may also be verified by direct calculation.) Thus,

$\bar{x} =$ ________ and $\bar{y} =$ ________

give the coordinates for the center of mass.

14. Suppose we wish to find the volume of the ellipsoid $9x^2 + 9y^2 + z^2 = 9$. In Cartesian coordinates the volume is given by

$$V = 2 \int_{-1}^{1} \int_{-\sqrt{1-x^2}}^{\sqrt{1-x^2}} z\, dy\, dz, \quad \text{where} \quad z = 3\sqrt{1 - x^2 - y^2}$$

(the factor 2 occurs because we selected $z \geq 0$, and the ellipsoid is symmetric across the plane $z = 0$). We see that this iterated integral would be very cumbersome to calculate. Let us try the integration in polar coordinates: $x = r \cos \theta$ and $y = r \sin \theta$ transform the equation $9x^2 + 9y^2 + z^2 = 9$ into the polar equation ____________. Thus, when $z = 0$ (in the xy-plane), $r =$ ______. Therefore, in terms of polar coordinates the volume is given by

---

13. $\int_0^{\pi} \int_0^{a}$, $\frac{\pi k a^4}{4}$, $kr^2(r \sin \theta)$, $\frac{ka^5}{5} \sin \theta$, 0, $\frac{8a}{5\pi}$

$$V = 2 \int_{\_\_\_}^{\_\_\_} \int_{\_\_\_}^{\_\_\_} 3\sqrt{1 - r^2} \cdot r\, dr\, d\theta$$

$$= 2 \int_0^{2\pi} \underline{\qquad\qquad\qquad} \Big]_{r=0}^{r=1} d\theta = 2 \int_0^{2\pi} d\theta = 4\pi .$$

13.4 TRIPLE INTEGRALS IN RECTANGULAR COORDINATES: VOLUMES AND AVERAGE VALUES

OBJECTIVE A: Evaluate a given iterated triple integral.

15. $\int_0^2 \int_0^x \int_0^{1-2x+y} e^z \, dz\, dy\, dx$

$$= \int_0^2 \int_0^x e^z \Big|_{z=0}^{z=1-2x+y} dy\, dx$$

$$= \int_0^2 \int_0^x \underline{\qquad\qquad\qquad\qquad} \, dy\, dx$$

$$= \int_0^2 \left[e^{1-2x+y} - \underline{\qquad}\right]_{y=0}^{y=x} dx$$

$$= \int_0^2 \left[(\underline{\qquad\qquad\qquad}) - e^{1-2x}\right] dx$$

$$= -e^{1-x} - \tfrac{1}{2}x^2 + \underline{\qquad\qquad}\Big]_{x=0}^{x=2}$$

$$= \left(e^{-1} - 2 + \tfrac{1}{2}e^{-3}\right) - \left(\underline{\qquad\qquad}\right)$$

$$\approx -0.984 .$$

OBJECTIVE B: By triple integration, find the volume of a specified region D in xyz-space.

16. Let us calculate the volume of the region in space bounded by the cylinders $z = x^2$ and $z = 4 - x^2$, and the planes $y = 0$, $y = 5$. A sketch of the region is shown at the right.

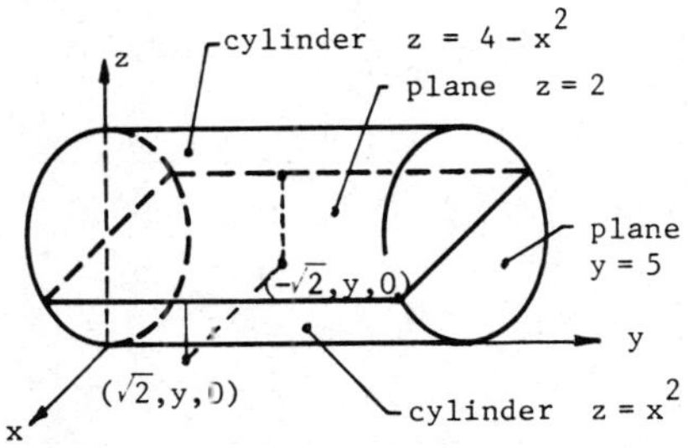

The two surfaces intersect when $4 - x^2 = x^2$, or $x^2 = 2$; that is they intersect on the plane

---

14. $z^2 + 9r^2 = 9$, 1, $\int_0^{2\pi} \int_0^1$, $-\left(1 - r^2\right)^{3/2}$

15. $e^{1-2x+y} - 1$, y, $e^{1-x} - x$, $\frac{1}{2}e^{1-2x}$, $-e + \frac{1}{2}e$

$z = 2$. The volume projects into the region R in the xy-plane described by $-\sqrt{2} \le x \le \sqrt{2}$ and $0 \le y \le 5$. Thus, the volume is given by the triple iterated integral,

$$V = \int_{\_\_\_}^{\_\_\_} \int_{\_\_\_}^{\_\_\_} \int_{\_\_\_}^{\_\_\_} dz\, dy\, dx$$

$$= \int_{-\sqrt{2}}^{\sqrt{2}} \int_0^5 \_\_\_\_\_\_\_\_ \, dy\, dx = \int_{-\sqrt{2}}^{\sqrt{2}} \_\_\_\_\_\_\_\_ \Big]_{y=0}^{y=5} dx$$

$$= \int_{-\sqrt{2}}^{\sqrt{2}} \_\_\_\_\_\_\_\_ \, dx = \_\_\_\_\_\_\_\_ \Big]_{x=-\sqrt{2}}^{x=\sqrt{2}} = \_\_\_\_\_\_\_\_ .$$

OBJECTIVE C: Find the average value of a given function $F(x,y,z)$ over a specified region in xyz-space.

17. To find the average value of $F(x,y,z) = x + y$ over the region bounded by the cylinders $z = x^2$ and $z = 4 - x^2$ in Problem 16, we evaluate the integral

Average value of F over D = ________

$$= \frac{3}{80\sqrt{2}} \int_{-\sqrt{2}}^{\sqrt{2}} \int_0^5 \_\_\_\_\_\_\_\_ \, dy\, dx$$

$$= \frac{3}{80\sqrt{2}} \int_{-\sqrt{2}}^{\sqrt{2}} [(4x - 2x^3)y + \_\_\_\_\_\_\_\_]_0^5 \, dx$$

$$= \frac{3}{80\sqrt{2}} \int_{-\sqrt{2}}^{\sqrt{2}} (20x - 10x^3 + \_\_\_\_\_\_\_\_)\, dx$$

$$= \frac{3}{80\sqrt{2}} \left[10x^2 - \frac{5}{2}x^4 + 50x - \frac{25}{3}x^3\right]_{-\sqrt{2}}^{\sqrt{2}}$$

$$= \frac{3}{80\sqrt{2}} (\_\_\_\_\_\_\_\_)$$

$$= \_\_\_\_\_\_\_\_ .$$

---

16. $\int_{-\sqrt{2}}^{\sqrt{2}} \int_0^5 \int_{x^2}^{4-x^2}$, $4 - 2x^2$, $y(4 - 2x^2)$, $5(4 - 2x^2)$, $20x - \frac{10}{3}x^3$, $\frac{80\sqrt{2}}{3}$

17. $\frac{3}{80\sqrt{2}} \int_{-\sqrt{2}}^{\sqrt{2}} \int_0^5 \int_{x^2}^{4-x^2} (x + y)\, dz\, dy\, dx$, $(4 - 2x^2)(x + y)$, $\frac{1}{2}y^2(4 - 2x^2)$, $50 - 25x^2$, $\frac{200}{3}\sqrt{2}$, $\frac{5}{2}$

13.5 MASSES AND MOMENTS IN THREE DIMENSIONS

OBJECTIVE: By triple integration, find the mass, the center of mass, or the moments of inertia of an object distributed over a region D of xyz-space and having density $\delta = \delta(x,y,z)$ at the point (x,y,z) of D.

18. Find the center of mass of the homogeneous solid bounded below by the cone $x^2 + y^2 = z^2$ and above by the plane $z = 4$.

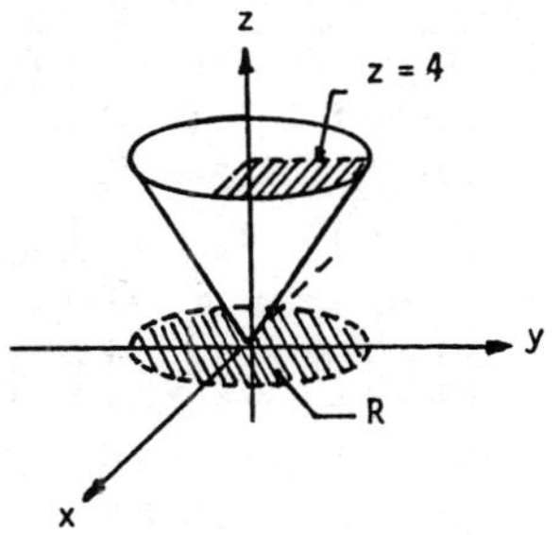

Solution. The solid region is sketched at the right. Since the region is geometrical we take the density to be unity, $\delta \equiv 1$. By symmetry $\bar{x} =$ _____ and $\bar{y} =$ _____. To find $\bar{z}$ we first calculate

$$M_{xy} = \iint_R \int_{z=0}^{z=4} z\delta \, dz\, dy\, dx$$

$$= \iint_R \left[\tfrac{1}{2}z^2\right]_{z=0}^{z=4} dy\, dx$$

$$= \iint_R \text{\_\_\_\_\_\_\_\_} \, dy\, dx$$

$$= 8 \cdot \text{area of planar region } R$$

$$= \text{\_\_\_\_\_\_\_\_\_\_\_\_} .$$

The mass of the object is

$$M = \iint_R \int_{z=0}^{z=4} \delta \, dz\, dy\, dx$$

$$= \iint_R \text{\_\_\_\_\_\_\_\_} \, dy\, dx$$

$$= \text{\_\_\_\_\_\_\_\_\_\_\_\_} .$$

Therefore,

$$\bar{z} = \frac{M_{xy}}{M} = \text{\_\_\_\_\_\_\_\_} .$$

The center of mass is ____________________ .

13.6 TRIPLE INTEGRALS IN CYLINDRICAL AND SPHERICAL COORDINATES

OBJECTIVE A: Find by triple integration, in cylindrical coordinates, the volume of a specified region in space. (The region may be described in Cartesian coordinates.)

---

18. 0, 0, 8, 128π, 4, 64π, 2, (0,0,2)

19. Consider the region in space that lies inside the sphere $x^2 + y^2 + z^2 = 9$, but <u>outside</u> the cylinder $x^2 + y^2 = 1$. The region is sketched in the figure below. The z-axis is an axis of symmetry so that cylindrical coordinates should be useful for finding the volume of the region by triple integration. The equation of the sphere in cylindrical coordinates is $z^2 =$ __________. The projection of the volume within the sphere and outside the cylinder in the xy-plane is a washer with inner radius $r = 1$ and outer radius $r =$ ______. This is the shaded shown in the diagram, and in polar coordinates it is described by the inequalities ______ $\le r \le$ ______ and ______ $\le \theta \le$ ______. For a point (x,y), or (r,θ), in this washer, the altitude z of the solid region varies from $z = -\sqrt{9 - r^2}$ (the surface of the sphere below the xy-plane) to $z =$ __________ (that portion of the surface above the xy-plane). Then the volume of the solid region in cylindrical coordinates is given by

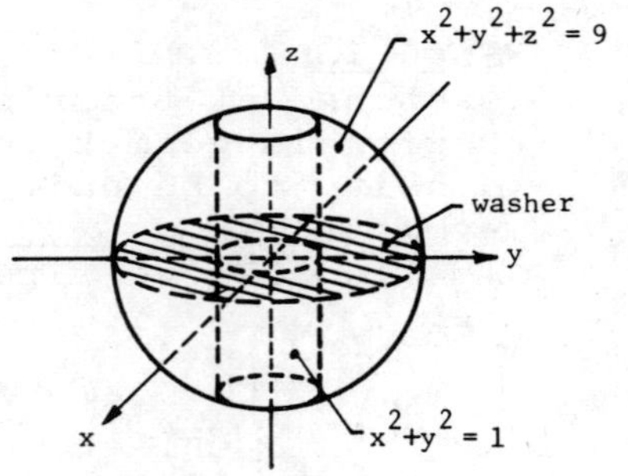

$$V = \int_1^3 \int_{\_\_\_}^{2\pi} \int_{-\sqrt{9-r^2}}^{\_\_\_\_} \_\_\_\_\_\_\_\_\_\_ = \int_1^3 \int_0^{2\pi} \_\_\_\_\_\_\_\_\_\_ \, d\theta \, dr$$

$$= \int_1^3 4\pi r\sqrt{9 - r^2} \, dr = \_\_\_\_\_\_\_\_\_\_ \Big]_{r=1}^{r=3} = \frac{64\pi\sqrt{2}}{3} \approx 94.78.$$

OBJECTIVE B: Find by triple integration, in spherical coordinates, the volume of a specified region in space. (The region may be described in Cartesian coordinates.)

20. Consider the region in space that lies inside the sphere $x^2 + y^2 + z^2 = 4$, but outside the cone $x^2 + y^2 = z^2$. The region is sketched in the figure at the right. The origin is a point of symmetry of the solid so that spherical coordinates should be useful for finding the volume of the region by triple integration.

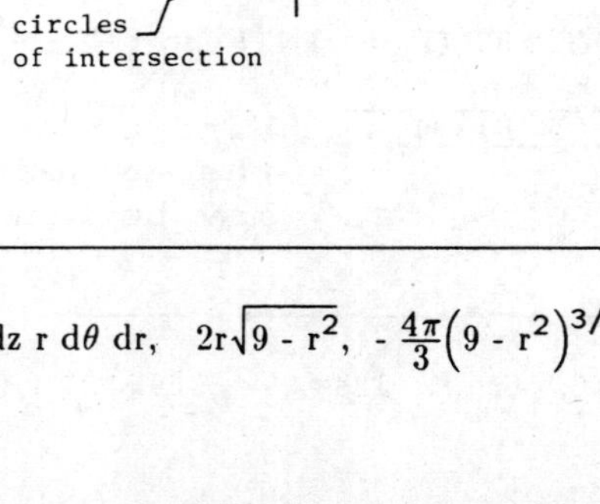

To find the intersection of the sphere and the cone, we substitute $x^2 + y^2 = z^2$ into the

---

19. $9 - r^2$, 3, $1 \le r \le 3$, $0 \le \theta \le 2\pi$, $\sqrt{9 - r^2}$, $\int_1^3 \int_0^{2\pi} \int_{-\sqrt{9-r^2}}^{\sqrt{9-r^2}} dz \, r \, d\theta \, dr$, $2r\sqrt{9 - r^2}$, $-\frac{4\pi}{3}\left(9 - r^2\right)^{3/2}$

equation of the sphere obtaining $z^2 + z^2 = 4$ or $z^2 =$ _____. Thus, $z = -\sqrt{2}$, or $z = \sqrt{2}$. The plane $z = -\sqrt{2}$ gives the circle of intersection $x^2 + y^2 = 2$ on the sphere which lies $\sqrt{2}$ units below the xy-plane; and $z = \sqrt{2}$ provides the corresponding circle of intersection above the xy-plane. In spherical coordinates, $z = \rho \cos \phi$, so the plane $z = \sqrt{2}$ corresponds to $\sqrt{2} = \rho \cos \phi$. Since the circles of intersection lie on the sphere where $\rho = 2$, the angle ϕ (see figure) for the upper circle satisfies the equation $\sqrt{2} = 2 \cos \phi$. Thus, $\phi =$ ______ radians. Similarly, the angle for the lower circle satisfies $-\sqrt{2} = 2 \cos \phi$, or $\phi = \frac{3\pi}{4}$ radians. Therefore, the volume of the region inside the sphere but outside the cone is given in spherical coordinates by

$$V = \int_{\_\_\_}^{\_\_\_} \int_{\_\_\_}^{\_\_\_} \int_{\_\_\_}^{\_\_\_} \rho^2 \sin \phi \; d\rho \; d\theta \; d\phi$$

$$= \int_{\pi/4}^{3\pi/4} \int_0^{2\pi} \tfrac{1}{3} \rho^3 \sin \phi \Big]_{\rho=0}^{\rho=2} d\theta \; d\phi = \int_{\pi/4}^{3\pi/4} \int_0^{2\pi} \_\_\_\_\_\_\_\_ \; d\theta \; d\phi$$

$$= \int_{\pi/4}^{3\pi/4} \_\_\_\_\_\_\_\_\_\_ \; d\phi = \frac{16\pi\sqrt{2}}{3} \approx 23.70.$$

OBJECTIVE C: By triple integration, using cylindrical or spherical coordinates, find the mass, the center of mass, or the moments of inertia of an object distributed over a region D of xyz-space and having density $\delta = \delta(x,y,z)$ at the point (x,y,z) of D.

21. Let us find the center of mass of a solid hemisphere of radius a if the density at any point is proportional to the distance of the point from the axis of the solid. We choose coordinates so that the origin is at the center of the sphere, the z-axis is the axis of the hemisphere, and consider the hemisphere that lies above the xy-plane. In spherical coordinates the hemisphere may be described by $\rho = a$, $0 \le \phi \le \frac{\pi}{2}$, and _____ $\le \theta \le$ _____. The distance $r = \rho \sin \phi$ is measured from the z-axis parallel to the xy-plane, and we are given that $\delta = k\rho \sin \phi$ for some constant k of proportionality. Therefore, the mass of the solid is given by the triple integral (in spherical coordinates),

$$M = \int_{\_\_\_}^{\_\_\_} \int_{\_\_\_}^{\_\_\_} \int_{\_\_\_}^{\_\_\_} (k\rho \sin \phi) \; \rho^2 \sin \phi \; d\rho \; d\phi \; d\theta$$

$$= \int_0^{2\pi} \int_0^{\pi/2} \_\_\_\_\_\_\_\_\_\_ \; d\phi \; d\theta$$

---

20. 2, $\frac{\pi}{4}$, $\int_{\pi/4}^{3\pi/4} \int_0^{2\pi} \int_0^2$, $\frac{8}{3} \sin \phi$, $\frac{16\pi}{3} \sin \phi$

$$= \frac{ka^4}{4} \int_0^{2\pi} [\frac{\phi}{2} - \frac{1}{4}\sin 2\phi]_{\phi=0}^{\phi=\pi/2} \, d\theta = \_\_\_\_\_\_\_\_\_\_ .$$

Because of the symmetry of the solid about the z-axis in both shape and density, $\bar{x} = \bar{y} = 0$. We calculate $\bar{z}$:

$$\iiint z\delta \, dV = \int_0^{2\pi} \int_0^{\pi/2} \int_0^a \_\_\_\_\_\_\_\_\_\_\_\_\_\_\_\_\_\_\_\_ \, d\rho \, d\phi \, d\theta$$

$$= \int_0^{2\pi} \int_0^{\pi/2} \_\_\_\_\_\_\_\_\_\_\_\_\_\_\_\_ \, d\phi \, d\theta$$

$$= \int_0^{2\pi} \frac{ka^5}{15} \sin^3\phi]_{\phi=0}^{\phi=\pi/2} \, d\theta = \_\_\_\_\_\_\_\_ .$$

Therefore, $\bar{z} = \frac{2\pi ka^5}{15M} = \_\_\_\_\_\_\_\_\_\_$.

22. Find the center of mass of the homogenous solid inside the paraboloid $x^2 + y^2 = z$ and <u>outside</u> the cone $x^2 + y^2 = z^2$.

<u>Solution</u>. The solid region is sketched at the right. A slice through the solid by a plane parallel to the xy-plane produces a washer-shaped area like that shaded area shown in the figure. The cone and the paraboloid intersect when $z = z^2$, or $z = 0$ (the base) or $z =$ ______ (the top rim of the solid). Since the region is geometrical we take the density as unity. Because the z-axis is an axis of symmetry it will be convenient to use cylindrical coordinates. In cylindrical coordinates, the equation $x^2 + y^2 = z^2$ of the cone becomes __________ and the equation for the paraboloid becomes __________. The projection of the solid into the xy-plane is the interior of a circle centered at the origin of radius $r =$ _______ (since $r = z$ for the top rim of the solid). In polar coordinates this circular disk is expressed by the inequalities _____ $\le r \le$ _____ and _____ $\le \theta \le$ _____. For a point (x,y), or (r,θ), in this disk the altitude of the solid region varies from the paraboloid $z =$ _______ to the surface of the cone $z =$ _______, both expressed in terms of cylindrical coordinates. Therefore, the mass of the solid is given by the triple integral

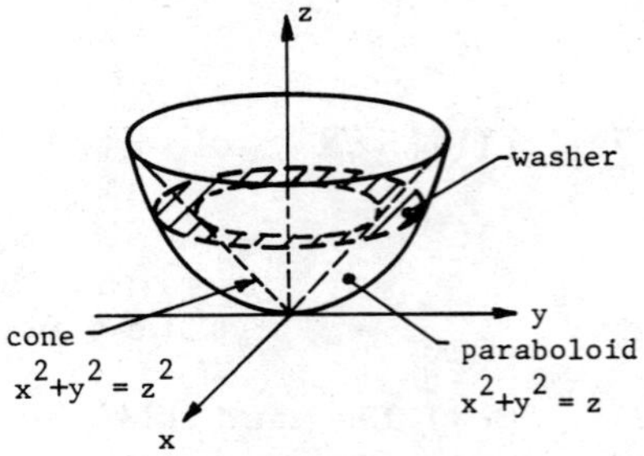

---

21. $0 \le \theta \le 2\pi$, $\int_0^{2\pi} \int_0^{\pi/2} \int_0^a$, $\frac{1}{4}ka^4 \sin^2\phi$, $\frac{ka^4\pi^2}{8}$, $(\rho \cos\phi)(k\rho \sin\phi)\rho^2 \sin\phi$, $\frac{1}{5}ka^5 \sin^2\phi \cos\phi$, $\frac{2\pi ka^5}{15}$, $\frac{16a}{15\pi}$

$$M = \iiint dV = \int_{\_\_\_}^{\_\_\_} \int_{\_\_\_}^{\_\_\_} \int_{\_\_\_}^{\_\_\_} dz\ r\ dr\ d\theta$$

$$= \int_0^{2\pi} \int_0^1 \_\_\_\_\_\_\_\_ \ dr\ d\theta = \int_0^{2\pi} \_\_\_\_\_\_\_\_ \Big]_{r=0}^{r=1} d\theta = \frac{\pi}{6} .$$

From the symmetry of the solid, it is clear that the center of mass must lie on the z-axis. Thus, $\bar{x} =$ ______ and $\bar{y} =$ ______. We calculate $\bar{z}$.

$$\iiint z\ dV = \int_{\_\_\_}^{\_\_\_} \int_{\_\_\_}^{\_\_\_} \int_{\_\_\_}^{\_\_\_} z\ dz\ r\ dr\ d\theta$$

$$= \int_0^{2\pi} \int_0^1 \_\_\_\_\_\_\_\_ \Big]_{z=r^2}^{z=r} dr\ d\theta = \frac{1}{2} \int_0^{2\pi} \int_0^1 (r^3 - r^5)\ dr\ d\theta$$

$$= \frac{1}{2} \int_0^{2\pi} \left(\frac{1}{4}r^4 - \frac{1}{6}r^6\right)\Big]_{r=0}^{r=1} d\theta = \frac{\pi}{12}.$$

Therefore, $\bar{z} =$ ________.

23. To calculate the moment of inertia about the z-axis of the solid in Problem 22 above, we find

$$I_z = \iiint \left(x^2 + y^2\right)\delta\ dV \qquad (\text{where } \delta \equiv 1)$$

$$= \int_{\_\_\_}^{\_\_\_} \int_{\_\_\_}^{\_\_\_} \int_{\_\_\_}^{\_\_\_} \_\_\_\_\_\_\_\_ \ dz\ r\ dr\ d\theta$$

$$= \int_0^{2\pi} \int_0^1 \_\_\_\_\_\_\_\_ \ dr\ d\theta$$

$$= \int_0^{2\pi} \_\_\_\_\_\_\_\_ \Big]_{r=0}^{r=1} d\theta = \_\_\_\_\_\_\_\_ .$$

13.7 SUBSTITUTIONS IN MULTIPLE INTEGRALS

24. If $f(x,y)$, $x = g(u,v)$, and $y = h(u,v)$ are continuous and have continuous partial derivatives, then substitution for x and y in the double integral

$$\iint_R f(x,y)\ dx\ dy$$

results in the integral

---

22. 1, $r^2 = z^2$, $r^2 = z$, 1, $0 \le r \le 1$, $0 \le \theta \le 2\pi$, r^2, r, $\int_0^{2\pi} \int_0^1 \int_{r^2}^{r}$, $r(r - r^2)$, $\frac{1}{3}r^3 - \frac{1}{4}r^4$, 0, 0, $\int_0^{2\pi} \int_0^1 \int_{r^2}^{r}$, $\frac{1}{2}rz^2$, $\frac{1}{2}$

23. $\int_0^{2\pi} \int_0^1 \int_{r^2}^{r}$, r^2, $r^3(r - r^2)$, $\frac{1}{5}r^5 - \frac{1}{6}r^6$, $\frac{\pi}{15}$

$$\iint_G f(g(u,v),h(u,v))\,|J(u,v)|\,du\,dv$$

where

$$J(u,v) = \frac{\partial(x,y)}{\partial(u,v)} = \underline{\hspace{4cm}} .$$

Here the region G in the uv-plane is transformed ________ into the region R in the xy-plane by the functions g and ______.

OBJECTIVE: Evaluate a double integral over a specified region R in the xy-plane by changing variables $x = g(u,v)$ and $y = h(u,v)$ and integrating over a region G in the uv-plane.

25. Let R be the region in the first quadrant of the xy-plane bounded by the parallel lines $y = 2x - 2$, $y = 2x + 1$, and the lines $x + y = 1$, $x + y = 3$. A sketch of R is shown in the figure at the right. Use the transformation $u = x + y$, $v = y - 2x$ with $u \geq 1$ and $v \geq -2$ to evaluate

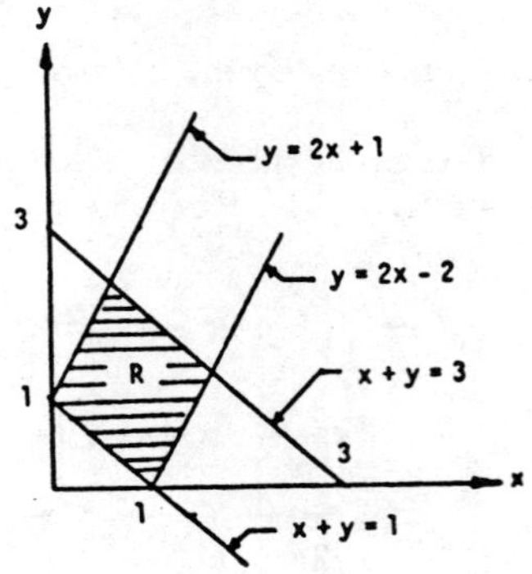

$$\iint_R \frac{3x}{x+y}\,dy\,dx .$$

Solution. First solve the transformation equations for x and y in terms of u and v. Routine algebra gives

$$x = \underline{\hspace{3cm}} , \quad y = \underline{\hspace{3cm}} .$$

The Jacobian of the transformation is

$$J(u,v) = \begin{vmatrix} \_\_ & \_\_ \\ \_\_ & \_\_ \end{vmatrix} = \frac{1}{3} .$$

The boundaries of the region R correspond to: $x + y = u = 1$, $x + y = u =$ ____, $y - 2x = v = -2$, $y - 2x = v =$ ____. Thus substitution in the double integral gives

---

24. $\begin{vmatrix} \frac{\partial x}{\partial u} & \frac{\partial x}{\partial v} \\ \frac{\partial y}{\partial u} & \frac{\partial y}{\partial v} \end{vmatrix}$, one-to-one, h

$$\iint_R \frac{3x}{x + y}\, dy\, dx = \int_1^3 \int_{-2}^1 \underline{\hspace{3cm}} \cdot \frac{1}{3}\, dv\, du$$

$$= \frac{1}{3} \int_1^3 \int_{-2}^1 \left(1 - \frac{v}{u}\right) dv\, du$$

$$= \frac{1}{3} \int_1^3 \left[\underline{\hspace{2.5cm}}\right]_{v=-2}^{v=1} du$$

$$= \frac{1}{3} \int_1^3 \left(1 - \frac{1}{2u} + \underline{\hspace{2cm}}\right) du$$

$$= \int_1^3 \left(\underline{\hspace{3cm}}\right) du$$

$$= u + \underline{\hspace{2.5cm}}\Big]_{u=1}^{u=3}$$

$$= 3 + \frac{1}{2} \ln 3 - 1 - \frac{1}{2} \ln 1 \approx 2.55 .$$

---

25. $\frac{1}{3}(u - v)$, $\frac{1}{3}(2u + v)$, $\begin{vmatrix} \frac{1}{3} & -\frac{1}{3} \\ \frac{2}{3} & \frac{1}{3} \end{vmatrix}$, 3, 1, $\frac{u - v}{u}$, $v - \frac{1}{2u}v^2$, $2 + \frac{2}{u}$, $1 + \frac{1}{2u}$, $\frac{1}{2} \ln u$

CHAPTER 13 SELF-TEST

1. Evaluate the following double integrals, and sketch the region over which the integration extends.

   (a) $\int_1^3 \int_{-y}^{2y} xe^{y^3} \, dx \, dy$ (b) $\int_0^{\pi/2} \int_0^{\cos x} e^y \sin x \, dy \, dx$

2. Write an equivalent double integral with the order of integration reversed for each of the following. Sketch the region over which the integration extends and evaluate the new integral.

   (a) $\int_1^2 \int_{x^2}^{x^3} dy \, dx$ (b) $\int_0^2 \int_0^{\sqrt{4-y^2}} \sqrt{4 - x^2} \, dx \, dy$

3. Find, by double integration, the volume of the solid under the paraboloid $z = x^2 + y^2$ and lying above the region in the xy-plane bounded by the curves $y = x$ and $y = x^2$.

4. Find, by double integration, the area of the region in the xy-plane bounded by the curves $y = x^2$ and $y = 4x - x^2$.

5. Find the center of mass of the region in the first quadrant of the xy-plane bounded by the curve $y = \sqrt{x}$ and the line $x = 4$, if the density at (x,y) is $\delta(x,y) = xy$.

6. Find the moments of inertia about the x- and y-axes for the region in Problem 5 (with the same density).

7. Change the double integral $\int_0^{2a} \int_0^{\sqrt{2ay-y^2}} x \, dx \, dy$ to an equivalent double integral in polar coordinates, and then evaluate.

8. By double integration, find the volume of the solid under the hemisphere $x^2 + y^2 + z^2 = 4$, $z \geq 0$, and lying above the region in the xy-plane within the cylinder $(x - 1)^2 + y^2 = 1$.

9. By triple integration, find the volume of the solid within the sphere $x^2 + y^2 + z^2 = z$ and above the cone $z^2 = x^2 + y^2$.

10. Find the center of mass of the wedge cut out of the cylinder $x^2 + y^2 = 1$ by the plane $z = y$ above, and the plane $z = 0$ below.

11. Find the moment of inertia of a right circular cone of base radius a, altitude h, and constant density $\delta = 1$, about its axis (i.e., the axis through the vertex and perpendicular to the base).

12. Evaluate the integral

$$\iint_R \cos\left(\frac{x - y}{x + y}\right) dx\, dy$$

over the region $R = \{(x,y):\ 0 \le x \le 1,\ 0 \le y \le 1,\ x + y \le 1\}$ by means of the transformation $x - y = u$ and $x + y = v$.

SOLUTIONS TO CHAPTER 13 SELF-TEST

1. (a) The region of integration is shown in the figure at the right. Evaluation of the integral leads to,

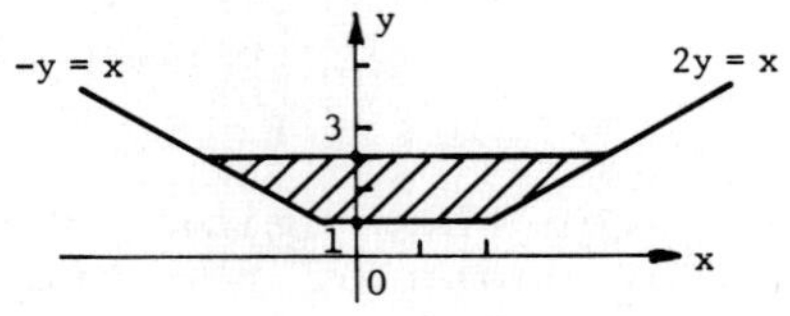

$$\int_1^3 \int_{-y}^{2y} xe^{y^3}\,dx\,dy$$

$$= \int_1^3 \tfrac{1}{2}x^2e^{y^3}\Big]_{x=-y}^{x=2y}\,dy = \int_1^3 \tfrac{1}{2}(4y^2 - y^2)e^{y^3}dy$$

$$= \int_1^3 \tfrac{3}{2}y^2e^{y^3}\,dy = \tfrac{1}{2}e^{y^3}\Big]_{y=1}^{y=3} = \tfrac{1}{2}\left(e^{27} - e\right).$$

(b) The region of integration is sketched at the right. Evaluation of the integral gives

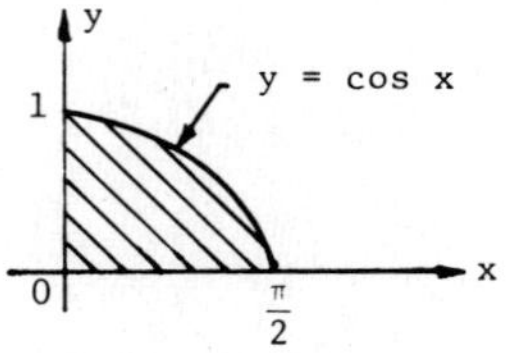

$$\int_0^{\pi/2}\int_0^{\cos x} e^y \sin x\,dy\,dx$$

$$= \int_0^{\pi/2} e^y \sin x\Big]_{y=0}^{y=\cos x}\,dx$$

$$= \int_0^{\pi/2} (\sin x\, e^{\cos x} - \sin x)\,dx = -e^{\cos x} + \cos x\Big]_{x=0}^{x=\pi/2}$$

$= e - 2 \approx 0.718.$

2. (a) The region of integration is sketched at the right. As y varies from $y = 1$ to $y = 4$, x varies from $x = y^{1/3}$ to $x = y^{1/2}$; but as y varies from $y = 4$ to $y = 8$, x varies from $x = y^{1/3}$ to $x = 2$. Thus, the integral becomes the sum of two integrals when the order of integration is reversed:

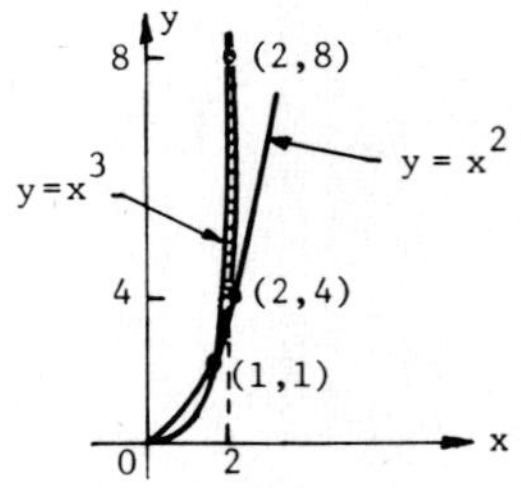

$$\int_1^2\int_{x^2}^{x^3} dy\,dx = \int_1^4\int_{y^{1/3}}^{y^{1/2}} dx\,dy + \int_4^8\int_{y^{1/3}}^{2} dx\,dy$$

$$= \int_1^4 (y^{1/2} - y^{1/3})\,dy + \int_4^8 (2 - y^{1/3})\,dy = \frac{17}{12}.$$

(b) The region of integration is sketched at the right. Reversing the order of integration gives

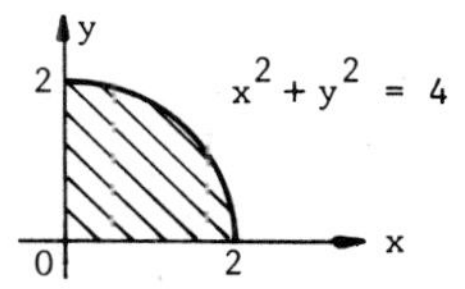

$$\int_0^2 \int_0^{\sqrt{4-y^2}} \sqrt{4 - x^2}\, dx\, dy$$

$$= \int_0^2 \int_0^{\sqrt{4-x^2}} \sqrt{4 - x^2}\, dy\, dx = \int_0^2 y(4 - x^2)^{1/2}\Big]_{y=0}^{y=\sqrt{4-x^2}} dx$$

$$= \int_0^2 (4 - x^2)\, dx = 4x - \tfrac{1}{3}x^3\Big]_{x=0}^{x=2}$$

$$= \frac{16}{3} .$$

3. The region of integration is sketched at the right. The volume is given by,

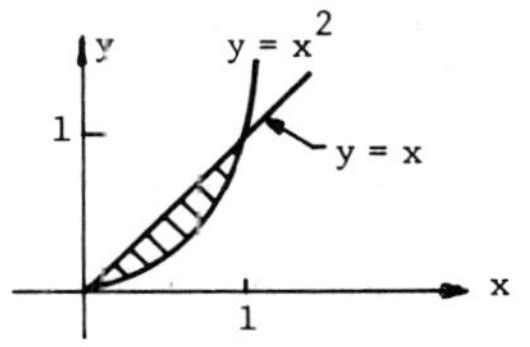

$$V = \iint z\, dA = \int_0^1 \int_{x^2}^{x} (x^2 + y^2)\, dy\, dx$$

$$= \int_0^1 (x^2 y + \tfrac{1}{3}y^3)\Big]_{y=x^2}^{y=x} dx$$

$$= \int_0^1 (\tfrac{4}{3}x^3 - x^4 - \tfrac{1}{3}x^6)\, dx = \tfrac{1}{3}x^4 - \tfrac{1}{5}x^5 - \tfrac{1}{21}x^7\Big]_{x=0}^{x=1}$$

$$= \frac{9}{105} \approx 0.086.$$

4. A sketch of the region is shown at the right. To determine the points of intersection of the two curves, we equate $y = x^2$ and $y = 4x - x^2$:

$x^2 = 4x - x^2$ or, $2x(x - 2) = 0$.

The points of intersection are therefore (0,0) and (2,4). The area of the region is given by

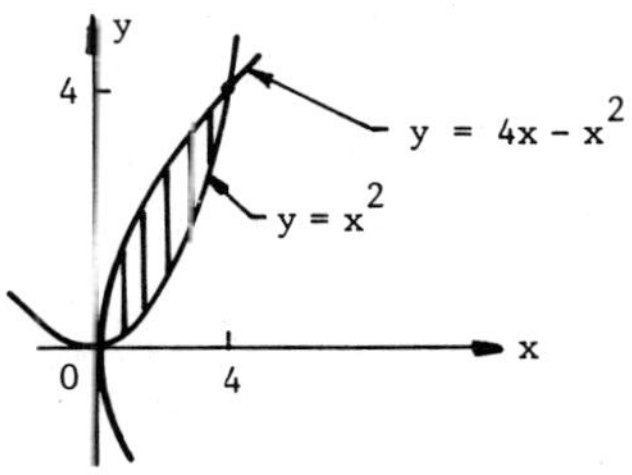

$$A = \iint dA = \int_0^2 \int_{x^2}^{4x-x^2} dy\, dx$$

$$= \int_0^2 (4x - x^2 - x^2)\, dx = \frac{8}{3}.$$

5. The mass of the region is given by,

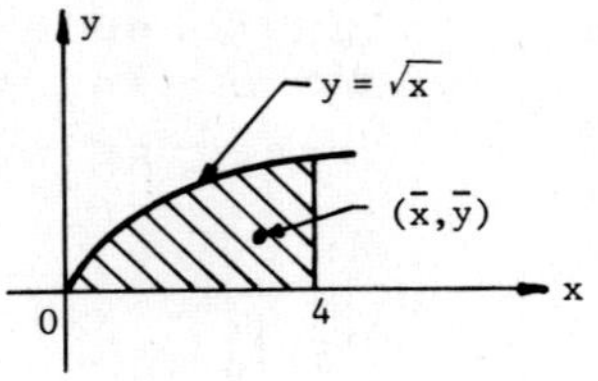

$$M = \iint \delta \, dA = \int_0^4 \int_0^{\sqrt{x}} xy \, dy \, dx$$

$$= \int_0^4 \tfrac{1}{2}xy^2\Big]_{y=0}^{y=\sqrt{x}} dx$$

$$= \tfrac{1}{2}\int_0^4 x^2 \, dx = \tfrac{32}{3} .$$

Calculation of the first moments gives,

$$M_x = \iint y\delta \, dA = \int_0^4 \int_0^{\sqrt{x}} xy^2 \, dy \, dx = \int_0^4 \tfrac{1}{3}xy^3\Big]_{y=0}^{y=\sqrt{x}} dx$$

$$= \tfrac{1}{3}\int_0^4 x^{5/2} \, dx = \tfrac{256}{21} ,$$

and

$$M_y = \iint x\delta \, dA = \int_0^4 \int_0^{\sqrt{x}} x^2 y \, dy \, dx = \int_0^4 \tfrac{1}{2}x^2y^2\Big]_{y=0}^{y=\sqrt{x}} dx$$

$$= \tfrac{1}{2}\int_0^4 x^3 \, dx = \tfrac{256}{8} = 32 .$$

Therefore,

$$\bar{x} = \frac{M_y}{M} = 3 \quad \text{and} \quad \bar{y} = \frac{M_x}{M} = \frac{8}{7}.$$

6. The moment of inertia about the x-axis is given by,

$$I_x = \iint y^2\delta \, dA = \int_0^4 \int_0^{\sqrt{x}} xy^3 \, dy \, dx$$

$$= \int_0^4 \tfrac{1}{4}y^4x\Big]_{y=0}^{y=\sqrt{x}} dx = \tfrac{1}{4}\int_0^4 x^3 \, dx = 16 .$$

The moment of inertia about the y-axis is given by,

$$I_y = \iint x^2\delta \, dA = \int_0^4 \int_0^{\sqrt{x}} x^3 y \, dy \, dx$$

$$= \int_0^4 \tfrac{1}{2}x^3y^2\Big]_{y=0}^{y=\sqrt{x}} dx = \tfrac{1}{2}\int_0^4 x^4 \, dx = 102.4.$$

Thus, the polar moment of inertia is given by

$$I_0 = I_x + I_y = 118.4.$$

7. For the region of integration, as y varies from $y = 0$ to $y = 2a$, x varies from $x = 0$ to $x = \sqrt{2ay - y^2}$. The equation $x = \sqrt{2ay - y^2}$ describes the right semi-circle $x^2 + (y - a)^2 = a^2$, $x \geq 0$. The region of integration is the shaded portion in the figure at the right. A polar equation for the circle is $r = 2a \sin \theta$. Then the region of integration may be described in terms of polar coordinates as follows: θ varies from $\theta = 0$ to $\theta = \frac{\pi}{2}$, and r varies from $r = 0$ to $r = 2a \sin \theta$. Thus, the double integral becomes,

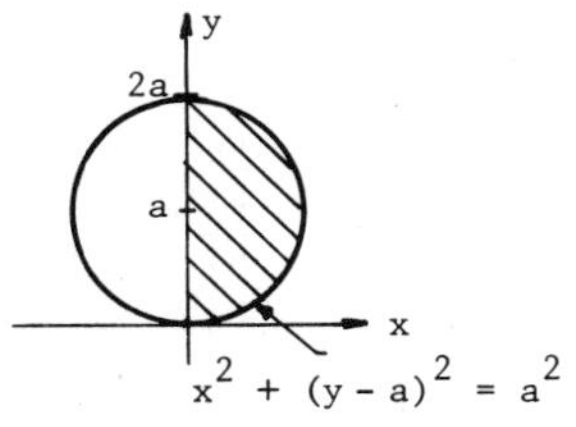

$$\int_0^{2a} \int_0^{\sqrt{2ay-y^2}} x \, dx \, dy = \int_0^{\pi/2} \int_0^{2a\sin\theta} r \cos \theta \cdot r \, dr \, d\theta$$

$$= \int_0^{\pi/2} \frac{8a^3}{3} \sin^3 \theta \cos \theta \, d\theta = \frac{2a^3}{3} \sin^4\theta \Big]_{\theta=0}^{\theta=\pi/2} = \frac{2a^3}{3} .$$

8. The Cartesian equation $z = \sqrt{4 - x^2 - y^2}$ can be written as $z = \sqrt{4 - r^2}$ using polar coordinates for x and y. The region of integration in the xy-plane is the interior of the circle $(x - 1)^2 + y^2 = 1$. In terms of polar coordinates this region is described by the inequalities $-\frac{\pi}{2} \leq \theta \leq \frac{\pi}{2}$ and $0 \leq r \leq 2 \cos \theta$. Because of the symmetry of the solid we need only compute the volume lying above the interior of the semi-circle in the first quadrant of the xy-plane, and then multiply by 2. Then the total volume is given by

$$V = \iint z \, dA = 2 \int_0^{\pi/2} \int_0^{2\cos\theta} \sqrt{4 - r^2} \cdot r \, dr \, d\theta$$

$$= 2 \int_0^{\pi/2} -\frac{1}{3}\left(4 - r^2\right)^{3/2}\Big]_{r=0}^{r=2\cos\theta} d\theta = -\frac{16}{3} \int_0^{\pi/2} (\sin^3 \theta - 1) \, d\theta$$

$$= -\frac{16}{3}\left[-\frac{1}{3} \cos \theta(\sin^2 \theta + 2) - \theta\right]_{\theta=0}^{\theta=\pi/2} = \frac{8\pi}{3} - \frac{32}{9} \approx 4.82 .$$

9. The solid region resembles an ice cream cone, and is sketched below. The sphere is centered at $(0, 0, \frac{1}{2})$ and has radius $a = \frac{1}{2}$. The cone and the sphere intersect when $z^2 + z^2 = z$, or $z = 0$ (the bottom tip of the cone), or $z = \frac{1}{2}$ (at the rim of the cone). The equation of the cone can be written in spherical

coordinates as $\rho^2 \cos^2\phi = \rho^2 \sin^2\phi$ or, for $\rho \neq 0$, $\phi = \frac{\pi}{4}$ (since $0 \leq \phi \leq \pi$ by definition). In spherical coordinates the equation of the sphere is $\rho^2 = \rho \cos \phi$, or $\rho = \cos \phi$ (since $\rho \neq 0$ for the top of the region). Therefore, the volume of the region is given in spherical coordinates by the triple integral

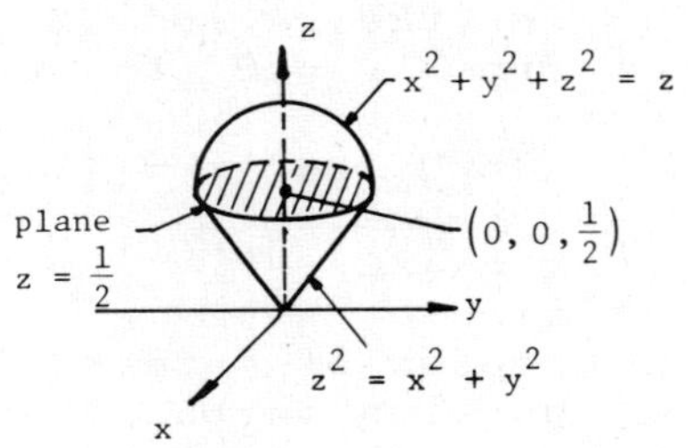

$$V = \iiint dV = \int_0^{2\pi} \int_0^{\pi/4} \int_0^{\cos \phi} \rho^2 \sin \phi \, d\rho \, d\phi \, d\theta$$

$$= \int_0^{2\pi} \int_0^{\pi/4} \frac{1}{3} \cos^3\phi \sin \phi \, d\phi \, d\theta$$

$$= -\frac{1}{12} \int_0^{2\pi} \cos^4 \phi \Big]_{\phi=0}^{\phi=\pi/4} d\theta = \frac{\pi}{8} \approx 0.39 .$$

10. A sketch of the solid is shown in the figure at the right. We will use cylindrical coordinates. The plane $z = y$ becomes $z = r \sin \theta$ in cylindrical coordinates. The region of integration in the xy-plane is the interior of the semi-circle $y = \sqrt{1 - x^2}$. In cylindrical coordinates this region is given by $0 \leq \theta \leq \pi$ and $0 \leq r \leq 1$. Since the region is geometrical we take the density as unity. Then the mass is given by,

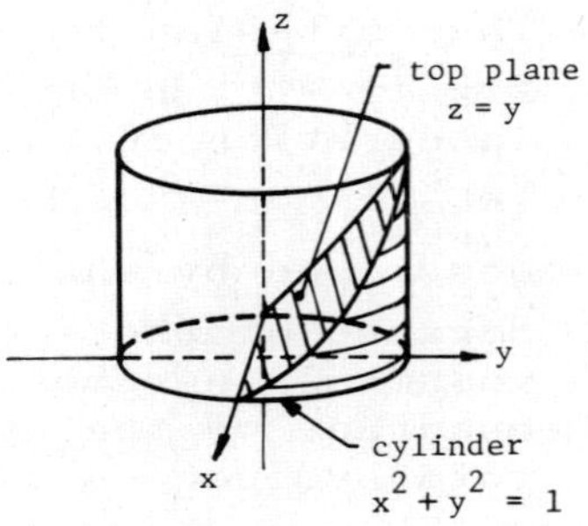

$$M = \iiint \delta \, dV$$

$$= \int_0^{\pi} \int_0^1 \int_0^{r \sin \theta} dz \, r \, dr \, d\theta$$

$$= \int_0^{\pi} \int_0^1 r^2 \sin \theta \, dr \, d\theta = \frac{1}{3} \int_0^{\pi} \sin \theta \, d\theta = \frac{2}{3} .$$

From the symmetry of the solid across the yz-plane, $\bar{x} = 0$. To find $\bar{y}$ and $\bar{z}$ we calculate the first moments:

$$\iiint y\delta \, dV = \int_0^{\pi} \int_0^1 \int_0^{r \sin \theta} r \sin \theta \, dz \, r \, dr \, d\theta$$

$$= \int_0^{\pi} \int_0^1 r^3 \sin^2\theta \, dr \, d\theta = \frac{1}{4} \int_0^{\pi} \sin^2\theta \, d\theta$$

$$= \frac{1}{4}\left(\frac{\theta}{2} - \frac{1}{4} \sin 2\theta\right)\Big]_{\theta=0}^{\theta=\pi} = \frac{\pi}{8}$$

so that $\bar{y} = \frac{\pi}{8} \div \frac{2}{3} = \frac{3\pi}{16}$.

Also,

$$\iiint z\delta \, dV = \int_0^{\pi} \int_0^1 \int_0^{r\sin\theta} z \, dz \, r \, dr \, d\theta$$

$$= \int_0^{\pi} \int_0^1 \tfrac{1}{2}z^2\Big]_{z=0}^{z=r\sin\theta} r \, dr \, d\theta$$

$$= \int_0^{\pi} \int_0^1 \tfrac{1}{2}r^3\sin^2\theta \, dr \, d\theta = \tfrac{1}{8}\int_0^{\pi} \sin^2\theta \, d\theta = \tfrac{\pi}{16}$$

from which it follows that $\bar{z} = \frac{\pi}{16} \div \frac{2}{3} = \frac{3\pi}{32}$.

11. We may choose the origin at the vertex of the cone with the z-axis as the axis of the cone. Then an equation for the cone in Cartesian coordinates is given by $z = \sqrt{x^2 + y^2}$, $0 \le z \le h$. A portion of the cone is shown at the right. From the geometry of the figure we see that the vertex angle α of the cone satisfies $\tan\alpha = \frac{a}{h}$. In spherical coordinates, the Cartesian equation $z = h$ for the base of the cone becomes $\rho\cos\phi = h$ or, $\rho = h\sec\phi$. Thus, the moment of inertia about the z-axis is given in spherical coordinates by the triple integral,

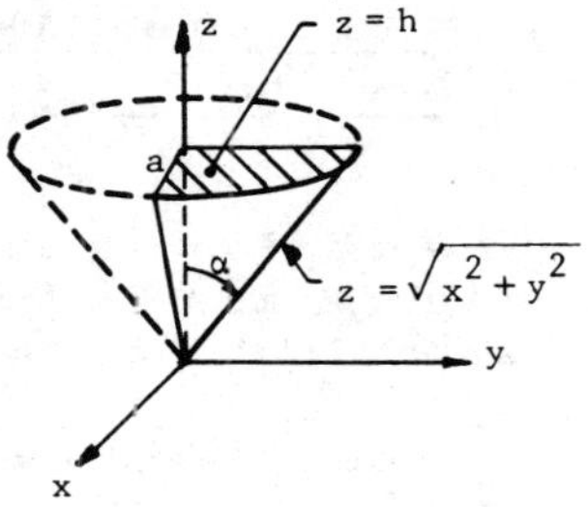

$$I_z = \iiint (x^2 + y^2)\,\delta \, dV \qquad (\delta \equiv 1)$$

$$= \int_0^{2\pi} \int_0^{\alpha} \int_0^{h\sec\phi} (\rho^2\sin^2\phi)\,\rho^2\sin\phi \, d\rho \, d\phi \, d\theta$$

$$= \frac{h^5}{5} \int_0^{2\pi} \int_0^{\alpha} \tan^3\phi \, \sec^2 {}_{2}\phi \, d\phi \, d\theta$$

$$= \frac{h^5}{5} \int_0^{2\pi} \frac{1}{4}\tan^4\alpha \, d\theta = \frac{\pi h^5}{10}\tan^4\alpha = \frac{\pi a^4 h}{10}$$

since $\alpha = \tan^{-1}\left(\frac{a}{h}\right)$.

12. The region R is sketched in the figure at the right. From the transformation equations

$$u = x - y \quad \text{and} \quad v = x + y$$

we find by routine algebra

$$x = \frac{1}{2}(u + v)$$

$$y = \frac{1}{2}(v - u)\ .$$

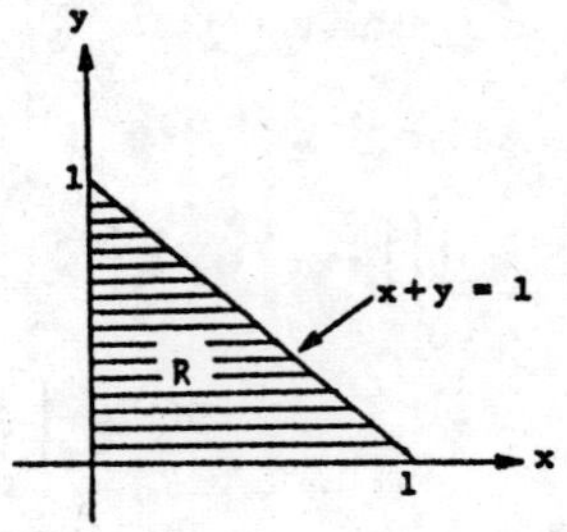

The Jacobian of the transformation is

$$J(u,v) = \frac{\partial(x,y)}{\partial(u,v)} = \begin{vmatrix} 1/2 & 1/2 \\ -1/2 & 1/2 \end{vmatrix} = \frac{1}{2}\ .$$

The region R is transformed to the region G in the uv-plane as follows:

<u>left boundary</u> $x = 0,\ 0 \le y \le 1$ becomes $u = -y$ and $v = y$ or $v = -u$;

<u>right boundary</u> (hypotenuse) $x + y = 1$ becomes $v = 1$;

<u>base boundary</u> $y = 0,\ 0 \le x \le 1$ becomes $u = x$ and $v = x$ or $v = u$.

The region is sketched in the figure at the right. Thus substitution in the integral gives

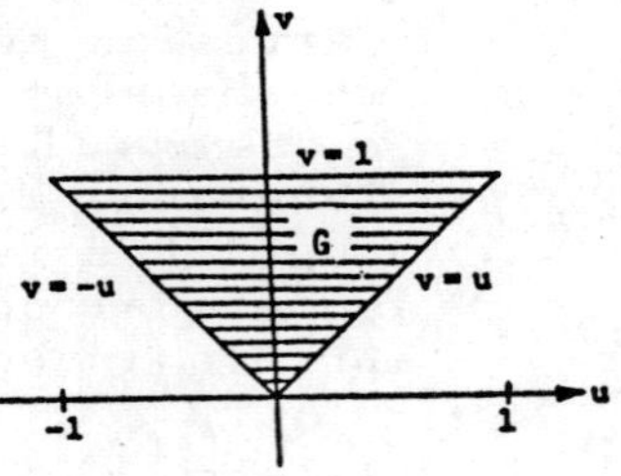

$$\iint_R \cos\left(\frac{x - y}{x + y}\right) dx\, dy = \iint_G \cos\left(\frac{u}{v}\right) \cdot \frac{1}{2}\, du\, dv$$

$$= \frac{1}{2} \int_0^1 \int_{-v}^{v} \cos\left(\frac{u}{v}\right) du\, dv$$

$$= \frac{1}{2} \int_0^1 v \sin\left(\frac{u}{v}\right)\Big|_{u=-v}^{u=v} dv$$

$$= \int_0^1 v \sin 1\, dv$$

$$= \frac{1}{2} v^2 \sin 1 \Big|_{v=0}^{v=1}$$

$$= \frac{1}{2} \sin 1 \approx 0.42074\ .$$

CHAPTER 14 INTEGRATION IN VECTOR FIELDS

14.1 LINE INTEGRALS

OBJECTIVE: For a curve C specified by the position vector
$$\vec{r}(t) = g(t)\vec{i} + h(t)\vec{j} + k(t)\vec{k}, \quad a \le t \le b$$
evaluate the line integral
$$\int_C f(x,y,z)\ ds$$
for a given function f along C.

1. Evaluate the integral of $f(x,y,z) = x - z$ along the curve $\vec{r}(t) = t\vec{i} + (1 - t)\vec{j} + \vec{k}$, $0 \le t \le 1$.

Solution. First we express ds in terms of dt:

$$ds = \sqrt{\left(\frac{dx}{dt}\right)^2 + \left(\frac{dy}{dt}\right)^2 + \left(\frac{dz}{dt}\right)^2}\ dt$$
$$= \sqrt{(1)^2 + (\_\_\_\_)^2 + (\_\_\_\_)^2}\ dt$$
$$= \sqrt{2}\ dt\ .$$

Thus,

$$\int_C f(x,y,z)\ ds = \int_{\_\_\_}^{\_\_\_} f[x(t),y(t),z(t)]\sqrt{2}\ dt$$
$$= \sqrt{2}\int_0^1 [x(t) - z(t)]dt$$
$$= \sqrt{2} \cdot \_\_\_\_\_\_\_\_\_\_\_\_$$
$$= \sqrt{2} \cdot \tfrac{1}{2}(t - 1)^2\Big]_0^1 = \_\_\_\_\_\_\_\_ .$$

2. Integrate $f(x,y,z) = x + y - z$ over the path from $(0,0,0)$ to $(1,1,1)$ shown in the figure on the next page.

Solution. The path in the xy-plane is described by

$$\vec{r}_1(t) = \_\_\_\_\_\_\_\_\_\_\_\_,\quad 0 \le t \le 1$$
$$|\vec{v}_1(t)| = \_\_\_\_\_\_\_\_\_\_ .$$

---

1. -1, 0, $\int_0^1$, $\int_0^1 (t - 1)\ dt$, $-\frac{\sqrt{2}}{2}$

The second path is given by

$\vec{r}_2(t) = \vec{i} + \vec{j} + t\vec{k}$, ____ $\leq t \leq$ ____

$|\vec{v}_2(t)| =$ ________ .

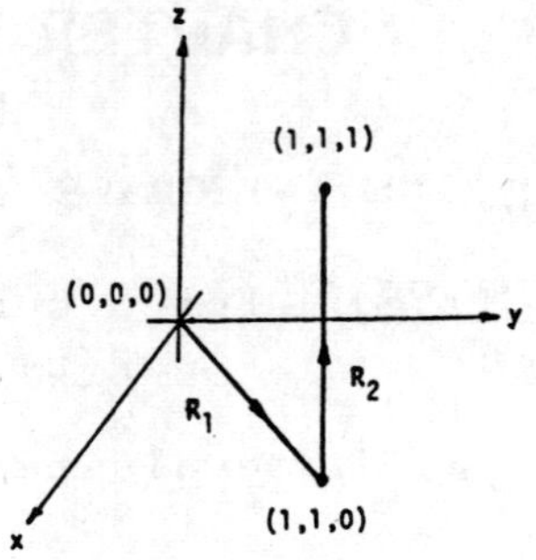

Having decided on the parameterization, we integrate $f(x,y,z) = x + y - z$ along each path in the direction of increasing t:

$$\int_{C_1 \cup C_2} f(x,y,z)\, ds = \int_0^1 (t + t - 0)\sqrt{2}\, dt$$

$$+ \int_{\_\_\_}^{\_\_\_} \_\_\_\_\_\_\_\_ \, dt$$

$$= \_\_\_\_\_\_\_\_ \Big]_0^1 + \left[2t - \frac{t^2}{2}\right]_0^1$$

$$= \_\_\_\_\_\_ + \frac{3}{2} .$$

14.2 VECTOR FIELDS, WORK, CIRCULATION, AND FLUX

OBJECTIVE A: Define the term vector field and give several examples of vector fields.

3. Let D be a region of 3-space. If, to each point P in D, a ________ $\vec{F}(P)$ is assigned, the collection of all such ________ is called a vector ________.

4. For a fluid flowing with steady-state flow in a region D, a vector field is given by the assignment of a ________ vector $\vec{v}$ indicating the flow at each point of D. This vector field may be described by writing a vector equation for the velocity at each point $P(x,y,z)$ of D.

5. If the gradient vector of a scalar function is attached to each point of a level curve, or level surface, of the function, a vector field is obtained. If the function is $z = f(x,y)$, this vector field lies in ____________; if $w = f(x,y,z)$ the vector field lies ____________. In the latter case we have a three-dimensional vector field on ________________.

---

2. $t\vec{i} + t\vec{j}$, $\sqrt{2}$, $0 \leq t \leq 1$, 1, $\int_0^1 (1 + 1 - t) \cdot 1\, dt$, $\sqrt{2}t^2$, $\sqrt{2}$

3. vector, vectors, field

4. velocity

5. the xy-plane, in space, the level surface

OBJECTIVE B: For a specified curve C evaluate the line integral

$$\int_C \vec{F} \cdot d\vec{r}$$

where $\vec{F} = M(x,y,z)\vec{i} + N(x,y,z)\vec{j} + P(x,y,z)\vec{k}$ is a given vector field with continuous components throughout some connected region D that contains C. Assume $\vec{r} = x\vec{i} + y\vec{j} + z\vec{k}$ is the position vector from the origin to the point (x,y,z).

6. If $\vec{F}$ is interpreted as a force whose point of application moves along the curve C from a point A to a point B, then the line integral

$$\int_C \vec{F} \cdot d\vec{r}$$

is the ________ done by the ________ along the curve.

7. If we calculate the dot product of the vectors $\vec{F}$ and $d\vec{r}$, an alternate form for the line integral in the Objecitve B is

________________________ .

8. Let us calculate $\int_C \vec{F} \cdot d\vec{r}$ for the force

$\vec{F} = (x - z)\vec{i} + (1 - xy)\vec{j} + y\vec{k}$ as its point of application moves from the origin to the point $A(1,1,1)$
(a) along the straight line $x = y = z$, and
(b) along the curve
$$x = t^2, \quad y = t, \quad z = t^3, \quad 0 \le t \le 1.$$

Solution. (a) The integral to be evaluated is

$$\int_C \vec{F} \cdot d\vec{r} = \int_C (x - z)\, dx + (1 - xy)\, dy + y\, dz ,$$

which, for the straight line path $x = y = z$, becomes

$$\int_C \vec{F} \cdot d\vec{r} = \int_{\_\_}^{\_\_} \_\_\_\_\_\_\_\_\_\_ \, dy = \_\_\_\_\_\_ .$$

(b) Along the curve $x = t^2$, $y = t$, $z = t^3$, $0 \le t \le 1$ we get

$$\int_C \vec{F} \cdot d\vec{r} = \int_{\_\_}^{\_\_} \_\_\_\_\_\_\_\_\_\_\_\_\_\_\_\_\_\_\_\_ \, dt$$

$$= \int_0^1 \left(1 + 4t^3 - 2t^4\right) dt = \_\_\_\_\_\_ .$$

---

6. work, force

7. $\int_C M\, dx + N\, dy + P\, dz$

8. (a) $\int_0^1 (1 + y - y^2)\, dy$, $\frac{7}{6}$ (b) $\int_0^1 (t^2 - t^3)2t\, dt + (1 - t^3)\, dt + t \cdot 3t^2\, dt$, $\frac{8}{5}$

Notice that the line integral depends on the path C joining the origin to A(1,1,1) since the values obtained in parts (a) and (b) are different.

9. Suppose a particle moves upward along the helix whose vector equation is given by

$$\vec{r}(t) = \cos t\vec{i} + \sin t\vec{j} + t\vec{k}, \quad 0 \le t \le 2\pi .$$

Find the work done on the particle by the force

$$\vec{F} = (-zy)\vec{i} + (zx)\vec{j} + (xy)\vec{k}$$

as the point of application moves along C from the point A(1,0,0) to the point B(1,0,2π).

Solution. The work done is given by the integral

$$W = \int_C \vec{F} \cdot d\vec{r} = \int_a^b \vec{F}\big(x(t),y(t),z(t)\big) \cdot \frac{d\vec{r}}{dt}\, dt .$$

Now, in terms of the parameter t, the force $\vec{F}$ with point of application on the helix C is given by

$\vec{F}\big(x(t),y(t),z(t)\big) =$ ____________________ .

Also, $\frac{d\vec{r}}{dt} = (-\sin t)\vec{i} +$ ________ $\vec{j} + \vec{k}$ so that

$\vec{F} \cdot \frac{d\vec{r}}{dt} = t \sin^2 t +$ ____________ = ____________ .

As t varies from t = 0 to t = 2π, the point P(x,y,z) on C varies from ________ to ________. Therefore, the work done by $\vec{F}$ from A to B is given by,

$W = \int_{\_\_}^{\_\_}$ ____________ dt = ____________]$_{\_\_}^{\_\_}$ $= 2\pi^2$.

10. Find the work done by the force

$$\vec{F} = y\vec{i} + z^2\vec{j} + x\vec{k} ,$$

as the point of application moves from A(0,0,0) along the y-axis to (0,-5,0), then in a straight line to the point B(0,1,1).

Solution. Let C_1 denote the line segment from A(0,0,0) to (0,-5,0), and let C_2 denote the straight line segment from (0,-5,0) to B(0,1,1). The path is sketched at the right. The total work done is the sum of two line integrals,

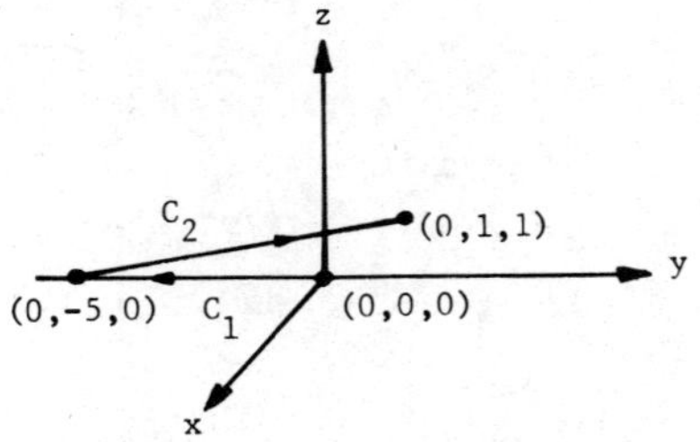

$$W = \int_{C_2} \vec{F} \cdot d\vec{r} + \int_{C_2} \vec{F} \cdot d\vec{r} .$$

---

9. $(-t \sin t)\vec{i} + (t \cos t)\vec{j} + (\sin t \cos t)\vec{k}$, $\cos t$, $t \cos^2 t + \sin t \cos t$, $t + \sin t \cos t$, A(1,0,0), B(1,0,2π), $\int_0^{2\pi} (t + \sin t \cos t)\, dt$, $\frac{1}{2}t^2 + \frac{1}{2}\sin^2 t\Big]_0^{2\pi}$

We want to find parametric representations for C_1 and C_2. The line segment C_1 is given by $x = 0$, $y = -t$, $z = 0$ for $0 \le t \le 5$. Notice that as t varies from $t = 0$ to $t = 5$, we move from the point ________ to the point ________. A parametric representation for C_2 is given by $x = 0$, $y = 1 + 6t$, $z =$ ________. As t varies from $t =$ ______ to $t =$ ______, we move from the point $(0,-5,0)$ to the point $(0,1,1)$. Thus,

on C_1: $\vec{r} = \vec{r}_1(t) = -t\vec{j}$, $\dfrac{d\vec{r}_1}{dt} =$ ________,

$\vec{F} = \vec{F}_1(t) =$ ________, and $\vec{F}_1 \cdot \dfrac{d\vec{r}_1}{dt} = 0$;

on C_2: $\vec{r} = \vec{r}_2(t) = (1 + 6t)\vec{j} +$ ______$\vec{k}$, $\dfrac{d\vec{r}_2}{dt} =$ ________,

$\vec{F} = \vec{F}_2(t) =$ ________________, and

$\vec{F}_2 \cdot \dfrac{d\vec{r}_2}{dt} =$ ________________.

Therefore, the work done is

$$W = \int_0^5 \text{\_\_\_\_\_\_\_\_}\, dt + \int_{\_\_}^{\_\_} 6(1 + t)^2\, dt = \text{\_\_\_\_\_\_\_\_\_\_}.$$

11. Suppose $\vec{F}(x,y,z)$ is the velocity field of a fluid flowing through a region in space and that

$$C: \quad \vec{r}(t) = x(t)\vec{i} + y(t)\vec{j} + z(t)\vec{k}, \quad a \le t \le b,$$

is a curve lying in the region. Then the integral

$$\int_C \vec{F} \cdot d\vec{r}$$

is called the ______________ of $\vec{F}$ along C. If C is a closed curve, the value of the flow integral is called the ______________ around the curve.

OBJECTIVE C: Given a continuous two-dimensional vector flow field $\vec{F}$, find the flux of $\vec{F}$ across a specified curve C in the xy-plane. Assume that C is piecewise smooth enough to have a tangent and that the direction across C is specified.

12. If $\vec{n}$ is a unit normal vector indicating the direction of flow across C, then the flux of $\vec{F}$ across C is given as a line integral

________________.

---

10. $(0,0,0)$ $(0,-5,0)$, $1 + t$, -1, 0, $-\vec{j}$, $-t\vec{i}$, $1 + t$, $6\vec{j} + \vec{k}$, $(1 + 6t)\vec{i} + (1 + t)^2\vec{j} + 0\vec{k}$, $6(1 + t)^2$, 0, $\int_{-1}^{0}$, 2 11. flow integral, circulation 12. $\int_C \vec{F} \cdot \vec{n}\, ds$

13. If C is a simple closed curve in the xy-plane, and if the counterclockwise direction on C is taken as the positive direction (as the direction of increasing arc length), then the flux of the field $\vec{F}(x,y) = M(x,y)\vec{i} + N(x,y)\vec{j}$ outward across C can be given by the line integral

________________ .

This integral has the advantage that it can be evaluated using ________ parameterization of C, provided we integrate in the positive direction along C.

14. Find the flux of the field $\vec{F} = xy^2\vec{i} + x^2y\vec{j}$ outward across the circle $x^2 + y^2 = a^2$.

Solution. A parameterization of the circle is $x = a \cos t$, $y =$ ________, $0 \le t \le$ ______. Using the line integral in Problem 13 for the flux we have,

$$\oint_C (M\,dy - N\,dx) = \oint_C \_\_\_\_\_\_\_\_\_\_\_\_$$

$$= \int_0^{2\pi} \_\_\_\_\_\_\_\_\_\_\_\_ \, dt$$

$$= 2a^4 \int_0^{2\pi} \tfrac{1}{4}(1 + \cos 2t) \_\_\_\_\_\_\_\_ \, dt$$

$$= 2a^4 \int_0^{2\pi} \tfrac{1}{4}(1 - \cos^2 2t)\, dt$$

$$= 2a^4 \int_0^{2\pi} \tfrac{1}{4}[1 - \tfrac{1}{2}(1 + \cos 4t)]\, dt$$

$$= 2a^4 \int_0^{2\pi} \_\_\_\_\_\_\_\_\_\_ \, dt$$

$$= 2a^4 [\tfrac{t}{8} - \tfrac{1}{32} \sin 4t]_0^{2\pi} = \_\_\_\_\_\_\_\_ .$$

The positive answer means that the net flux is __________.

14.3 GREEN'S THEOREM IN THE PLANE

15. In mathematics, the flux density is called the __________ of a vector flow field $\vec{F}$. If $\vec{F}(x,y) = M(x,y)\vec{i} + N(x,y)\vec{j}$, then

div $\vec{F}$ = ________________ .

---

13. $\oint_C (M\,dy - N\,dx)$, any

14. $a \sin t$, 2π, $xy^2\,dy - x^2y\,dx$, $2a^4 \cos^2 t \sin^2 t$, $1 - \cos 2t$, $\frac{1}{8} - \frac{1}{8}\cos 4t$, $\frac{\pi a^4}{2}$, outward

15. divergence, $\frac{\partial M}{\partial x} + \frac{\partial N}{\partial y}$

16. The divergence of a vector field $\vec{F}(x,y)$ is a ________-valued function.

[OBJECTIVE A]: Find the divergence of a given vector field $\vec{F}(x,y)$.

17. For the vector field $\vec{F}(x,y) = (e^x + y^2)\vec{i} + (x^2y - y)\vec{j}$ the divergence is given by

$$\text{div } \vec{F} = \frac{\partial M}{\partial x} + \frac{\partial N}{\partial y}$$

$$= \_\_\_\_\_\_ + x^2 - 1$$

$$= \_\_\_\_\_\_\_\_\_\_ .$$

18. In mathematics, the circulation density is called the ________ of a vector flow field $\vec{F}$. If $\vec{F}(x,y) = M(x,y)\vec{i} + N(x,y)\vec{j}$, then

$$\text{curl } \vec{F} = \_\_\_\_\_\_\_\_\_\_ .$$

19. The curl of a vector field $\vec{F}(x,y)$ is a ________-valued function.

[OBJECTIVE B]: Find the curl of a given vector field $\vec{F}(x,y)$.

20. For the vector field in Problem 17, the curl is given by

$$\text{curl } \vec{F} = \frac{\partial N}{\partial x} - \frac{\partial M}{\partial y}$$

$$= 2xy - \_\_\_\_\_\_$$

$$= \_\_\_\_\_\_\_\_\_\_ .$$

21. In the flux-divergence form, Green's theorem is

$$\oint_C M\,dy - N\,dx = \iint_R \_\_\_\_\_\_\_\_\_\_\_\_ \,dx\,dy.$$

That is, under suitable conditions the ______ of $\vec{F} = M\vec{i} + N\vec{j}$ outward across a simple closed curve C equals the double integral of the ____________ over the region R enclosed by C.

22. In the circulation curl form, Green's theorem is

$$\oint_C M\,dx + N\,dy = \iint_R \_\_\_\_\_\_\_\_\_\_\_\_ \,dx\,dy.$$

---

16. scalar

17. e^x, $e^x + x^2 - 1$

18. curl, $\frac{\partial N}{\partial x} - \frac{\partial M}{\partial y}$

19. scalar

20. $2y$, $2y(x - 1)$

21. $\frac{\partial M}{\partial x} + \frac{\partial N}{\partial y}$, flux, divergence of $\vec{F}$

That is, the counterclockwise ______________ of $\vec{F} = M\vec{i} + N\vec{j}$ around C equals the double integral of the ______________ over the region R enclosed by C.

OBJECTIVE C: Use Green's theorem to evaluate a given line integral around a simple closed curve C. Assume all hypotheses of the theorem are satisfied, and that the curve C is oriented in the counterclockwise direction in the xy-plane.

23. If C is a suitable simple __________ curve in the xy-plane containing the region R as its interior, and if M, N, $\frac{\partial M}{\partial y}$, and $\frac{\partial N}{\partial x}$ are ______________ functions of (x,y) in R and on C, then

$$\oint_C (M\,dx + N\,dy) = \_\_\_\_\_\_\_\_\_\_\_\_\_\_\_\_\_\_ .$$

24. Give some examples of "suitable" regions R with a piecewise smooth boundary C in the xy-plane for which Green's theorem applies.

(a) ____,

(b) ____,

(c) ____,

(d) ____.

25. Let C be the closed curve bounded by $x = 0$, $y = \sqrt{1 - x^2}$ and $y = 0$, oriented counterclockwise. Evaluate the line integral

$$\oint_C 3y^4\,dx + (x^2 + 12y^3x)\,dy$$

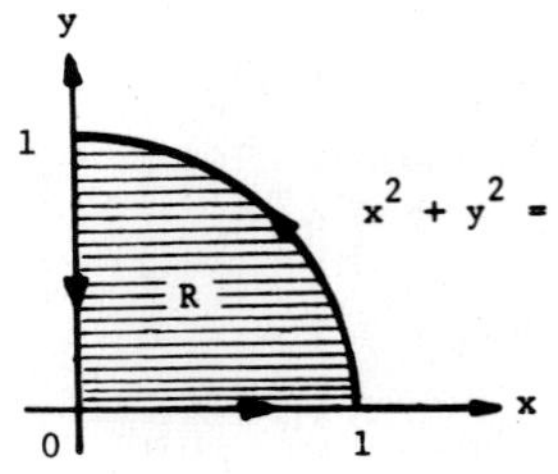

Solution. We will use Green's theorem. Thus, for $M = 3y^4$ and $N = x^2 + 12y^3x$,

$$\frac{\partial N}{\partial x} - \frac{\partial M}{\partial y} = (\_\_\_\_\_\_\_\_) - 12y^3 = \_\_\_\_\_\_\_\_ .$$ Hence,

---

22. $\frac{\partial N}{\partial x} - \frac{\partial M}{\partial y}$, circulation, curl of $\vec{F}$

23. closed, continuous, $\iint_R \left[\frac{\partial N}{\partial x} - \frac{\partial M}{\partial y}\right] dx\,dy$

24. (a) R is bounded by a simple closed curve C such that a line parallel to either axis cuts C in at most two points
(b) R is a rectangle
(c) R is an annulus
(d) R combines regions like those in (a), (b), or (c)

$$\oint_C 3y^4\ dx + (x^2 + 12y^3x)\ dy = \int_{\_\_\_}^{\_\_\_} \int_{\_\_\_}^{\_\_\_} \underline{\qquad\qquad}\ dy\ dx$$

$$= \int_0^1 \underline{\qquad\qquad}\ dx = \underline{\qquad\qquad}\ .$$

26. Let us evaluate the line integral

$$\oint_C xy\ dx + \left(x^{3/2} + y^{3/2}\right)\ dy\ ,$$

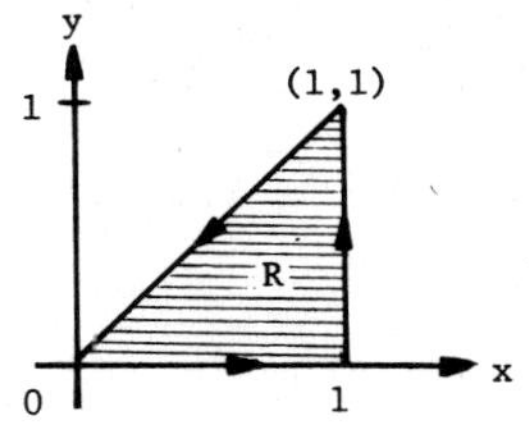

where C is the triangle with vertices $(0,0)$, $(1,0)$, $(1,1)$ oriented counterclockwise. Using Green's theorem,

$$\oint_C xy\ dx + \left(x^{3/2} + y^{3/2}\right)\ dy$$

$$= \iint_R \underline{\qquad\qquad}\ dA = \int_{\_\_\_}^{\_\_\_} \int_{\_\_\_}^{\_\_\_} \left(\tfrac{3}{2}x^{1/2} - x\right)\ dy\ dx$$

$$= \int_0^1 \underline{\qquad\qquad}\ dx = \tfrac{3}{5}x^{5/2} - \underline{\qquad\qquad}\Big]_0^1 = \underline{\qquad\qquad}\ .$$

OBJECTIVE D: Use Green's theorem to find the area of a given suitable region R in the xy-plane with a piecewise smooth boundary C.

27. For regions R, like those specified in Problem 24 above, the area of R can be calculated via Green's theorem as the line integral __________________. (See Problems 35-38 in Section 14.3 of Thomas/Finney.)

28. Let us find the area of the region bounded below by the x-axis and above by one arch of the cycloid parameterized by

$$x = a(\phi - \sin\phi),$$
$$y = a(1 - \cos\phi),$$

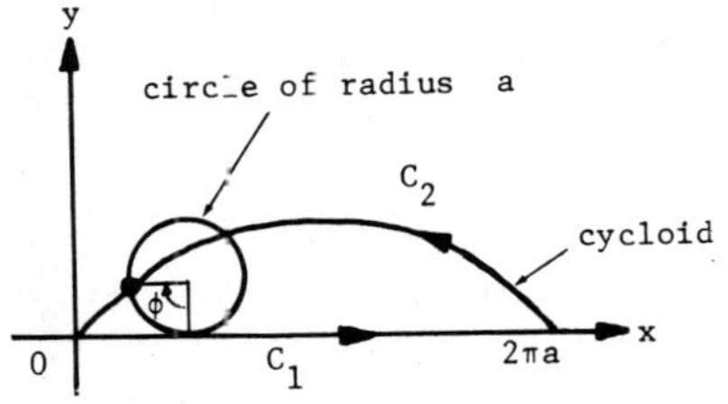

$0 \le \phi \le 2\pi$. (See the figure at the right.) We take the counterclockwise orientation on the curve C bounding the region. The curve C is made up of two smooth curves: the x-axis C_1, and the cycloid arch C_2. Now,

---

25. $2x + 12y^3$, $2x$, $\int_0^1 \int_0^{\sqrt{1-x^2}} 2x\ dy\ dx$, $2x\sqrt{1 - x^2}$, $\frac{2}{3}$

26. $\frac{3}{2}x^{1/2} - x$, $\int_0^1 \int_0^x$, $x\left(\frac{3}{2}x^{1/2} - x\right)$, $\frac{1}{3}x^3$, $\frac{4}{15}$

27. $\frac{1}{2}\oint_C x\ dy - y\ dx$

on C_1: $x\,dy - y\,dx$ = ______________ = 0, and

on C_2: $x\,dy - y\,dx = a(\phi - \sin\phi)(a \sin\phi\, d\phi)$

− ______________________

= ____________ .

Therefore, the area of the region is given by (use the correct orientation),

$$A = \frac{1}{2}\oint_C x\,dy - y\,dx$$

$$= \frac{a^2}{2}\int_{\_\_\_}^{\_\_\_} \_\_\_\_\_\_\_\_\_\_\_\_\_\_\_\_\_\_\_\_ \, d\phi$$

$$= \frac{a^2}{2}\left[\sin\phi - \cos\phi + \_\_\_\_\_\_\_\_\_\_\_\_\right]_{2\pi}^{0} = \_\_\_\_\_\_\_\_\_\_ .$$

14.4 SURFACE AREA AND SURFACE INTEGRALS

OBJECTIVE A: Using integration, find the area of a specified surface $f(x,y,z) = c$ in space.

29. Suppose $f(x,y,z) = c$ is a surface in space. Let R denote the region representing the "shadow" of the surface over some plane whose normal is the vector $\vec{p}$. Let γ be the angle between $\vec{\nabla}f$ and $\vec{p}$. Then, assuming $\vec{\nabla}f$ is not parallel to the plane, so that $\vec{\nabla}f \cdot \vec{p} \neq 0$, the area of the surface over R is given by

$$\text{Surface area} = \iint_R \frac{1}{|\cos\gamma|}\, dA$$

$$= \iint_R \_\_\_\_\_\_\_\_\_\_\_\_\_\_\_\_\_\_ \, dA .$$

30. Let us find the area of the surface of that portion of the sphere $x^2 + y^2 + z^2 = a^2$ that lies inside the elliptic cylinder $4y^2 + x^2 = a^2$. The figure at the top of the next page shows that portion which lies above the first quadrant of the xy-plane. Because of the symmetries of the ellipse and the sphere, the total surface area is equal to 8 times that shown in the figure. The gradient vector $\vec{\nabla}f$ = ____________ is normal to the surface of the sphere, and the unit vector $\vec{k}$ is

---

28. $x \cdot 0 - 0 \cdot dx$, $a(1 - \cos\phi)(a - a\cos\phi)\, d\phi$, $a^2(\phi \sin\phi + 2\cos\phi - 2)$, $\int_{2\pi}^{0} (\phi\sin\phi + 2\cos\phi - 2)\, d\phi$, $2\sin\phi - 2\phi$, $3\pi a^2$

29. $\dfrac{|\vec{\nabla}f|}{|\vec{\nabla}f \cdot \vec{p}|}$

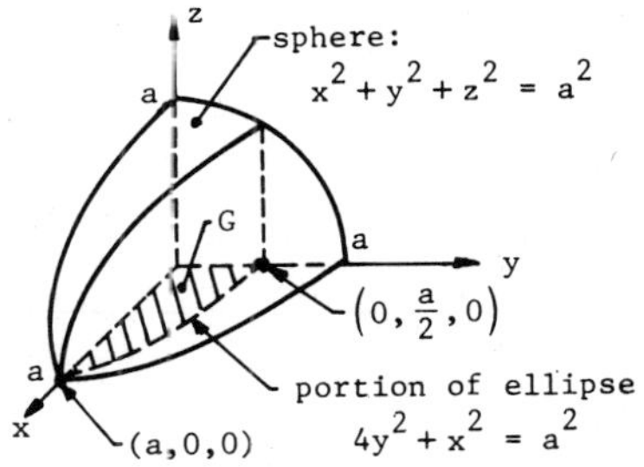

perpendicular to the ground plane. The region of integration R is described by the inequalities $0 \le x \le a$ and ______ $< y \le$ ______________ . Therefore, the total surface area is given by

$$S = 8 \iint_R \frac{|\vec{\nabla} f|}{|\vec{\nabla} f \cdot \vec{k}|}\, dA$$

$$= 8 \iint_R \underline{\qquad\qquad\qquad}\, dA$$

$$= 8 \int_{\underline{\quad}}^{\underline{\quad}} \int_{\underline{\quad}}^{\underline{\quad}} \frac{a}{\sqrt{a^2 - x^2 - y^2}}\, dy\, dx$$

(since $x^2 + y^2 + z^2 = a^2$, $z \ge 0$)

$$= 8a \int_0^a \sin^{-1} \frac{y}{\sqrt{a^2 - x^2}} \Big]_{y=0}^{(a^2-x^2)^{1/2}/2} dx$$

$$= 8a \int_0^a \underline{\qquad\qquad}\, dx = \underline{\qquad\qquad} .$$

31. If the surface is given in the form $z = f(x,y)$, we define the function $F(x,y) = f(x,y) - z = 0$. In this situation

$$\vec{\nabla} F = \underline{\qquad\qquad\qquad\qquad} .$$

Let R denote the region in the xy-plane representing the "shadow" of the surface $z = f(x,y)$. From Problem 29, the surface area is given by

$$\text{Surface area} = \iint_R \frac{|\vec{\nabla} F|}{|\vec{\nabla} F \cdot \vec{k}|}\, dA$$

$$= \iint_R \underline{\qquad\qquad\qquad\qquad}\, dx\, dy .$$

(See Problems 37-42 in Section 14.4 of Thomas/Finney.)

32. Suppose we wish to find the surface area of that part of the cylinder $z^2 + x^2 = a^2$, $a > 0$, which lies above the triangle in the xy-plane bounded by $x = 0$, $y = 0$, and $x + y = a$. A sketch of the surface is shown at the top of the next page. Since $z \ge 0$, we can take $z = \sqrt{a^2 - x^2}$ as the function

---

30. $2x\vec{i} + 2y\vec{j} + 2z\vec{k}$, $0 \le y \le \frac{1}{2}\sqrt{a^2 - x^2}$, $\dfrac{\sqrt{4x^2 + 4y^2 + 4z^2}}{2z}$, $\displaystyle\int_0^a \int_0^{\sqrt{a^2-x^2}/2}$, $\dfrac{\pi}{6}$, $\dfrac{4\pi a^2}{3}$

31. $\vec{\nabla} F = \dfrac{\partial f}{\partial x}\vec{i} + \dfrac{\partial f}{\partial y}\vec{j} - \vec{k}$, $\sqrt{f_x^2 + f_y^2 + 1}$

$z = f(x,y)$ describing the surface over the triangular region R in the xy-plane. Then,

$\frac{\partial z}{\partial x}$ = ____________ and

$\frac{\partial z}{\partial y}$ = ________ . Thus,

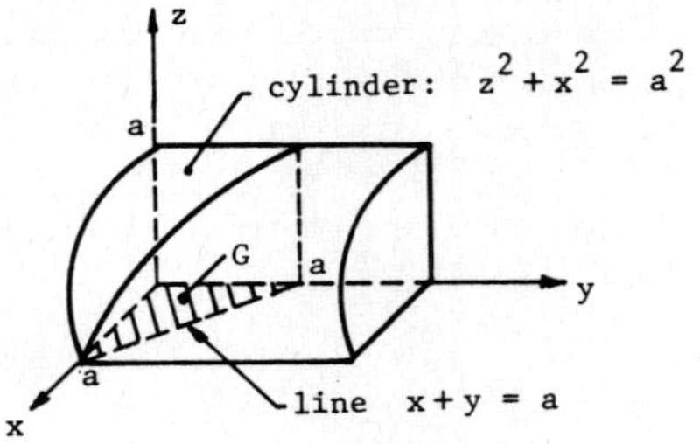

$\sqrt{\left(\frac{\partial z}{\partial x}\right)^2 + \left(\frac{\partial z}{\partial y}\right)^2 + 1}$

= ______________ .

The region of integration R is described by the inequalities _____ $\le x \le$ _____ and _____ $\le y \le$ _____. Therefore, from Problem 31, the surface area is given by the integral

Surface area = $\int_{\_\_\_}^{\_\_\_} \int_{\_\_\_}^{\_\_\_}$ ________________ dy dx

$$= a \int_0^a \frac{a - x}{\sqrt{a^2 - x^2}} \, dx$$

$$= a^2 \int_0^a \frac{dx}{\sqrt{a^2 - x^2}} - a \int_0^a \frac{x \, dx}{\sqrt{a^2 - x^2}}$$

$$= a^2 \left(\_\_\_\_\_\_\_\_\right) + a\sqrt{a^2 - x^2}\Big]_{x=0}^{x=a} = \_\_\_\_\_\_\_\_\_\_ .$$

OBJECTIVE B: Let S denote a specified surface in space. Assuming that $g(x,y,z)$ is a given continuous function on S, find the surface integral

$$\iint_S g(x,y,z) \, d\sigma .$$

33. Consider the surface integral $\iint_S z^2 \, d\sigma$, where S is the portion of the cone $z^2 = x^2 + y^2$ between the planes $z = 2$ and $z = 5$. The surface S and its projection R onto the xy-plane are sketched at the right. Observe that R is the ring _____ $\le x^2 + y^2 \le$ _____. The function $z =$ ________ defines the surface S over R.

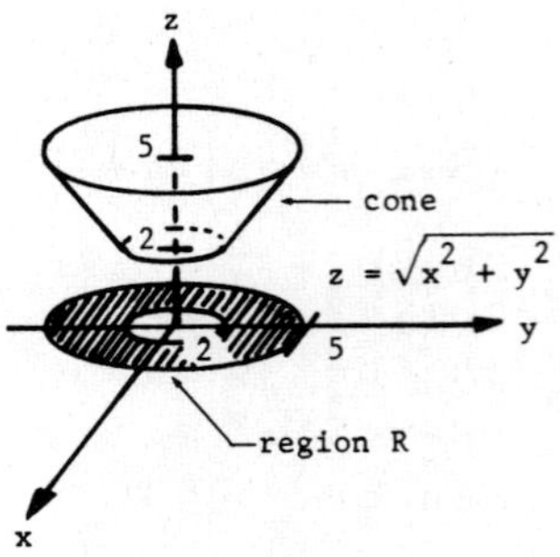

---

32. $\frac{-x}{\sqrt{a^2 - x^2}}$, 0, $\frac{a}{\sqrt{a^2 - x^2}}$, $0 \le x \le a$, $0 \le y \le a - x$, $\int_0^a \int_0^{a-x} \frac{a}{\sqrt{a^2 - x^2}} \, dy \, dx$, $\sin^{-1} \frac{x}{a}$, $\frac{a^2}{2}(\pi - 2)$

Thus, from Problem 31, we use the gradient

$$\vec{\nabla}z = \frac{\partial z}{\partial x}\vec{i} + \frac{\partial z}{\partial y}\vec{j} - \vec{k}\ .$$

Now,

$$\frac{\partial z}{\partial x} = \underline{\qquad\qquad} = \frac{x}{z} \quad \text{and} \quad \frac{\partial z}{\partial y} = \underline{\qquad\qquad} = \underline{\qquad\qquad}\ .$$

Hence,

$$d\sigma = \sqrt{1 + \left(\frac{x^2}{z^2}\right) + (\underline{\qquad\qquad})}\ dA = \underline{\qquad\qquad}\ dA$$

because $x^2 + y^2 + z^2 = 2z^2$ on S. Therefore

$$\iint_S z^2\ d\sigma = \iint_R (x^2 + y^2)\sqrt{2}\ dA = \int_{\_\_}^{\_\_} \int_{\_\_}^{\_\_} \underline{\qquad\qquad\qquad}\ dr\ d\theta$$

$$= \underline{\qquad\qquad\qquad} (5^4 - 2^4) = \frac{609\pi\sqrt{2}}{2} \approx 1352.86.$$

OBJECTIVE C: Evaluate the flux integral

$$\iint_S \vec{F} \cdot \vec{n}\ d\sigma\ ,$$

for a specified vector field $\vec{F}$ and surface S, where $\vec{n}$ is a unit vector normal to S and pointing in a consistent way (e.g., always outward or always inward). Assume that the components of $\vec{F}$ are continuous on S.

34. Let S be the paraboloid $z = 1 - x^2 - y^2$ above the xy-plane, and let $\vec{n}$ be a unit normal to S at each point, which is directed upward. Let $\vec{F}$ be the vector field on S given by $\vec{F} = x\vec{i} + y\vec{j} + z\vec{k}$. We want to find the surface integral

$$\iint_S \vec{F} \cdot \vec{n}\ d\sigma\ .$$

Let us first calculate the vector $\vec{n}$. If we define $g(x,y,z) = z - (1 - x^2 - y^2)$, then the gradient vector $\vec{\nabla}g = 2x\vec{i} + \underline{\qquad}\vec{j} + \vec{k}$ is perpendicular to the surface S at each point. Moreover, it is directed upward and outward so it is pointing in the direction specified for $\vec{n}$. The unit normal $\vec{n}$ can be written as

$$\vec{n} = \frac{\vec{\nabla}g}{|\vec{\nabla}g|} = \underline{\qquad\qquad\qquad\qquad}\ .$$

Therefore,

$$\vec{F} \cdot \vec{n} = \underline{\qquad\qquad\qquad\qquad} = \frac{1 + x^2 + y^2}{\sqrt{4x^2 + 4y^2 + 1}}$$

---

33. $4 \le x^2 + y^2 \le 25$, $\sqrt{x^2 + y^2}$, $\frac{x}{\sqrt{x^2 + y^2}}$, $\frac{y}{\sqrt{x^2 + y^2}}$, $\frac{y}{z}$, $\frac{y^2}{z^2}$, $\sqrt{2}$, $\int_0^{2\pi} \int_2^5 \sqrt{2}\, r^3\ dr\ d\theta$, $\frac{\sqrt{2}\pi}{2}$

because $z = 1 - x^2 - y^2$ on the surface S. Next,

$$d\sigma = \sqrt{1 + z_x^2 + z_y^2}\, dA = \underline{\hspace{3cm}}\, dA.$$

The surface S projects onto the region R in the xy-plane described by ______________. Therefore

$$\iint_S \vec{F} \cdot \vec{n}\, d\sigma = \iint_R (\underline{\hspace{5cm}})\, dA$$

$$= \int_{\_\_}^{\_\_} \int_{\_\_}^{\_\_} \underline{\hspace{4cm}}\, dr\, d\theta$$

↑___ in polar coordinates

$$= \underline{\hspace{2cm}} \approx 4.71.$$

14.5 THE DIVERGENCE THEOREM

OBJECTIVE A: Given a vector field $\vec{F} = M\vec{i} + N\vec{j} + P\vec{k}$ with suitable continuity conditions, verify the divergence theorem

$$\iint_S \vec{F} \cdot \vec{n}\, d\sigma = \iiint_D \text{div } \vec{F}\, dV .$$

Assume that D is a convex region with no holes or bubbles enclosed by a piecewise smooth surface S with outward normal $\vec{n}$.

35. Let us verify the divergence theorem for the field $\vec{F} = (2xyz)\vec{i} + (x^2z)\vec{j} + (x^2y + 1)\vec{k}$ and the cube with center at the origin and faces in the planes $x = \pm 1$, $y = \pm 1$, $z = \pm 1$. First,

$$\text{div } \vec{F} = \frac{\partial M}{\partial x} + \frac{\partial N}{\partial y} + \frac{\partial P}{\partial z} = 2yz + \underline{\hspace{2cm}} + 0 = \underline{\hspace{2cm}} .$$

Thus, if D is the region enclosed by the cube,

$$\iiint_D \text{div } \vec{F}\, dV = \int_{-1}^{1} \int_{-1}^{1} \int_{-1}^{1} 2yz\, dz\, dy\, dx$$

$$= \int_{-1}^{1} \int_{-1}^{1} \underline{\hspace{2.5cm}}\Big]_{z=-1}^{z=1} dy\, dx = \underline{\hspace{2cm}} .$$

Next, we compute $\iint \vec{F} \cdot \vec{n}\, d\sigma$ as the sum of the integrals over the six faces separately. We begin with the two faces perpendicular to the x-axis. For the face $x = -1$ and the face $x = +1$, respectively, we have the first and second lines of the following table (complete the table):

---

34. $2y$, $\dfrac{2x\vec{i} + 2y\vec{j} + \vec{k}}{\sqrt{4x^2 + 4y^2 + 1}}$, $\dfrac{2x^2 + 2y^2 + z}{\sqrt{4x^2 + 4y^2 + 1}}$, $\sqrt{4x^2 + 4y^2 + 1}$, $0 \le x^2 + y^2 \le 1$, $1 + x^2 + y^2$,

$\displaystyle\int_0^{2\pi} \int_0^1 (1 + r^2)\, r\, dr\, d\theta$, $\dfrac{3\pi}{2}$

range of integration	outward unit normal	field $\vec{F}$
$-1 \le y \le 1,\ -1 \le z \le 1$	$-\vec{i}$	$(-2yz)\vec{i} + z\vec{j} + (y+1)\vec{k}$
________________	______	________________

For each of these planes, $x = x(y,z)$ is a constant function of (y,z) so that

$$d\sigma = \sqrt{1 + \left(\frac{\partial x}{\partial y}\right)^2 + \left(\frac{\partial x}{\partial z}\right)^2}\ dy\ dz = \underline{\qquad\qquad}\ .$$

Therefore, the sum of the integrals over these two faces is

$$\iint \vec{F} \cdot \vec{n}\ d\sigma = \int_{-1}^{1}\int_{-1}^{1} 2yz\ dz\ dy + \underline{\qquad\qquad\qquad\qquad}$$

$$= 2\int_{-1}^{1} yz^2\Big]_{z=-1}^{z=1}\ dy = \underline{\qquad\qquad}\ .$$

Now consider the two faces perpendicular to the y-axis. For the face $y = -1$ and the face $y = +1$, respectively, complete the first and second lines of the following table:

range of integration	outward unit normal	field $\vec{F}$
$-1 \le x \le 1,\ -1 \le z \le 1$	$-\vec{j}$	$(-2xz)\vec{i} + (x^2z)\vec{j} + (-x^2+1)\vec{k}$
________________	______	________________

For each of these planes $d\sigma = \underline{\qquad\qquad}$. Therefore, the sum of the surface integrals over these two faces is

$$\iint \vec{F} \cdot \vec{n}\ d\sigma = \int_{-1}^{1}\int_{-1}^{1} (-x^2z)\ dz\ dx + \underline{\qquad\qquad\qquad\qquad}$$

$$= \underline{\qquad\qquad}\ .$$

Finally, we take the two faces perpendicular to the z-axis. For the face $z = -1$ and the face $z = +1$, respectively, we obtain the first and second lines of the following table:

range of integration	outward unit normal	field $\vec{F}$
$-1 \le x \le 1,\ -1 \le y \le 1$	$-\vec{k}$	$(-2xy)\vec{i} + (-x^2)\vec{j} + (x^2y+1)\vec{k}$
$-1 \le x \le 1,\ -1 \le y \le 1$	$\vec{k}$	$(2xy)\vec{i} + x^2\vec{j} + (x^2y + 1)\vec{k}$

---

35. 0, $2yz$, yz^2, 0, $-1 \le y \le 1$, $-1 \le z \le 1$, $\vec{i}$, $(2yz)\vec{i} + z\vec{j} + (y+1)\vec{k}$, dy dz, $\int_{-1}^{1}\int_{-1}^{1} 2yz\ dz\ dy$, 0, $-1 \le x \le 1$, $-1 \le z \le 1$, $\vec{j}$, $(2xz)\vec{i} + (x^2z)\vec{j} + (x^2+1)\vec{k}$, dz dx, $\int_{-1}^{1}\int_{-1}^{1} x^2z\ dz\ dx$, 0, 0

For each of these planes $d\sigma = dx\ dy$, and the sum of the surface integrals over these two faces is

$$\iint \vec{F} \cdot \vec{n}\ d\sigma = \int_{-1}^{1} \int_{-1}^{1} -(x^2y + 1)\ dx\ dy + \int_{-1}^{1} \int_{-1}^{1} (x^2y + 1)\ dx\ dy$$

$$= 0 .$$

Therefore, the surface integral over the six faces of the cube is

$$\iiint_D \text{div}\ \vec{F}\ dV = \underline{\qquad\qquad} = \iint_S \vec{F} \cdot \vec{n}\ d\sigma .$$

36. Give some examples of "suitable" regions D enclosed by a piecewise smooth bounding surface S for which the divergence theorem applies. One example is when D is a convex region with no holes such that when D is projected into a coordinate plane it produces a simply connected region R, with the property that any line perpendicular to that coordinate plane at an interior point of R intersects the bounding surface S in at most ______ points. Other examples are:

(a) ________________,

(b) ________________________,

(c) ____
______________________________________ .

37. Let us verify the divergence for the vector field $\vec{F} = x\vec{i} + y\vec{j} + z\vec{k}$, where D is the region inside the cylinder $x^2 + y^2 = 1$ and between the planes $z = 0$ and $z = 2$. Now,

$$\text{div}\ \vec{F} = \frac{\partial M}{\partial x} + \frac{\partial N}{\partial y} + \frac{\partial P}{\partial z} = \underline{\qquad\qquad} ,$$

so that

$$\iiint_D \text{div}\ \vec{F}\ dV = 3 \iiint_D dV = \underline{\qquad\qquad} = 6\pi .$$

The surface integral $\iint \vec{F} \cdot \vec{n}\ d\sigma$ is the sum of three integrals: one over the top, another one over the bottom, and a third one over the side of the cylinder. We calculate each of these separately.

<u>The top</u>: $z = 2$, $0 \le x^2 + y^2 \le 1$, $\vec{n} = \underline{\qquad\qquad}$ is the outer normal, and

$$\vec{F} = \underline{\qquad\qquad\qquad} .$$

---

36. two, (a) cubes
(b) two concentric spheres
(c) regions that can be split up into a finite number of simple regions of the type described above

Then,

$$\iint \vec{F} \cdot \vec{n}\, d\sigma = \iint \_\_\_\_\_\_ \, d\sigma = 2 \times \text{area of top} = \_\_\_\_\_\_ .$$

<u>The bottom</u>: $z = 0$, $0 \le x^2 + y^2 \le 1$, $\vec{n} = \_\_\_\_\_\_$ is the outer normal, and

$$\vec{F} = \_\_\_\_\_\_\_\_\_\_ .$$

Then,

$$\iint \vec{F} \cdot \vec{n}\, d\sigma = \iint \_\_\_\_\_\_ \, d\sigma = 0 .$$

<u>The side</u>: $x^2 + y^2 = 1$, $0 \le z \le 2$, $\vec{F} = \_\_\_\_\_\_\_\_$ and

$\vec{n} = \dfrac{x\vec{i} + y\vec{j}}{\sqrt{x^2 + y^2}} = x\vec{i} + y\vec{j}$ is the outer normal. Hence,

$$\iint \vec{F} \cdot n\, d\sigma = \iint \_\_\_\_\_\_\_\_ \, d\sigma = \iint d\sigma = \_\_\_\_\_\_\_\_ = 4\pi .$$

Therefore, the surface integral over the entire cylindrical can is

$$\iiint_D \text{div}\, \vec{F}\, dV = \_\_\_\_\_\_ + 0 + 4\pi = \iint_S \vec{F} \cdot \vec{n}\, d\sigma .$$

OBJECTIVE B: Given a continuous three-dimensional vector flow field $\vec{F}$, find the flux of $\vec{F}$ outward through a specified smooth closed surface S enclosing a region D.

38. Consider the flow field $\vec{F} = y\vec{i} - x\vec{j} + (x^2 + y^2)\vec{k}$ through the portion of the paraboloid $z = 9 - x^2 - y^2$ above the xy-plane, and directed outward through the surface. We want to find the flux outward. Therefore, we seek to evaluate the surface integral

$$\_\_\_\_\_\_\_\_\_\_\_\_ ,$$

where $\vec{n}$ is the outward-pointing unit normal to the paraboloid. Let us first calculate this vector $\vec{n}$. If we define $g(x,y,z) = z - (9 - x^2 - y^2)$, then the vector $\_\_\_\_\_\_$ is a unit vector normal to the surface at each point. We find this vector to be $\dfrac{\vec{\nabla} g}{|\vec{\nabla} g|} = \dfrac{2x\vec{i} + 2y\vec{j} + \vec{k}}{\_\_\_\_\_\_\_\_}$, and it is directed upward from the surface of the paraboloid. Thus we can take $\vec{n} = \dfrac{\vec{\nabla} g}{|\vec{\nabla} g|}$. Then,

$$\vec{F} \cdot \vec{n} = \frac{\_\_\_\_\_\_\_\_}{\sqrt{4x^2 + 4y^2 + 1}} .$$

---

37. 3, $3\pi(1)^2(2)$, $\vec{k}$, $x\vec{i} + y\vec{j} + 2\vec{k}$, 2, 2π, $-\vec{k}$, $x\vec{i} + y\vec{j}$, 0, $x\vec{i} + y\vec{j} + z\vec{k}$, $x^2 + y^2$, $2\pi(1)(2)$, 2π

Next,

$$d\sigma = \sqrt{1 + \left(\frac{\partial z}{\partial x}\right)^2 + \left(\frac{\partial z}{\partial y}\right)^2}\, dA = \text{\_\_\_\_\_\_\_\_\_\_\_\_\_\_\_\_}\ dx\, dy\ .$$

The paraboloid S projects onto the region R in the xy-plane bounded by the circle $x^2 + y^2 = 9$. Therefore, the flux of $\vec{F}$ is,

$$\iint_S \vec{F} \cdot \vec{n}\, d\sigma = \iint_R \left(\frac{x^2 + y^2}{\sqrt{4x^2 + 4y^2 + 1}}\right) \sqrt{4x^2 + 4y^2 + 1}\ dx\, dy$$

$$= \int_{\_\_}^{\_\_} \int_{\_\_}^{\_\_} \text{\_\_\_\_\_\_}\ dr\, d\theta = \frac{\pi 3^4}{2} \approx 127.23\ .$$

↳ in polar coordinates

14.6 STOKES'S THEOREM

OBJECTIVE A: Given a vector field $\vec{F} = M\vec{i} + N\vec{j} + P\vec{k}$, where M, N, and P are continuous functions of (x,y,z), together with their first-order partial derivatives, throughout a region D containing a specified smooth, simply connected, orientable surface S bounded by a simple closed curve C, verify Stokes's theorem. Assume that the positive direction around C is the one induced by the positive orientation of S.

39. Under the hypotheses stated in the above Objective, if $\vec{n}$ is a positive unit vector normal to S, then

$$\oint_C \vec{F} \cdot d\vec{r} = \text{\_\_\_\_\_\_\_\_\_\_\_\_\_\_\_\_\_\_\_\_}\ .$$

40. Consider the oriented triangle shown in the figure at the right. Let

$$\vec{F} = y^2\vec{i} + xy\vec{j} - 2xz\vec{k}\ .$$

We will verify Stokes's theorem for the triangular plane bounded by the sides C_1, C_2, C_3 directed as shown. First, let us find the positive unit vector normal to the plane that agrees with the orienta-tion around the triangle. A vector normal to the plane is

$2\vec{i} \times (2\vec{j} + \vec{k}) = \text{\_\_\_\_\_\_\_\_\_\_\_\_}$.

Notice that this vector points

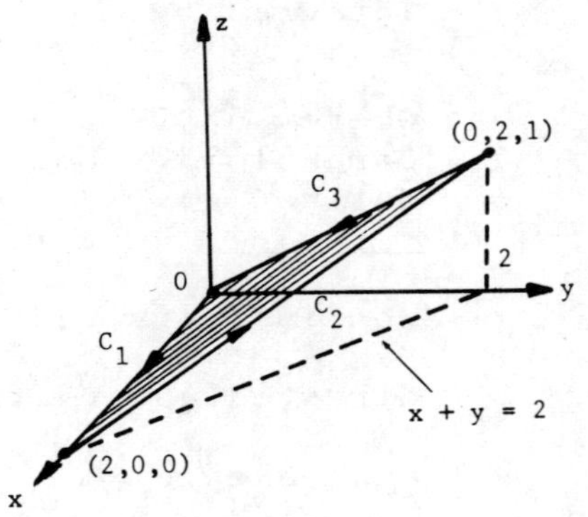

---

38. $\iint_S \vec{F} \cdot \vec{n}\, d\sigma$, $\frac{\vec{\nabla} g}{|\vec{\nabla} g|}$, $\sqrt{4x^2 + 4y^2 + 1}$, $2xy - 2xy + x^2 + y^2$, $\sqrt{4x^2 + 4y^2 + 1}$, $\int_0^{2\pi} \int_0^3 r^3\, dr\, d\theta$

39. $\iint_S (\text{curl}\ \vec{F}) \cdot \vec{n}\, d\sigma$

upward (positive $\vec{k}$ component) and toward the left in the figure (negative $\vec{j}$ component), so it points in the positive direction relative to the counterclockwise direction around the boundary. Therefore, the unit vector $\vec{n}$ is given by $\vec{n}$ = ____________. An equation of the plane is $-2(y - 0) + 4(z - 0) = 0$, or z = ________. Also,

$$\text{curl } \vec{F} = \begin{vmatrix} \vec{i} & \vec{j} & \vec{k} \\ \frac{\partial}{\partial x} & \frac{\partial}{\partial y} & \frac{\partial}{\partial z} \\ y^2 & xy & -2xz \end{vmatrix} = \_\_\_\_\_\_\_\_\_\_\_\_\_\_ .$$

For the element of surface area we use,

$$d\sigma = \sqrt{1 + \left(\frac{\partial z}{\partial x}\right)^2 + \left(\frac{\partial z}{\partial y}\right)^2}\, dx\, dy = \_\_\_\_\_\_\_\_\_\_\_\_\_\_ \, dx\, dy$$

or $d\sigma = \frac{1}{2}\sqrt{5}\, dx\, dy$. Therefore,

$$\text{curl } \vec{F} \cdot \vec{n}\, d\sigma = (2z\vec{j} - y\vec{k}) \cdot (-\tfrac{1}{2}\vec{j} + \vec{k})dx\, dy = (-z - y)dx\, dy$$
$$= \_\_\_\_\_\_\_\_\_\_ \, dx\, dy \quad \text{on the plane.}$$

Hence,

$$\iint_S \text{curl } \vec{F} \cdot \vec{n}\, d\sigma = \int_{\_\_}^{\_\_} \int_{\_\_}^{\_\_} -\tfrac{3}{2}y\, dy\, dx = \int_0^2 -\tfrac{3}{4}(2 - x)^2\, dx$$
$$= \_\_\_\_\_\_\_ .$$

Now, to find the line integral $\oint_C \vec{F} \cdot d\vec{r}$, we will calculate three integrals, one for C_1, C_2, and C_3 separately, and sum them. The integrand in the line integral is

$$\vec{F} \cdot (dx\vec{i} + dy\vec{j} + dz\vec{k}) = \_\_\_\_\_\_\_\_\_\_\_\_\_\_ .$$

On C_1: $z = 0$, $y = 0$, $0 \le x \le 2$, and thus

$$\vec{F} \cdot d\vec{r} = \_\_\_\_\_\_\_ . \quad \text{Hence} \int_{C_1} \vec{F} \cdot d\vec{r} = 0 .$$

On C_2: The line segment from $(2,0,0)$ to $(0,2,1)$ can be represented parametrically by $x = 2 - 2t$, $y = 2t$, $z = t$ for $0 \le t \le 1$. Then, $\vec{F} \cdot d\vec{r}$ on the segment can be expressed in terms of t by,

$$\vec{F} \cdot d\vec{r} = (2t)^2(-2\, dt) + \_\_\_\_\_\_\_\_\_ - 2(2 - 2t)t\, dt$$
$$= \_\_\_\_\_\_\_\_\_ \, dt, \quad \text{and therefore}$$

$$\int_{C_2} \vec{F} \cdot d\vec{r} = \int_{\_\_}^{\_\_} 4(-3t^2 + t)dt = \_\_\_\_\_\_ .$$

(check the orientation for C_2 here)

40. $-2\vec{j} + 4\vec{k}$, $\frac{-\vec{j} + 2\vec{k}}{\sqrt{5}}$, $\frac{y}{2}$, $2z\vec{j} - y\vec{k}$, $\sqrt{1 + 0 + \frac{1}{4}}$, $-\frac{3}{2}y$, $\int_0^2 \int_0^{2-x}$, -2, $y^2\, dx + xy\, dy - 2xz\, dz$, 0, $(2 - 2t)(2t)(2\, dt)$, $4(-3t^2 + t)$, $\int_0^1$, -2, 0, -2

On C_3: $x = 0,\ z = \frac{y}{2},\ 2 \geq y \geq 0,$ and thus

$$\vec{F} \cdot d\vec{r} = y^2 \cdot 0 + 0dy - 0dz = \underline{\qquad\qquad} \quad \text{and}$$

$$\int_{C_3} \vec{F} \cdot d\vec{r} = 0 .$$

Therefore, summing the three line integrals,

$$\oint_C \vec{F} \cdot d\vec{r} = \underline{\qquad\qquad} = \iint_S \text{curl } \vec{F} \cdot \vec{n}\, d\sigma .$$

41. Stokes's theorem says that, under conditions normally met in practice, the ______________ of a vector field $\vec{F}$ around the boundary of a surface in space, in a direction counterclockwise with respect to the ________ vector $\vec{n}$ of the surface, is equal to the double integral of ____________ over the surface.

42. An important vector identity states that

$$\text{curl grad } f \quad \text{or} \quad \vec{\nabla} \times \vec{\nabla} f$$

equals ____________________. The identity holds for any function $f(x,y,z)$ having ____.

OBJECTIVE B: Use the surface integral in Stokes's theorem to calculate the circulation of a specified vector field $\vec{F}$ around a space curve C in an indicated direction.

43. Find the circulation of $\vec{F} = z\vec{i} - x\vec{j} + y\vec{k}$ around C: the circle $x^2 + y^2 = 4$ in the xy-plane, counterclockwise when viewed from above.

Solution. According to Stokes's theorem, the circulation is given by the integral

$$\iint_S \text{curl } \vec{F} \cdot \vec{n}\, d\sigma$$

where S is the hemisphere __________________. For the curl of $\vec{F} = z\vec{i} - x\vec{j} + y\vec{k}$, we have

$$\vec{\nabla} \times \vec{F} = \begin{vmatrix} \vec{i} & \vec{j} & \vec{k} \\ \frac{\partial}{\partial x} & \frac{\partial}{\partial y} & \frac{\partial}{\partial z} \\ z & -x & y \end{vmatrix} = \underline{\qquad\qquad\qquad} .$$

The outer unit normal of S is the vector

$$\vec{n} = \frac{x\vec{i} + y\vec{j} + z\vec{k}}{\sqrt{x^2 + y^2 + z^2}} = \underline{\qquad\qquad\qquad} .$$

---

41. circulation, normal, curl $\vec{F} \cdot \vec{n}$

42. the zero vector, continuous first and second partial derivatives

Next, we calculate the element of surface area. The gradient to the surface S satisfies

$$|\vec{\nabla}F| = |2x\vec{i} + 2y\vec{j} + 2z\vec{k}| = 2\sqrt{x^2 + y^2 + z^2} = 4 ,$$
$$|\vec{\nabla}F \cdot \vec{p}| = |\vec{\nabla}F \cdot \vec{k}| = |2z| = 2z ,$$
$$d\sigma = \frac{|\vec{\nabla}F|}{|\vec{\nabla}F \cdot \vec{p}|} \, dA = \frac{2}{z} \, dA .$$

(Note $F(x,y,z) = x^2 + y^2 + z^2 = 4$ is the <u>surface</u> S and <u>not</u> the vector field $\vec{F} = z\vec{i} - x\vec{i} + y\vec{k}$.) Thus,

$$\iint_S \text{curl } \vec{F} \cdot \vec{n} \, d\sigma = \iint_S \underline{\hspace{3cm}} \, d\sigma$$
$$= \iint_{x^2+y^2 \le 4} \underline{\hspace{3cm}}$$
$$= \underline{\hspace{3cm}} .$$

14.7 PATH INDEPENDENCE, POTENTIAL FUNCTIONS, AND CONSERVATIVE FIELDS

OBJECTIVE A: Know the meaning of a conservative field $\vec{F}$ throughout an open connected region D in space, and the basic implications of conservative fields.

44. A vector field $\vec{F}$ is said to be <u>conservative</u> on D if there is a scalar function f on D such that

$$\vec{F} = \underline{\hspace{3cm}} .$$

The function f is called a ______________________ for $\vec{F}$.

45. If $\vec{F}$ is conservative on D, then

$$\text{curl } \vec{F} = \underline{\hspace{4cm}}$$

throughout D.

46. Whenever $\vec{F}$ is conservative on D, the work integral over <u>any</u> closed path in D has value ________.

47. If the components of $\vec{F} = M\vec{i} + N\vec{j} + P\vec{k}$ are continuous throughout D, then $\vec{F}$ is conservative if and only if for all points A and B in D the value of

$$\int_A^B \vec{F} \cdot d\vec{r}$$

is ______________________________ joining A to B in D.

---

43. $x^2 + y^2 + z^2 = 4$, $\vec{i} + \vec{j} - \vec{k}$, $\frac{x\vec{i} + y\vec{j} + z\vec{k}}{2}$, $-\frac{z}{2}$, $-dA$, -4π

44. $\vec{\nabla}f$, potential function

45. the zero vector $\vec{0}$

46. zero

47. independent of the path

48. If the integral is independent of the path from A to B, its value is

$$\int_A^B \vec{F} \cdot d\vec{r} = \underline{\hspace{3cm}}$$

where $\vec{F} = \underline{\hspace{2cm}}$.

49. Whenever a field $\vec{F}$ is conservative, the integrand in the work integral,

$$\vec{F} \cdot d\vec{r} = M dx + N dy + P dz$$

is an ____________________ .

50. If $M(x,y,z)$, $N(x,y,z)$, and $P(x,y,z)$ are continuous, together with their ____________ partial derivatives, then a necessary and sufficient condition for the expression

$$M\,dx + N\,dy + P\,dz$$

to be an exact differential is that the following equations all be satisfied:

__________, __________, __________ .

OBJECTIVE B: Determine if a specified force field $\vec{F} = M\vec{i} + N\vec{j} + P\vec{k}$ is conservative. If so, find a potential function f for the field.

51. Consider the vector field

$$\vec{F}(x,y,z) = (2xyz)\vec{i} + (x^2z)\vec{j} + (x^2y + 1)\vec{k} .$$

Let us determine if $\vec{F}$ is conservative. First, $\vec{F} \cdot d\vec{r} = (2xyz)dx + (x^2z)dy + (x^2y + 1)dz$. Then, applying the test in Problem 50 above, with $M = 2xyz$, $N = \underline{\hspace{1.5cm}}$, and $P = x^2y + 1$, we obtain

$$\frac{\partial M}{\partial z} = 2xy = \frac{\partial P}{\partial x}, \quad \frac{\partial M}{\partial y} = \underline{\hspace{1.5cm}} = \frac{\partial N}{\partial x}, \quad \text{and} \quad \frac{\partial \underline{\hspace{0.7cm}}}{\partial y} = x^2 = \frac{\partial N}{\partial z} .$$

Therefore, we conclude that $\vec{F}$ is conservative and there is a function $f(x,y,z)$ such that $\vec{F} \cdot d\vec{r} = df$. We want to find the potential function f. Now f satisfies

$$\frac{\partial f}{\partial x} = 2xyz, \quad \frac{\partial f}{\partial y} = \underline{\hspace{1.5cm}}, \quad \text{and} \quad \frac{\partial f}{\partial z} = \underline{\hspace{2cm}}.$$

To find f we integrate the first of these equations with respect to x, holding y and z constant, obtaining

---

48. $f(B) - f(A)$, $\vec{F} = \vec{\nabla} f$

49. exact differential

50. first-order, $\frac{\partial M}{\partial y} = \frac{\partial N}{\partial x}$, $\frac{\partial M}{\partial z} = \frac{\partial P}{\partial x}$, $\frac{\partial N}{\partial z} = \frac{\partial P}{\partial y}$

$$f(x,y,z) = \_\_\_\_\_\_\_\_\_\_ + g(y,z) ,$$

where $g(y,z)$ is an arbitrary function acting as the "constant of integration." Next, we differentiate the last equation with respect to y, holding x and z constant, equate this to $\frac{\partial f}{\partial y}$, and solve for $\frac{\partial g}{\partial y}$:

$$\_\_\_\_\_\_\_\_ + \frac{\partial g(y,z)}{\partial y} = x^2 z, \quad \text{so that} \quad \frac{\partial g(y,z)}{\partial y} = \_\_\_\_\_\_\_\_ .$$

Therefore, $g(y,z) = h(z)$ is a function of z alone. The expression for f then becomes

$$f(x,y,z) = \_\_\_\_\_\_\_\_\_\_ + h(z) .$$

We differentiate this last equation with respect to z, holding x and y constant, equate this to $\frac{\partial f}{\partial z}$, and solve for $h'(z)$:

$$\_\_\_\_\_\_\_\_ + h'(z) = x^2 y + 1, \quad \text{so that} \quad h'(z) = \_\_\_\_\_\_\_\_ .$$

Therefore, $h(z) = \_\_\_\_\_\_\_\_ + c$ for some arbitrary constant c. Hence we may write f as

$$f(x,y,z) = \_\_\_\_\_\_\_\_\_\_\_\_ .$$

It is easy to verify that $\vec{F} = \vec{\nabla} f$.

52. Suppose it is required to find the line integral $\int_C \vec{F} \cdot d\vec{r}$ for the force field $\vec{F}$ in Problem 51 above, where C is composed of the line segments $A(0,0,0)$ to $(0,-1,-3)$ and from $(0,-1,-3)$ to $B(-1,1,2)$. Then,

$$\int_C \vec{F} \cdot d\vec{r} = f(\_\_\_\_\_\_\_\_) - f(\_\_\_\_\_\_\_\_\_\_) = \_\_\_\_\_\_\_\_ .$$

53. Let C be a directed curve that is continuous and has bounded and piecewise-continuous first derivatives from $A(-2,1,0)$ to $B(1,0,1)$. Let $\vec{F}$ be the gravitational field of a mass M located at the origin. Find the work W done by $\vec{F}$ on a unit point mass that traverses C.

Solution. We know from Problem 5 of this chapter that the gravitational field $\vec{F}$ is the gradient of the function

$$f(x,y,z) = \frac{GM}{\sqrt{x^2 + y^2 + z^2}}$$

where G is the gravitational constant. Consequently,

$$W = \int_C \vec{F} \cdot d\vec{R} = f(\_\_\_\_\_\_\_\_) - f(\_\_\_\_\_\_\_\_) = \_\_\_\_\_\_\_\_\_\_\_\_ .$$

---

51. x^2z, $2xz$, P, x^2z, $x^2y + 1$, x^2yz, x^2z, 0, x^2yz, x^2y, 1, z, $x^2yz + z + c$

52. $(-1,1,2)$, $(0,0,0)$, 4

53. $(1,0,1)$, $(-2,1,0)$, $GM\left(\frac{1}{\sqrt{2}} - \frac{1}{\sqrt{5}}\right) \approx 0.26\ GM$

CHAPTER 14 SELF-TEST

1. Evaluate the following line integrals:

   (a) $\int_C \sqrt{x + z}\, ds$, where C is the line segment from the point $A(0,0,0)$ to $B(4,5,6)$

   (b) $\int_C y^2 dx + x^2 dy$, where C is the right semi-circle $x = \sqrt{1 - y^2}$ directed from the point $A(0,-1)$ to $B(0,1)$

2. Find the work done by the force

   $$\vec{F} = \left(\frac{1}{x + 3y + 2z} - 5x\right)\vec{i} + \left(\frac{3}{x + 3y + 2z} + 3y^2\right)\vec{j} + \left(\frac{2}{x + 3y + 2z}\right)\vec{k}$$

   as the point of application moves from $A(0,2,0)$ along the y-axis to $(0,1,0)$, and from there in a straight line to $B(1,1,1)$. <u>Hint</u>: Is the field conservative?

3. Use Green's theorem to evaluate the line integral $\oint_C y\,dx - x\,dy$, where C is the cardioid $r = 1 - \cos\theta$ directed in counter-clockwise direction.

4. Use Green's theorem to find the area of the region bounded by the hypocycloid parameterized by $x = a\cos^3 t$, $y = a\sin^3 t$, for $0 \le t \le 2\pi$. Assume the boundary is directed in the counterclockwise direction.

5. A force is given by $\vec{F} = (x^2 - xy^3)\vec{i} + (y^2 - 2xy)\vec{j}$, and its point of application moves counterclockwise around the square in the xy-plane with vertices $(0,0)$, $(3,0)$, $(3,3)$, and $(0,3)$. Find the work done.

6. Find the surface area of that part of the cylinder $x^2 + z^2 = a^2$ that lies inside the cylinder $x^2 + y^2 = a^2$.

7. Let S be the portion of the cylinder $z = \frac{1}{2}y^2$ for which $x \ge 0$, $y \ge 0$, and $x + y \le 1$. Find the surface integral

   $$\iint_S \sqrt{x(1 + 2z)}\, d\sigma .$$

8. Evaluate the flux integral

   $$\iint_S \vec{F} \cdot \vec{n}\, d\sigma ,$$

   for $\vec{F} = x\vec{i} + y\vec{j} + z\vec{k}$, given that S is the plane of the triangle with vertices $(a,0,0)$, $(0,a,0)$, $(0,0,a)$, $a > 0$, lying in the first octant, and $\vec{n}$ is the upper normal unit vector.

9. Use the divergence theorem to find the flux of $\vec{F}$ outward through the region inside the sphere $x^2 + y^2 + z^2 = 4$ and outside the cylinder $x^2 + y^2 = 1$, if the vector flow field is $\vec{F} = 6x\vec{i} - 13y\vec{j} + 12z\vec{k}$.

10. Let C be the intersection of the sphere $x^2 + y^2 + z^2 = 1$ and the cone $z = \sqrt{x^2 + y^2}$, directed in the counterclockwise sense around the z-axis. For the field

$$\vec{F} = (x^2 + z)\vec{i} + (y^2 + 2x)\vec{j} + (z^2 - y)\vec{k} ,$$

use Stokes's theorem to calculate the circulation of $\vec{F}$ around C.

11. Find the flux of the vector field $\vec{F} = -y\vec{i} + x\vec{j} + z^4\vec{k}$ outward through the sphere $x^2 + y^2 + z^2 = 4$.

12. Determine if the force field

$$\vec{F} = (2xz + 1)\vec{i} + 2y(z + 1)\vec{j} + (x^2 + y^2 + 3z^2)\vec{k}$$

is conservative. If so, find a potential function f for the field.

SOLUTIONS TO CHAPTER 14 SELF-TEST

1. (a) A parametric representation for the line segment C is $x = 4t$, $y = 5t$, and $z = 6t$ with $0 \le t \le 1$. Thus,

$$\int_C \sqrt{x + z}\, ds = \int_0^1 \sqrt{4t + 6t} \cdot \sqrt{\left(\frac{dx}{dt}\right)^2 + \left(\frac{dy}{dt}\right)^2 + \left(\frac{dz}{dt}\right)^2}\, dt$$

$$= \int_0^1 \sqrt{10t}\,\sqrt{77}\, dt = \frac{2}{3}\sqrt{770} \approx 18.50.$$

(b) A parametric representation for the semi-circle is $x = \cos\theta$ and $y = \sin\theta$ with $-\frac{\pi}{2} \le \theta \le \frac{\pi}{2}$. (Note the orientation.) Thus,

$$\int_C y^2 dx + x^2 dy = \int_{-\pi/2}^{\pi/2} [\sin^2\theta(-\sin\theta) + \cos^2\theta(\cos\theta)]\, d\theta$$

$$= \int_{-\pi/2}^{\pi/2} (\cos^3\theta - \sin^3\theta)\, d\theta = \int_{-\pi/2}^{\pi/2} \cos^3\theta\, d\theta$$

↑ (since $\sin^3\theta$ is an odd function)

$$= \frac{1}{3}(\sin\theta)(\cos^2\theta + 2)\Big]_{-\pi/2}^{\pi/2} = \frac{4}{3}.$$

2. From a little observation of the components of $\vec{F}$, it is easy to see that $\vec{F} = \vec{\nabla} f$, where

$$f(x,y,z) = \ln|x + 3y + 2z| - \frac{5}{2}x^2 + y^3.$$

Therefore, $\vec{F}$ is a conservative force field so that the work done by $\vec{F}$ from A to B is independent of the path joining them. The work done is

$$W = \int_A^B \vec{F} \cdot d\vec{r} = f(1,1,1) - f(0,2,0)$$

$$= (\ln 6 - \frac{5}{2} + 1) - (\ln 6 - 0 + 8) = -\frac{19}{2}.$$

3. Let R denote the region that lies inside the cardioid. Then,

$$\oint_C y\,dx - x\,dy = -2\iint_R dx\,dy = -2\int_0^{2\pi}\int_0^{1-\cos\theta} r\,dr\,d\theta$$

↳ note the orientation and polar coordinates

$$= \int_{2\pi}^{0} (1 - 2\cos\theta + \cos^2\theta)\, d\theta$$

$$= \theta - 2\sin\theta + \frac{\theta}{2} + \frac{1}{4}\sin 2\theta\Big]_{2\pi}^{0} = -3\pi.$$

4. A sketch of the region is given at the right. From the symmetry of the region we can calculate the area of the region in the first quadrant and multiply by 4. We use the area formula from Green's theorem. For the parameterization

$x = a\cos^3 t$ and $y = a\sin^3 t$,

$dx = -3a \sin t \cos^2 t\ dt$ and

$dy = 3a \cos t \sin^2 t\ dt$.

Thus, the area of the entire region is given by

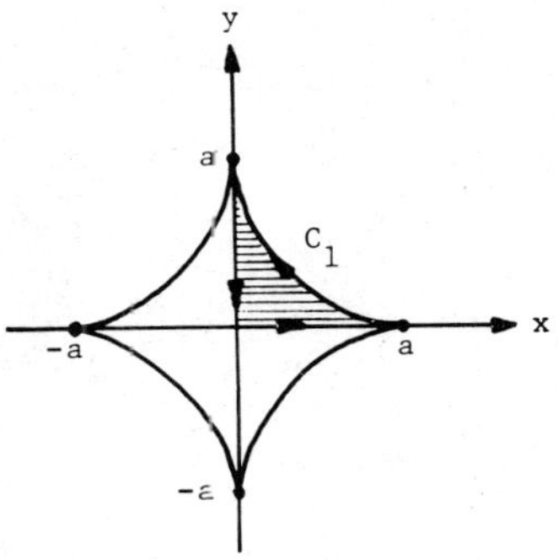

$$A = \oint \frac{1}{2}(x\,dy - y\,dx)$$

$$= 4\int_{C_1} \frac{1}{2}(x\,dy - y\,dx)$$

$$= 4\int_0^{\pi/2} \frac{1}{2}(3a^2 \cos^4 t \sin^2 t + 3a^2 \sin^4 t \cos^2 t)\ dt$$

$$= 6a^2 \int_0^{\pi/2} \cos^2 t \sin^2 t\ dt = 6a^2\left[\frac{t}{8} - \frac{1}{32}\sin 4t\right]_0^{\pi/2} = \frac{3\pi}{8}a^2 \ .$$

(as in Problem 14 of this chapter)

5. According to Green's theorem, the work done is

$$W = \oint_C \vec{F} \cdot d\vec{r} = \int_0^3 \int_0^3 \left[\frac{\partial}{\partial x}(y^2 - 2xy) - \frac{\partial}{\partial y}(x^2 - xy^3)\right] dy\ dx$$

$$= \int_0^3 \int_0^3 (-2y + 3xy^2)\ dy\ dx$$

$$= \int_0^3 (-9 + 27x)\ dx = \frac{189}{2} \ .$$

6. A sketch of the intersecting cylinders is below. By the symmetry of the surface we need only calculate the area of the top surface (above the xy-plane), and multiply this by 2. In that case, $z = \sqrt{a^2 - x^2}$ and this yields

$\dfrac{\partial z}{\partial x} = \dfrac{-x}{\sqrt{a^2 - x^2}}$ and $\dfrac{\partial z}{\partial y} = 0$. Therefore,

$\sqrt{(f_x)^2 + (f_y)^2 + 1}$

$$= \sqrt{\frac{x^2}{a^2 - x^2} + 1} = \frac{a}{\sqrt{a^2 - x^2}} .$$

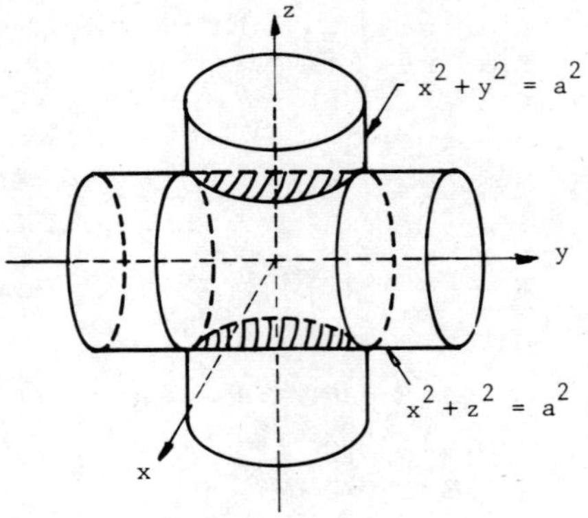

The region in the xy-plane over which the surface lies is the interior of the circle $x^2 + y^2 = a^2$. Thus, the total surface area is given by the double integral,

$$S = 2 \int_{-a}^{a} \int_{-\sqrt{a^2-x^2}}^{\sqrt{a^2-x^2}} \frac{a}{\sqrt{a^2 - x^2}}\, dy\, dx$$

$$= 2a \int_{-a}^{a} 2\, dx = 8a^2 .$$

7. The portion of the cylindrical surface is sketched below. For the element of surface area $d\sigma$ we use

$$d\sigma = \sqrt{1 + \left(\frac{\partial z}{\partial x}\right)^2 + \left(\frac{\partial z}{\partial y}\right)^2}\, dx\, dy = \sqrt{1 + 0 + y^2}\, dx\, dy .$$

The surface integral becomes

$$\iint_S \sqrt{x(1 + 2z)}\, d\sigma$$

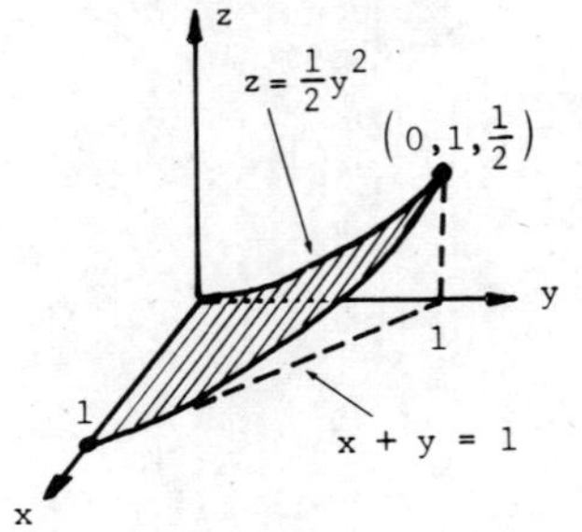

$$= \int_0^1 \int_0^{1-x} \sqrt{x}(1 + y^2)\, dy\, dx$$

$$= \int_0^1 \sqrt{x}[(1 - x) + \tfrac{1}{3}(1 - x)^3]\, dx$$

$$= \int_0^1 (\tfrac{4}{3}x^{1/2} - 2x^{3/2} + x^{5/2} - \tfrac{1}{3}x^{7/2})\, dx$$

$$= \frac{8}{9} - \frac{4}{5} + \frac{2}{7} - \frac{2}{27} \approx 0.30 .$$

8. The triangular shaped surface S is shown at the right. An equation of the plane is

$$x + y + z = a, \quad \text{or} \quad z = a - x - y \, .$$

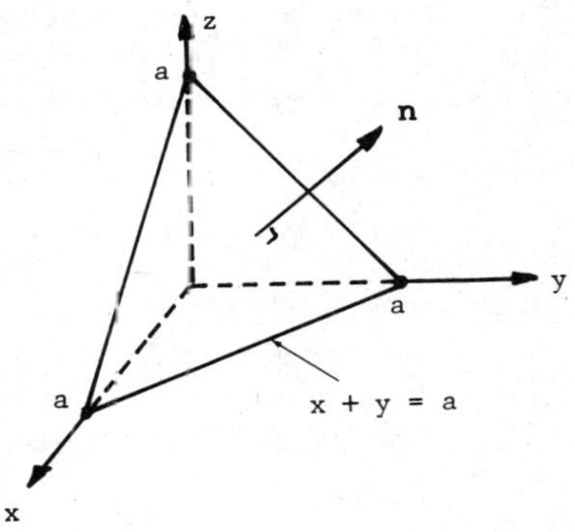

A vector normal to the plane is $\vec{N} = \vec{i} + \vec{j} + \vec{k}$, and this vector points in the upward direction. Thus,

$$\vec{n} = \frac{\vec{i} + \vec{j} + \vec{k}}{\sqrt{3}} \, .$$

For the element of surface area we have,

$$d\sigma = \sqrt{1 + \left(\frac{\partial z}{\partial x}\right)^2 + \left(\frac{\partial z}{\partial y}\right)^2}$$

$$= \sqrt{3} \, dx \, dy \, .$$

The projection of the surface onto the xy-plane is the region described by $x \geq 0$, $y \geq 0$, and $x + y \leq a$ (see figure). Thus,

$$\iint_S \vec{F} \cdot \vec{n} \, d\sigma = \iint_S \frac{1}{\sqrt{3}}(x + y + z) \, d\sigma$$

$$= \int_0^a \int_0^{a-x} (x + y + a - x - y) \, dy \, dx$$

$$= a \int_0^a (a - x) \, dx = \tfrac{1}{2}a^3 \, .$$

9. Evaluation of $\iint_S \vec{F} \cdot \vec{n} \, d\sigma$ itself would involve finding two surface integrals, one for the sphere and one for the inside cylinder. Instead we use the divergence theorem:

$$\iint_S \vec{F} \cdot \vec{n} \, d\sigma = \iiint_D \operatorname{div} \vec{F} \, dV = \iiint_D (6 - 13 + 12) \, dV$$

$$= 5 \int_0^{2\pi} \int_1^2 \int_{-\sqrt{4-r^2}}^{\sqrt{4-r^2}} dz \, r \, dr \, d\theta$$

cylindrical ⤴
coordinates

$$= 5 \int_0^{2\pi} \int_1^2 2r\sqrt{4 - r^2} \, dr \, d\theta$$

$$= 5 \int_0^{2\pi} -\tfrac{2}{3}\left(4 - r^2\right)^{3/2}\Big]_{r=1}^{r=2} d\theta = 20\pi\sqrt{3} \approx 108.83 \, .$$

10. The intersection of the sphere and the cone is shown at the right. The sphere and cone intersect when

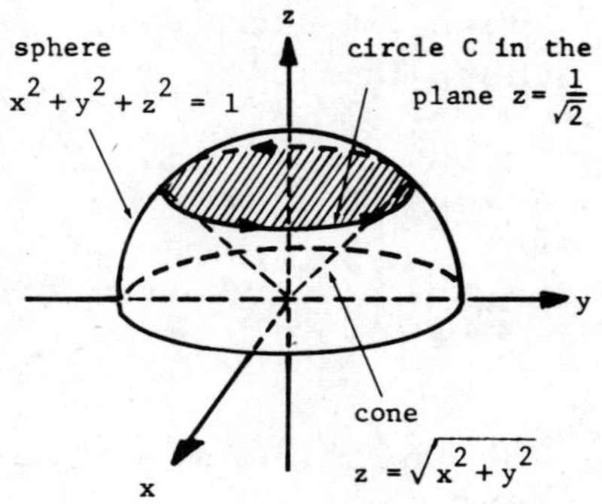

$$x^2 + y^2 + \left(\sqrt{x^2 + y^2}\right)^2 = 1$$

or

$$x^2 + y^2 = \tfrac{1}{2} \quad \text{and} \quad z = \frac{1}{\sqrt{2}} .$$

We can apply Stokes's theorem using the circle $C: \ x^2 + y^2 = \frac{1}{2}$ considered in the <u>plane</u> $z = \frac{1}{\sqrt{2}}$ (rather than using the spherical cap above it for S.) The reason for this choice of the surface is that its unit normal is the constant vector $\vec{n} = \vec{k}$ (rather than the varying unit normal on the cap). Then,

$$\text{curl } \vec{F} = \begin{vmatrix} \vec{i} & \vec{j} & \vec{k} \\ \frac{\partial}{\partial x} & \frac{\partial}{\partial y} & \frac{\partial}{\partial z} \\ x^2+z & y^2+2x & z^2-y \end{vmatrix} = -\vec{i} + \vec{j} + 2\vec{k} \ ,$$

and Stokes's theorem gives the circulation of $\vec{F}$ around C as

$$\oint_C \vec{F} \cdot d\vec{r} = \iint_S \text{curl } \vec{F} \cdot \vec{n} \, d\sigma$$

$$= \iint_S 2 \, d\sigma = 2 \cdot \text{area enclosed by the circle } C$$

$$= 2 \cdot \pi\left(\frac{1}{\sqrt{2}}\right)^2 = \pi .$$

11. We divide the sphere into the upper hemisphere $S_1: \ z = \sqrt{4 - x^2 - y^2}$ and the lower hemisphere $S_2: \ z = -\sqrt{4 - x^2 - y^2}$. In either case, a unit outer normal is given by

$$\vec{n} = \frac{x\vec{i} + y\vec{j} + z\vec{k}}{\sqrt{x^2 + y^2 + z^2}} = \frac{\vec{\nabla} w}{|\vec{\nabla} w|} \quad \text{for} \quad w = x^2 + y^2 + z^2 - 4 .$$

Thus, $\vec{n} = \frac{1}{2}(x\vec{i} + y\vec{j} + z\vec{k})$ since $x^2 + y^2 + z^2 = 4$ on the sphere. Notice that $\vec{n}$ points in the outward direction (upward for $z > 0$ and downward for $z < 0$).

An element of surface area for S_1 or S_2 is given by

$$d\sigma = \sqrt{1 + \left(\frac{\partial z}{\partial x}\right)^2 + \left(\frac{\partial z}{\partial y}\right)^2}\ dx\ dy = \sqrt{1 + \frac{x^2}{z^2} + \frac{y^2}{z^2}}\ dx\ dy$$

$$= \sqrt{\frac{x^2 + y^2 + z^2}{z^2}}\ dx\ dy = \frac{2}{|z|} .$$

Thus, the flux of $\vec{F}$ outward through the sphere S is,

$$\iint_{S_1 \cup S_2} \vec{F} \cdot \vec{n}\ d\sigma = \iint_{S_1} \vec{F} \cdot \vec{n}\ d\sigma + \iint_{S_2} \vec{F} \cdot \vec{n}\ d\sigma$$

$$= \iint_{S_1} \tfrac{1}{2}z^5 \cdot \frac{2}{|z|}\ dx\ dy + \iint_{S_2} \tfrac{1}{2}z^5 \cdot \frac{2}{|z|}\ dx\ dy$$

$$= \iint_{x^2+y^2 \le 4} z^4\ dx\ dy + \iint_{x^2+y^2 \le 4} -\ z^4\ dx\ dy = 0 .$$

12. If $M = 2xz + 1$, $N = 2y(z + 1)$, and $P = x^2 + y^2 + 3z^2$, then

$$\frac{\partial M}{\partial z} = 2z = \frac{\partial P}{\partial x}, \quad \frac{\partial N}{\partial z} = 2y = \frac{\partial P}{\partial y}, \quad \frac{\partial M}{\partial y} = 0 = \frac{\partial N}{\partial x} .$$

Thus, the field is conservative and there is a potential function $f(x,y,z)$ with $\vec{F} = \vec{\nabla} f$. Now, f satisfies

$$\frac{\partial f}{\partial x} = 2xz + 1, \quad \frac{\partial f}{\partial y} = 2y(z + 1), \quad \text{and} \quad \frac{\partial f}{\partial z} = x^2 + y^2 + 3z^2 .$$

Integration of the first of these equations with respect to x, holding y and z fixed, gives

"constant of integration" ↓

$$f(x,y,z) = x^2 z + x + g(y,z) .$$

Then,

$$2y(z + 1) = \frac{\partial f}{\partial y} = \frac{\partial g(y,z)}{\partial y} \quad \text{so} \quad g(y,z) = y^2(z + 1) + h(z) ,$$

where $h(z)$ is the "constant of integration" obtained when $\frac{\partial g}{\partial y} = 2y(z + 1)$ is integrated with respect to y with z fixed.
Then,

$$f(x,y,z) = x^2 z + x + y^2(z + 1) + h(z) ,$$

and

$$x^2 + y^2 + 3z^2 = \frac{\partial f}{\partial z} = x^2 + y^2 + h'(z)$$

so $h'(z) = 3z^2$. Hence, $h(z) = z^3 + c$ and

$$f(x,y,z) = x(xz + 1) + y^2(z + 1) + z^3 + c,$$

where c is an arbitrary constant.

NOTES.

CHAPTER 15 DIFFERENTIAL EQUATIONS

15.1 SEPARABLE FIRST ORDER EQUATIONS

1. A differential equation is an equation that contains one or more ______________ of a ______________ function.

2. Differential equations are classified by ______________ and ______________.

3. The <u>order</u> of a differential equation is the order of the highest ______________ that occurs in the equation.

4. A differential equation is ______________ if it can be put in the form

$$a_n(x)\frac{d^ny}{dx^n} + a_{n-1}(x)\frac{d^{n-1}y}{dx^{n-1}} + \dots + a_1(x)\frac{dy}{dx} + a_0(x)y = F(x)$$

where the a's are functions of x.

5. The differential equation

$$x\frac{d^3y}{dx^3} + \left(\frac{dy}{dx}\right)^2 - e^x y = 0$$

is an ______________ differential equation of order ______________.
It is not ______________.

6. The differential equation

$$\frac{\partial u}{\partial t} = \left(h^2\frac{\partial^2 u}{\partial x^2} + \frac{\partial^2 u}{\partial y^2}\right)$$

is a ______________ differential equation of order ______________.

7. A function $y = f(x)$ is said to be a ______________ of a differential equation if the latter is satisfied when ______________ and its ______________ are replaced throughout by ______________ and its corresponding derivatives.

OBJECTIVE A: Show that a given function is a solution to a specified (ordinary) differential equation.

8. Consider the differential equation

$$3xy' - y = \ln x + 1, \quad x > 0,$$

---

1. derivatives, differentiable
2. type, order
3. derivative
4. linear
5. ordinary, three, linear
6. partial, two
7. solution, y, derivatives, f(x)

and the function

$$y = f(x) = Cx^{1/3} - \ln x - 4,$$

where C is any constant. Then,

$$\frac{dy}{dx} = f'(x) = \underline{\qquad\qquad\qquad},$$

and

$$3xy' = \underline{\qquad\qquad\qquad}.$$

Thus,

$$3xy' - y = (Cx^{1/3} - 3) - (Cx^{1/3} - \ln x - 4)$$
$$= \underline{\qquad\qquad}.$$

Therefore, the function $f(x) = Cx^{1/3} - \ln x - 4$, and its derivative, satisfy the differential equation. We have verified that $y = f(x)$ is a solution.

9. Consider the second order differential equation

$$2xy'' + (1 - 4x)y' + (2x - 1)y = e^x,$$

and the function

$$y = f(x) = (c_1 + c_2\sqrt{x} + x)e^x, \quad x > 0,$$

where c_1 and c_2 are any constants. Then,

$$y' = (\underline{\qquad\qquad\qquad})\, e^x,$$

and

$$y'' = (\underline{\qquad\qquad\qquad})\, e^x.$$

Then,

$$2xy'' = [(2c_1 + 4)x + 2x^2 - \tfrac{1}{2}c_2x^{-1/2} + 2c_2x^{1/2} + 2c_2x^{3/2}]e^x,$$

$$(1 - 4x)y' = [\underline{\qquad\qquad\qquad\qquad\qquad\qquad\qquad\qquad}]e^x,$$

$$(2x - 1)y = [-c_1 + (2c_1 - 1)x + 2x^2 - c_2x^{1/2} + 2c_2x^{3/2}]e^x.$$

Therefore,

$$2xy'' + (1 - 4x)y' + (2x - 1)y = \underline{\qquad\qquad}.$$

We conclude that $y = (c_1 + c_2\sqrt{x} + x)e^x$ ______ a solution to the differential equation.

---

8. $\frac{1}{3}Cx^{-2/3} - \frac{1}{x}$, $Cx^{1/3} - 3$, $\ln x + 1$

9. $c_1 + c_2\sqrt{x} + x + 1 + \frac{1}{2}c_2x^{-1/2}$, $c_1 + c_2\sqrt{x} + x + 2 + c_2x^{-1/2} - \frac{1}{4}c_2x^{-3/2}$, $c_1 + 1 - (4c_1 + 3)x - 4x^2 + \frac{1}{2}c_2x^{-1/2} - c_2x^{1/2} - 4c_2x^{3/2}$, e^x, is

OBJECTIVE B: Solve first order differential equations in which the variables can be separated. If initial conditions are prescribed, determine the value of the constant of integration.

10. Solve the differential equation

$$(xy - x)\,dx + (xy + y)\,dy = 0 .$$

Solution. We separate the variables and integrate:

$$x(y - 1)\,dx + y(x + 1)\,dy = 0 ,$$

$$\frac{y\,dy}{y - 1} = \underline{\qquad\qquad} .$$

Then,

$$\int \left(1 + \frac{1}{y - 1}\right) dy = \underline{\qquad\qquad}$$

$$y + \ln|y - 1| = \underline{\qquad\qquad} + \ln C.$$

We introduce $\ln C$, $C > 0$, as the constant of integration in order to simplify the form of the solution. Thus, by algebra,

$$x + y = \ln C\left|\frac{x + 1}{y - 1}\right| \quad \text{or,} \quad |y - 1|e^{x+y} = \underline{\qquad\qquad} .$$

11. Solve the differential equation

$$x^2yy' = e^y \ ; \quad \text{when} \quad x = 2, \quad y = 0 .$$

Solution: We change to differential form, separate the variables, and integrate:

$$x^2y\,dy = e^y dx \quad \text{or,} \quad \int ye^{-y} dy = \underline{\qquad\qquad} .$$

We integrate the left side by parts, using $u = y$ and $dv = e^{-y}dy$:

$$\underline{\qquad\qquad\qquad} = -\frac{1}{x} + C$$

$$-e^{-y}(\underline{\qquad\qquad}) = -\frac{1}{x} + C ,$$

or simplifying algebraically,

$$x(y + 1) = \underline{\qquad\qquad} .$$

Using the initial condition $x = 2$ and $y = 0$ gives,

$$2(0 + 1) = \underline{\qquad\qquad}, \quad \text{or} \quad C = \underline{\qquad\qquad} .$$

Thus, the solution is given by $x(y + 1) = \left(1 + \frac{x}{2}\right)e^y$.

---

10. $-\frac{x\,dx}{x + 1}$, $-\left(1 - \frac{1}{x + 1}\right) dx$, $-x + \ln|x + 1|$, $C|x + 1|$

11. $x^{-2}\,dx$, $-ye^{-y} + \int e^{-y}dy$, $y + 1$, $(1 - Cx)e^y$, $1 - 2C$, $-\frac{1}{2}$

OBJECTIVE C: Determine if a differential equation is homogeneous, and if it is, solve it.

12. If a differential equation can be put into the form $\frac{dy}{dx}$ = ________, then the equation is called homogeneous. The equation becomes separable in the variables x and v by defining v = ________.

13. Solve the differential equation

$$3xy^2\,dy = (4y^3 - x^3)\,dx .$$

Solution. From the given equation, we have

$$\frac{dy}{dx} = \frac{4y^3 - x^3}{3xy^2} = \frac{1}{3}\left[4\left(\frac{y}{x}\right) - \text{\_\_\_\_\_\_\_\_}\right] .$$

The equation is homogeneous, and we let $v = \frac{y}{x}$, or $y = vx$. Then $\frac{dy}{dx}$ = ________ and the differential equation becomes,

$$v + x\frac{dv}{dx} = \text{\_\_\_\_\_\_\_\_\_\_\_\_} ,$$

or separating the variables x and v,

$$\frac{dx}{x} = 3\left(\frac{v^2\,dv}{\text{\_\_\_\_\_\_}}\right) .$$

The solution of this is,

$$\ln|x| = \text{\_\_\_\_\_\_\_\_\_\_\_\_} + \ln C$$

so that

$$|x| = C|v^3 - 1| .$$

In terms of x and y, the solution is

________________________ .

OBJECTIVE D: Find the family of solutions of a given differential equation and the family of orthogonal trajectories (defined in the Exercise section).

14. Consider the differential equation $x + y\frac{dy}{dx} = 0$. Separating the variables, and integrating, gives

$$x\,dx + y\,dy = 0, \quad \text{and} \quad \text{\_\_\_\_\_\_\_\_} = C_1, \quad \text{where } C_1 > 0 .$$

Thus, the family of solutions is a family of ________ centered at ________. To find the family of orthogonal trajectories, we solve the differential equation ________.

---

12. $F\left(\frac{y}{x}\right)$, $\frac{y}{x}$

13. $\left(\frac{x}{y}\right)^2$, $v + x\frac{dv}{dx}$, $\frac{1}{3}(4v - v^{-2})$, $v^3 - 1$, $\ln|v^3 - 1|$, $|x| = C\left|\frac{y^3}{x^3} - 1\right|$

Separating the variables, and integrating, gives

$$\frac{dy}{y} = \_\_\_\_\_\_\_\_ \quad \text{and} \quad \ln |y| = \_\_\_\_\_\_\_\_ + \ln C_2 ,$$

or

$$y = \pm C_2 x, \quad C_2 > 0 .$$

Notice that $y = 0$, the x-axis, also solves the differential equation for the orthogonal trajectories; so does $x = 0$, the y-axis. Thus, the orthogonal trajectories are the family of ____________ passing through the origin. A sketch of the solution family, and the family of orthogonal trajectories, is given at the right.

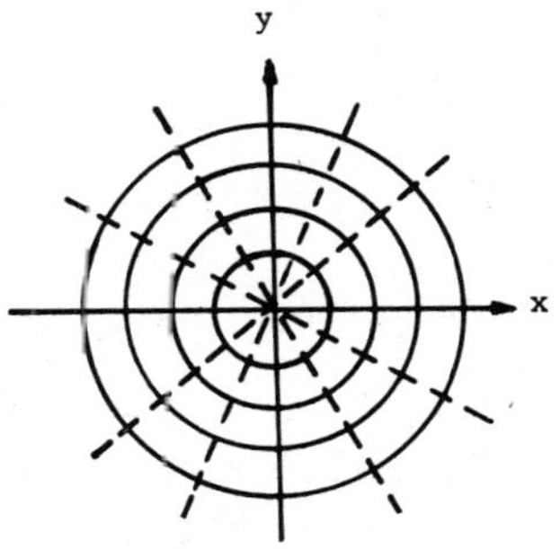

15.2 EXACT DIFFERENTIAL EQUATIONS

OBJECTIVE: Solve a differential equation that is exact. It might be necessary to make the given equation exact by multiplication by a suitable integrating factor $\rho(x,y)$.

15. Show the differential equation

$$\cos y \, dx - (x \sin y - y^2) \, dy = 0$$

is exact and solve it.

Solution. $\frac{\partial}{\partial y}(\cos y) = - \sin y$ and $\frac{\partial}{\partial x}(-x \sin y + y^2) =$ __________ so the equation is exact: that is, the left side is an exact differential $df(x,y)$. Now, $\frac{\partial f}{\partial x} =$ ________ so $f(x,y) =$ __________ $+ g(y)$. Differentiating the last equation with respect to y with x held constant gives,

$$\frac{\partial f}{\partial y} = \_\_\_\_\_\_\_\_\_\_\_\_\_\_ .$$

Thus, $g'(y) =$ ________. Hence, $g(y) =$ __________ $+ C_1$ and

$$f(x,y) = -x \sin y + \frac{y^3}{3} + C_1 .$$

Therefore,

$$-x \sin y + \frac{y^3}{3} = C,$$

where C is an arbitrary constant, solves the differential equation.

---

14. $x^2 + y^2$, circles, the origin, $y\,dx - x\,dy = 0$, $\frac{dx}{x}$, $\ln |x|$, lines

15. $- \sin y$, $\cos y$, $x \cos y$, $-x \sin y + g'(y)$, y^2, $\frac{1}{3} y^3$

16. Let us solve $3x^2y\,dx + (y^4 - x^3)\,dy = 0$.
Since $\frac{\partial}{\partial y}(3x^2y) = 3x^2 \neq -3x^2 = \frac{\partial}{\partial x}(y^4 - x^3)$, the equation, as it stands, is not exact. However, two terms in the coefficients of dx and dy are of degree three and the other coefficient is not of degree three, so we try regrouping the terms as

$$(3x^2y\,dx - x^3\,dy) + y^4\,dy = 0 .$$

If we rewrite this last equation as

$$[y\,d(x^3) - x^3\,dy] + y^4\,dy = 0 ,$$

The first two terms are suggestive of $d(\frac{u}{v}) =$ ____________.
Therefore, we might divide the rewritten equation by __________, obtaining

$$\frac{y\,d(x^3) - x^3\,dy}{y^2} + y^2\,dy = 0.$$

Thus,

$$d(\_\_\_\_\_\_) + y^2\,dy = 0 \quad \text{gives} \quad \_\_\_\_\_\_\_\_\_\_ + C .$$

15.3 LINEAR FIRST ORDER EQUATIONS

OBJECTIVE: Determine if a differential equation of first order is linear, and if it is, solve it.

17. A differential equation of first order, which is linear in the dependent variable y, can always be put in the standard form

________________,

where P and Q are functions of x.

18. Assuming that P and Q are continuous functions of x, we can solve a linear differential equation $y' + Py = Q$ by finding an integrating factor,

$$\rho(x) = \_\_\_\_\_\_\_\_\_\_\_\_ ,$$

providing a solution $\rho y =$ __________________.

---

16. $\frac{v\,du - u\,dv}{v^2}$, y^2, $\frac{x^3}{y}$, $\frac{x^3}{y} + \frac{1}{3}y^3$

17. $\frac{dy}{dx} + Py = Q$

18. $e^{\int P(x)dx}$, $\int \rho(x)Q(x)\,dx + C$

19. Let us solve the equation $x\frac{dy}{dx} + (x - 2)y = 3x^3e^{-x}$. In standard form,

$$\frac{dy}{dx} + \left(1 - \frac{2}{x}\right)y = 3x^2e^{-x} .$$

Here $P =$ ________ and $Q =$ ________, and the differential equation is linear. An integrating factor is given by

$$\rho = e^{\int P\,dx} = e^{\int (1-\frac{2}{x})dx} = e^{\_\_\_\_\_\_} = x^{\_\_\_\_} e^x .$$

Hence a solution is given by

$$x^{-2}e^xy = \int \_\_\_\_\_\_\_\_\_\_\_\_ dx + C = \int \_\_\_\_\_\_\_\_\_\_ dx + C$$

$$= \_\_\_\_\_\_\_\_\_\_\_\_ .$$

Thus,

$$y = \_\_\_\_\_\_\_\_\_\_\_\_\_\_\_\_\_\_\_\_ .$$

20. The differential equation $y' = x - 4xy$ can be written in standard form as

$$y' + 4xy = x ,$$

so it is linear. The equation may also be written in the form

$$\frac{dy}{1 - 4y} = \_\_\_\_\_\_\_\_\_ ,$$

so it is separable in the variables x and y. Thus we have a choice of methods of solution. As a separable equation, we integrate the last equation, and find

$$-\frac{1}{4}\ln|1 - 4y| = \frac{1}{2}x^2 + \ln C ,$$

or

$$|1 - 4y| = C_1 \_\_\_\_\_\_\_\_ , \quad \text{where} \quad C_1 = C^{-4} .$$

If we consider the differential equation as linear, an integrating factor is

$$\rho = e^{\int 4x\,dx} = \_\_\_\_\_\_\_\_\_\_\_\_\_\_ ,$$

from which we get

$$ye^{2x^2} = \int \_\_\_\_\_\_\_\_\_ dx + C_2 = \_\_\_\_\_\_\_\_\_\_ + C_2$$

or

$$4y = \_\_\_\_\_\_\_\_\_\_\_\_\_\_ .$$

---

19. $1 - \frac{2}{x}$, $3x^2e^{-x}$, $x - 2\ln x$, -2, $x^{-2}e^x \cdot 3x^2e^{-x}$, 3, $3x + C$, $(3x^3 + Cx^2)e^{-x}$

If $1 - 4y < 0$, we choose $4C_2 = C_1$, and if $1 - 4y \geq 0$, we choose $4C_2 = -C_1$. Thus both solution forms agree.

15.4 LINEAR HOMOGENEOUS SECOND ORDER EQUATIONS

21. A linear equation of order n can be written in the form

____ .

The coefficients $a_1, a_2, \ldots, a_n$ may be functions of x. If F(x) is ____________ the equation is said to be homogeneous; otherwise it is called ______________.

22. The symbol D is introduced to represent differentiation with respect to ____, and powers of D mean taking successive derivatives:

$$D^2f(x) = \_\_\_\_\_\_ \quad \text{and} \quad D^nf(x) = \_\_\_\_\_\_, \quad n \geq 2 .$$

23. Let us find $(2D^2 - D + 3)(e^x + \sin x)$:

$(2D^2 - D + 3)(e^x + \sin x)$

$= 2D^2(e^x + \sin x) - D(\_\_\_\_\_\_) + 3(e^x + \sin x)$

$= 2D(\_\_\_\_\_\_) - (e^x + \cos x) + 3(e^x + \sin x)$

$= 2(\_\_\_\_\_\_) + 2e^x + 3 \sin x - \cos x$

$= \_\_\_\_\_\_\_\_\_\_ .$

24. Linear differential operators that are polynomials in D with constant coefficients satisfy basic algebraic laws that make it possible to treat them as ______________ so far as ________, multiplication, and ________ are concerned.

OBJECTIVE: Solve linear second order homogeneous equations with constant coefficients. The roots of the characteristic equation of the differential equation may be real and unequal, real and equal, or a pair of complex conjugate numbers.

25. Solve the equation

$$2\frac{d^2y}{dx^2} + 5\frac{dy}{dx} - 3y = 0 .$$

---

20. $x\,dx$, e^{-2x^2}, e^{2x^2}, xe^{2x^2}, $\frac{1}{4}e^{2x^2}$, $1 + 4C_2e^{-2x^2}$

21. $a_n\frac{d^ny}{dx^n} + a_{n-1}\frac{d^{n-1}y}{dx^{n-1}} + \ldots + a_1\frac{dy}{dx} + a_0y = F(x)$, identically zero, nonhomogeneous

22. x, $\frac{d^2f(x)}{dx^2}$, $\frac{d^nf(x)}{dx^n}$

23. $e^x + \sin x$, $e^x + \cos x$, $e^x - \sin x$, $4e^x + \sin x - \cos x$

24. ordinary polynomials, addition, factoring

Solution. The associated characteristic equation is given by ______________. This equation factors into $(2r - 1)($ ________ $) = 0$, so the roots are $r_1 =$ ________ and $r_2 =$ ________. Since these roots are real and unequal, the solution of the differential equation is

$y =$ ______________________________ .

26. Solve the equation

$$\frac{d^2y}{dx^2} - 4\frac{dy}{dx} + 4y = 0 .$$

Solution. The characteristic equation is ______________, and has roots $r_1 =$ ______ and $r_2 =$ ______. Since these roots are real and equal, the solution of the differential equation is

$y =$ ______________________________ .

27. Solve the equation

$$\frac{d^2y}{dx^2} - 6\frac{dy}{dx} + 13y = 0 .$$

Solution. The characteristic equation is ______________, and has roots $r_1 =$ ________ and $r_2 =$ ________. Thus, these roots are a pair of conjugate complex numbers with $\alpha =$ ______ and $\beta =$ ______. The solution of the differential equation is

$y =$ ______________________________ .

15.5 SECOND ORDER EQUATIONS; REDUCTION OF ORDER

OBJECTIVE A: Use the method of variation of parameters to solve linear, second order, nonhomogeneous equations with constant coefficients.

28. A method for solving the nonhomogeneous equation

$$\frac{d^2y}{dx^2} + 2a\frac{dy}{dx} + by = F(x) ,$$

is first to obtain the general solution y_h of the related homogeneous equation obtained by replacing ______________. Let this solution be denoted by

$$y_h = C_1u_1(x) + C_2u_2(x) .$$

Next, determine two functions $v_1 = v_1(x)$ and $v_2 = v_2(x)$ in the following way: the derivatives v_1' and v_2' must satisfy

---

25. $2r^2 + 5r - 3 = 0$, $r + 3$, $\frac{1}{2}$, -3, $C_1e^{x/2} + C_2e^{-3x}$

26. $r^2 - 4r + 4 = 0$, 2, 2, $(C_1 + C_2x)e^{2x}$

27. $r^2 - 6r + 13 = 0$, $3 + 2i$, $3 - 2i$, 3, 2, $e^{3x}(C_1 \cos 2x + C_2 \sin 2x)$

the two equations

______________ and ______________ .

Solve this pair of simultaneous equations for v_1' and v_2', and integrate these functions to obtain the functions $v_1 = v_1(x)$ and $v_2 = v_2(x)$ (don't forget the constants of integration). Then, the general solution of the nonhomogeneous differential equation is given by

$y =$ ______________ .

The method described above is known as ______________.

29. Let us solve the equation $\dfrac{d^2y}{dx^2} - y = \dfrac{2}{e^x + 1}$ by variation of parameters. We first solve the associated homogeneous equation: $\dfrac{d^2y}{dx^2} - y = 0$ gives the characteristic equation ______________, which has the roots $r_1 =$ ________ and $r_2 =$ ________. Thus, we find the solutions

$u_1(x) =$ ________ and $u_2(x) =$ ________

to the homogeneous equation. Next, we demand that the functions v_1 and v_2 satisfy the equations

$v_1' e^{-x} + v_2' e^x = 0,$ and ______________ .

Solving for v_1' and v_2' we find,

$$v_1' = \frac{\begin{vmatrix} 0 & e^x \\ \frac{2}{e^x+1} & e^x \end{vmatrix}}{\begin{vmatrix} e^{-x} & e^x \\ -e^{-x} & e^x \end{vmatrix}} = \frac{-e^x[2/(e^x + 1)]}{\underline{\qquad}} = \underline{\qquad\qquad},$$

and

$$v_2' = \frac{\begin{vmatrix} e^{-x} & 0 \\ -e^{-x} & \frac{2}{e^x+1} \end{vmatrix}}{\begin{vmatrix} e^{-x} & e^x \\ -e^{-x} & e^x \end{vmatrix}} = \frac{\underline{\qquad\qquad}}{2} = \frac{e^{-x}}{e^x + 1} .$$

Integration then gives:

$$v_1 = \int \frac{-e^x\,dx}{e^x + 1} = \underline{\qquad\qquad} + C_1 ,$$

---

28. F(x) by zero, $v_1'u_1 + v_2'u_2 = 0$, $v_1'u_1' + v_2'u_2' = F(x)$, $v_1(x)u_1(x) + v_2(x)u_2(x)$, variation of parameters

and

$$v_2 = \int \frac{e^{-x}\,dx}{e^x + 1} = \int \frac{-u\,du}{u + 1} \qquad (u = e^{-x})$$

$$= \int \left(-1 + \frac{1}{u + 1}\right) du = \underline{\hspace{3cm}} + C_2 .$$

Therefore, the general solution is given by

$$y = v_1u_1 + \underline{\hspace{2cm}}$$

$$= [-\ln(e^x + 1) + C_1]\underline{\hspace{1.5cm}} + [-e^{-x} + \ln(e^{-x} + 1) + C_2]\underline{\hspace{1.5cm}}$$

$$= C_1e^{-x} + C_2e^x - 1 - e^{-x}\ln(e^x + 1) + e^x\ln(e^{-x} + 1) .$$

OBJECTIVE B: Use the method of undetermined coefficients to solve linear second order nonhomogeneous equations with constant coefficients when the right-hand side is a sum of one or more terms like

$$e^{rx}, \quad \cos kx, \quad \sin kx, \quad ax^2 + bx + c .$$

30. Let's find a particular solution of $y'' + 3y' + 2y = 12x^2$. The characteristic equation is __________ and its roots are $r =$ ______ and $r =$ ______. Thus the general solution to the related homogeneous equation is $y_h =$ __________. To find a particular solution y_p that will produce $12x^2$ we choose our trial to be

$$y_p = Ax^2 + Bx + C$$

because ______ is not a root of the characteristic equation. Substitution of y_p, $y_p' = 2Ax + B$, and $y_p'' =$ ______ into the original equation yields

$$2A + 3(2Ax + B) + 2(Ax^2 + Bx + C) = 12x^2 .$$

This equation will hold if $2A =$ ______, $6A + 2B =$ ______, and __________ $= 0$. Thus, $A =$ ______, $B = -18$, and $C =$ ______. Our particular solution is __________.

OBJECTIVE C: Solve second-order differential equations in which the dependent variable, or the independent variable, is missing.

31. If a second-order equation has the special form

$$F\left(x, \frac{dy}{dx}, \frac{d^2y}{dx^2}\right) = 0 ,$$

---

29. $r^2 - 1 = 0$, -1, 1, e^{-x}, e^x, $-v_1'e^{-x} + v_2'e^x = \frac{2}{e^x + 1}$, 2, $\frac{-e^x}{e^x + 1}$, $\frac{2e^{-x}}{e^x + 1}$, $-\ln(e^x + 1)$, $-e^{-x} + \ln(e^{-x} + 1)$, v_2u_2, e^{-x}, e^x

30. $r^2 + 3r + 2 = 0$, -2, -1, $C_1e^{-2x} + C_2e^{-x}$, 0, $2A$, 12, 0, $2A + 3B + 2C$, 6, 21, $6x^2 - 18x + 21$

in which the ____________ variable is missing, we can reduce it to a first-order equation by substituting ____________ and ____________ .

32. To solve $\frac{d^2y}{dx^2} = x\left(\frac{dy}{dx}\right)^3$, we substitute $p = \frac{dy}{dx}$ and $\frac{dp}{dx} = \frac{d^2y}{dx^2}$.

This gives, $\frac{dp}{dx} =$ ________ or $p^{-3}\ dp =$ ________, $p^{-2} = -x^2 + C_1^2$,

$p = \frac{dy}{dx} =$ _______ . Thus, $y + C_2 = \sin^{-1} \frac{x}{C_1}$ or $y + C_2 =$ ______ .

That is,

$$x = \text{\_\_\_\_\_\_\_\_\_\_\_\_\_\_\_\_\_\_} \quad \text{or} \quad x = C_1 \cos (y + C_2) \ .$$

However, since $\cos (y + C_2) = \sin (y + C_2 + \frac{\pi}{2})$, and C_2 is an arbitrary constant, the second result is redundant, and we have $x = C_1 \sin (y + C_2)$ as the general solution.

33. If a second-order equation has the special form

$$F\left(y, \frac{dy}{dx}, \frac{d^2y}{dx^2}\right) = 0 \ ,$$

in which the ______________ variable is missing, the substitutions to use are

$$p = \text{\_\_\_\_\_\_\_\_} \quad \text{and} \quad \frac{d^2y}{dx^2} = \text{\_\_\_\_\_\_\_\_\_\_} \ .$$

34. Consider the equation $y \frac{d^2y}{dx^2} + \left(\frac{dy}{dx}\right)^2 + 1 = 0$. Let $\frac{dy}{dx} = p$,

$\frac{d^2y}{dx^2} = p \frac{dp}{dy}$, and we have __________ $+ p^2 + 1 = 0$.

We can separate the variables in the preceding equation, obtaining

$$\frac{p\ dp}{p^2 + 1} + \text{\_\_\_\_\_\_\_\_} = 0 \ .$$

Integration gives, $\frac{1}{2} \ln (p^2 + 1) +$ __________ $= \ln C_1$.

Solving the previous equation for p yields $\frac{dy}{dx} = p =$ $\pm$ ____________ . Therefore,

$$\pm y\left(C_1^2 - y^2\right)^{-1/2} dy = dx \ ,$$

$$\pm \text{\_\_\_\_\_\_\_\_\_\_\_\_} = x + C_2, \quad \text{or} \quad (x + C_2)^2 = \text{\_\_\_\_\_\_\_\_\_\_}$$

is the general solution.

---

31. dependent, $p = \frac{dy}{dx}$, $\frac{d^2y}{dx^2} = \frac{dp}{dx}$

32. xp^3, $x\,dx$, $\frac{\pm 1}{\sqrt{C_1^2 - x^2}}$, $\cos^{-1} \frac{x}{C_1}$, $C_1 \sin (y + C_2)$

33. independent, $\frac{dy}{dx}$, $p \frac{dp}{dy}$

34. $yp \frac{dp}{dy}$, $\frac{dy}{y}$, $\ln |y|$, $\frac{\sqrt{C_1^2 - y^2}}{y}$, $\left(C_1^2 - y^2\right)^{1/2}$, $C_1^2 - y^2$

OBJECTIVE D: Use a known solution $y = u(x)$ to a linear second order homogeneous equation to find the equation's general solution.

35. It is easy to verify that $y = \sqrt{x}$, $x > 0$, solves the equation

$$2x^2y'' + 3xy' - y = 0 .$$

Convince yourself this is true, and find the general solution.

Solution. Substitute $y = ux^{1/2}$, $y' = u'x^{1/2} + \frac{1}{2}x^{-1/2}u$, and $y'' =$ ______________ into the second order equation.

Then,

$$2x^2(u''x^{1/2} + x^{-1/2}u' - \tfrac{1}{4}x^{-3/2}u) + 3x(\text{______________}) - ux^{1/2} = 0.$$

Simplifying the left-hand side algebraically gives

$$x^{3/2}(\text{______________}) = 0 .$$

Let $w = u'$ in the last equation to obtain the first-order equation

$$x^{3/2}(\text{______________}) = 0 .$$

The expression inside the parentheses must be zero since $x > 0$ yielding the separable equation

$$\frac{dw}{w} = \text{__________}\ dx .$$

Thus,

$$\ln w = \text{__________} \quad \text{and} \quad w = x^{-5/2} .$$

Then, $u = \int w\,dx =$ __________ and $y = ux^{1/2} = -\frac{2}{3}x^{-1}$, a second solution. The general solution is

$$y = C_1x^{1/2} + C_2\left(-\tfrac{2}{3}x^{-1}\right) .$$

15.6 OSCILLATION

OBJECTIVE: Find an equation for a given vibratory motion specified by a linear second order differential equation with constant coefficients. The motion may be damped or undamped.

36. An object weighing 2-lbs is suspended from the lower end of a spring, immersed in a medium, with its upper end attached to a rigid support. The object extends the spring 32 inches. After the object has come to rest in its equilibrium position, it is given an additional pull downward of 1 ft and released.

---

35. $u''x^{1/2} + x^{-1/2}u' - \frac{1}{4}x^{-3/2}u$, $u'x^{1/2} + \frac{1}{2}x^{-1/2}u$, $2u''x + 5u'$, $2w'x + 5x$, $-\frac{5}{2}x^{-1}$, $-\frac{5}{2}\ln x$, $-\frac{2}{3}x^{-3/2}$

As it moves up and down, its motion, taking into account the resistance of the medium, is described by the differential equation

$$m\frac{d^2x}{dt^2} = -kx - \frac{1}{2}\frac{dx}{dt} ,$$

where m is the mass of the object and k is the spring constant. Find its subsequent motion.

<u>Solution</u>. Let us first determine the spring constant k. Since 2 lbs stretches the spring 32 in $= \frac{8}{3}$ ft, by Hooke's law $ks = mg$ we find,

$$\_\_\_\_\_\_\_\_ = 2, \quad \text{or} \quad k = \_\_\_\_\_\_\_\_ .$$

The mass m of the object is m = ________, and so the differential equation of the motion becomes

$$\frac{1}{16}\frac{d^2x}{dt^2} + \frac{1}{2}\frac{dx}{dt} + \frac{3}{4}x = 0,$$

or

$$\frac{d^2x}{dt^2} + 8\frac{dx}{dt} + 12x = 0 .$$

The characteristic equation is $r^2 + 8r + 12 = 0$, and it has the two roots r_1 = ________ and r_2 = ________. Thus, the general solution is

$$x = \_\_\_\_\_\_\_\_\_\_\_\_\_\_\_\_, \quad \text{with} \quad \frac{dx}{dt} = -2C_1e^{-2t} - 6C_2e^{-6t} .$$

The initial conditions are $t = 0$, x = ________, and $\frac{dx}{dt}$ = ________. Substituting these values into the general solution and its derivative, we find

$$1 = C_1 + C_2 \quad \text{and} \quad \_\_\_\_\_\_\_\_\_\_\_\_\_\_\_\_ .$$

Solving these equations simultaneously gives C_1 = ________ and C_2 = ________. Therefore, an equation of the motion is

$$x = \frac{3}{2}e^{-2t} - \frac{1}{2}e^{-6t} .$$

Notice that as $t \to +\infty$, $x \to 0$. The motion is nonoscillatory and we have ____________ damping.

37. For the same spring system as in Problem 36 above, suppose the resistance of the medium is such that the motion is described by the differential equation

$$m\frac{d^2x}{dt^2} = -kx - \frac{3}{8}\frac{dx}{dt} .$$

As before, $k = \frac{3}{4}$ and $m = \frac{1}{16}$ so the equation becomes

---

36. $\frac{8}{3}k$, $\frac{3}{4}$, $\frac{2}{32}$, -2, -6, $C_1e^{-2t} + C_2e^{-6t}$, 1, 0, $0 = -2C_1 - 6C_2$, $\frac{3}{2}$, $-\frac{1}{2}$, overcritical

$$\frac{1}{16}\frac{d^2x}{dt^2} + \frac{3}{8}\frac{dx}{dt} + \frac{3}{4}x = 0 ,$$

or

$$\frac{d^2x}{dt^2} + 6\frac{dx}{dt} + 12x = 0 .$$

In this case the roots of the characteristic equation are $r_1 =$ ________ and $r_2 =$ ________. Thus, the general solution is

$$x = \text{\_\_\_\_\_\_\_\_\_\_\_\_\_\_\_\_\_\_\_\_\_\_\_\_},$$

or

$$x = Ce^{-3t} \sin(\sqrt{3}t + \phi) .$$

We will use the initial conditions $t = 0$, $x = 1$, and $\frac{dx}{dt} = 0$ to determine the constants C and ϕ.

Differentiation of the general solution with respect to t yields

$$\frac{dx}{dt} = -3Ce^{-3t} \sin(\sqrt{3}t + \phi) + C\sqrt{3}e^{-3t} \cos(\sqrt{3}t + \phi) ,$$

and substitution of the values for the initial conditions into these equations for x and $\frac{dx}{dt}$ gives,

$$1 = \text{\_\_\_\_\_\_\_\_} \quad \text{and} \quad 0 = -3C \sin \phi + \sqrt{3}C \cos \phi .$$

Substituting $C = \csc \phi$ from the first of these equations into the second, we find

$$\cot \phi = \text{\_\_\_\_\_\_\_\_}, \quad \text{so} \quad \phi = \frac{\pi}{6} \quad \text{or} \quad \frac{7\pi}{6} .$$

Choosing $\phi = \frac{\pi}{6}$ and $\sin \phi = \frac{1}{2}$ gives $C =$ ________. Therefore, the equation of the motion becomes

$$x = 2e^{-3t} \sin(\sqrt{3}t + \frac{\pi}{6}) .$$

As $t \to +\infty$, $x \to 0$. The motion is oscillatory and we have ____________ damping. The damped period of the motion is $T =$ ________.

15.7 POWER SERIES SOLUTIONS

OBJECTIVE: Find a power series solution to a second order differential equation of the form

$$y'' + p(x)y' + q(x)y = 0$$

where $p(x)$ and $q(x)$ are polynomial functions. Determine at least four nonzero terms in the series.

---

37. $-3 + \sqrt{3}i$, $-3 - \sqrt{3}i$, $e^{-3t}[C_1 \cos \sqrt{3}t + C_2 \sin \sqrt{3}t]$, $C \sin \phi$, $\sqrt{3}$, 2, undercritical, $\frac{2\pi}{\sqrt{3}}$

38. Find a power series solution for

$$y'' + xy' + y = 0 .$$

Solution. Assume there is a solution of the form

$$y = a_0 + a_1x + a_2x^2 + \dots + a_nx^n + \dots = \sum_{n=0}^{\infty} a_nx^n .$$

Then $y' = \sum_{n=1}^{\infty} na_nx^{n-1}$ and $y'' =$ ______________. Substitution into the differential equation gives

$$\sum_{n=2}^{\infty} n(n - 1)a_nx^{n-2} + x \sum_{n=1}^{\infty} na_nx^{n-1} + \sum_{n=0}^{\infty} a_nx^n = 0 .$$

We next collect like powers of x on the left-hand side and set each coefficient equal to 0:

Power of x	Associated coefficient
x^0	$2(1)a_2 + a_0 = 0$ so $a_2 =$ ____________
x^1	$3(2)a_3 + a_1 + a_1 = 0$ so $a_3 =$ ____________
x^2	________________ $= 0$ so $a_4 = -\frac{1}{4}a_2$
x^3	________________ $= 0$ so $a_5 = -\frac{1}{5}a_3$
x^4	________________ $= 0$ so $a_6 = -\frac{1}{6}a_4$

Thus, a_0 and a_1 are arbitrary with $a_2 = -\frac{1}{2}a_0$, $a_3 = -\frac{1}{3}a_1$, $a_4 = -\frac{1}{4}a_2 = \frac{1}{2\cdot4}a_0$, $a_5 =$ ________ a_1, $a_6 =$ ________ a_0. Therefore, the series solution is given by

$$y = a_0(1 - \tfrac{1}{2}x^2 + \tfrac{1}{8}x^4 - \tfrac{1}{48}x^6 + \dots) + a_1\ (\text{\_\_\_\_\_\_\_\_\_\_\_\_\_\_\_\_\_\_\_\_\_\_})$$

Remark: If you calculate the coefficient of the power x^{2k-2} you will find $a_{2k} = -\frac{1}{2k}a_{2k-2}$; likewise, the power x^{2k-1} produces the equation $a_{2k+1} = -\frac{1}{2k+1}a_{2k-1}$. Hence the even coefficients will be expressed (ultimately) in terms of a_0 and the odd coefficients in terms of a_1. In fact,

$$a_{2k} = \frac{(-1)^k}{2\cdot4\cdot6\cdots2k}a_0 , \quad k = 1,2,3, \dots$$

$$a_{2k+1} = \text{\_\_\_\_\_\_\_\_\_\_\_\_\_\_\_\_}\ a_1 , \quad k = 1,2,3, \dots$$

---

38. $\sum_{n=2}^{\infty} n(n-1)a_nx^{n-2}$, $-\frac{1}{2}a_0$, $-\frac{1}{3}a_1$, $4(3)a_4 + 2a_2 + a_2$, $5(4)a_5 + 3a_3 + a_3$, $6(5)a_6 + 4a_4 + a_4$, $\frac{1}{3\cdot5}$, $\frac{-1}{2\cdot4\cdot6}$, $x - \frac{1}{3}x^3 + \frac{1}{15}x^5 - \dots$, $\frac{(-1)^k}{3\cdot5\cdot7\cdots(2k+1)}$

Then the solution becomes

$$y = a_0 \sum_{k=0}^{\infty} (-1)^k \frac{x^{2k}}{2^k \cdot k!} + a_1 \sum_{k=0}^{\infty} (-1)^k \frac{x^{2k+1}}{1 \cdot 3 \cdot 5 \cdots (2k+1)} .$$

15.8 SLOPE FIELDS AND PICARD'S EXISTENCE AND UNIQUENESS THEOREM

OBJECTIVE: Use Picard's iteration scheme to find the approximations $y_n(x)$, for $n = 0, 1, 2, 3,$ to the initial value problem $y' = f(x,y)$ and $y(x_0) = y_0$.

39. Consider the initial value problem

$$y' = x^2 - y , \quad y(1) = 2 .$$

Now Picard's iteration formula is given by

$$y_{n+1}(x) = y_0 + \underline{\hspace{5cm}} .$$

Setting $y_0(x) = y_0 = 2$ and applying Picard's formula gives,

$$y_1(x) = 2 + \underline{\hspace{4cm}} = \frac{x^3}{3} - 2x + \frac{11}{3} .$$

The next iteration with $n = 1$ gives

$$y_2(x) = 2 + \int_1^x [t^2 - (\underline{\hspace{4cm}})] \, dt$$

$$= \underline{\hspace{6cm}} .$$

Next,

$$y_3(x) = \underline{\hspace{6cm}}$$

$$= -\frac{x^4}{12} + \frac{x^5}{60} + \frac{11}{6}x^2 + \frac{53}{12}x - \frac{251}{60} .$$

15.9 NUMERICAL METHODS

40. Consider the initial value problem $y' = f(x,y)$ and $y(x_0) = y_0$. Then Euler's method allows you to approximate the solution by stepping along the tangent lines in increments $\Delta x = h$ according to the formula

$$x_{n+1} = x_n + h \quad \text{and} \quad y_{n+1} = \underline{\hspace{5cm}} .$$

---

39. $\int_{x_0}^{x} f[t, y_n(t)]\, dt$, $\int_1^x (t^2 - 2)\, dt$, $\frac{t^3}{3} - 2t + \frac{11}{3}$, $\frac{x^3}{3} - \frac{x^4}{12} + x^2 - \frac{11}{3}x + \frac{53}{12}$,

$2 + \int_1^x [t^2 - \left(\frac{t^3}{3} - \frac{t^4}{12} + t^2 - \frac{11}{3}t + \frac{53}{12}\right)]\, dt$

40. $y_n + hf(x_n, y_n)$

41. In the improved Euler method you use the formulas

$$x_{n+1} = x_n + h,$$
$$z_{n+1} = y_n + hf(x_n, y_n), \quad \text{and}$$
$$y_{n+1} = \_\_\_\_\_\_\_\_\_\_\_\_\_\_\_\_\_\_\_\_.$$

The formula schemes outlined in Problems 40 and 41 are easily implemented on a computer.

---

41. $y_n + \frac{h}{2}[f(x_n, y_n) + f(x_n, z_{n+1})]$

CHAPTER 15 SELF-TEST

1. Show that the function $f(x) = 4 + 2x + x^2e^x$ is a solution to the differential equation

$$\frac{d^2y}{dx^2} - 2\frac{dy}{dx} + y = 2e^x + 2x \ .$$

In Problems 2-5, solve the given differential equation.

2. $[x \cos^2(\frac{y}{x}) - y]\, dx + x\, dy = 0$

3. $\frac{dy}{dx} = x^3e^x + \frac{2y}{x} - 1, \quad x > 0$

4. $e^x(y - 1)\, dx + 2(e^x + 4)\, dy = 0$

5. $y(y^3 - x)\, dx + x(y^3 + x)\, dy = 0$

6. Find the family of orthogonal trajectories to the family of curves given by

$$e^x + e^{-y} = C \ .$$

7. Solve the following second order differential equations.

(a) $\frac{d^2y}{dx^2} = 2y\left(\frac{dy}{dx}\right)^3$ (b) $x\frac{d^2y}{dx^2} + \frac{dy}{dx} + x = 0$

In Problems 8-11, solve the given differential equation.

8. $2y'' - y' - 3y = 0$

9. $9y'' - 12y' + 4y = 0$

10. $y'' + 4y' + 9y = 0$

11. $\frac{d^2y}{dx^2} + y = \sec^3 x$

12. Find a particular solution of the equation

$$y'' - 9y = x + 2e^{3x} \ .$$

13. A spring is stretched 4 inches by a 2-lb weight. After the weight has come to rest in its new equilibrium position, it is struck a sharp blow that starts it downward at a velocity of 4 ft/sec. If air resistance furnishes a retarding force of magnitude 0.02 of the velocity, find its subsequent motion.

14. Find a power series solution to

$$2y'' + xy' - 4y = 0 \ .$$

15. Use Picard's iteration scheme to find $y_n(x)$ for $n = 0, 1, 2$ in the initial value problem

$$y' = 3x + y^2 \ , \quad y(0) = 1 \ .$$

SOLUTIONS TO CHAPTER 15 SELF-TEST

1. $f(x) = 4 + 2x + x^2e^x$, $f'(x) = 2 + 2xe^x + x^2e^x$, and

$f''(x) = 2e^x + 4xe^x + x^2e^x$. Thus,

$$f'' - 2f' + f = (2 + 4x + x^2)e^x - (4 + 4xe^x + 2x^2e^x) + (4 + 2x + x^2e^x) = 2e^x + 2x .$$

Thus, $y = f(x)$ satisfies the differential equation and is, by definition, a solution.

2. From the given equation, we have

$$\frac{dy}{dx} = \frac{y}{x} - \cos^2\left(\frac{y}{x}\right) = F\left(\frac{y}{x}\right), \quad \text{where} \quad F(v) = v - \cos^2 v \quad \text{and} \quad v = \frac{y}{x} .$$

Thus, $\frac{dx}{x} + \frac{dv}{v - F(v)} = 0$ becomes $\frac{dx}{x} + \frac{dv}{\cos^2 v} = 0$. The solution of this is

$$\ln |x| + \tan v = \ln C ,$$

or, in terms of x and y,

$$\tan\left(\frac{y}{x}\right) = \ln \frac{C}{|x|} .$$

3. $y' - \frac{2}{x}y = x^3e^x - 1$, $x > 0$ is linear. An integrating factor is

$$\rho = e^{\int -\frac{2}{x}\,dx} = e^{-2 \ln x} = x^{-2}, \quad x > 0 .$$

Thus,

$$\begin{aligned} x^{-2}y &= \int x^{-2}(x^3e^x - 1)\,dx \\ &= \int xe^{-x}\,dx - \int x^{-2}\,dx \\ &= -(x + 1)e^{-x} + x^{-1} + C \end{aligned}$$

or

$$y = Cx^2 + x - x^2(x + 1)e^{-x} .$$

4. The variables are separable, and the differential equation can be written as

$$\frac{e^x}{e^x + 4}\,dx + \frac{2}{y - 1}\,dy = 0 .$$

Integration gives,

$$\ln(e^x + 4) + 2 \ln |y - 1| = \ln C, \quad \text{or} \quad (y - 1)^2(e^x + 4) = C .$$

5. $\frac{\partial}{\partial y}[y(y^3 - x)] = 4y^3 - x$ and $\frac{\partial}{\partial x}[x(y^3 + x)] = y^3 + 2x$,

so the equation is not exact. However, the equation can be rewritten as

$$x\left(\frac{x\ dy - y\ dx}{y^2}\right) + y(x\ dy + y\ dx) = 0 ,$$

or

$$\left(-\frac{x}{y}\right) d\left(\frac{x}{y}\right) + d(xy) = 0 ,$$

or

$$-u\ du + d(xy) = 0 , \quad \text{where} \quad u = \frac{x}{y} .$$

Integration gives,

$$-\frac{1}{2}\left(\frac{x}{y}\right)^2 + xy = C , \quad \text{or} \quad 2xy^3 - x^2 = 2Cy^2 .$$

6. The given family of curves satisfies the differential equation

$$e^x\ dx - e^{-y}\ dy = 0 .$$

The family of orthogonal trajectories satisfies the differential equation

$$e^{-y}\ dx + e^x\ dy = 0 , \quad \text{or} \quad e^{-x}\ dx + e^y\ dy = 0 ,$$

whose solution is

$$e^y - e^{-x} = C_1 ,$$

the family of orthogonal trajectories.

7. (a) The independent variable is missing. We substitute $p = \frac{dy}{dx}$ and $\frac{d^2y}{dx^2} = p\frac{dp}{dy}$, and obtain $p\frac{dp}{dy} = 2yp^3$, or $p^{-2}\ dp = 2y\ dy$. Integration gives $-\frac{1}{p} = y^2 + C_1$, or $(y^2 + C_1)\ dy = -dx$. Thus,

$$\frac{1}{3}y^3 + C_1y = -x + C_2 , \quad \text{or} \quad y^3 = 3(C_2 - x - C_1y) .$$

(b) The dependent variable is missing. We substitute $p = \frac{dy}{dx}$ and $\frac{dp}{dx} = \frac{d^2y}{dx^2}$, and obtain $x\frac{dp}{dx} + p + x = 0$, or $\frac{dp}{dx} + \frac{1}{x}p = -1$. This last equation is linear in p, and an integrating factor is $\rho = e^{\int dx/x} = x$. Thus

$$px = \int -x\ dx + C_1, \quad \text{or} \quad x\frac{dy}{dx} = -\frac{1}{2}x^2 + C_1.$$

The variables are separable, and we find

$$dy = \left(-\tfrac{1}{2}x + \tfrac{1}{x}C_1\right) dx \quad \text{gives} \quad y = -\tfrac{1}{4}x^2 + C_1 \ln |x| + C_2 .$$

8. The characteristic equation is

$$2r^2 - r - 3 = 0$$
$$(2r - 3)(r + 1) = 0$$

or $r = -1, \frac{3}{2}$. The general solution is

$$y = C_1e^{-x} + C_2e^{3x/2} .$$

9. $9r^2 - 12r + 4 = 0$

$$(3r - 2)^2 = 0$$

or $r = \frac{2}{3}, \frac{2}{3}$. The general solution is

$$y = C_1e^{2x/3} + C_2xe^{2x/3} .$$

10. $r^2 + 4r + 9 = 0$

The roots to the characteristic equation are

$$r = \frac{-4 \pm \sqrt{16 - 36}}{2} = -2 \pm \sqrt{5}i .$$

The general solution is

$$y = C_1e^{-2x} \cos \sqrt{5}x + C_2e^{-2x} \sin \sqrt{5}x .$$

11. The associated homogeneous equation has the solutions

$$u_1(x) = \cos x \quad \text{and} \quad u_2(x) = \sin x .$$

We then have

$$v_1' \cos x + v_2' \sin x = 0$$
$$-v_1' \sin x + v_2' \cos x = \sec^3 x .$$

By Cramer's rule:

$$v_1' = \frac{\begin{vmatrix} 0 & \sin x \\ \sec^3 x & \cos x \end{vmatrix}}{\begin{vmatrix} \cos x & \sin x \\ -\sin x & \cos x \end{vmatrix}} = -\frac{\sin x}{\cos^3 x} ,$$

$$v_2' = \frac{\begin{vmatrix} \cos x & 0 \\ -\sin x & \sec^3 x \end{vmatrix}}{\begin{vmatrix} \cos x & \sin x \\ -\sin x & \cos x \end{vmatrix}} = \sec^2 x .$$

Hence,

$$v_1 = \int \frac{-\sin x\,dx}{\cos^3 x} = -\frac{1}{2}\cos^{-2}x + C_1 = -\frac{1}{2}\sec^2 x + C_1 ,$$

$$v_2 = \int \sec^2 x\,dx = \tan x + C_2 ,$$

and

$$\begin{aligned} y &= v_1u_1 + v_2u_2 \\ &= -\frac{1}{2}\sec x + C_1\cos x + \sin^2 x \sec x + C_2 \sin x \\ &= \sec x\,(\sin^2 x - \tfrac{1}{2}) + C_1\cos x + C_2\sin x \\ &= \sec x\,(\tfrac{1}{2} - \cos^2 x) + C_1\cos x + C_2\sin x \\ &= \frac{1}{2}\sec x + C_3\cos x + C_2\sin x . \end{aligned}$$

12. The general solution to the homogeneous equation $y'' - 9y = 0$ is

$$y_h = C_1e^{-3x} + C_2e^{3x} .$$

Because e^{3x} appears as a term in y_h, we will need a term xe^{3x} in our trial solution. Thus we try

$$y_p = Axe^{3x} + Bx + C .$$

The first and second derivatives of y_p are

$$y_p' = 3Axe^{3x} + Ae^{3x} + B$$

$$y_p'' = 9Axe^{3x} + 6Ae^{3x} .$$

The result of substituting y_p and its derivatives into the nonhomogeneous equation

$$y'' - 9y = x + 2e^{3x}$$

is

$$\left(9Axe^{3x} + 6Ae^{3x}\right) - 9\left(Axe^{3x} + Bx + C\right) = x + 2e^{3x}$$

$$6Ae^{3x} - 9Bx - 9C = x + 2e^{3x} .$$

The last equation is an identity in x if

$$6A = 2, \quad -9B = 1, \quad -9C = 0 .$$

Thus, $A = \frac{1}{3}$, $B = -\frac{1}{9}$ and $C = 0$.

Therefore,

$$y_p = \frac{1}{3}xe^{3x} - \frac{1}{9}x$$

is a particular solution.

13. A differential equation of the motion is

$$m\frac{d^2x}{dt^2} = -kx - 0.02\frac{dx}{dt} ,$$

where $\frac{1}{3}k = 2$ or $k = 6$ (by Hooke's law), and $m = \frac{2}{32}$. Thus,

$$\frac{d^2x}{dt^2} + \frac{8}{25}\frac{dx}{dt} + 96x = 0 ,$$

is the differential equation of motion, and the general solution is (see the Thomas/Finney text for undercritical damping)

$$x = Ce^{-0.16t} \sin (9.8t + \phi) .$$

The derivative of the motion is

$$\frac{dx}{dt} = -0.16Ce^{-0.16t} \sin (9.8t + \phi) + 9.8Ce^{-0.16t} \cos (9.8t + \phi) .$$

From the initial conditions $t = 0$, $x = 0$, $\frac{dx}{dt} = 4$, we find

$$0 = C \sin \phi \quad \text{and} \quad 9.8C \cos \phi = 4 .$$

Thus, $\phi = 0$ and $C \approx 0.41$. Hence,

$$x = 0.41e^{-0.16t} \sin (9.8t)$$

describes the motion. The motion is oscillatory with undercritical damping.

14. Let $y = \sum_{n=0}^{\infty} a_nx^n$ and the differential equation becomes

$$2\sum_{n=2}^{\infty} n(n - 1)a_nx^{n-2} + x\sum_{n=1}^{\infty} na_nx^{n-1} - 4\sum_{n=0}^{\infty} a_nx^n = 0 ,$$

or

$$\sum_{n=2}^{\infty} 2n(n - 1)a_nx^{n-2} + \sum_{n=1}^{\infty} na_nx^n - 4\sum_{n=0}^{\infty} a_nx^n = 0 .$$

Equating the coefficients of each power of x to zero gives:

x^0: $2\cdot2(1)a_2 - 4a_0 = 0$ or $a_2 = a_0$

x^1: $2\cdot3(2)a_3 + a_1 - 4a_1 = 0$ or $a_3 = \frac{1}{4}a_1$

x^2: $2\cdot4(3)a_4 + 2a_2 - 4a_2 = 0$ or $a_4 = \frac{1}{12}a_2$

x^3: $2\cdot5(4)a_5 + 3a_3 - 4a_3 = 0$ or $a_5 = \frac{1}{40}a_3$

x^4: $2 \cdot 6(5)a_6 + 4a_4 - 4a_4 = 0$ or $a_6 = 0$

x^5: $2 \cdot 7(6)a_7 + 5a_5 - 4a_5 = 0$ or $a_7 = -\frac{1}{84}a_5$

x^6: $2 \cdot 8(7)a_8 + 6a_6 - 4a_6 = 0$ or $a_8 = 0$

Note: $a_{2k} = 0$ for $k \geq 3$.

x^{2k-1}: $2 \cdot (2k + 1)(2k)a_{2k+1} + (2k - 1)a_{2k-1} - 4a_{2k-1} = 0$

$$a_{2k+1} = \frac{5 - 2k}{4k(2k + 1)} a_{2k-1}, \quad k \geq 1 .$$

We can write the first few terms of the series solution:

$$y = a_0(1 + x^2 + \tfrac{1}{12}x^4) + a_1(x + \tfrac{1}{4}x^3 + \tfrac{1}{160}x^5 - \tfrac{1}{13,440}x^7 + \ldots)$$

15. $y_{n+1}(x) = 1 + \int_0^x (3t + y_n^2)\, dt$ so that $y_0 = 1$ and

$$y_1 = 1 + \int_0^x (3t + 1)\, dt = \tfrac{3}{2}x^2 + x + 1$$

$$y_2 = 1 + \int_0^x [3t + (\tfrac{3}{2}t^2 + t + 1)^2]\, dt$$

$$= 1 + \int_0^x (\tfrac{9}{4}t^4 + 3t^3 + 4t^2 + 5t + 1)\, dt$$

$$= \tfrac{9}{20}x^5 + \tfrac{3}{4}x^4 + \tfrac{4}{3}x^3 + \tfrac{5}{2}x^2 + x + 1 .$$